Reprints of Economic Classics

AN ANALYSIS

OF THE

OCCUPATIONS OF THE PEOPLE

AN ANALYSIS

OF THE

OCCUPATIONS OF THE PEOPLE

SHOWING THE RELATIVE IMPORTANCE OF THE

AGRICULTURAL, MANUFACTURING, SHIPPING, COLONIAL, COMMERCIAL & MINING INTERESTS

OF THE

UNITED KINGDOM OF GREAT BRITAIN

AND ITS DEPENDENCIES

BY

FREDERICK W. SPACKMAN

[1847]

REPRINTS OF ECONOMIC CLASSICS

AUGUSTUS M. KELLEY · PUBLISHERS

NEW YORK 1969

First Edition 1847

(London: *Published by and for* The Author. *And
Sold by* Richardson, *Cornhill* & Ollivier, *Pall
Mall*, 1847)

Reprinted 1969 by
AUGUSTUS M. KELLEY · PUBLISHERS
New York   New York   10001

.   .   .   .

S B N   678 00573 7

L C N   68 58020

.   .   .   .

PRINTED IN THE UNITED STATES OF AMERICA
by SENTRY PRESS, NEW YORK, N. Y. 10019

AN ANALYSIS

OF THE

OCCUPATIONS OF THE PEOPLE,

SHOWING THE RELATIVE IMPORTANCE OF THE

AGRICULTURAL, MANUFACTURING, SHIPPING, COLONIAL, COMMERCIAL,
AND MINING INTERESTS,

OF THE

UNITED KINGDOM OF GREAT BRITAIN

AND ITS DEPENDENCIES,

IN NUMBERS, CAPITAL, AND ANNUAL PRODUCTIONS;

AND ALSO THE PROPORTION WHICH THE AGRICULTURAL AND MANUFACTURING INTERESTS
RESPECTIVELY PAY OF THE DIRECT AND LOCAL TAXATION OF THE COUNTRY.

COMPILED FROM THE

CENSUS OF 1841 AND OTHER OFFICIAL RETURNS.

By WILLIAM FREDERICK SPACKMAN,

AUTHOR OF AN ANNUAL PUBLICATION ON THE STATISTICS OF THE BRITISH EMPIRE.

" In every country the FIRST CREDITOR is the PLOUGH. This original indefeasible claim supersedes every other demand."
Edmund Burke.

LONDON:

PUBLISHED BY AND FOR THE AUTHOR,

AND SOLD BY

RICHARDSON, CORNHILL.—OLLIVIER, PALL MALL.

M.DCCC.XLVII.

My Lords and Gentlemen,

THE relative importance of the Agricultural and Manufacturing Interests having long been the subject of discussion, both in and out of Parliament, and public opinion being much divided thereon, the present work has been undertaken with a view to set the question finally at rest.

In this Analysis of the occupations of the People, compiled from the best and only authorities we can have in such matters, the public, it is presumed, will find abundant

proof, that from its paramount importance in all that constitutes the strength, wealth, and stability of a nation, the
Agricultural Interest of the United Kingdom is entitled to
the special favour and consideration of the Legislature.

I have the honour to remain,

My Lords and Gentlemen,

Your most Obedient and most Obliged Servant,

WILLIAM FREDERICK SPACKMAN.

Tollington Park, Hornsey Road,
May 16*th*, 1847.

PREFACE.

THE greatness of a nation is not made up or dependent on any one particular section of the community, but is the result of the prosperity of the whole; and the object of the present work in ascertaining and defining the exact status of each interest in the body politic is not so much to give a triumph to any as to do justice to all.

It is unnecessary to enlarge on the importance of promoting agriculture by all the means in our power, as it must be obvious to every one that it is the first duty of all governments to provide food for the people. The nation must be fed, at whatever cost ; and the only question at issue between the two great parties is, whether you can produce at home the food necessary to sustain the population, or obtain it from abroad, with greater collateral advantages to the whole community.

This is the all-important question that has so long engaged the attention of our people, and which our present circumstances continue to impress on the public mind with greater force than ever. Its gravity, as compared with others, will, in all probability, render it an all-absorbing matter of interest, until the policy of free trade shall have been confirmed or abandoned, as the results of our experience may dictate.

The considerations which necessarily enter into so important a subject are many ; and so far as they bear on the interests of each class in society and the importance of the agricultural, as compared with the manufacturing interest, our labours will probably not be in vain in the present attempt to place them fully and fairly before the public.

We have no intention to decry the importance of the mechanical arts or the value of our manufacturing industry. To do either would be as unworthy of the statician as it would be fatal to the statesman. No one can deny the great advantages of a constant source of employment for a large amount of our population, or the benefits derived from exchanging their productions for those of other nations.

It were something too much, however, to expect that in a time of profound peace the rivalry of other nations and the interests of all mankind should be concentrated in furthering British industry ; and it is therefore not less our duty than our interest to ascertain with some degree of certainty what have been the primary causes of our past success as well as the real character of the principles on which we are to rely for the future in meeting the competition of other nations.

The times and events which gave to Great Britain a monopoly of the manufacturing and commercial trade of the world have long since passed away ; and, from the year 1815, there has been a constant struggle going on between the statesmen of this and other countries as to the extent to which the exclusive privileges acquired by us up to that time shall be surrendered for the common benefit of all.

On all hands we 'find this antagonistic principle in full operation. Nearly all the nations of Europe and the two Americas, without having any corresponding advantages to offer, have severally put in claims for the removal of those restrictions which have hitherto governed our intercourse with them, and, failing to obtain these, have, by countervailing duties, sought to exclude us from their own markets.

It is not, therefore, so much reciprocity as a demand for the surrender of a principle,— a demand to be admitted to a participation of profits, to an equality of rights ; and the only difficulty on our part in at once conceding all that is required of us is, that there is no equality in the circumstances of the two parties.

During the late war, it is true we enjoyed many advantages, and almost exclusive possession of the whole commerce of the seas, but this desperate struggle left us with a debt of 800 millions. It no doubt operated as a scourge on other nations. For a time it paralysed every interest, and swept off generations of their people: agriculture with them made no progress, their manufactures were abandoned, and the arts and sciences only followed the chariot-wheels of the

conqueror to record his triumphs and to perpetuate his
fame.

The sacrifice on the part of those countries was, however,
a present, not a prospective one; with us it has operated as a
mortgage of the present possessions and future labour of the
whole population down to the latest posterity.

To dispute the validity of this mortgage we imagine to
be altogether out of the question. It would entail individual
ruin and national dishonour. The taxes necessary to dis-
charge the obligation must therefore be paid, and the labour
which does pay them, we contend, is entitled to protection
against that which has neither part nor lot in the matter.

Some men indeed are sanguine enough to imagine that
even with such an incubus on our exertions, we can leave all
competition far behind us. However highly one may estimate
the energy and industry of our people, it is difficult to
be satisfied with such a conclusion, and the pages of
this work, we venture to say, afford abundant evidence,
from the progress made by other countries, of its being a
most unjust one. It is the same with nations as with individuals—capital may do much, but not everything, and it is
only indispensably necessary where taxation is high. Large
farms prevail in England because the application of capital
is essential to secure an increase of production on a given
amount of land. In the United States, small arable farms
are the rule throughout the Union, and both, in all countries,
are determined by the presence or absence of taxation. Large
factories may enable the manufacturers of one country to

compete successfully with those of another, provided there be any parity in their circumstances; but if the one is heavily taxed and the other is comparatively untaxed, the cheaper labour of the latter will, in many cases, completely set all the multiplying powers of machinery at defiance.

The national burdens of a people, inasmuch as they enter into everything that is conducive to their daily strength, must retard their progress in proportion as they are easy or otherwise, and it was just as reasonable to expect that the Israelites of old could make bricks without straw, as it would be that the labour of individuals in this country could compete with the untaxed labour of the Swiss, the Germans, and the Saxons in respect of manufactures, or with that of the provinces of the Baltic in respect of agricultural productions.

A writer in one of the most distinguished of our periodicals, has, with peculiar felicity, enumerated the items of taxation which the labour of our people is made to contribute to the necessities of the State, and shown that it embraces everything within the compass of our wants and wishes, from our entrance into the world to our final exit from it. The beer, tea, coffee, sugar, and everything else that we either eat or drink, the hat which covers the head, the shoes that enclose the feet, the raiment wherewith we are clothed, nay, all that is necessary to support the strength and gratify the senses, must pay an enormous government toll before it can reach the individual who has nothing but his labour to sustain him. In health or in sickness he contributes to the taxation of the State, and after he has departed this life, should his virtues be chronicled at all, the knowledge of them must be handed down to posterity on taxed marble, and then, but only then, can it be said that he is gathered to his fathers, to be taxed no more.

Since, then, the taxation of a country is so unlimited in its operation and so imperative in its effects, the actual importance of each class in the same community must be determined by the amount which they severally contribute to the national burdens, and this we have endeavoured to ascertain and define.

Of the number of persons actually employed by the agriculturists and manufacturers, no difference of opinion can exist, as we have adopted the government classification in every instance, and copied the figures given in the returns. We believe this classification to be correct in principle, and but slightly erroneous in details.

Political economists may exercise their ingenuity by calling in question this classification, but we believe it is the only one that accurately traces the dependence of an individual on the one or the other interest, and as this is the primary object of all such matters, if it attains this end, it is sufficient for all purposes. By the Landed Interest, we mean not only the proprietors of the soil, but all that are engaged in its cultivation, and all the interests that are dependent on and supported by both landlord and tenant. An Agriculturist is one who grows the raw material. The Manufacturer changes the fabric from cotton into calico ; flax into linen ; wool into cloth ; raw into manufactured silk ; mineral ores into various combinations of metals ; and the skin of an animal into leather.

All besides the Agriculturists and the Manufacturers, are auxiliaries, not principals ; thus the handicraftsman alters the form, but not the substance, and adapts the article to the use of the consumer,—so, the miller, baker, and butcher ; the tailor, milliner, and shoemaker.

There is also a very numerous class, who neither produce, manufacture, nor alter the shape or substance of an article, and these are called merchants, if they buy and sell in a wholesale manner, or shopkeepers and retail dealers, if they sell by retail. The business of these is to distribute all articles imported from abroad or produced at home, through every city, town, and village in the United Kingdom ; and the Government definition of all these auxillaries is, " Engaged in Trade and Commerce."

The dependence of any particular class engaged in trade and commerce, or in handicraft, is not upon the party who produces, alters, or supplies the article, but upon the individual who consumes it, and if there is any tax whatever on the raw material, or on any thing used in its manufacture, adaptation, or distribution, it is on him that all and every item of such tax, together with all profits and charges, must ultimately fall.

Inasmuch, however, as there is no wealth in this country of any amount, but what has been derived either from Agriculture or Manufactures, nor any of which the value is not determined by the success of these; so, again, this consumer, whatever his rank or position in society may be, is mainly dependent on them. The rental of land, the income from houses, or investments in the public funds, are merely the represen-

tatives of so much labour, and the means necessary to pay
them are principally drawn from either Agriculture or Manufactures.

Our annual creation of wealth may be thus stated:

Agriculture -	£250,000,000
Manufactures, deducting the value of the raw material	127,000,000
Mining Interest -	37,000,000
Colonial Interest -	18,000,000
Foreign Commerce (including the Shipping Interest), 10 per Cent. on the amount of our Exports and Imports	15,000,000
Fisheries - -	3,000,000
	£450,000,000

And from one or the other of these does every individual in
the land derive his income or means of support. The Peer
of the realm, the landed proprietor, the Government annui-
tant, the clergyman, the medical, and the legal adviser, with the
banker, merchant, dealer, and handicraftsman of every class
and kind,—derive what is necessary to support their state
and condition and their daily sustenance from these spring-
heads of national wealth. This is the substance of the nation;
and what we call money consists merely of the counters we use
to denote and measure the value of this substance as it passes
from one to another.

To do equal justice to all classes, the legislation of a
country ought therefore to keep steadily in view their relative importance, not only as regards numbers, but also their
powers of production and the proportion which they severally

bear of the national burdens. Unless this is the governing principle, it strikes at the root of their prosperity, and the injury inflicted on a class is evinced in the gradual decay of the whole community.

We live in an age when mankind place but little reliance on opinions, however authoritatively expressed. The statements of a Prime Minister are subjected, as they ought to be, to the strictest scrutiny; and when opposed to the policy of a long political career, are received by all parties with suspicion. The opinions of men, almost gifted with the spirit of prophecy, who have grown gray in writing voluminous works on all conceivable subjects, are set at nought ; for the present generation is a matter of fact one, and nothing short of demonstration will satisfy it.

We submit the present work to its decision, in the full confidence that, however imperfectly we may have executed the task, in this particular it will be found to be in accordance with the public taste. We are also not without the hope that it will disabuse the public mind of much of the error which so generally prevails on this matter, and reconcile both parties to the maintenance in all their integrity of the most important interests of the British Empire.

CONTENTS.

Advance in Value of Lard.—Coasting Trade.—Foreign Trade.—Colonial Trade. Capital invested in Shipping.—Annual Profits.
The Colonial Interests.—The Political Importance of our Colonies.—Opinions of Mr M'Culloch and Mr Porter.—List of our Colonies —Shipping.—Exports.
The Foreign Trade.—Comparative Tables of the Imports and Exports of England, France, and the United States from 1801 to 1844.—Exports of Great Britain to all Countries in 1844.—Official and Declared Value of the Exports and Imports of Great Britain from 1801 to 1846 . . . Pages 101 to 120

CHAPTER X.
CONCLUSION.

Review of the whole subject . . . . . Pages 121 to 128

APPENDIX.
List of the AUTHORITIES referred to in the compilation of this Work.

ERRATA.

PAGE 9, for " overwhelming *number*," read " overwhelming *numbers*."
,, 14, for " *six* midland and northern counties," read " *eight*."
,, 14, for " *six* out of the fifty-two counties," read " *eight*."
,, 26, for " Mr M'Culloch estimates the capital employed in the cotton trade
       at *thirty-four* millions," read " *forty-seven* millions."
,, 27, for " *six* midland and northern counties," read " *eight*."
,, 28, for " produces annually *three hundred* millions," &c., read " *two hun-
       dred and fifty* millions."
,, 38, for " if low prices *out* are," &c., read " for if low prices *only*."
,, 90, for " the returns in the census for 1811," read " 1841."

IN THE APPENDIX :—

PAGE 27, Northumberland, Property tax on land is omitted. Amount, £24,378.
,, 28, Nottingham, Property tax on land is omitted. Amount, £20,641.
,, 176, for " the rental of the land of the United Kingdom is about *fifty-two*
       millions," read " *fifty-eight* millions, that of houses forty millions,
       government annuitants thirty millions, making together *one hundred
       and twenty-eight millions*," &c.

AN ANALYSIS

OCCUPATIONS OF THE PEOPLE.

CHAPTER I.

Introduction.—Necessity for the present Inquiry.

IT has been the subject of remark with writers in all ages, that many of the most important changes which have been wrought, whether for evil, or for good, in the social and political institutions of mankind, have sprung from very inadequate causes in the first instance, and have often been carried out without the slightest reference to any deduction which could be drawn from the experience of the past, or which the facts relating to the present would justify.

The passions of the multitude are easily influenced to this end. The long continuance in one line of policy or course of trade oftentimes produces a desire of change, and at such a moment the slightest pressure on the circumstances of a people is sufficient to turn the current, or direct the course, of public opinion which decides the fate of the question. If to this we add, that, should at any time popular agitation have for its object, the transfer of political power from the few to the many,—the reduction of the price of food,—or an increase in the price of labour, the arguments in support of such propositions, however impracticable, however absurd in the abstract, or pernicious in their effects, are seldom examined by

the masses in the first instance, because, *prima facie*, they themselves appear to have a direct interest in bringing about such
results, and thus a handful of demagogues agitating for their own
selfish ends have not unfrequently overturned what the practical
wisdom of ages had established.

The same remark will apply not only to the masses, but to those
who are entrusted with their government.   Ministers of state in
their struggles for political power,—senators whose adherence to a
party, or an interest, is the condition of their election,—and even
the public press, desirous of retaining its hold on the popular will,
have all frequently exhibited the most remarkable conversions to
opinions which, through a long political career, they had previously
opposed.

It is not within our province nor is it our intention in any such
case to impute motives, but to deal with the data put forward in
justification of such conversions, and, so far as the relative importance of the Agricultural and Manufacturing Interests is concerned, to show that they have no foundation in honesty or truth.

With no better security, however, for the stability of any
particular system than the popular will, it is nothing extraordinary
that the most important interest of a country should for a time be
decried, neglected, or sacrificed, or that, in such a state of things,
some of the most time-honoured institutions of a country should
disappear.

If universal peace and good-will always prevailed among the
nations of the earth, and the civil and political circumstances of
every country were alike ; or even if the relative importance of
each class in the same community were so nicely balanced, that
the trial of any new principle of national policy would equally
affect all; the argument against violent changes, although still un-
answered, would lose much of its force; but, unfortunately for
this assumption, perfect equality is not a principle in nature.   It is
not to be found in the dispensations of Providence, in the civil or
political condition of nations, or in the external or internal circumstances of those several classes of mankind who collectively constitute the separate kingdoms of which the earth is composed.

We have not the slightest wish to derogate from the importance of manufactures, the value of new inventions, or the use of machinery, but it will be a part of our duty to ascertain how far these have been carried on respectively of the labour which some suppose they have a tendency to supplant, and, above all, we desire to estimate them at their real value.

It has been often said that a purely agricultural country never could be a rich one; but, at all events, Britain exercised a great and powerful influence among the nations when manufactures were but yet in their infancy, and it is a matter of record that for the extension of her power over an empire which has no parallel in history, and for her dominion of the seas, she is indebted to

> " A bold peasantry, their country's pride,"

which,

> " When once destroyed, can never be supplied."

On the other hand, were it possible to realize the most sanguine assertions of the free-traders, and to make these fair islands the workshop of the world, we should have but a very slight security for the continuance of any prosperity derived from such a source ; for, independent of the competition of other countries with whom Cotton, Fine Wool, and Silk are natural productions—assisted as they are by recent discoveries of Coal and Minerals—the very principle of our success in the first instance, viz., the increase and perfection of our mechanical power, would be certain, by its multiplication, to insure its own destruction; for, as we shall presently demonstrate, the increase in the production of manufactured goods, and the employment of the population, proceed in an inverse ratio to each other.

For these reasons a mixed community of agriculturists and manufacturers, and a system that under all circumstances shall induce the cultivation of the soil to the greatest possible extent, and that altogether irrespectively of other markets, we believe to be the best for any nation and people,—the only security for the supply of their own wants,—the only certain means of maintaining their own independence.

It is also our firm conviction that the one interest cannot suffer loss and depression for any length of time without reacting on the other, and in the end involving it in the same consequences. The two are therefore interested in mutual protection and support, and any false principle of legislation which shall endanger the security of agriculture will undoubtedly seal the fate of manufactures.

It behoves us, then, to take especial care that we depart not from first principles, for, in national as well as individual instances, there is a moral retribution which never fails to exact a heavy penalty in all such cases: thus, the excess of public liberty is licentiousness, in the end producing a grinding despotism; and freedom of trade, although when carried out on just and equitable principles, may be considered the perfection of political economy, and perhaps of human wisdom; yet, if not based on this principle of justice to all classes, it may produce the very evils it was intended to check, and, by damaging the most important member of the body politic, may have the effect of laying every other prostrate in the dust.

We propose to show that these remarks are applicable to the false estimate which has been made, and which very generally prevails, of the status of the agricultural interest of the United Kingdom.

Much of the ignorance which exists on this matter may be ascribed to the very uninviting character of the Government publications. To investigate and analyze the formidable array of figures which form the population returns of the census of 1841, and a host of others made by Church, Tithe, Poor-law, and Tax Commissioners, and to collate and concentrate the whole, is a task indeed which few will undertake for themselves, and which we believe is now for the first time attempted.

The principles of division and sub-division, the incompleteness of the details, and the want of uniformity in the returns for Great Britain and those for the kingdom of Ireland, have been the subject of much doubt and difficulty to most persons who have ventured on the inquiry, and in some instances have only stultified it when made.

Hence men, well informed and intelligent on all other subjects, have been deplorably deficient in a knowledge of that which ought to be the foundation of all and every argument affecting the interests of those two great classes of mankind, the agriculturists and the manufacturers; viz., the exact proportion which they respectively bear to each other and to the whole population of the country. They have thus been led to adopt and argue on general assumptions as extravagant and absurd as they are fallacious and inconsequential.

The Commissioners for taking the census of 1841 have in their "Abstract" departed from the practice of their predecessors. This has deceived many superficial readers, and furnished many designing men with an argument to depreciate the real strength and importance of the agricultural interest. The orators of the League, for instance, in all their speeches and writings, took especial care to exclude from consideration nearly one-third of the population of the United Kingdom living in Ireland, seven-eighths of whom are wholly dependent on agriculture.

To correct these errors, whether of design or misconception, and to bring before the public the statistical facts which bear on the condition and circumstances of each interest, is the object of the present work. In the execution of the task, we shall confine ourselves to facts, and not to opinions,—to figures extracted from the government returns in every instance, and not to assertions,—leaving our readers to draw such inferences from these as the strict justice of the case may in each instance require.

Our first duty will be to define the general principles on which this inquiry is to be conducted.

Political economists may differ in their definitions of productive and unproductive labour, but it is quite clear that there are two great divisions of mankind—the producer and the non-producer; and also two great sources from which all mankind derive their wealth— the raw material and the manufactured one.

The producers of the raw material are certainly the first and most important class in all communities, not only because, having no machinery to assist their labours, they must of necessity be the most numerous, but because they are in truth the root from whence all others derive their origin.

In the condition assigned to this class by Providence, they realize the primeval curse inflicted on our first parents, that man should cultivate the soil by the sweat of his brow. They are, in every instance, the pioneers of human civilization, and compel the earth in many a barren and desolate wilderness to assume the appearance of an earthly paradise, and to yield up her countless stores of corn, wine, and oil, of fruits, vegetables, and flowers in endless variety to sustain the wants, to supply the necessities, and to gratify the senses of man. Machinery, as applied to the cultivation of the soil, is yet in its infancy, and contributes little or nothing to the saving of labour, or to the production of those great results which enable us in all seasons, except when it shall please Providence to afflict us in common with other countries with a deficient crop, to feed twice the amount of population which existed in the year 1800, this increased production giving at the same time a corresponding amount of employment to the working classes, and thus ministering to their wants, instead of supplanting their labour.

The next in importance is the manufacturer, who by his skill can give additional lustre to the diamond, can not only transmute ores into precious metals, but form and fashion them into every variety of shape for the use, convenience, and luxury of mankind, and who also by the multitude of his inventions, can turn the production of a moth, and the gossamer of a cotton tree, into the most costly and useful fabrics that either minister to the comforts, or add to the substantial riches of society.

The manufacturer, however, differs from the agriculturist in one very important particular. While, with the gigantic and unlimited power of machinery, he can almost realize the wonders of Aladdin's lamp, and produce goods to any extent which the demand of a world might require, he at the same time supersedes nearly an equal amount of human labour, so that, if this mighty power of production could be carried on *ad infinitum*, it would present the extraordinary anomaly of the accumulation of great wealth on the part of the mill-owner, with the condition of the labouring classes in a course of gradual deterioration, hence, except in times when the opening up of new markets gave a great additional stimulus to trade, the destitution of the lower classes, with every return of adversity, would become deeper and deeper still, until at last it formed an aggregate of human misery that would dissolve the entire framework of society.

These, then, are the two great sections into which a community necessarily and naturally divides itself; all others, by whatever name called, are not principals but auxiliaries to these, and therefore all persons engaged in Trade and Commerce—the Mining Interest, —the Shipping Interest, and all other classes, must be referred to these as to a common root, on which they are dependent for their means of support, and without which they could not exist.

After noticing certain objections to the form of the Government returns, and the fallacies which have been adopted by many of our public writers in consequence thereof, we shall proceed to ascertain the relative strength and importance of each interest, and the exact degree of dependence, on the one or the other, of every other class of the community. In other words, we shall range each under their respective standards, and proceed to number the people.

CHAPTER II.

Objections to the form of the Government Returns.—Notice of the Fallacies of public Writers thereon.—Examination of the terms Trade and Commerce.

The object of taking a Census of the people every ten years we imagine to be three-fold :—

1st. In order to ascertain the numerical strength of the nation as a whole, and the causes operating to an increase or decrease of the population.

2nd. To ascertain the progress of each separate interest in the community, so that, by the application of wise and judicious legislation, we may protect each according to its importance as compared with the whole.

3rd. To trace the relative degree of dependence of one class upon another.

It is a little remarkable that in the accomplishment of this object any difficulty should arise. At first sight it would appear to be simple enough, and in truth it is as simple an affair as can well be to those who will take the trouble of examining the details for themselves; but the Commissioners for taking the Census and several of our public writers have so perverted the figures which they themselves have placed on record, that without this examination the "*most abstruse and fanciful theories*" imaginable have been palmed off on the public as the most veritable of truths, and these form the foundation of nearly all the arguments which have been adduced in support of the new system of political economy.

What a security for the realization of that millennium of prosperity which free trade is to confer on mankind!

But first in reference to the returns made by the Commissioners:

The return of 1831 was made under three main heads, viz.—

AGRICULTURE,

MANUFACTURES,

ALL OTHER CLASSES;

and the returns under these heads were as follows, viz. —

AGRICULTURE.	GREAT. BRITAIN.	IRELAND.
Agricultural Occupiers employing Labourers - -	187,075	95,339
Occupiers not employing Labourers - - -	168,815	564,274
Labourers employed in Agriculture - - -	887,167	567,441
Total employed in Agriculture - - -	1,243,057	1,227,054
MANUFACTURES.		
Employed in Manufactures, or in making Manufacturing Machinery - - - - - -	404,317	25,746
ALL OTHER CLASSES.		
Employed in Retail Trade or in Handicraft, as Masters or Workmen - - - - -	1,159,867	298,838
Capitalists, Bankers, Professional and other educated Men	214,390	61,514
Labourers employed in Labour not Agricultural, as Miners, Quarriers, Fishermen, Porters, &c. - -	608,712	89,876
Other Males twenty years of Age except Servants -	235,499	110,595
Male Servants - - - - - -	78,669	54,142
	3,944,511	1,867,765
Total number of Males of the age of 20 years and upwards in the United Kingdom - -	5,812,276	

This was the state of things in 1831; but between this period and 1841 a new theory had been propounded, and much new light appears to have broken in upon gentlemen holding high official situations, and some others of our public writers. Many of these had sent forth publications assigning such overwhelming numb er to each branch of manufactures as to form a total perfectly irreconcilable with the above fact that only 430,063 males of all ages above that of twenty were engaged in their production. This was only about one-sixth of the number engaged in agriculture, and about one-thirteenth of the whole; and although these figures were perfectly correct and fully confirmed by the Census of 1841, yet the form in which the fact was presented to the public was fatal to any argument touching the numerical strength and importance of the manufacturing interest.

It was also fatal to any conclusion that it would be safe or politic to legislate for so small an interest at the expense of one which preponderated to such an extent as it is here shown the agricultural interest did at this period.

No course, therefore, was left but to quarrel with the returns themselves, and to show that, like other statistical returns, they contained many apparent fallacies, which it required no great stretch of ingenuity to use on the one or the other side of an argument at the will and pleasure of a writer; but, at the same time, although so used, and that with much subtlety, the said returns might still be perfectly correct.

On this head the Commissioners report as follows, page 8 :—

> " In some cases the accuracy of returns of this kind has been impugned, in consequence of the small numbers returned as engaged in making or selling articles of very general consumption. Thus, the assertion that any large place contains but one spectacle-maker, two pork-butchers, three coffin-makers, or four hatters, has been quoted as incorrect or ridiculous; whereas it should be borne in mind, that only in places of such importance and commercial activity as to require and support great subdivision of trades, would any such occupations be separately carried on at all. In many small country towns, the spectacle-maker would merge in the optician, who would perhaps be also the watch-maker, the barometer-seller, and the bell-hanger of his neighbourhood. The coffin-maker would be doing the last offices to his former customers in the cabinet-making line; while the hatter would figure in the list as draper, grocer, bookseller, or shopkeeper, according as he might prefer one name to the other."

And yet, notwithstanding this very proper explanatory remark of the Commissioners, which accounts for and embraces the whole argument, Mr Porter, in his " Progress of the Nation" for 1847, endeavours to show that such a classification is perfectly useless because it does not correspond in all instances with the number of Excise Licences granted for carrying on particular trades. Why, how can any return or classification do so, when as every body knows, many tradesmen in large towns, and all tradesmen in small towns, carry on half a dozen or a dozen trades, requiring for each a particular licence from the Excise : thus, an individual may be a tea-dealer, tobacco-dealer, wine-dealer, spirit-dealer, soap-maker, tallow-chandler, vender of patent medicines, and brewer, and many other trades, all requiring a licence, and yet in the returns of the Census he may be called by that which in a country town includes the whole, *a grocer.*

Had Mr Porter shown us that these were improperly classed as dealers, and that they were in truth manufacturers, there would have been something in the argument; but the objection that they are called by one of the trades in which they deal, instead of another, is puerile indeed, and in fact amounts to nothing.

This, however, was only intended to raise a difficulty where none actually existed; a trader or dealer in an article, and a manufacturer of it, are two callings as distinct as any two things well can be, and about which there could be no mistake.

But it had a far different object, and this will be found in Mr Porter's books, both of 1837 and 1847.

In both editions we have the following paragraph :—

> " By adopting only two divisions or classes, this difficulty is removed, and a greater degree of certainty upon the subject is attained. The persons appointed to prepare the returns might easily fall into errors in classing traders and followers of professions, but could hardly fail to distinguish from all others those families who drew their support from agricultural occupations."

And so, because it was possible that the enumerator might have some doubt about the class to which a few trades or callings belonged, whether they were dealers or manufacturers, Mr Porter in 1837 recommended that for the future the population should be divided into two divisions or classes, viz., Agriculturists, and those engaged in Trade, Commerce, *and Manufactures ;* and in the Census of 1841 the Government adopted the suggestion, and the returns have consequently been made in this form. Throughout the editions of the " Progress of the Nation," in 1837 and 1847, we have accordingly the occupations of the people treated in reference to two classes only, which for any practical purpose is as great an absurdity as if we were to call the Agriculturists themselves Manufacturers. One of the principal objects of taking the Census, as we have before said, is to trace the relative degree of dependence of one class upon another; but how can this be done if all the trade and commerce of the country is to be mixed up and classed with manufactures ?

The real object of this manœuvre was to conceal the weakness of the manufacturing interest, and at the same time to oust the agricultural interest from that precedence which, in all former times, had been accorded to it in the National Accounts, and which

it is the object of this work to show it is still pre-eminently entitled to hold in the Statistics of the British Empire.

Mr Porter would have us to consider Trade and Commerce, *and
Manufactures* as synonymous terms, and that 'together they only
form one class; and he seems to be so thoroughly haunted with the
numerical weakness of the manufacturing interest, that his fear of
its being discovered peeps out in every paragraph, and by mixing
them up, in every table in which they are mentioned in his book,
with those engaged in trade and commerce, he has effectually
succeeded in his object.

The gross injustice of confounding all persons engaged in trade
and commerce with the manufacturers, is very strikingly illustrated
by the four first counties in the Government summary, which, in
that document, stand thus:—

COUNTIES.	Trade, Commerce, and Manufactures.	Agriculture.
Bedford - - -	14,333	14,933
Berks - - - -	16,479	21.249
Bucks - - - -	19,669	21,897
Cambridge - - -	14,744	22,918
	65,225	80,997

This would lead us to the conclusion, that in these four counties
the two interests are nearly balanced, when in truth, if we separate
those engaged in manufactures from those engaged in trade and
commerce, and then divide all other classes between the agriculturists and the manufacturers, in the proportion which these bear
to each other, we arrive at the fact that five-sixths of the whole are
dependent on agriculture, as will be seen by the following table :—

COUNTIES.	AGRICULTURE.			MANUFACTURES.		
	Engaged in :	Dependent on :	TOTAL.	Engaged in :	Dependent on :	TOTAL.
Bedford - -	14,933	62,703	77,636	5,828	24,472	30,300
Berks - -	21,249	127,695	148,944	1,741	10,462	12,203
Bucks - -	21,897	92,989	114,886	7,833	33,264	41,097
Cambridge -	22,918	135,981	158,899	802	4,758	5,560
	80,997	419,368	500,365	16,204	72,956	89,160

Total engaged in, and dependent on, Agriculture   -   500,365
Total engaged in, and dependent on, Manufactures   -   89.160

Total of the four Counties   -   589.525

Could anything be more unreasonable, and in fact more absurd, than to tell us that the population of a county is dependent on manufactures where no manufactures exist, or that all the retail dealers and those engaged in handicraft in such a county are not dependent on the landed interest, and the numerous trades and occupations which the cultivation of the soil in the first instance, and the distribution of its productions in the second, necessarily give rise to in every class of which society is composed ?

The relative strength of these classes in each county will be treated of under their proper heads, but it will be sufficient for our present purpose to call the attention of the reader to the actual strength of these three classes, treated, as they ought to be, as separate and distinct interests :—

AGRICULTURE - -	see Appendix, page 144 - -	3,344,207
TRADE and COMMERCE -	see Appendix, page 160 - - -	2,413,951
MANUFACTURES - -	see Appendix, page 152, Great Britain -	1,140,906
	Ireland - -	300,000
		1,440,906

This leads us to the consideration of what constitutes

TRADE AND COMMERCE.

The number of persons engaged in Trade and Commerce, it will be seen, is 2,413,951. This is about two-thirds of the number actually employed in Agriculture, and nearly double the whole number employed in Manufactures.

In this very numerous class are included the merchants, brokers, agents, wholesale and retail dealers, and all persons engaged in trade or in handicraft as masters or workmen. Our general proposition in respect of this class is, we imagine, a self-evident one— that all charges, whether of cost or profit, on the production, sale, conveyance, and distribution of every article, whether imported from abroad or manufactured at home, are paid by the consumer ; and *ergo*, that all and every one of the classes enumerated in the table given in the Appendix, at page 155, are supported by the Agriculturists and the Manufacturers in the proportion which these respectively bear to each other.

The tea, sugar, coffee, wine, and every other article of foreign production brought to these islands, are not consumed by any particular class, or limited to any particular district, but diffused over the whole surface of the United Kingdom; and although there may be some slight inequalities in the distribution of luxuries, and even of necessaries, as in the case of Ireland, yet it will be seen that these are not of sufficient importance to affect the general argument, but on the contrary, they prove that all the incidents of the condition of the agricultural population, and of those who draw their means of support from it, as retail dealers, or persons engaged in handicraft as masters or workmen, of necessity induce a greater amount of what is called Trade and Commerce than any other interest can possibly do.

For instance, the agricultural population extends over the entire surface of the three kingdoms. The manufacturing population of England and Wales is represented by that of the six midland and northern counties (see Article on Manufactures), and more than two-thirds of the whole are resident in these six out of the fifty-two counties composing England and Wales. The same remark will apply to Scotland : the city of Glasgow, and the towns of Paisley, Dundee, Kilmarnock, and a very few others, comprise the total of their population engaged in manufactures, while the same amount of agricultural population is spread over thirty-two counties, extending from the Orkneys to Berwick-upon-Tweed. In Ireland, if we except those engaged in the linen trade in the town of Belfast and the immediate locality, there is little that is worthy of notice.

It is also certain that a very large proportion of the manufactures exported are shipped in the immediate locality of the place in which they are produced; and the same remark will apply to all the foreign produce consumed by this interest, three-fourths of which is imported at Liverpool and Hull, and distributed throughout the immediate district at a trifling expense as compared with the larger proportion required by the agricultural population, and all the classes dependent on and supported by it, and which is sent to them by every conveyance that circulates throughout the United Kingdom.

Again, large masses of population congregated in cities and towns do not support or maintain even *pro ratâ* the same number of Retail Tradesmen, Professional Persons (see Appendix, page 174), Persons engaged in the Government Civil Service (see Appendix, page 177), Parochial, Town, and Church Officers (see Appendix, page 178), or Domestic Servants (see Appendix, page 179), as the same amount of population would if spread over the agricultural districts, and for this very obvious reason, that one individual can supply the wants, superintend the affairs, or be the professional adviser of a much greater number so situated than under any other circumstances whatever.

But it may be said that although the manufacturers have these advantages in respect of their own productions, still the agricultural produce required for their consumption must be brought from a distance, and this is perfectly true to the extent of their numbers, but nothing more. For it must be taken into consideration, that the agricultural produce of their own localities nearly supplies their wants, and that the cost of conveying all that they may require from a distance is but an unit as compared with that of distributing 300 millions of agricultural produce, and 100 millions of manufactured goods throughout the three kingdoms: the cost or profit of the production, and the sale, conveyance, and ultimate distribution by the retail dealer, being in every instance, as we have already observed, paid by the consumers, and these consumers being the agriculturists and the manufacturers, and those dependent on them, in the exact proportion which they bear to each other in the whole population of the United Kingdom.

Trade and Commerce are not, therefore, necessarily identified, or synonymous, with Manufactures, as Mr Porter and many other writers would have us believe. So far as the internal commerce of the country is concerned, they form a separate and distinct interest from either agriculture or manufactures, and are dependent on each in the exact proportion of their respective numbers, and the relative value of the contribution which each interest makes annually to the common stock of the community.

If there is any one branch of our national interests in which manufactures may be said to be predominant, it is in the external or foreign trade of the country; but this only forms about one-tenth of the whole, and into all particulars relating to its importance we shall inquire under the head of "Manufactures."

We, therefore, contend that the classing of all persons engaged in trade and commerce with those engaged in manufactures is not warranted in any statistical or economical sense; and that, so far as regards the returns made by the Commissioners appointed to take the Census for Great Britain, whoever gave the directions for such a classification must have done so with the predetermination to perpetrate an act of great injustice to the agricultural interest, and with a view of preparing the public mind for a change in policy which the facts bearing on these two great interests would in no way justify.

The returns for Ireland, like everything else in that unfortunate country, fairly defy analysis. The Commissioners for Ireland, instead of following the form appointed for Great Britain, appear to have acted without any definite instructions in the matter, and to have set up one of their own, of so arbitrary, fanciful, and peculiar a structure as to resemble nothing of the kind known among men.

For the purpose of legislation, indeed, these returns are worse than useless, because they conceal the fact of the amount of individual dependence on the one interest or the other, the primary object of all such returns. It is also a remarkable fact, that they have made no return of any class as Independent, and thus, as to their *dependence* or *independence* we are left equally in the dark. The English Commissioners fixed twenty years of age as the period when dependence on the parent generally ceases, and separation takes place. The Commissioners for Ireland, without assigning any reason, have reduced this to fifteen years of age, which has so confounded the relative numbers of each class that it has made it next to impossible to make any comparison between the corresponding classes of the two countries.

Again, instead of ranging the population under the respective heads of Agriculture, Manufactures, Trade and Commerce, and the several other divisions given in the returns for Great Britain, they have made use of a classification which confounds all the distinctions hitherto observed by political economists. According to it, we have the various occupations of the people defined as follows : —

MINISTERING TO FOOD.
MINISTERING TO CLOTHING.
MINISTERING TO LODGING, FURNITURE, MACHINERY, &c.
MINISTERING TO HEALTH.
MINISTERING TO CHARITY.
MINISTERING TO JUSTICE.
MINISTERING TO EDUCATION.
MINISTERING TO RELIGION.
VARIOUS ARTS AND EMPLOYMENTS NOT INCLUDED IN THE FOREGOING.
RESIDUE OF POPULATION.

To show the extreme fallacy of such a classification, it is only necessary to make the following extract from the Report of the Commissioners for Great Britain :—

" We would willingly have given a classification of the occupations of the inhabitants of Great Britain into the various wants to which they respectively minister, but, in attempting this, we were stopped by the various anomalies and uncertainties to which such a classification seemed necessarily to lead, from the fact that many persons supply more than one want, though they can only be classed under one head. Thus to give but a single instance,—the farmer and grazier may be deemed to minister quite as much to clothing by the fleece and hides as he does to food by the flesh of his sheep and cattle."

Mr Porter, at page 68 of his new edition, has adopted this Irish classification, and given us a table in which, under the head of "Ministering to Clothing," it is gravely stated that no less than 669,310 persons are engaged in the "manufacture of materials." If this were true, it would be more than the number employed in the manufacture of the textile fabrics in the whole of England and Wales, and be equal to nearly seven-eighths of the whole number employed in Great Britain. (See Appendix, page 147.)

It is hardly necessary to controvert such a statement, but under the head of Manufactures we shall endeavour to show, notwithstanding the deficiency in these returns, what is the extent of the manufacturing interest in the kingdom of Ireland, as also the number dependent on those actually employed.

The division of the two interests of Agriculture and Manufactures in Ireland is so distinct, and the support and dependency of all other classes on the one ˚or the other is so strongly marked, as to leave no doubt of our being able to get at a correct result. Our principal object in referring thus to the returns for Ireland has been to point out the fallacy of such a classification, the errors it has given rise to, and the necessity of adopting on future occasions one uniform system for the whole of the United Kingdom.

Such are the returns we have to deal with on the present occasion, and we shall now proceed to analyse them in strict conformity with the Government definition of what constitutes Trade and Commerce, and what Manufactures.

Dividing those engaged in Trade and Commerce between the Agriculturists and the Manufacturers in each county of the three kingdoms, on the rule we have laid down, we shall thus arrive at a complete knowledge of the local circumstances of the population of each county and be able to ascertain the precise numbers *actually employed in,* and *actually dependent on,* each interest.

We shall adopt the same rule in reference to the local and direct taxation of the several counties, and although we believe that in nearly every instance it will materially underrate the actual proportion which is paid by the Agriculturists, yet it is the only general rule applicable to such an argument, and is the nearest approximation to the truth which the nature of the subject will admit of.

The tables which form the Appendix to this work have been compiled from the Government returns with great care and fidelity. As regards the number of Agriculturists in each county no question or difficulty could arise, because they are strictly defined, and the precise numbers are copied.

With respect to manufactures, the principal and leading branches carried on in each county have been extracted, and are given with great correctness, and the last line under this head includes all the miscellaneous branches of too small an amount to deserve a more particular enumeration.

That we have done perfect justice to the manufacturing interest will be admitted from the fact, that in the summary of all the counties in Great Britain we make the total number employed by this interest 42,780 more than the Government returns. It is probable that we may have included some particular class which the Commissioners rejected, but they have given no abstract of the number of persons employed in manufactures in the several counties, by which the mistake, if there is one, could be detected.

The authorities from which the amount of taxation paid in each county have been taken are given at the commencement of the Appendix; and we believe they will be found to be the latest published by the Government on the several subjects to which they refer.

The three metropolitan counties of Middlesex, Edinburgh, and Dublin, we consider to be the representatives of all the interests of each kingdom, and have so treated them. Thus, the population of Middlesex is divided between the Agriculturists and the Manufacturers, in the proportion which these bear to each other, in the whole population of England and Wales, and the same of Edinburgh, in reference to Scotland, and Dublin is treated in like manner, as representing the interests of all Ireland. Any other rule than this, we apprehend, would be perfect nonsense; for instance, the nobility, landed gentry, and persons of independent means resident in London, Edinburgh, and Dublin, are drawn from all parts of the United Kingdom. As regards London it may be said, that these classes, with the members of the learned professions, have taken possession of all west of Temple Bar, and support the thousands of tradesmen living within this district.

The learned professions are not the representatives of any particular interest but of the whole community, and one thing is quite certain, that the conveyance and management of real property is the most lucrative and important branch of the legal profession. The seat of Government and the Court of Appeal in the last resort being always held in the City of Westminster, it follows that it is the representative of the whole empire, and those of Edinburgh and Dublin, for the same reason, are the representatives of all the interests of their respective kingdoms.

The merchants and dealers of the City do not represent any particular interest, whether Agricultural or Manufacturing; but the entire trade and commerce of the country, foreign and domestic, and inasmuch as the merchant or dealer derives his profit not from the manufacturer but from the consumer of an article, it necessarily follows that he is dependent on each of these interests in the proportion which they bear to each other.

Again, the east end of the metropolis is both occupied and supported by the shipping interest, which derives its profits from three sources; first, in regard to a vast amount of external commerce which is carried on in making trading voyages from one port to another, all over the globe, and in conveying colonial produce to the Continent of Europe, without any reference to either Agriculture or Manufactures. Secondly, as to the Manufactures exported from this to all other countries; but, thirdly, and mainly, in reference to the return cargoes, or the imports into this country, which we shall show under its proper head, principally consists of articles of general consumption by all classes. The shipping interest is consequently the representative of all and every interest in the British Empire.

On reference to page 22, in the Appendix, it will be seen that the county of Middlesex contains only 18,164 Agriculturists, and 48,435 Manufacturers, and if to these we add the county of Surrey, in order to include Southwark, the state of the case will not be much altered (see Appendix, page 36), so that any division based on a reference to the actual circumstances of these interests in the county of Middlesex, would be an absurdity, and the one we have adopted in respect of the metropolis of each kingdom is the only one that can do equal justice to both interests, and is the nearest in accordance with the fact.

We shall thus have furnished the reader with the statistical details touching the population and taxation of the several districts into which the United Kingdom is divided, and enabled him to test the general accuracy of the work, and the application of the rule we have laid down, by a reference to the circumstances of the particular county in which he may happen to reside.

CHAPTER III.

THE AGRICULTURAL INTEREST.

Notice of Free Trade Fallacies in respect of the natural Laws governing the Production of Food.—Superiority of the Agricultural as compared with the Manufacturing Interest as regards Numbers, Sex, and Age.—Comparison of the Amount of Employment given to the Labouring Classes by each Interest.—Review of the Circumstances of each and of the Numbers of all other Classes in the Population dependent on each.

IT requires no great insight into the affairs of mankind to arrive at the conclusion that the cultivation of the soil is at all times and under all circumstances a matter of primary importance. Calculations, therefore, such as Mr Porter refers to in opening his Chapter on Agriculture, of the amount of shipping which would be required to convey the food of thirty millions of people from a foreign land to our own shores would only be the demonstration of an absurdity in itself impracticable.

It has, however, been propounded as a maxim of the highest political wisdom that we should buy in the cheapest market, even that which nature has ordained every country should produce for itself, namely, the food of the people. In this respect, man is governed by the same natural laws as the lower animals, and every country brings forth different varieties of food suited to the inhabitants thereof; but, the governing principle of all is, that the productions of the soil shall sustain that which is born on its surface, and any system which in its results is opposed to this is a compact unnatural in its essence, and equally opposed to the laws of God and the ordinations of nature.

We belong not to that class who, to support an argument, would wish to connect the dispensations of an all-wise Providence with the legislation of man; but, if ever there was a practical commentary on his presumption and ignorance, it is to be found in the fact that in this, the first year of free trade, a whole nation should be placed in jeopardy by a calamity which, unless counteracted by a forced cultivation of the soil, and that too at any cost whatever, and altogether irrespective of cheaper markets, will be rendered perpetual, and sap the foundations of England's prosperity.

Seasons of scarcity are common to all times, and to all people; and to suspend the laws which, in such an emergency, may interfere with the supply of food from foreign countries, is not less the duty than it has been the practice of all governments.

Any deduction, therefore, from the fact that in such a state of things we are dependent on others, or that in the present crisis we have received supplies of the utmost importance from distant countries, does not touch the principle of protection, and is only an exception to the rule.

The rule itself is incontrovertible, and is this: that it is the first and most important duty of all governments by wise legislation to induce the cultivation of the soil to the greatest possible extent, so that under all and every contingency of human affairs, in seasons of plenty and of scarcity, in times of war and of peace, we may possess within our own borders enough to satisfy the wants of the people, and be as little dependent on others as possible for a supply of the first necessaries of life.

Luxuries, the natural productions of more favoured climates, could be dispensed with, or taxed much more heavily than they are at present with but little detriment to the public interest. Mechanical inventions or productions may for a time be suspended or reduced without materially affecting the security of a country, but anything that shall endanger or render precarious a supply of food for the people would give a fluctuating and uncertain character to every other interest, endanger the manufacturing class itself, and place our very existence as a nation continually in jeopardy.

Mr Porter, with the certainty before him that, with the first good harvest throughout Europe and America, the prices of grain in this country will be depressed far below anything ever yet known, recommends the *stimulus of low prices* as the only one calculated to ensure an increase in the amount of our agricultural productions. Without intending any disrespect to so eminent an authority in these matters, we must be excused for saying that this looks very much like the prescription of a celebrated quack doctor, who, when his patients began to decline, commenced a system of counter irritation, which soon exhausted what little vitality was left, and worked off the unfortunate sufferer in a very short time.

Discoveries of this kind, both on the part of the League and other political economists, are numerous and novel, and were it not that the property and safety of millions are at issue, they might be safely left to excite the risibility of the reader.

We imagine, however, that we shall give the best refutation to such theories by destroying the premises on which they are based : by proving the paramount importance of the interest they seek to depreciate, and by reducing to its own proper standard the one they propose to exalt at its expense.

We shall therefore proceed to demonstrate what is the actual status of the agricultural interest in the United Kingdom at the present time, and the inquiry will be conducted under two heads :—

1st. What is the numerical strength of the persons *actually employed* in agriculture, as compared with those *actually employed* in manufactures ?

2nd. To what extent are " All other Classes " *dependent* on the one or the other of these interests ?

1st.—EMPLOYMENT.

How it could ever have entered into the heads of public men to conceive that there existed any interest in the three kingdoms that for its importance, either nationally or numerically, would bear a comparison with the agricultural, it is difficult to imagine ; and yet at Covent Garden Theatre, night after night, and at all the gatherings of Messrs Cobden and Bright throughout the country, the superiority of the manufacturing in all these particulars was the burden of their song. In both Houses of Parliament the same assertions were made by those opposed to protection, and the form of the Government returns materially assisted all parties in giving currency to the delusion.

To controvert these statements, the tables referring to each county in the United Kingdom, which form the Appendix to this work, have been carefully compiled from those returns, and agree with them in every instance except one, referred to at page 19 ; and we now present the result of the evidence collected from them on the several points of numbers, sex, and age, of the persons actually employed in agriculture and manufactures.

NUMBERS.

Agriculture, see Appendix, page 143 -	- 3,344,207
Manufactures, ,, ,, ,, 152 -	- *1,865,927

SEX.

MALES -	Agriculture, see Appendix, page 144 -	- 3,118,557
,,	Manufactures, ,, ,, ,, 152 -	- 886,744
FEMALES	Agriculture, see Appendix, page 144 -	- 225,650
,,	Manufactures, ,, ,, ,, 152 -	- *979,183

AGE.

MALES above 20	Agriculture, see Appendix, page 144 -	- 2,810,384
,, ,, ,,	Manufactures, ,, ,, ,, 152 -	- 717,780
MALES under 20	Agriculture, see Appendix, page 144 -	- 308,173
,, ,, ,,	Manufactures, ,, ,, ,, 152 -	- 168,964
FEMALES above 20	Agriculture, see Appendix, page 144 -	- 192,654
,, ,, ,,	Manufactures, ,, ,, ,, 152 -	- *788,246
FEMALES under 20	Agriculture, see Appendix, page 144 -	- 32.996
,, ,, ,,	Manufactures, ,, ,, ,, 152 -	- 190,937

In order that full justice may be done to the Manufacturing Interest we have given the whole numbers returned, but from each of these items marked thus *, we imagine that 425,287 persons must be deducted, for the reasons given at page 152 of the Appendix.

From these figures it will be seen that, taking the whole of the persons actually employed in the two occupations, the numbers are as follows—

AGRICULTURE - - - 3,344,207 - ⎫ or 33 as to 14 in
MANUFACTURES, estimating those ⎰ 1,440,906 ⎬ favour of Agri-
   in Ireland at 300,000, - ⎱ - ⎭ culture.

It is, however, of the utmost importance that we should call the attention of our readers to the numerical strength of the *male* population actually employed in each interest, as we shall presently have occasion to speak of the circumstances of each, in reference to the degree of dependence of other interests on these two classes. The numbers are as follows:—

AGRICULTURE.		MANUFACTURES.	
Farmers and Graziers -	737,206	Above 20 - - - -	717,780
Agricultural Labourers -	2,312.388	Under 20 - - - -	168,964
Gardeners, Nurserymen, &c.	60,767		
All other classes - - -	9,196		
Total males - - -	3,118,557	Total males of all classes -	886,744

    (*See Appendix, page* 144.)   (*See Appendix, page* 152.)

It will thus be seen that the Farmers' and Graziers alone, as a body, are more in number than all the males above twenty years of age employed in manufactures, and only 150,000 short of the whole number of males of all ages so employed. If we add the 2¼ millions of labourers which these farmers and graziers give employment to, the *male* population employed in agriculture are nearly as four to one compared with those employed in manufactures. The same remark will also apply as to age: those above twenty are four to one, those under twenty are nearly two to one.

To sum up this division of our subject, it may be further said, that in nearly all instances the Agriculturists are the heads and fathers of thriving families following the most healthy of all occupations, are of full age and able-bodied, and, whether for security against foreign aggression or internal dissensions, they form the right arm of England's power.

2nd.—DEPENDENCE.

Our definition of what constitutes " Trade and Commerce" is given in the preceding chapter, and having ascertained the numerical strength of those actually employed in Agriculture and Manufactures, we now proceed to trace the degree of dependence of those engaged in " Trade and Commerce," and of " All other Classes," on the one or the other of these two divisions of mankind. To enable us to do this with any degree of certainty or justice, it is necessary in the first instance that we should inquire what are their respective circumstances, and we think the following will be found a correct review of the facts relating to each as they exist in society at the present moment.

LANDED INTEREST.

The Peerage.

A large proportion of the Members of both Houses of Parliament.

Those returned as of Independent means.

The Endowments of the Church.

Four-fifths of the property of all the Charitable Institutions in Great Britain. (See Appendix, page 183.)

The first two classes are, of course, included in the last, in the returns of the census; and these, for Great Britain, are stated to be 511,540. If to these we add 50,000 for Ireland, we have a total of 561,540.

These are in possession of the fee-simple of the land, which, at 25 years' purchase, is worth 1,500 millions, independent of their property in houses and in the funds.

MANUFACTURING INTEREST.

There is no return of the exact number of Mill Owners and Master Manufacturers given in the returns of the census; but the number of mills, including Cotton, Woollen, Flax, and Silk, is given in 1839 at 5,281. If we average the number of partners at two to each, we have about 10,500 persons interested as principals in these, the principal branches of our manufactures. Birmingham and Sheffield undoubtedly abound with small manufacturers, many of them working at their own trade, but we are quite certain that we over-estimate the number, when we say that the master manufacturers of every class and kind in the United Kingdom do not exceed 25,000.

Mr M'Culloch estimates the capital employed in the cotton trade at 34 millions; and this employing the most expensive machinery of any, and being about one-fifth of the whole, we may estimate according to this rule, the actual capital employed in Manufactures at about 170 millions.

We use these figures for the purpose of making a comparison in the present instance; but, under the head of Manufactures, we shall presently show there is no such an amount in existence among them.

Annual Income from the Rental of the Land, £58,753,615. (See Chapter iv.)

Annual Income, say 10 per cent. on 170 millions, the amount of their annual productions, and about 2½ millions, the rental of all the mills, factories, &c., making together about 20 millions. It is impossible to state this precisely, because there is no distinction between the classes in the Returns of the Income Tax, but in a return made in April, 1815, the proportions were given as follows :—

Land - - -	68·8
Dwelling-houses - -	26·1
Mills, Factories, &c. -	3·7
Manorial Profits, &c. -	1·4
	100·0

Making a great allowance for increase since then, the amount we have given would be about the present amount.

The Landed Interest occupies the entire surface of the three kingdoms.

The Manufacturing Interest is located in the principal towns of the six Midland and Northern Counties, and in some other places, but the whole number in England and Wales, either employed or dependent on manufactures, is represented by the population of these counties.

Supports 779,881 Farmers and Graziers, in possession of stock and capital amounting to 250 millions, and all the trades dependent on and supported by them.

This item is, of course, included in the number given in the next paragraph, as employed; but they are here described as an Interest possessing an amount of capital for which there is nothing to set off or compare them with in the manufacturing interest.

Employs	2,810,384	Males above 20.
„	308,173	„ under 20.
„	192,654	Females above 20.
„	32,996	„ under 20.
Total -	3,344,207	

Employs	717,780	Males above 20.
„	168,964	„ under 20.
„	*788,246	Females above 20.
„	190,937	„ under 20.
Total -	1,865,927	

---

* Subject to the reduction of 425,287, as stated at p. 24, and in Appendix, p. 152.

Produces annually 300 millions of Food, and materials for clothing the people. (See next Chapter.)

Produces annually about 170 to 180 millions, two-thirds of which is consumed at home, and one-third shipped to foreign parts.

Pays, of the Direct and Local Taxation, £13,881,911. (See Appendix, p. 141.)

Pays, of the Direct and Local Taxation, £4,432,997. (See Appendix, p. 141.)

Such are the circumstances of the two interests as they appear on the surface of things; but let us examine these facts a little closer, and we shall find there is a still greater disparity.

The nobility, resident gentry, and persons living in a state of independence, make use of all the superfluities and luxuries of this life in a much greater proportion than the manufacturers, who, however wealthy and respectable in society, do not, from their rank, station, connexions, habits, or business, either require or use them to the same extent, or in the same degree. Carriages, horses, servants, town and country residences, on which enormous sums are expended, are all necessary to the rank and station of a nobleman, a landed proprietor, or a gentleman living in independence, but would be a superfluity to, if not a positive drawback on the circumstances of, nineteen-twentieths of the Manufacturers.

The same may be said in respect of the patronage of the Fine Arts. The painter, the sculptor, the engraver, and a host of others, draw their support principally from persons of independent means, and these are resident in the Agricultural and Manufacturing districts in the proportions given in the Appendix, p. 175.

But without pursuing the inquiry farther as to the higher classes, about which there can be no doubt whatever, let us make a comparison of the middling and lower classes.

The Farmers and Graziers, as we have shown, are 779,881, with a capital of at least 250 millions; and whether we consider their numbers, strength, occupation, or wealth, they are unique, and there is no class in the United Kingdom will bear a comparison with them, in fact there is no corresponding class among the Manufacturers to compare them with.

We must, therefore, descend to those they give employment to, and these for the greater part are able-bodied men, in most instances with wives and families, and in number 2,810,384, spread over the whole kingdom. The same class engaged in manufactures, and living in towns, amount to 717,780, but all the rest, with the exception of 168,964 boys under twenty years of age, are females, for the most part unmarried, earning but small wages, and having no families dependent on their labour for support.

These are the positive facts which bear on the condition and circumstances of the two interests, and it appears to us that we have done the Agriculturists a great injustice by the adoption of the rule we have laid down, that of dividing all other classes between them and the Manufacturers in the proportion which these bear to each other in the whole population; for as we have already observed there is not a single incident in the condition of the Agricultural Interest, and those supported by and dependent on it, but what must of necessity give rise to a greater amount of Trade and Commerce than the corresponding class among the Manufacturers. The rank and position of the parties, their daily and hourly expenditure, their residence in every part of the United Kingdom, their annual income, numbers, and capital employed, all point to one conclusion—that the land and its productions constitute an interest on which not only the comparative numbers here given are dependent, but on the prosperity of which the well being of the whole population of this country mainly, vitally, essentially depends.

The inference, therefore, which the Government returns would have us to draw by mixing up those engaged in Trade and Commerce with those engaged in Manufactures, namely, that the two interests are nearly balanced, or that the manufacturing preponderates, is a fiction which has not the slightest foundation in fact, and exists only in the political dishonesty of such a return.

CHAPTER IV.

THE AGRICULTURAL INTEREST.—(*Continued.*)

Erroneous Opinions of Mr Cobden and Mr Bright respecting the Farming Interest.—Inclosure of Land since 1800. *—Improvement in Cultivation and Increased Productions.—Mr Couling's Tables of the Land of the United Kingdom.—Average Price of Wheat and Number of Inclosure Bills passed since* 1760.—*Import and Export of Grain from* 1695.—*Prices of Grain in Foreign Countries.— Rental of the United Kingdom.—Capital employed in Agriculture. —Estimate of the Annual Productions of Agriculture.—Conclusion.*

WITH what degree of justice the Agricultural Interest is to be decried our readers will now be able to judge for themselves; but it has long been the practice of certain parties to hold it forth as one possessing neither intellect nor energy. The present race of farmers have been denounced by the orators of the League as little better than the serfs of the soil they cultivated, incapable of being excited to emulation or interested in the march of improvement.

Mr Cobden would sometimes amuse his audience by comparing the ploughs now used in some parts of the country to that followed by Cincinnatus, and in his speech in the House of Commons so late as the 27th of February, 1846, he made the following statement in derogation of the numbers of the Agriculturists and their importance in the body politic:—

> "But I can give you some information on the subject. There are about 150,000 tenants who form the basis of your political power, and who are distributed throughout the counties of this country. You should bear in mind that less than one-half of the money invested in the Savings' Banks (£15,000,000) laid out at better interest in the purchase of freeholds, would give qualifications to more persons than your 150,000 tenant farmers."

And all this of a class of men numbering more than 700,000, and in possession of 250 millions of capital of their own, and who, whether we consider their improvements in the breed of cattle, or in the cultivation of the soil for the production of grain, have made greater, more substantial, and more enduring progress than any other interest in the kingdom.

Mr Bright, who occasionally talked of rolling the Crown and the aristocracy in the dust, has often indulged in vagaries of the same character, and would hardly give them credit for being anything except a mass of pauperism. " It was nothing but protection which had damaged them. The farmers had been protected into a state of decrepitude, and this unfortunate system of legislation had destroyed the vitality of agriculture."

Mr Porter also, strongly imbued with free-trade opinions, at the same time that he admits the vast increase in the amount of agricultural productions since the commencement of the present century, comes to the conclusion, in direct opposition to his own figures, as we shall presently show, that Protection is the bane of Agriculture, and that it is only by the *stimulus of low prices* that we can hope to keep pace with the wants of the people.

Let us examine on what this hypothesis rests. In the year 1801 the population of Great Britain was 10,472,048. In the census of 1841 it was 18,664,761, and at the present moment it may be estimated in round numbers at twenty millions.

The population has consequently doubled itself in the last forty-six years.

The number of acres of land inclosed and brought under cultivation in the same period is as follows:—

	INCLOSURE BILLS.	ACRES.
1801 to 1810 inclusive - - -	906	1,657,980
1811 to 1820 ,, - - - -	771	1,410,930
1821 to 1830 ,, - - - -	186	340,380
1831 to 1840 ,, - - - -	129	236,070
1841 to 1844 ,, - - - -	52	95,160
	2,044	3,740,520

This is about one-twelfth of the whole now under cultivation; so that evidence of the extent of improvement which has taken place in the cultivation of the soil, may at once be deduced from this fact: Thus in the year 1800 we had under cultivation forty-two millions of acres which produced food for ten millions of people; whereas by adding one-twelfth to this quantity in a period of forty-six years, we now produce food for twenty millions of people, and that too, as every one will admit, of a very superior quality. Nothing, indeed, can more clearly show the degree of improvement which has taken place in this respect than the fact that wheaten bread of the best quality is now common to all classes, and that the middling and lower orders during this period of protection have made greater progress than at any other period of our history.

Mr Porter says in a note at page 159, " This calculation proceeds upon the supposition that not any of the land enclosed was previously cultivated, which, however, is far from having been the case." So much the better for our argument, and we want nothing more conclusive than this to prove the extraordinary degree of improvement that must have been carried into every branch of agriculture to have enabled it to double its productions within the period referred to.

We decline following Mr Porter through all his calculations of pecks and gallons more or less to each individual, and we also refuse to divide the period of time into sections to suit one argument or another, in the presence of so grand and important a fact as this, that the improved culture of eleven-twelfths of the land now under cultivation has been carried to such a degree of perfection, since the year 1800, as to have added annually at least 100 millions of produce to the common stock of the community.

In order that the reader may judge of our capability to effect even much more than this under the same system of protection, we now present Mr Couling's statement of the land in the United Kingdom, delivered into a Committee of the House of Commons in the year 1827.

ENGLAND.				
COUNTIES.	CULTIVATED.	UNCULTIVATED.	UNPROFITABLE.	SUMMARY.
	Acres.	Acres.	Acres.	Acres.
Bedford - -	248,000	31,000	17,320	296,320
Berks - -	380,000	75,000	28,840	483,840
Buckingham -	440,000	5,000	28,600	473,600
Cambridge - -	500,000	17,000	32,120	549,120
Chester -	594,000	40,000	39,280	673,280
Cornwall - -	550,000	190,000	109,280	849,280
Cumberland -	670,000	150,000	125,920	945,920
Derby - -	500,000	100,000	56,640	656 640
Devon - -	1,200,000	300,000	150.560	1,650,560
Dorset - -	573,000	25,000	45,200	643,200
Durham - -	500,000	100,000	79,040	679,040
Essex - -	900,000	10,000	70,480	980,480
Gloucester - -	750,000	6,000	47,840	803,840
Hants - -	900,000	80,000	61,920	1,041,920
Hereford - -	495,000	24,000	31,400	550,400
Hertford - -	310,000	8,000	19,920	337,920
Huntingdon -	220,000	3,000	13,800	236,800
Kent - - -	900,000	20,000	63,680	983,680
Lancaster - -	850,000	200,000	121,840	1,171,840
Leicester - -	480,000	5,000	29,560	514,560
Lincoln - -	1,465,000	180,000	113,720	1,758,720
Middlesex - -	155,000	17,000	8,480	180,480
Monmouth - -	270,000	30,000	18,720	318,720
Norfolk - -	1,180,000	78,000	80,880	1,338,880
Northampton -	555,000	50,000	45.880	650,880
Northumberland -	900,000	160,000	137,440	1,197,440
Nottingham -	470,000	28,000	37,680	535,680
Oxford - -	403,000	50,000	28,280	481,280
Rutland - -	89,000	1,000	5,360	95,360
Salop - -	790,000	20,000	48,240	858,240
Somerset - -	900,000	88,000	62,880	1,050,880
Stafford - -	560,000	85,000	89,720	734,720
Suffolk - -	820,000	88,000	59,680	967.680
Surrey - -	400,000	50,000	35,120	485,120
Sussex - -	625,000	170,000	141,320	936,320
Warwick - -	510,000	30,000	37,280	577,280
Westmoreland -	180,000	110,000	198,320	488,320
Wilts - -	500,000	200.000	182,560	882,560
Worcester - -	400,000	30,000	36,560	466,560
York - -	2,500,000	600,000	715,040	3,815,040
	25,632,000	3,454,000	3,256,400	32,342,400

WALES.				
COUNTIES.	CULTIVATED.	UNCULTIVATED.	UNPROFITABLE.	SUMMARY.
Anglesea - -	150,000	10,000	13,440	173,440
Brecknock - -	300,000	80,000	102,560	482,560
Cardigan - -	245,000	80,000	107,000	432,000
Carmarthen - -	342,000	60,000	221,360	632,360
Carnarvon - -	160.000	60,000	128,160	348,160
Denbigh - -	360,000	20,000	25,120	405,120
Flint - -	130,000	10,000	16,160	156,160
Glamorgan - -	305,000	60,000	141,880	506,880
Merioneth - -	350,000	20,000	54,320	424,320
Montgomery - -	240.000	100,000	196 960	536.960
Pembroke - -	300,000	20,000	70,400	390,400
Radnor - -	235,000	10,000	27,640	272,640
	3,117,000	530,000	1,105,000	4,752,000

SCOTLAND.				
COUNTIES.	CULTIVATED.	UNCULTIVATED.	UNPROFITABLE.	SUMMARY.
	Acres.	Acres.	Acres.	Acres.
Aberdeen - -	300,000	450,000	520,740	1,270,740
Argyle - -	308,000	600,000	1,524,000	2,432,000
Ayr - -	292,000	300,000	432,000	1,024,000
Banff - - -	120,000	130,000	70,000	320,000
Berwick - -	160,000	100,000	25,600	285,600
Bute - - -	60,000	40,000	65,000	165,000
Caithness - -	70,000	75,000	250,680	395,680
Clackmannan - -	22,000	5,000	3,720	30,720
Cromarty - -	20,000	5,000	14,690	39,690
Dumbarton - -	70,000	50,000	27,200	147,200
Dumfries - -	212,000	320,000	620,000	1,152,000
Edinburgh - -	181,000	20,000	29,400	230,400
Elgin -	120,000	200,000	217,600	537,600
Fife - - -	200,000	85,000	37,560	322,560
Forfar - -	200,000	220,000	117,600	537,600
Haddington - -	100,000	30,000	30,000	160,000
Inverness - -	500,000	750,000	1,694,000	2,944.000
Kincardine - -	110,000	50,000	42,870	202,870
Kinross - -	30,000	10,000	13,120	53,120
Kirkcudbright - -	110,000	200,000	254,480	564,480
Lanark -	220,000	195,000	141,800	556,800
Linlithgow - -	50,000	10,000	11,680	71,680
Nairn - -	70,000	30,000	28,000	128,000
Peebles - -	104,000	80,000	46,400	230,400
Perth - -	500,000	550,000	606,320	1,656,320
Renfrew - -	100,000	20,000	34,240	154,240
Ross - -	301,000	545,000	929,830	1,775.830
Roxburgh - -	200,000	100,000	157,600	457,600
Selkirk - -	85,000	30,000	53,320	168,320
Stirling - -	200,000	50,000	62,960	312,960
Sutherland -	150,000	600,000	372 560	1,122,560
Wigton - -	100,000	100,000	88,960	288,960
	5,265,000	5,950.000	8,523,930	19,738,930

IRELAND.				
COUNTIES.	CULTIVATED.	UNCULTIVATED.	UNPROFITABLE.	SUMMARY.
Antrim - -	336,400	218,870	119.136	674,406
Armagh - -	166.000	92,430	51,233	309,663
Carlow - -	173,000	34,000	15.021	222,021
Cavan - -	265,400	160;500	61,720	487,620
Clare - -	579,000	104,400	88.044	771,444
Cork - - -	1,188,000	361,000	150,056	1,699.056
Donegal - -	507,000	417,920	175.951	1,100,871
Down - -	349,000	126,170	89,481	564,651
Dublin - -	159,130	49,920	21,071	230,121
East Meath - -	465,000	40,120	26,078	531,198
Fermanagh -	254,000	120,500	84,689	459,189
Galway - -	829,200	532,040	242,479	1,603,719
Kerry - -	556,300	348,410	144,483	1,049,193
Kildare - -	259,990	87,670	35,875	383,535
Kilkenny - -	403,100	58.100	25,367	486,567
King's County - -	341,310	80.900	34.954	457,164
Leitrim - -	222,250	128,200	64,189	414,689
Limerick - -	460,000	114,110	52.425	626,535
Londonderry -	279,400	172,070	80.214	531,684
Longford - -	121,900	41,460	53,963	217,323

IRELAND —(*Continued.*)			
COUNTIES,	CULTIVATED.	UNCULTIVATED.	UNPROFITABLE.	SUMMARY.

COUNTIES,	CULTIVATED.	UNCULTIVATED.	UNPROFITABLE.	SUMMARY.
	Acres.	Acres.	Acres.	Acres.
Louth - -	157,000	12,000	10,415	179,415
Mayo - -	502,900	565,570	212,302	1,280.772
Monaghan - -	257,000	12,000	21,952	290,952
Queen's County -	311,100	47,120	22,966	381,186
Roscommon -	348,000	122,460	91,113	561,573
Sligo - -	143,500	189,930	66,953	400,383
Tipperary - -	693,200	113,490	92,329	899.019
Tyrone - -	539,900	135,020	91,988	766,908
Waterford - -	348,500	44,220	33,016	425,736
West Meath -	287,330	51,200	36,581	375,111
Wexford - -	340,470	156,200	58,828	555,498
Wicklow - -	281,000	162,000	61,792	504,792
	12,125,280	4,900,000	2,416,664	19,441,944

BRITISH ISLANDS.

COUNTIES.	CULTIVATED.	UNCULTIVATED.	UNPROFITABLE.	SUMMARY.
Man - -	95,000	23,000	22,800	140,800
Scilly, Jersey, Guernsey, Alderney, Sark, &c. -	68,690	31,000	30,669	130,359
Orkneys and Shetland	220,000	112,000	516,000	848,000
	383,690	166,000	569,469	1,119,159

RECAPITULATION.

	CULTIVATED.	UNCULTIVATED.	UNPROFITABLE.	SUMMARY.
ENGLAND - -	25,632,000	3,454,000	3,256,400	32,342,400
WALES - -	3,117,000	530,000	1,105,000	4,752,000
SCOTLAND - -	5,265,000	5,950,000	8.523,930	19,738,930
IRELAND - -	12,125.280	4,900,000	2,416,664	19,441,944
BRITISH ISLES -	383,690	166,000	569,469	1,119,159
	46,522,970	15,000,000	15,871,463	77,394,433

	Arable and Gardens.	Meadows, Pastures, and Marshes.	Wastes capable of Improvement.	Annual Value of Wastes in their present state.	Incapable of Improvement.	SUMMARY.
	Statute Acres.	Statute Acres.	Statute Acres.	Pounds Sterling.	Statute Acres.	Statute Acres.
ENGLAND -	10,252,800	15,379,200	3.454,000	1,700,000	3,256,400	32,342,400
WALES - -	890.570	2,226,430	530,000	200,000	1,105.000	4,752,000
SCOTLAND -	2,493,950	2,771,050	5.950.000	1,680,000	8,523,930	19,738,930
IRELAND -	5,389,040	6,736,240	4.900,000	1,395,000	2,416,664	19,441,944
BRITISH ISLES -	109,630	274,060	166,000	25,000	569,469	1,119,159
	19,135,990	27,386,980	15,000,000	5,000,000	15,871,463	77,394,433

The following are Mr Porter's remarks on this statement :—

" This statement which was drawn up by Mr William Couling, a civil engineer and surveyor, was delivered in by him when examined before the Select Committee of the House of Commons, appointed in that year to inquire into the subject of Emigration from the United Kingdom. It does not pretend to absolute accuracy, but considerable knowledge and industry having been employed in preparing it, the statement may be received as a near approximation to the truth, and as the best evidence that can be adduced on the subject. In support of his statement, Mr Couling told the Committee that his calculations were for the most part the result of personal inspection, he having carefully examined the greater part of 106 counties, and partially travelled over the remaining 11, the aggregate length of his journeys, for the purpose, having exceeded 50,000 miles. Mr Couling further assured the Committee, that when he had not enjoyed the means of making personal inspection, he had consulted and availed himself of the very best authorities for completing his estimates."

From these very valuable tables, it will be seen that we have still fifteen millions of land, waste and capable of improvement ; and, dividing it between arable and pasture, in the proportion which at present exists, Mr Porter estimates that it would add six millions to the arable, capable of producing food for 8,726,000 people ; but that if all England were as well cultivated as Northumberland and Lincoln, the quantity now produced would be more than doubled.

We now present Mr Porter's table of the progress of inclosure, and the average prices of wheat since the year 1760, which we imagine disposes of his own conclusion, that protection has been the bane of agriculture, and that low prices are the only stimulus to increased production.

The number of Inclosure Bills passed from 1801 to 1844 was 2,044 ; and the total number of acres inclosed was 3,740,520, as follows :—

	BILLS.	ACRES.
1801 to 1810 inclusive	906	1,657,980
1811 to 1820 ,,	771	1,410,930
1821 to 1830 ,,	186	340,380
1831 to 1840 ,,	129	236,070
1841 to 1844 ,,	52	95,160
	2,044	3,740,520

TABLE of the NUMBER of INCLOSURE BILLS passed by Parliament, and of the AVERAGE PRICES of WHEAT in the several Years from 1760 to 1844.

YEARS.	Number of Inclosure Bills.	Average Price of Wheat.		YEARS.	Number of Inclosure Bills.	Average Price of Wheat.	
		s.	*d.*			*s.*	*d.*
1760	24	36	6	1800	63	110	5
1761	21	30	3	1801	80	115	11
1762	39	39	0	1802	122	67	9
1763	31	40	9	1803	96	57	1
1764	66	46	9	1804	104	60	5
1765	60	52	0	1805	52	87	1
1766	49	43	1	1806	71	76	9
1767	35	64	6	1807	76	73	1
1768 } 1769 }	60	{ 60 { 45	6 8	1808	91	78	11
				1809	92	94	5
	385	**45**	**10**		**847**	**82**	**2**
1770	63	41	4	1810	122	103	3
1771	67	47	2	1811	107	92	5
1772	70	50	8	1812	133	122	8
1773	65	51	0	1813	119	106	6
1774	62	52	8	1814	120	72	1
1775	42	48	4	1815	81	63	8
1776	58	38	2	1816	47	76	2
1777	99	45	6	1817	34	94	0
1778	66	42	0	1818	46	83	8
1779	68	33	8	1819	44	72	3
	660	**45**	**0**		**853**	**88**	**8**
1780	45	35	8	1820	40	65	10
1781	25	44	8	1821	25	54	5
1782	15	47	10	1822	13	43	3
1783	18	52	8	1823	9	51	9
1784	15	48	10	1824	12	62	0
1785	23	51	10	1825	24	66	6
1786	25	38	10	1826	20	56	11
1787	22	41	2	1827	22	56	9
1788	34	45	0	1828	16	60	5
1789	24	57	2	1829	24	66	3
	246	**45**	**9**		**205**	**58**	**5**
1790	26	53	2	1830	21	64	3
1791 } 1792 }	38	{ 47 { 41	2 9	1831	9	66	4
				1832	12	58	8
1793	46	47	10	1833	15	52	11
1794	42	50	8	1834	16	46	2
1795	39	72	11	1835	4	39	4
1796	75	76	3	1836	10	48	6
1797	86	52	2	1837	10	55	10
1798	52	50	4	1838	19	64	7
1799	65	66	11	1839	20	70	8
	469	**·55**	**11**		**136**	**56**	**9**

YEARS.	Number of Inclosure Bills.	Average Price of Wheat.	
		s.	*d.*
1840	14	66	4
1841	22	64	4
1842	11	57	3
1843	11	50	1
1844	8	51	3

It will be seen from this last table that, from the years 1800 to 1820, the high average prices of that period caused the inclosure of land to an extent never equalled before or since, and that, just in the proportion of the decline in prices, inclosure has also gradually declined, so that, at this moment, a man must be mad indeed to venture on the experiment of inclosing poor lands for the purpose of converting them into arable, in order to grow grain in competition with the produce of other countries, if, for the future, it is to be admitted duty free.

Applications for assistance to drain and improve waste lands may continue to be made, and the English yeoman will adopt whatever improvements can be suggested by experience, or by men of skill and science, so as to overcome all and every obstacle that may oppose his onward course; nay, he will struggle long against adverse circumstances; but if low prices out are to be the motive by which he is to be stimulated to action, the world will have grown old in the discovery of a principle in political economy, which, if true, and it had been propounded in past ages, would have made a philosopher immortal.

Our reading of the foregoing table is this, that the high prices of produce from 1800 to 1820 gave rise to great improvements in the science of agriculture, both as regards the growth of grain and the breeding of cattle; and that the abundance of the last twenty-six years, and the lower average prices of produce, have been a natural consequence of the high state of cultivation induced by the high prices of the preceding twenty years, and of nothing else.

But it has been said, that, even with this increased production of our own soil, we are still dependent on other countries for a part of our supplies. On this head we present the following table of the imports and exports of grain for the last 150 years. In the compilation of this we have taken the returns made by the Custom-House authorities, dated Feb. 8, 1842, for the quantities imported and exported, deducting from these the quantities received from Ireland. There are some descrepancies between this statement and the quantities given in Mr Porter's book, but the whole difference is very trifling, and of not sufficient importance in any way to affect the argument.

IMPORT OF FOREIGN WHEAT AND FLOUR.

STATEMENT of the TOTAL QUANTITIES of WHEAT and WHEAT FLOUR IMPORTED INTO and EXPORTED FROM GREAT BRITAIN in each Year, from 1697 to 1846.

YEARS.	IMPORTED.	EXPORTED.	YEARS.	IMPORTED.	EXPORTED.
	Quarters.	Quarters.		Quarters.	Quarters.
1697	400	14,698	1749	382	631,007
1698	1,689	6,886	1750	280	950,483
1699	486	557	1751	3	662,957
1700	5	49,057	1752	—	430,117
1701	1	98,324	1753	—	300,754
1702	—	90,230	1754	201	356,781
1703	50	106,615	1755	—	237,466
1704	2	90,314	1756	5	102,752
1705	—	96,185	1757	141,562	11,545
1706	77	188,332	1758	20,353	9,234
1707	—	174,155	1759	162	227,641
1708	86	83,969	1760	3	393,614
1709	1,552	71,618	1761	—	441,956
1710	400	16,607	1762	56	295,385
1711	—	80,941	1763	72	429,538
1712	—	148,539	1764	1	396,857
1713	—	179,969	1765	104,547	167,126
1714	16	180,665	1766	11,020	164,939
1715	—	173,237	1767	497,905	5,071
1716	—	75,876	1768	349,268	7,433
1717	—	25,637	1769	4,378	49,892
1718	—	74,381	1770	34	75,449
1719	20	130,533	1771	2,510	10,089
1720	—	84,343	1772	25,474	6,959
1721	—	82,748	1773	56,857	7,637
1722	—	178,915	1774	289,149	15,928
1723	—	158,082	1775	560,988	91,037
1724	148	247,162	1776	20,578	210,664
1725	12	211,175	1777	233,323	87,686
1726	—	143,626	1778	106,394	141,070
1727	—	31,030	1779	5,039	222,261
1728	74,574	3,935	1780	3,915	224,059
1729	40,315	18,993	1781	159,866	103,021
1730	76	94,530	1782	80,695	145,152
1731	4	130,650	1783	584,183	51,945
1732	—	202,612	1784	216,947	89,288
1733	7	427,425	1785	110,863	132,685
1734	7	498,747	1786	51,463	205,466
1735	9	155,280	1787	59,339	120,536
1736	18	118,218	1788	148,710	82,971
1737	32	466,671	1789	112,656	140,014
1738	3	588,284	1790	222,577	30,892
1739	23	285,492	1791	469,056	70,626
1740	5,469	54,391	1792	22,417	300,278
1741	7,540	45,417	1793	490,398	76,869
1742	1	295,698	1794	327,902	155,048
1743	3	375,979	1795	313,793	18,836
1744	2	234,274	1796	879,200	24,679
1745	8	325,340	1797	461,767	54,525
1746	—	131,105	1798	396,721	59,782
1747	—	270,491	1799	463,185	39,362
1748	6	545,240	1800	1,264,520	22,013

Years.	Imported.	Exported.	Years.	Imported.	Exported.
	Quarters.	Quarters.		Quarters.	Quarters.
1801	1,424,765	28,406	1824	85,183	61,680
1802	647,663	149,304	1825	391,588	38,796
1803	373,725	76,580	1826	582,276	20,054
1804	461,140	63,073	1827	306,615	57,323
1805	920,834	77,955	1828	757,716	76,489
1806	310,342	29,566	1829	1,670,602	75,097
1807	404,946	25,113	1830	1,676,034	37,149
1808	84,889	98,005	1831	2,310,340	65,875
1809	455,987	31,278	1832	681,765	289,558
1810	1,567,126	75,785	1833	322,256	96,222
1811	336,131	97,765	1834	201,982	159,482
1812	290,710	46,325	1835	89,035	134,076
1813	559,000	133,441	1836	264,400	256,978
1814	852,567	111,477	1837	575,027	308,420
1815	194,931	227,947	1838	1,380,817	158,621
1816	210,861	121,611	1839	2,852,398	42,512
1817	1,030,830	317,534	1840	2,352,205	87,242
1818	1,586,031	58,668	1841	2,691,555	30,390
1819	471,607	44,689	1842	2,916,835	175,958
1820	591,732	94,657	1843	1,064,942	90,679
1821	137,684	199,846	1844	1,379,261	76,285
1822	47,598	160,499	1845	1,142,927	59,841
1823	23,951	145,751	1846	2,351,908	132.758

The best exposition of our opinions in respect of the above table may be given in Mr Porter's own words, applied to another period of time. At page 139 he says, " In the closing years of the last century there occurred a succession of deficient harvests, which caused a considerable importation of corn into this country; but previous to that time the production of wheat had been about adequate, taking one year with another, for the feeding of the inhabitants." Between the period referred to by Mr Porter and the years from 1838 to 1842, the parallel is complete. The importations in fact in all other years have been too unimportant to affect the general argument, that except in seasons of scarcity, the agriculturists could, if their interests were protected, provide food for the people. In the years 1800 and 1801, we imported about 1,300,000 quarters in each year, and considering that the population at that period was only one half what it is at present, our deficiency in seasons of scarcity is not, *pro rata*, greater now than it was fifty years ago. The whole quantity taken for home consumption from 1800 to 1844, was 36,085,957 quarters or an average of 784,477 quarters per annum; but if we except the five years of scarcity from 1838 to 1842, the total number of quarters imported is 24,386,870, giving an average for the thirty-nine years of only 625,304 quarters, which is very little indeed above that of the preceding twenty years, and as compared with the fifty millions of grain of all kinds which we annually produce ourselves, is unworthy of an argument. But even supposing our deficiency much greater, and that it may be necessary to import a million or a million-and-a-half of quarters annually, still this sinks into utter insignificance when compared with other considerations of great and weighty importance. The rental of the land of the three kingdoms is estimated at 58,753,615*l.* (see Rental). The direct and local taxation amounts to 18,314,908*l.*, of which 13,881,911*l.* is paid by the landed interest, and 4,432,997*l.* by the manufacturing interest (see Appendix, page 141). Such being the preponderance of the landed interest and those dependent on it, we have a right to assume, for the reasons given in chap. 3, that the same proportion of the Government taxes on all articles of consumption, whether of excise or customs, direct or indirect, amounting in round numbers, independently of the income tax, to fifty millions per annum, is paid from profits derived from the cultivation of the soil in respect of its rental and productions.

In addition to this, we have also to consider the amount of capital embarked in the cultivation of the soil, and this we estimate at 250 millions. The quantity of land under cultivation is stated to be 46,522,970 acres, and we estimate the average amount of capital employed at from 5*l.* to 6*l.* per acre. In some counties it is very much more than this, while in others it is somewhat less. Some authors have made estimates of three times this amount, but there can be no foundation for such assertions. It is a matter much regretted by all who have written on the subject that we have no statistical information of the amount of the annual productions of the agricultural interest on which perfect reliance can be placed. We can therefore only collect the opinions of those most conversant with such matters, and we believe the following to be the nearest approximation to the quantities of the several crops and stock that can be made.

The notes which we shall append to each article will contain the authority for the statement, and show also the amount of supplies drawn from Ireland and foreign Countries, so that the reader will be able to embrace at a glance all the considerations which attach to the several articles enumerated:—

ESTIMATE OF THE ANNUAL PRODUCE OF THE UNITED KINGDOM.

22,000,000 quarters of WHEAT at 60s. - - - £66,000,000

	Quarters.
England - -	18,000,000
Scotland - -	1,750,000
Ireland - -	2,250,000

	Quarters.
Average Imports from foreign countries since 1800 - - - - -	784,477
Average of the same period, deducting 5 years of scarcity from 1838 to 1842 - - -	625,304
Imports from Ireland in 1845 - - -	779,113
Ditto , ditto 1846 - - -	186,730
Mr McCulloch estimates the quantity at -	15,000,000

34,000,000 quarters of ALL OTHER GRAIN at 30s. - - 51,000,000

	Barley.	Oats & Rye.	Beans & Peas
	Qrs.	Qrs.	Qrs.
England and Wales -	6,000,000	10,500,000	1,500,000
Scotland - - -	1,560,000	5,500,000	120,000
Ireland - - -	1,320,000	7,500,000	
	8,880,000	23,500,000	1,620,000
Total - - - -		34,000,000	

Mr McCulloch's estimate of these quantities amounts to 36,608,572 quarters.

Imports from Ireland in 1845 - 2,353,985 qrs. of Oats.
     „   „   „   - 93,095 „ Barley.

HAY, SEEDS, GARDEN and GREEN CROPS - - - 30,000,000

    Mr McCulloch estimates Meadow and Grass, for work and pleasure horses, at 13,000,000l. To this must be added the value of all the seed crops grown.

2,000,000 head of CATTLE - - - - 30,000,000

    Mr McCulloch's estimate is not so high. He considers the number of Cattle of all kinds in Great Britain to be about 5,620,000, and in Ireland the returns of the census give the number at 1,863,116, making a total of 7,483,116 for the United Kingdom. Of these one-fourth are slaughtered annually.

Carried forward - - £177,000,000

Brought forward - -		£177,000,000
Sent to Smithfield market in 1845 - - -	192,180	
Imported from Ireland in 1846 - - -	186,483	
„ foreign parts in 1842 - -	4,264	
„ „ 1843 - -	1,521	
„ „ 1844 - -	4,889	
„ „ 1845 - -	16,870	
„ „ 1846 - -	42,562	

10,000,000 SHEEP and LAMBS - - - - £15,000,000

Mr Luccock, in 1800, estimated the number of sheep in England and Wales at 19,007,601.

Mr McCulloch is of opinion that this number has not materially varied for nearly fifty years; a conclusion, we think, very much at variance with the fact.

Mr Porter estimates the number at - -	25,343,476	
In Scotland the number is estimated at - -	3,500,000	
In Ireland the number returned in the census of		
1841 - - - - - -	2,106,189	
Imported from Ireland in 1846 - - -	259,257	
Imported from foreign parts in 1842 - -	644	
„ 1843 - -	217	
„ 1844 - -	2,817	
„ 1845 - -	15,958	
„ 1846 - •	94,567	

POTATOES - - - - - - - 25,000,000

Mr Labouchere, in his speech in the House of Commons, on Irish distress, adopted an estimate of Mr Griffith, that the potato crop of Ireland was worth 15,000,000*l.*, to which must be added at least 10,000,000*l.* for Great Britain.

WOOL - - - - - - - 8,000,000

Mr M'Culloch estimates the quantity of British wool annually produced at 110,000,000 lb.; Mr Porter .' at 145,724,880lb., which, at present prices, would yield this amount

Imported from foreign parts in 1846 - 63,117,668 lb.

BUTTER - - - - - - - 5,000,000

Mr McCulloch estimates the consumption of London annually at 1,410,000*l.*

Imported from foreign parts in 1846 .. - 257,777 cwt.

CHEESE - - - - - - - 5,000,000

Imported from foreign parts in 1846 - - 336,185 cwt.

POULTRY, MILK, EGGS, FRUIT, and VEGETABLES - - 3,000,000

Mr McCulloch estimates the consumption of milk in London at 800,000*l.* per annum.

Mr Porter estimates the quantity of eggs imported from Ireland at 100,000*l.* per annum.

Imported from foreign parts in 1846, Eggs - 72,299,632

Carried forward - - £238,000,000

Brought forward - -	£238,000,000
HORSES, 200,000 - - - - - -	3,000,000

The number of horses of all kinds kept in England and Wales in 1821, was 1,161,430, of which 832,726 were wholly employed in husbandry, and 135,542 partially. Mr McCulloch estimates the whole number at 1,500,000, of the average value of 12*l.* to 15*l.*, or from 18,000,000*l.* to 22,500,000*l.* In 1822 the duty on horses employed in husbandry was taken off, and since then no return has been made, but it is clear from the return we have given, that five-sixths of all the horses in the United Kingdom are employed by the Agricultural Interest.

PIGS - - - - - - - 2,000,000

Mr McCulloch estimates the number annually produced in England and Wales at 555,000; but this must be much too low.

Imported from Ireland in 1846	-	-	-	480,827
Imported from foreign parts in 1842		-	-	410
„	1843	-	-	361
„	1844	-	-	265
,,	1845	-	-	1,598
„	1846	-	-	3,443

ALL OTHER ANIMALS - - - - - 1,000,000

Including asses, mules, 386,063 dogs, deer, and game of all kinds.

HOPS. - - - - - - - 1,500,000

Duty at twopence per lb. in 1846, at 443,657*l.*
Mr. M'Culloch estimates the crop at 750,000*l.*

TIMBER - - - - - - - 2,500,000

Dr Beke estimates the timber of this country worth 80,000,000*l.* which at 4 per cent. would produce 3,200,000*l.* per annum.
Mr McCulloch says from 40,000,000*l.* to 50,000,000*l.*

Imported in 1846	-	1,221,096	loads, colonial.
		809,024	„ foreign.
		2,030,120	loads

VALUE OF UNCULTIVATED WASTES and WOODS - - - 2,000,000

Total - - £250,000,000

The foregoing is an approximation to the probable quantities and value of the annual productions of our agricultural interest, but if the estimate had been made at the present prices of produce, it would of course have added some fifty millions to the amount.

Such has been the course, and such the results of British Agriculture, up to the time when the grand discovery was made that we had been progressing in the wrong direction, and protection, which had been engrafted as a principle on our system, was surrendered on a plea of expediency to the clamour of a faction agitating for their own selfish interests.

Had protection been continued to our home and colonial markets, and the extension of trade with our natural enemies and rivals been treated as of secondary importance, it is not improbable that in a few years Mr Porter's assertion, that these quantities might be doubled, would have been realised by the cultivation of the entire surface of the three kingdoms to a degree of perfection equal to that of Lincoln or any other county; but the *stimulus* of low prices will only effect this, when the natural order of things shall be reversed, and mankind have learnt the lesson of living by the loss rather than the profit of their occupations.

Up to the present time our farmers have lived in a state of comfort, equally with other classes of the community; and none have a better title to do so, for, as we have shown at page 141 in the Appendix, they pay three-fourths of the direct and local taxation of the country. They are now called upon, with what degree of justice it is impossible to perceive, to compete with men unacquainted with the wants of a civilized life, who pay but a nominal rent for their land, and whose taxation, direct and indirect, is not one-twentieth of that paid by the English farmer.

The serfs of the lords of Poland and Russia, and a class of men just emerging from a state of half civilization, the farmers in America, are for the future to be their competitors; not in foreign markets, but in our own; not in Germany, France, or Belgium, but in Mark lane, Liverpool, Wakefield, and Devizes; and writers who wish to conceal the truth tell us, that the distance of these countries and the expense of freight are a sufficient protection for the agricultural interests of this country.

To show the degree of credit such assertions are entitled to, Mr Porter shall speak for himself, when writing on Foreign Commerce, and in support of the free-trade system: he thus proceeds:—

" The argument in favour of the greater comparative value to a country of its home
than of its foreign trade, which has been founded upon the greater economy and
celerity with which the operations of the former are conducted, is far from being
always correct when applied to England. The trading communication between
the south and east coast of Great Britain and the north and west shores of many
European countries, is kept up with greater facility and economy than the traffic
between some of our distant counties. The time and money expended in conveying a bale of goods from Manchester to London, by canal or by the ordinary road,
are greater than are required for its conveyance from London to Rotterdam, and
the charge made for the cartage of a puncheon of rum from the West India Docks
to Westminster exceeds the charge that would be made for conveying the same
puncheon of rum from those Docks to Hamburgh. Even in those branches of
foreign commerce, when, from the length of the voyage, a considerable time must
elapse between the shipment of goods, their reception and sale abroad, and
the transmission of returns to the hands of the shipper, a remedy for the evil
of delay has been found in the operation of commercial bankers, whose dealings
consist in the purchase and sale of bills of exchange, and are founded upon the
varying necessities of different individual traders."

The first year of free trade has falsified all the assertions of its
advocates, that in times of scarcity the superabundance of other
countries would keep down our own prices ; and the first year of
an abundant harvest throughout Europe will be sufficient to satisfy
our farmers, that wheat, oats, and barley can be transported from
the shores of the Baltic to any of our own markets, at nearly as
small an expense as from Lincolnshire to Mark lane, or from Cork,
Limerick, and Belfast, to the river Thames.

The additional facilities for the transmission of produce by
steam-boats, railroads, &c., which are every day springing up in all
directions, will soon reduce the expenses far below even the present estimate, and make it a merely nominal consideration whether
a cargo of grain is taken on board in the ports of the Baltic, or in
those of Scotland, Ireland, or the North of England. And it only
requires the suspension or abolition of the navigation laws, to
enable the grower of agricultural produce to avail himself of the
cheapest carrier, to give the *coup de grâce* to the argument, and
confirm Mr Porter's statement, that the operation between these
ports and some of our more distant counties may be conducted with
equal economy and celerity.

We have therefore to consider the probable degree of competition which, under these circumstances, the English farmer will
have to contend with ; and this will be best seen by a reference

to the following table of the prices of wheat in England and in foreign countries from 1834 to 1842, extracted from returns presented to Parliament:—

STATEMENT of the HIGHEST PRICES of CORN, per Winchester Quarter of 8 Bushels, in sterling, calculated at current rate of exchange, on the average of the first week of each of the months of January, April, July, and October, in each year from 1834 to 1842, compiled from the Consular Returns presented to Parliament.

	1834		1835		1836		1837		1838		1839		1840		1841		1842	
	s.	d.	s.	d.	s.	d.	s.	d.	s.	d.	s.	d.	s.	d.	s.	d.	s.	d.
Average Price in England	46	2	39	4	48	6	55	10	64	7	70	8	66	4	64	4	57	3
,, Antwerp	32	3	35	6	37	2	39	9	46	7	56	8	54	4	47	9	55	1
,, Amsterdam	28	11	27	3	27	1	32	9	35	1	55	6	46	2	37	9	40	3
,, Hamburgh	26	11	24	6	25	10	33	0	40	1	53	9	49	3	41	4	50	0
,, Denmark	20	4	21	6	33	9	33	9	46	10	43	9	—		—		—	
,, Dantzic	30	7	27	5	30	1	31	8	37	8	52	2	—		43	10	48	2
,, Riga	25	11	24	11	25	1	28	3	34	9	42	4	42	9	48	5	—	
,, Naples	27	6	22	9	26	10	31	2	34	6	38	2	37	0	34	6	35	11
,, Venice	29	4	29	0	32	4	38	2	35	8	42	11	39	6	35	10	39	10
,, Trieste	33	2	31	1	33	5	34	7	37	4	42	11	40	2	40	11	38	6
,, Odessa	32	8	23	5	20	5	21	8	24	0	49	7	28	6	27	6	29	4
,, New York	37	0	—		49	5	56	8	57	5	47	8	35	5	40	6	39	6
,, Philadelphia	37	6	41	1	52	5	—		55	5	48	10	32	7	34	4	41	4
,, Norfolk	32	10	—		49	3	—		—		—		31	1	38	0	35	4
,, Portsmouth (N. H.)	36	10	43	5	48	8	58	11	57	10	57	0	48	3	45	8	48	4

The average prices are about 10 to 15 per cent. under the above; and the lowest vary from 25 to 30 per cent.

We may flatter ourselves on our superior capital and skill, but so long as cause and effect have any relationship to each other, there can be but one deduction from the foregoing statement of facts, and it is this, — that, with a free trade in grain, all countries will be stimulated alike to increase their growth, and the countries nearest to our own shores will have so decided an advantage over those at a distance, as to leave them no chance of competing with them. The idea that America will ever supply us with any thing except flour, and with that only when prices are high, must be abandoned. Besides which, with a free trade in grain it matters not to our agriculturists from whence the supply may come. If from a great distance so much the worse, for it will only prove the superiority of such countries over ourselves to be of a more decided character; and for the farmer of this country there is no alternative but to descend to the level of those of other countries, or to raise them up to his own peculiar and hitherto superior standard. There is no middle course—no counteracting cause; and the first two or three years of abundance will painfully establish the truth of this conclusion. What an inducement for the investment of capital in the most uncertain and hazardous of all occupations! what a stimulus for exertion on the part of our farmers and landed gentry, is the social condition of the landed interests in the countries given in this list!

But whatever may be the result of this experiment, as regards Great Britain, how can it be justified in reference to our sister kingdom of Ireland? Struck down to the earth as she has been by one of the most awful calamities that ever afflicted a nation, and labouring under many other evils of long standing, which her union with this country has neither ameliorated nor redressed, she was yet gradually progressing in agricultural pursuits; and it is worthy of especial notice, that her trade with us is twice in amount, and of much greater importance, than that with the United States of America. On this head we present the following tables, which will show the proportion that Ireland has contributed to the supply of Great Britain, and the gradual progress of her exports to this country, which has been of course balanced by her imports of colonial produce and manufactured goods from us:—

STATEMENT of the QUANTITY of VARIOUS KINDS of GRAIN and MEAL brought into GREAT BRITAIN from IRELAND in each year from 1815 to 1845.

Years.	Wheat, and Wheat Flour.	Barley, and Barley Meal.	Rye.	Oats and Oatmeal.	Indian Corn.	Beans.	Peas.	Total of Grain and Meal.
	Qrs.	Qrs.	Qrs.	Qrs.	Qrs.	Qrs.		Qrs.
1815	189,544	27,108	207	597,537	—	6,796		821,192
1816	121,631	62,254	43	683,714	—	6,223		873,865
1817	59,025	26,766	614	611,117	—	2,287		699,809
1818	108,230	25,387	4	1,069,385	—	4,845		1,207,851
1819	154,031	20,311	2	789,613	—	3,904		967,861
1820	404,747	87,095	134	916,250	1	8,893		1,417,120
1821	569,700	82,884	550	1,162,249	—	7,433		1,822,816
1822	463,004	22,532	353	569.237	—	7,963		1,063,089
1823	400,068	19,274	198	1,102,487	—	6,126		1,528,153
1824	356,408	45,872	112	1,225,085	·—	6,547		1,634,024
1825	396,018	165,082	220	1,629,856	—	12,786		2,203,962
1826	314,851	64,885	77	1,303.734	—	7,190	1,452	1,692,189
1827	405,255	67,791	256	1,343,267	1,765	10,037	1,372	1,829,743
1828	652,584	84,204	1,424	2,075,631	280	7,068	4,944	2,826,135
1829	519,493	97,140	568	1,673,628	39	10,444	4,503	2,305,806
1830	529,717	189,745	414	1,471,252	28	19,053	2,520	2,212,729
1831	557,520	185,409	515	1,655,934	563	15,039	4,663	2,419,643
1832	572,586	123,068	294	1,890,321	3,037	14,512	1,916	2,605,734
1833	844,201	107,519	167	1,762,519	117	19,103	2,645	2,736,281
1834	779,504	217,568	982	1,713,971	75	18,770	2,176	2,733,046
1835	661,773	156,176	614	1,813,101	—	24,234	3,447	2,659,345
1836	598,756	182,867	483	2,126,693	Malt.	17,603	2,920	2,929,322
1837	534,465	187,473	1,016	2,274,675	4,174	25,630	2,860	3,030,293
1838	542,583	156,467	628	2,742,807	5,001	21,584	5,232	3,474,302
1839	258,331	61,675	2,331	1,904,933	2,552	11,535	1,484	2.242,841
1840	174,440	95,954	122	2,037,836	3,456	14,753	1,403	2,327,964
1841	218,708	75,568	172	2,539,380	4,935	15,907	855	2,855,525
1842	201,998	50,286	76	2,261,434	3,046	19,931	1,550	2,538,221
1843	413,466	110,449	371	2,648,033	8,643	24,329	1,192	3,206,483
1844	440,153	90,655	264	2,242,300	8,153	18,580	1,091	2,801,206
1845	779,113	93,095	165	2,353,985	11,154	12,745	1,644	3,251,901

IMPORTS AND EXPORTS.

IMPORTS and EXPORTS from IRELAND to GREAT BRITAIN in the years 1845 and 1846.			Imports into Ireland from Great Britain.	Exports from Ireland to Great Britain.
CORN, in 1845.				
779,113 Qrs. Wheat,	at 50s.	£1,942,782		
93,095 Barley and Meal,	30s.	139,642		
2,353,985 Oats,	20s.	2,353,985		
CATTLE, IN 1846.				
186,483 Black Cattle, at £16 - -		2,983,728	1801 £3,270,350	£3,537,725
6,363 Calves „ 45s. - -		14,316		
259,257 Sheep „ 40s. - -		518,514	1805 - 4,067,717	4,288,167
480,827 Pigs „ 50s. - -		1,202,067		
Horses and Mules, no return this year; but in 1837 they amounted to 70,802l., and, allowing for a small increase, we estimate them at - - -		80,000	1809 - 5,316,557	4,588,305
			1813 - 6,746,353	5,410,326
Total of Agricultural produce -		9,235,034		
			1817 - 4,722,766	5,696,613
LINEN MANUFACTURE, 12-13ths of which is sent to Great Britain - -		5,000,000	1821 - 5,338,838	7,117,452
Total Value -		- £14,235,034	1825 - 7,048,936	8 531,355

SHIPPING.

	ENTERED INWARDS.			ENTERED OUTWARDS.	
Years.	Ships.	Tonnage.	Years.	Ships.	Tonnage.
In 1801	5,360	456,026	In 1801	6,816	582,033
1825	8,922	741,182	1825	10,981	922,325
1844	10,147	1,349,273	1844	16,948	1,817,756

The Irish trade since 1825 has been assimilated to the coasting-trade, and no return of the exports and imports has been made; but it will be seen that the tonnage of the shipping employed between the two countries has nearly doubled since 1825; and that the trade now amounts to nearly fifteen millions per annum, or twice that carried on with the United States.

The state of Ireland at the present time bears a strong analogy to that of England in the reigns of Henry VIII and Elizabeth, when the land was overrun with beggars, and the most cruel enactments could not suppress the crime of mendicancy. By the 14th Elizabeth, cap. 5, it is declared, that

"All persons whole and mighty in body, able to labour, not having land or master, nor using any lawful merchandise, craft, or mystery, and all common labourers able in body, loitering and refusing to work for such reasonable wages as are commonly given, shall for the first offence be *grievously whipped and burned through the gristle of the right ear with a hot iron of the compass of an inch about,* for the second shall be deemed *felons,* and for the third shall *suffer death* as felons, without benefit of clergy."

The first law, however, which gave to the pauper a legal title to relief was the source from which have flowed nine-tenths of the improvements so favourably distinguishing this country from all others. Follow this example. Give to Ireland a sound and wholesome system of poor laws, and it will compel the landlord to reside on his estate, and dispense with the services and the tyranny of the middle man. It will also compel him to give employment to a long-neglected peasantry, by the application of capital and skill to the cultivation of the soil, and thus put an end to the worst of all evils, the sub-letting of the land, and the consequent degradation of the population.

And unless the minister, whoever he is, or may be, is powerful enough to carry out this great sovereign remedy for the social evils which afflict Ireland, he will do nothing for the salvation of the people. His feeding a whole nation on charity, however imperative as a duty, from the dire necessity of the case in the present instance, and however praiseworthy for the extent of its generosity, is calculated to leave the worst effect on the minds and habits of the people, and is, in truth, the most fearful remedy that could be applied to such a state of things, for it discloses an abyss of self-abandonment and degradation which it is fearful to contemplate.

It is the duty of the statesman to look far beyond this temporary measure of expediency, and at once to apply an efficient remedy; for, if this is not done, the agrarian outrages, which have so long been a foul stain on the national character of Ireland, may prove to have been only the forerunner, the type, the foreshadowing of some great convulsion, that, operating on those struggling for existence, will involve all classes in one common ruin.

" Better that a class should be ruined than that a nation should perish," said a writer in *The Times,* a few days ago, and we reiterate the sentiment; but better, far better, that, with improved institutions, and with protection for her productions, she should take her just rank by our side, and become a source of strength instead of weakness. Her capabilities are such, that she could increase the amount of her agricultural productions ten-fold. With great quantities of waste land unreclaimed, a fertile soil, a rapidly increasing population, noble harbours, easy of access from all parts of the island, Ireland ought to be, under good government,—what Sicily was to the Romans,—an inexhaustible storehouse of food for the people.

We have now presented a sketch of the Agricultural Interest in all its bearings, comparatively with the Manufacturing, and as an interest standing on its own individual importance. It is not necessary to repeat the exact figures here, as they will be found under the several heads of our division of the subject,—in the Tables of each of the counties given in the Appendix, and in the Summary of the whole at the conclusion of the work. But the results of this inquiry may be shortly re-stated thus:—

In the land of the United Kingdom is invested about two thousand millions of capital. It gives employment to three millions and a quarter of able-bodied persons, the mainstay and strength of our political power. Of the several classes who are dependent on those employed in the cultivation of the soil, or on the rental of the land, or on the circulation of its productions, it supports eighteen millions and three quarters, making a total of twenty-two millions in all. It pays three-fourths of the entire taxation of the country. It feeds and supports the poor, maintains the Church, is the great bulwark of the throne, and in it are embodied all the elements of national strength, wealth, order, and tranquillity.

CHAPTER V.

THE MANUFACTURING INTEREST.

Review of the Progress of Manufactures in Great Britain and Foreign Countries since the Peace.—Locality of the Manufacturing Interest in the United Kingdom.—Its Numerical Strength.—Number of Persons employed in the most important Branches.—Number employed in Ireland.—Tendency of Mechanical Power to abridge Labour.

THE Manufacturing Interest of this country is undoubtedly one of great importance, but it derives this importance, not from any principle of strength within itself, for it is in truth the weakest of all the members of the body politic. However much we may pride ourselves on the possession of coal and minerals, recent discoveries have placed other nations on the same level in respect of these; and as for natural productions, which constitute the raw material of our factories, Britain is one of the poorest nations in the universe.

It produces neither cotton, fine wool, nor silk; and for all the improvements which have latterly been made in the manufacture of our coarse wools, we are indebted to the ingenuity of our neighbours the French, who were the first to turn the long wools of this country to so good an account. The manufacture of hardware is also dependent on the superior quality of the iron imported from Sweden.

Possessing therefore no natural advantages over other countries, and subject to the competition of nations equally ingenious, industrious, and persevering as ourselves, and from many of whom we have borrowed the most important discoveries in the mechanical arts, we must trace the rise, the progress, and the present importance of the Manufacturing Interest to other causes than that of any inherent principle of originality or stability of its own.

The principal cause, undoubtedly, is the purely adventitious one of our having been the only nation in Europe whose territory was not involved in the horrors of a desolating war; and the fact, that during the night of adversity which afflicted other countries from 1790 to 1815, we enjoyed a monopoly of the trade of the world.

If, during this period, and with these political advantages, our manufactures had made no progress, or the skill of the parties engaged in them had not developed itself, it would have been extraordinary indeed; but the assertion that the spinning-jenny and the steam-engine have been the moving powers of our fleets and armies, and the chief support of a long-continued agricultural prosperity; and the boast of Arkwright, that give him but these and he would pay the taxation of the country, however flattering to the vanity of a party, we are under the necessity of maintaining have neither the one nor the other the slightest foundation in fact.

But whatever may have been the extent of their development during this period, let it be always remembered that it was, from first to last, under a system of *protection* that this took place. The productions of the soil, equally with those of the loom and the spindle, were protected by duties, which in almost all instances operated as a total prohibition of any competition from abroad. Independently of this, the kingdoms of Continental Europe, continually overrun by the armies of Napoleon, could offer no resistance to our success, and the United States were in too infantine a state of both capital and mechanical knowledge to compete with us, or even to manufacture for themselves.

With the return of peace in 1815, a new order of things arose, and the angry passions of mankind gave way to an earnest desire on the part of all to cultivate the arts of peace, and we were compelled by the force of circumstances to admit as competitors those whom we had hitherto regarded and treated as enemies.

France, to whom we are indebted for the most valuable of mechanical inventions, the Jacquard loom, and the art of cotton printing, and who has far surpassed us in her discoveries of the chemical properties of things, being no longer dazzled by the false glory of conquest, sat herself down to investigate the cause of our success, and to follow our example. And well has she succeeded. Her silks have sustained their ancient excellence, and her finer woollens and cambrics have a preference, and find a market, in every quarter of the globe; and even in the article of cotton, on the manufacture of which we so much pride ourselves, her progress during the last thirty years has been equal to our own. To show the degree of rivalry, and extent of the respective efforts, of the two nations in these important branches, we give the following table of their exports and imports at the conclusion of the war, and at the last period returned.

	Imports of Raw Cotton.	Exports of Manufactured Cotton.	Exports of Woollens.	Exports of Silks.
	lb.	£	£	£
ENGLAND, in 1815 -	92,525,951	20,620,956	9,381,426	In 1820 - 371,755
„ 1844 -	554,196,602	25,805,348	8,204,836	1844 - 736,455
FRANCE 1815 -	36,000,000	362,451	1,610,944	1820 - 2,700,000
„ 1844 -	132,000,000	3,440,701	3,287,522	1843 - 6,000,000

It will thus be seen, that although the import of raw cotton into France has not kept pace with that of England, yet her exports of manufactured cottons have increased ten-fold, while those of England in the same time have only increased one-fourth. The deficiency in the import of raw cotton is accounted for by the fact that an enormous amount of twist is every year smuggled from this country into France, with the connivance of the French Government.* Her exports of woollens have nearly doubled, while those of England have fallen off; and the export of silks from France has risen from three to six millions, while that of England has only struggled on from 371,755*l.* in 1820, to 736,455*l.* in 1844.

But the unkindest cut of all remains to be told; and it is one which Mr Porter says could hardly have been anticipated. Our

---

* The quantity so introduced is estimated by Messrs Villiers and Bowring at 12,000,000 lb. annually.

Government thought it "could be of no moment to the maker of machines, whether his customers reside in the United Kingdom, or in France or Germany," and therefore repealed the restrictions against the export of machinery made in England. The French Government, concluding that a drawing of any machine could be sent at a trifling expense by the post, and that their machinists were equal to our own, and that their labour required protection, instantly put on a heavy import duty, and thus rebuked the assertion made by many of our writers, that in the mechanical arts we excel all other countries.

The people of Germany, Belgium, Switzerland, and even Russia, excited by our example, have begun to develope their resources, and, benefiting by the experience of a few years, are now able to carry on a successful competition with us in every market in the world. On this subject, however, we prefer to use the language of Mr Porter himself, and therefore copy the entire passage from his volume, pages 246 and 247 :—

"A considerable impulse has been given to manufacturing industry in different parts of Germany within the last twelve years, and especially since the formation of the Prussian commercial league. In Prussia itself, many cotton spinning-mills have been erected since 1833, and large capitals have been invested in machinery. In Saxony the manufacture of hosiery has become considerable in amount, and the goods produced are so low in price that exports have been made to England in the face of a consumption duty of 10 per cent. on the value. The cotton manufacture has also been successfully undertaken in Bavaria, in Würtemberg, and in some others of the states included within the league. These attempts, however, are for the most part of such recent origin, that it is hardly possible to form any certain estimate as to their ultimate results. At present it is only through the imposition of a considerable import duty in the German states, that their cotton goods generally are able in any way to compete with English fabrics; but it is altogether impossible to say how long this state of things may continue, and it may reasonably be expected, that the German artisans will in time acquire a degree of skill and experience which, aided by the lower cost of subsistence in Germany, as compared with England, will render their rivalry formidable to Manchester and Paisley, at least in neighbouring countries, if not in more distant parts of the world.

"It has long been the policy of the Russian government to afford protection to its own manufacturers by prohibiting the goods of other countries. At present nearly the whole amount of the exports from this kingdom to Russia, consists of cotton yarn, which is there woven into all kinds of fabrics from the coarsest fustians to fine cambrics. The establishments for this purpose are under the immediate patronage of the Russian government, and it is said that the goods produced are so good in quality as to equal those of English make, but in regard to the cost of production, the advantage is still greatly with us, and so it will probably remain so long as Russia still maintains the policy of protecting its artisans from the competition of other countries.

" In several of the cantons of Switzerland the manufacture of woven fabrics has been steadily and prosperously pursued of late years. So little of what is called protection is accorded to the Swiss manufacturer, that there are not any custom houses in the cantons from which to obtain returns of imports and exports, whereby to ascertain the comparative progress of these branches of industry. Free trade, in the fullest extent of the term, has been tried in these cantons; and although, as already observed, we are unable to bring forward an array of figures in proof of its success, we know that in spite of the disadvantages of geographical position, and notwithstanding the comparative scarcity of capital, the cotton which is obtained by a tedious and expensive land carriage is converted into fabrics which compete successfully in every market with the products of our looms; and that the silk and linen goods of Switzerland which are excluded by fiscal regulations from neighbouring countries, find customers in a wider and more profitable field on the other side of the Atlantic. If we take into account the small natural resources of the Swiss manufacturers, it may with truth be asserted that no people have made greater, or even as great, progress as they have done during the last twenty years. Switzerland has been strongly urged to join the Prussian commercial league, and by that means to secure twenty-four millions of consumers for its cheap manufactures, but satisfied with their present condition and future prospects, and jealous as to the possible effect of permitting foreigners to interfere in any way with their concerns, the cantons have hitherto declined to accept the proffered advantage."

America, too, although restrained for a time by the paucity of her numbers, spread over a great extent of territory, and naturally preferring agricultural pursuits, has been stimulated by the rapid increase in her population to turn her attention to the manufacture of that which is a natural production of her own soil.

And not only has she made wonderful progress in the manufacture of cotton goods, but the determination of Congress to increase the import duties in preference to taxing tea and coffee, to pay the expenses of the war in Mexico, is indicative of her policy to protect and foster them by all the means in her power.

In addition to this, her discoveries of coal and iron have opened up a new branch of industry to her people, which bids fair to interfere with a very important item of our exports to that country:

" The first bar of American railroad iron was made in 1844, and an American paper now states that there are at present 16 or 18 mills, at which it is made at the rate of 120,000 tons per annum.

" This amount is sufficient to lay 4 miles of railway per day, or 1,200 miles per year; and hence the prospect of any large exportation from Great Britain, at the prices to which our inordinate railway speculations have driven this commodity, can hardly be looked for. The Trenton ironworks (New York) alone have entered into a contract to furnish the New York and Michigan lines with 9,000 tons of rails during the current year; and the capacity of their works will enable them in addition to supply the market with 200 tons per month.

"In Pennsylvania the use of the anthracite coal, which abounds in that state, appears to have stimulated this branch of manufacture, since there are now 40 furnaces in blast—many of them of the largest class—where this kind of fuel is consumed, although in 1840 none existed in successful operation. There is one iron manufacturing company in Pennsylvania, which alone consumes 60,000 of anthracite, and 100,000 bushels of bituminous coal annually."—*Extract from Times, March* 9.

It is thus that every day adds to her capital and knowledge, and brings us nearer to that crisis when she will demonstrate to the men of Lancashire that mechanical power and the skill to apply it are not the exclusive birthright of an Englishman, but the common property of all mankind.

If to this we add, that should she, at the same time, discover that the operation of our free-trade system will make it more profitable to grow corn than cotton for the supply of the English market, it is not improbable that the glory of Manchester may depart, and the staple of this country be again represented by woollens, which some suppose we manufactured in the days when Cincinnatus followed his plough.

Such are the external circumstances of the manufacturing interests, in which we are at a loss to perceive one single element of strength or stability. Dependent on other countries for the raw material in nearly every instance, a war with any of these would annihilate some branches and cripple others. Competition with countries also whose taxation is not to be compared with our own must be carried on with every advantage in favour of our rivals, and as it is impossible for us to call new worlds into existence to keep pace with the multiplication of our mechanical power, it behoves us to look well to the introduction of any new system of political economy, however speciously put forward, lest it should endanger the home and colonial markets, which have hitherto been the principal customers for our own productions.

Having thus examined the external circumstances of the Manufacturing Interest, let us now inquire into the facts which relate to its internal condition.

And, first, as to its

LOCALITY.

The Manufacturing Interest of the United Kingdom is distributed as follows:—

	Engaged in Manufactures.	Dependent on Manufactures.	Total.
England, (see Appendix, p. 46) - -	943,998	4,738,829	5,682,827
Wales, „ 60 - -	19,517	137,706	157,223
Scotland, „ 94 - -	220,171	1,011,417	1,231,588
British Isles, „ 96 - -	1,631	18,352	19,983
Ireland, „ 152 - -	300,000	700,000	1,000,000
	1,485,317	6,606,304	8,091,621
Total of the Manufacturing Interest in the United Kingdom		8,091,621	

and, so far as concerns England and Wales, it is principally located in the eight midland counties; viz.—

	Engaged in Agriculture.	Engaged in Manufactures.	Population.
Chester (see Appendix, p. 46) -	26,804	58,293	395,560
Derby „ „ -	19,333	27,968	272,217
Lancaster „ „ -	49,567	292,129	1,667,054
Leicester „ „ -	17,072	22,029	215,867
Nottingham „ „ -	20,358	27,710	249,910
Stafford „ „ -	29,120	53,249	510,504
Warwick „ „ -	24,239	38,451	401,715
Yorkshire „ „ -	93,159	176,249	1,591,480
	279,674	696,078	5,304,407
In all other parts of England and Wales -	- -	247,920	
Total - -		943,998	

The number of persons actually employed in agriculture in the above eight counties being 279,674, or 31,754 more than are employed in every branch of manufactures throughout all other parts of England and Wales, it follows that the population of these eight counties more than represents the entire Manufacturing Interest of this kingdom.

It is almost unnecessary to remark on the well-known fact, that in all other parts this interest is very thinly scattered; for instance:—

				Persons engaged in Manufactures.
In 8 Counties in the West there are only	-	-	61,096
„ 3	„	South	„	-	-	22,434
„ 9	„	East	„	-	-	34,869
„ 7	„	Midland	„	-	-	51,971
„ 4	„	North	„	-	-	29,115

Among the most important branches of manufactures are the following: —

			Number of Persons employed.	
Cotton -	(see Appendix, p. 147)	-	- 377,662
Wool and Worsted	„	-	- 167,296
Flax and Linen	„	-	- 85,213
Silk -	„	-	- 83,773
Hose -	„	-	- 50,955
Lace -	„	-	- 35,347
Total of the Textile Fabrics	-	-		800,246
Iron Manufactures - - -	-	-	- 29,496
Engineers - - - -	-	-	- 25,370
Pottery, China, and Earthenware	-	-	- 24,774
Factory Workers, manufactures not specified	-	-	22,478
Nail Makers - - - -	-	-	- 20,311
Brick and Tile Makers - - -	-	-	- 18,363
Hatters and Hat Manufacturers -	-	-	- 18,012
Printers (Cotton and Calico) -	-	-	- 15,303
Rope and Cord Spinners and Manufacturers	-	-	- 11,319
Straw Plait Manufacturers - -	-	-	- 11,217
				196,643
All other branches of Manufactures	-	-	-	144,017
Total of Great Britain	-	-		1,140,906

We have extracted all the numbers in the list above 10,000; and there is no branch of manufactures in Great Britain giving employment to more than that number, except those we have here enumerated.

But the returns for Ireland deserve a separate and distinct notice. There are only two branches of manufactures of any importance carried on in Ireland, and these are —

Flax and Linen (all branches) giving employment to	-	135,303 persons.
Woollen and Cloth (all branches) - - -	-	77,650 „
		212,953

The numbers given are described as including all branches of these trades, and of course spinners and weavers, and yet the same returns give—

Spinners (branch not specified) - - - - -		334,201
Weavers „ - - - - -		91,086
		425,287

We confess that we are utterly unable to understand this, and there is nothing in the returns which will solve the difficulty. It must therefore remain for the reader to reject or admit, as he may think proper; but for the reasons given at page 152 of the Appendix, we estimate the numbers employed in manufactures in Ireland at 300,000, making the total of the United Kingdom 1,440,906. Subject to this correction, the number of each sex would stand thus :—

	MALES.	FEMALES.	TOTAL.
Great Britain - - - -	741,872	399,034	1,140,906
Ireland - - - - -	60,000	240,000	300,000
Total of the United Kingdom -	791,872	639,034	1,440,906

and such is the numerical strength of the persons *employed* in manufactures.

DEPENDENCE.

It is unnecessary here to repeat the argument, that the incidents of the condition of our manufacturing population do not give rise to the same amount of trade and commerce as those of the agricultural, spread as it is over the entire surface of the country; but, assuming that there are the same number *pro ratâ* of all other classes dependent on them, this will give about five to one on the number employed, and confirm the correctness of the summary of manufactures, given at page 152 in the Appendix.

UNITED KINGDOM.

Total number employed in manufactures - - - -	1,440,906
Total number dependent on those employed in manufactures -	6,650,715
Total employed and dependent on the manufacturing interest of the United Kingdom - - - - - -	8,091,621

That there is a tendency in all improvements in mechanical power to abridge human labour is a conclusion that some have doubted. In 1835, the Committee on Hand-loom Weaving reported that 840,000 persons were either engaged in, or dependent on it; and these, as a separate branch, whether as regards cotton, woollen, silk, or any of the coarser fabrics, were at that time by far the most numerous of any class engaged in manufactures. Since then the introduction of the power loom has been gradually superseding their labour, and little doubt is entertained that but a short time can elapse before all fabrics, except those of extreme fineness and of fancy patterns, will be made entirely by it. The labour of the thousands and tens of thousands of weavers who formerly lived in the villages of the west and the south, was first drawn into the large towns of the north by the application of the steam engine or mechanical power in its first stage. In course of time, one improvement has been superadded to another, until the labour of those who left these villages and sought for employment in the towns is now carried on by mechanical power alone. In fact, all improvements point but to this one conclusion, that the whole manufacturing process of any given article should be concentrated within the walls of a factory or mill, and be conducted at the least possible expense and by the smallest number of persons.

The best illustration we can give is probably that of the making of paper; a bundle of rags is put in at one end of the mill, and at the other flows out an endless length of paper ready printed and fit for use in the next five minutes. We know that screws, nails, needles, and many other articles are made by a process similar in its operation and results; and in every department of manufactures the same principle is being acted upon and carried out to the fullest extent, having for its only object to economise the use of human labour, and to increase the production of goods.

It has been asserted, that, in proportion as new machines are invented and put into operation, the same amount of human labour which they supersede is required in the making of machines, in keeping them at work, and in the manufacturing of new articles and things which would not be made, or made only on a small scale or at a dear rate, but for such new inventions. In the returns of the census there is nothing to justify such a conclusion, either as applicable to any one branch of manufactures or the whole collectively.

We may differ as to the deductions to be made from these statistical facts, or on the principles which govern our present system of trade, but every well-wisher of his country must be desirous that the manufacturing interest should flourish, and that the productions of our mechanical skill should still continue to go forth to the uttermost ends of the earth. We have, however, a sterner duty to perform than to follow Mr M'Culloch's example, and to read a homily on the comparative moral and physical circumstances of this over other countries, much of which is illusory, and the whole of which belongs rather to history than to the present time. The rapid progress which other nations are making in the manufacture of the same articles is, in our opinion, the best and most conclusive evidence that a thirty years' peace has placed us on a common level with the nations of the continent, and sufficient, at all events, to induce a suspicion that it is possible we may have overrated these moral and physical advantages, and by so doing have mistaken the shadow for the substance.

Superiority in either mechanical skill or chemical knowledge we repudiate as an absurdity. In what, then, does it consist? The French surpass us in silks, cambrics, and woollens; and the best patterns of Mr Cobden's productions are only copies of foreign designs. The untaxed Swiss are beating us in our own markets in the article of watches; and these and the Germans undersell us in foreign markets in linen and hosiery, and are making great progress in many articles of hardware.

That our inventions in the mechanical arts have been numerous and valuable no one will for an instant dispute, but the rapid communication of ideas, and the transit of commodities in the present day, makes any invention the common property of Europe in a month; and if any climax was wanting to the argument, it would be found in the permission given to export both our artisans and our machinery if required.

With these facts fully before them, and with this competition to contend with, we should hope that our manufacturers will bestir themselves, and, without any reliance on our *moral and physical advantages*, will, by still greater exertion, maintain their present proud position; but if the labour of our factories should fail, and the cottons of Manchester and the woollens of Leeds should meet with successful rivals in markets hitherto their own, it must be owing to some evil principle at work in our own system, which it is the duty of all who feel an interest in the welfare of this interest to detect, and correct, if possible, lest it should subvert the whole.

We therefore propose to pass in review the several articles which form the staples of the Manufacturing Interest of this country, and in so doing we shall probably not only ascertain the actual status of this interest in the body politic, but also be able to trace the degree of its dependence on the home and foreign trade for the consumption of its productions.

CHAPTER VI.

THE MANUFACTURING INTEREST.—(*Continued.*)

The Manufacture of Cotton.—Review of the present Circumstances of this Trade.—Estimate of Capital invested and employed in the Manufacture.—Amount of annual Productions.—Comparison of Home and Export Trade.—Number of Persons employed and dependent.— Tables of Import of Raw Cotton, and the Official and Declared Value of the Exports of Manufactured Goods from 1820 to 1846.

It is quite true that " there is nothing in the history of industry to compare with the rapid growth of the American cotton trade, except that of the manufacture in this country." Notwithstanding, however, the rapid growth, and present importance of the manufacture of cotton, an incident has just occurred which shows how slight is the tenure by which we hold possession of it, how extremely sensitive it is of anything touching the source of its supplies; and how extensive is the suffering which, under present circumstances, any failure in these inevitably creates among those dependent on it for their means of subsistence.

The manufacturers of cotton have, during the past year, been struck in their most vital part, and, like all men keenly alive to their own interests, they discern in the distance a cloud, although no bigger than a man's hand, which portends them no good. The quantity of raw cotton imported in 1845 reached the enormous amount of 721,523,712 lb., having doubled itself in the short space of ten years. An unusually low price of the raw material, and an enormous increase in the production of manufactured goods, were the natural consequences. Had the supply of raw cotton gone on increasing, the same results would have followed, and a still further reduction in the value of both have taken place, until the rate of profit of the grower in America, and the manufacturer in England, had been estimated by the bale instead of the pound, and reduced to so small a fraction as to be scarcely discernible.

The importation of the year 1846, however, fell off to 467,748,624 lb., or to about three-fifths of the preceding year; while the export at the same time increased from 42,916,384 lb., to 65,930,704 lb.; and the same consequences that we have so often witnessed in this trade again followed: first, an advance in raw cotton, then a partial suspension of business, and working short time, and, as a matter of course, a corresponding amount of distress among the working classes.

It has been the practice of Mr Cobden and Mr Bright, and those entertaining their opinions, to assign as the primary cause of such a state of things the want of freedom of trade, the corn-laws, or the high price of food; but, as that excuse will no longer serve their purpose, the parties engaged in this trade have adopted a much more sensible course of proceeding, and, within a few days, we find that a meeting has been called in Manchester for the purpose of urging on Government the necessity of instituting an inquiry as to the extent to which the production of cotton in the East Indies could be profitably promoted.

This would seem to imply a suspicion on their part, that the supply of cotton from America at extreme low prices had reached its maximum; and it is not improbable that they have been assisted in coming to this conclusion by a consideration that the facilities for introducing the bread stuffs of the Americans into this country may induce them to prefer the cultivation of corn to cotton.

We should devoutly hope that none of these results will be realized; but it is incumbent on our manufacturers to watch the progress of the new system, lest it should produce effects which may, even in a year or two, endanger their own security. The real cause of the frequent depression in this business, we consider, has no connexion with or relation to the corn-laws, or the price of food, but may be clearly traced to our vast mechanical power, which can, with wonderful facility, exhaust a stock of raw cotton, however large, or glut the markets of the world with an amount of manufactured goods which, under other circumstances, would have found employment for the population for a long period of time.

In 1843, Mr Bright, addressing the electors of Durham, dwelt with great pathos on the decay of trade, and the desolation of the loom and the spindle. The words were hardly spoken before the opening up of the trade with China gave an impetus to the industry of the country which has never been surpassed; and the years 1844 and 1845, with the corn-laws still unrepealed, were equal in prosperity to any in our history.

It required not, however, the gift of prophecy to foretel that after such a state of things a period of great depression would follow, for great as our prosperity may be, our mechanical power is still greater ; and, as a consequence, the desolation of the loom and the spindle is the same in 1847 as when Mr Bright uttered his lamentations in 1843.

We shall now proceed to inquire into the capital embarked in the manufacture of

COTTON.

Mr M'Culloch estimates it as follows :—

Capital employed in the purchase of the raw material	£4,000,000
Capital employed in the payment of wages	8,000,000
Capital invested in spinning mills, power and hand looms, work-shops, warehouses, and stock on Hand	35,000,000
Total	£47,000,000

That the capital employed is very large, there can be no doubt, but we consider this estimate to be much beyond the truth, and our reasons for this conclusion are the following :—

Capital employed in the purchase of the raw material, 4,000,000*l*.— This sum would represent at the current prices of raw cotton for some years past about one-half the whole quantity imported in twelve months. In very speculative times, it is possible that the manufacturers may hold a larger proportion than usual, say one-half the stock on hand, the whole amount of which at any one time would not amount to more than about 4,000,000*l.* or 4,500,000*l.*

It is, however, a well known fact that with the increase in trade, the credit given in dealing, both for the raw material and the manufactured one, has been gradually curtailed until a very large proportion is now carried on for cash payment in fourteen days, and the remainder for bills at a very short date. The great bulk of manufactured goods are drawn for at two months, from the first of the month after the execution of the order. Hence there is no reason why the manufacturer should hold heavy stocks of the raw material on the one hand, while on the other there is every inducement for him to produce and send to market with all possible rapidity the manufactured article.

And in truth it is this facility of buying and selling from hand to mouth that has caused small manufacturers to spring up in all directions, whose returns are almost weekly, and who, unless this system prevailed, could neither pay for the raw material, nor the wages of manufacturing it. We therefore estimate the amount of capital required to represent the value of the raw material held by our manufacturers, and in progress through their mills at any one time, at about 2,500,000*l.*

Capital employed in the payment of wages, 8,000,000*l.*—This is an equally extravagant sum. A return was made in 1839 to the factory commissioners of the monthly wages of 225 cotton mills in Lancashire. The amount given is 141,635*l.*, and the number of persons employed 67,819, which being about one-fourth of the whole number of persons employed in cotton factories, although the number of mills is only one-eighth, proves that this return embraces the largest and most important concerns in the kingdom. Estimating, however, the whole number at the same rate, this would give about 7,300,000*l.* per annum as the wages of those employed within the mills, the most skilled and the highest priced labour of all. If to this we add 5,000,000*l.* for those employed out of the mills, which is far beyond the mark, we have a total of 12,300,000*l.* for the year.

The amount of capital actually employed in the payment of these wages must, however, depend on the system of credit which prevails in the sale of the goods, and this being so extremely short, it follows that a spinner of yarn, or a manufacturer of cloth, turns his capital four, five, and six times a year, and a very large proportion of them much oftener, so that we cannot estimate the amount of capital required to represent wages at more than 3,500,000*l.*

Capital invested in spinning mills, stock in trade, &c., 35,000,000*l.* —We cannot discover the slightest authority for this estimate. Mr M'Culloch in his former edition estimated their value at 20,000,000*l.*, but he has now advanced it to 37,000,000*l.* The number of cotton mills in the United Kingdom in 1839 was 1,819, of which 1,125 were situated in Lancashire. This would give an average of about 20,000*l.* to each; but the assessment to the poor rates of the rental of these mills and factories would not warrant any such conclusion.

In 1844, 314 cotton mills in Manchester and the surrounding districts made a return of their assessment to the poor rates, which amounted to 179,767*l.* These employed 116,281 persons, or more than one-third of the whole number in the United Kingdom, and therefore, as in the former instance, embraced the largest and most extensive concerns in this trade. This is about the same proportion which they bore to other property in the year 1815 ; and our estimate founded on this return is the following :—Annual rental of 1,819 mills, 450,000*l.*, which, at 6 per cent., would represent a capital of 7,500,000*l.* Allowing for every 100*l.* of rent 2,000*l.* for machinery, this would add 9,000,000*l.*, making in all, for the buildings and machinery, a total of 16,500,000*l.* If we add these items together, the capital required to represent the cotton interest in the United Kingdom may be thus stated :—

Capital employed in the purchase of the raw material	£2,500,000
Capital employed in the payment of wages	3,500,000
Capital invested in spinning mills, power looms, &c.	16,500,000
Capital required to represent stock on hand	2,000,000
Total	£24,500,000

The manufacturers of cotton, it is well known, have amassed great wealth, and with the above means may easily produce forty, fifty, or sixty millions' worth of goods per annum, according to the degree of fineness of the article manufactured; but this is no evidence that, with the present system of trade, a larger amount of capital than is here stated is required to effect it. As well might we consider the one thousand millions which pass through the London clearing house in the course of twelve months evidence of the amount of capital in trade, when, in fact, they have no relationship whatever to it. This large amount is merely evidence of the fact, that transactions in commerce are multiplied in proportion to the degree of briskness which prevails in trade, and which may arise equally from speculation or consumption.

On these grounds we altogether object to the estimate of Mr M'Culloch, and contend that it is not formed on any practical knowledge of the subject, we also deny that there are any official returns in existence which would justify his conclusions. It is a well-known fact that when trade is active the manufacturers hold no permanent stock of any amount, and can hardly deliver fast enough to supply the demand. In ordinary times the productions of these mills pass into the hands of the dealer and the shipper in an incredibly short space of time; and it is only in dull times, when business is in a state of stagnation, that capitalists are compelled to hold stock. In this state of things, however, the small manufacturer, whose weekly supplies are suspended immediately, ceases to work. The larger one, to keep his machinery in order, commences working short time, and thus nearly the whole pressure of the times is thrown back on the consignee of cotton at Liverpool, with whom the raw material rests until called into activity by a revival of trade.

We have further to consider the amount of cotton goods annually produced. Mr M'Culloch estimates it thus:—

Raw material, 500,000,000 lb. at 5*d*.	£10,000,000
Wages of 542,000 weavers, spinners, bleachers, &c., at 24*l*. a year each.	13,000,000
Wages of 80,000 engineers, machine-makers, smiths, masons, joiners, &c., at 50*l*. a year	4,000,000
Profits of the manufacturers, wages of superintendance, sums to purchase the materials of machinery, coals, &c.. . .	9,000,000
Total value of every description of cotton goods manufactured in Great Britain annually . .	£36,000,000

The data here given are certainly very loose and unsatisfactory, and throw but little light on a very important matter. Considering that 10,000,000*l.* of raw cotton forms the base, and that there are very few fabrics in manufactured goods in which the increase in the value of the raw material would not be much greater than is here given, while a large proportion is worked up to every conceivable degree of fineness, we consider this estimate to be much too low; but there are so many considerations attached to this matter that any guesses of the kind on data so unsatisfactory are of very little worth. The reduced price of the raw material, the improved machinery and increased facilities of production, and the reduced rate of profit, as compared with former periods, render it next to impossible to make a comparison in point of value between the present and past times.

There is one fact, however, which admits of no dispute, and that is, that the official value fixed in 1694, and continued down to the present time, measures the quantities exported, thus:—

YEARS.	Raw Cotton entered for Home Consumption.	Official Value of Cotton Goods Exported.	As compared with 1815, ought to have been
	lb.	£	£
1815	92,525,951	22,289,645	
1820	152,829,633	22,331,079	36,000,000
1825	202,546,869	29,495,281	48,000,000
1830	269,616,640	41,050,969	64,000,000
1835	326,407,692	52,333,278	78,000,000
1840	528,142,743	73,152,251	126,000 000
1844	554,198,602	91,039,574	132,000,000
1845	721,523,712		

It will be seen from these figures that the *quantities* exported have not kept pace with the quantities of raw cotton taken for home consumption, and that, with occasional fluctuations, the deficiency has gone on increasing, and consequently the home trade must have absorbed the difference. Whatever variety of opinion may exist as to the value of the manufacture, there can be no gainsaying this, that the home trade has increased in a greater proportion than the foreign.

But it is said that this is not conclusive, inasmuch as the finer qualities of goods are retained for the home consumption ; so that the quantity exported as measured with any fixed price, and the amount of raw cotton imported, would not show the precise fact, because the heavier and coarser goods, those consuming more raw cotton, would form the principal part of our export trade. Whatever truth there may be in this, it only proves that the home trade is the most important in value as well as quantity, for it consumes goods of the most costly description, and on which a much larger amount of labour is bestowed than any other; while white and plain calico, on which it is comparatively small, constitute one half of the whole export trade of manufactured cottons.

This we consider to be clearly proved by the following comparative Table of the Exports of White or Plain and Printed or Dyed Cottons at different periods, compared with 1820:—

Years.	White or Plain Cotton exported.	Declared Value.	Decrease in value as compared with 1820.	Printed or Dyed Cottons exported.	Declared Value.	Decrease in value as compared with 1820.
	Yards.	£	Per cent.	Yards.	£	Per cent.
1820	113,682,486	5,451,024		134,688,144	7,742,505	
1825	158,039,786	6,027,892	25	178,426,912	8,205,117	26
1830	244,799,032	6,562,397	81	199,799,466	7,557,373	50
1835	277,704,525	6,910,506	91	279,811,176	8,270,925	100
1840	433,114,273	7,803,772	170	357,517,624	8,498,448	150
1844	623,249,423	9,346,865	220	403,421,400	8,265,281	180

Again, with respect to our trade in twist, which, in 1846, amounted to 7,873,727*l.*, inasmuch as Germany, Holland, and Russia, take two-thirds of the whole, it is only an evidence of the rapid progress which our rivals are making in manufacturing for themselves; and this is more clearly shown by the fact, that while in 1846 the export of manufactured goods, as compared with 1845 fell off 1,429,130*l.* the export of yarn increased 910,492*l.*

Before parting with the manufacture of cotton, we cannot help noticing certain fallacies put forward as to the amount of employment it gives, and the number of all classes it supports. Mr M'Culloch has treated the statistical works of Dr Colquhoun as something nearly allied to the " Arabian Nights' Entertainments;" but we shall show that his own works recently published are not altogether free from the same charge, and that they abound with calculations thrown off in a very *ad captandum* style, which will hardly bear the test of inquiry. Among others, in his account of the capital invested in the manufacture of cotton, he gives us an estimate of the wages of 542,000 weavers, spinners, bleachers, &c., at 24*l.*, and of 80,000 engineers, machine-makers, smiths, masons, joiners, &c. at 50*l.* a year each. We should look in vain for any figures in the returns of the census to corroborate this statement. The whole number of every age and sex, employed in the cotton trade, is 302,376; and if we include their proportion of those returned under the head of "Fabric not specified," it only amounts to 377,662. Of these, 259,336 are employed within the mills, and Mr Porter gives a return made to the Factory Commissioners of the payments to all the persons employed in 225 factories, averaging 10*s.* 6*d.* per week each. Considering that the labour within the mills is the most skilled of all, this is much lower than we expected; but it is admitted on all hands that the earnings of the hand-loom weaver, and most others outside the walls, do not amount to anything like this, and that their condition for years together has been one of unmitigated destitution.

The whole number of engineers in the United Kingdom is 25,804, of whom only 4,505 are resident in the county of Lancaster; and as to machine-makers, the whole number in the three kingdoms is no more than 8,513, of whom 2,058 reside in this county; and if we include the smiths, masons, and joiners, it will be very difficult to make the numbers amount to two-thirds of Mr McCulloch's estimate.

Again, Mr McCulloch states that "allowance being made for old and infirm persons, children, &c. dependent upon those actually employed in the various departments of the cotton manufacture, and in the construction, repairs, &c. of the machinery and buildings required to carry it on," the entire cotton manufacture must furnish, on the most moderate computation, subsistence for from 1,200,000 to 1,300,000 persons. Where is the evidence in support of such an assertion? Certainly not in the returns of the census.

The sense in which the term subsistence is here used by Mr M'Culloch is, that the wages of the persons employed do directly support this number of 1,200,000. But the returns show that the number of males above twenty years of age is only 138,112, and that all the rest are either females, or under twenty years of age ; and therefore not only not heads of families, but it is very improbable that their small earnings can support any but themselves. Our estimate founded on these facts is as follows :—

138,112 MALES above 20 years of age.—Heads of Families, and representing three each, besides themselves	414,336
MALES under 20—not Heads of Families	59,171
FEMALES above 20—in most instances the wives of the males above mentioned, and their families, included in the same number	104,470
FEMALES under 20 years of age	75,909
	653,886
Add for the proportion of Females married to persons other than those included in the number above-mentioned, and for the mechanics and other artisans dependent on this branch	50,000
	703,886

Such is the number actually receiving wages or directly deriving support from the manufacture of cotton.

In this branch of the textile fabrics mechanical power has acquired a greater ascendancy than in any other. The manufacture of linens and woollens are fast approximating the same state of things, but in the article of silk the difficulty of applying machinery is found to be much greater.

Hence, in proportion to the amount of their productions, the manufacturers of cotton employ a less number of hands, and pay a smaller amount of wages, than any other interest in the kingdom ; —a consideration of vast importance, when taken in reference to the employment of the population or the taxation of the country.

TABLE of the IMPORTS and EXPORTS of RAW COTTON, and also of the MANUFACTURED GOODS EXPORTED, distinguishing YARN from other Manufactures, and giving the OFFICIAL and REAL VALUE of each in the several years from 1820 to 1846.

YEARS.	RAW COTTON.		MANUFACTURED GOODS EXPORTED.					
	IMPORTED.	EXPORTED.	YARN.		MANUFACTURES.		Official Value.	Real Value.
			Millions of Pounds.	Real Value.	Millions of Yards.	Real Value.	Including Hosiery and Small Wares.	
	lb.	lb.		£		£	£	£
1820	151,672,655	6,024,038	23	2,826,639	248¼	13,193,529	22,531,079	16,516 748
1821	132.536,620	14,589,477	21½	2,305,823	269¼	13,167,965	22,541.615	16,093.787
1822	142,387,628	18.267,786	26½	2,697,582	302	13 798,607	26,911.043	17.218 724
1823	191,402,503	9,318,402	27¼	2,625,946	301¾	12 980,644	26.544,770	16.326.604
1824	149,380,122	13 299,505	33½	3,135,396	344½	14,448,249	30,155,901	18,452,987
1825	228,005,291	18,204,953	32½	3 206,729	336¼	14,233,009	29,475,281	18.359,526
1826	177,607,401	24.474,920	42	3.491,338	267	9,866,534	25,194 270	14,093,369
1827	272 448,909	18,134,170	44¾	3,545.578	365¼	12,947,035	33,182,898	17 637 165
1828	227,760,642	17,396,776	50½	3 595,405	363¼	12,483,249	33,467,417	17,244 417
1829	222,767.411	30 289,115	61¼	3,976,874	402½	12,516.248	37,269,432	17,535,006
1830	263,961,452	8,534,976	64½	4,133 741	444½	14,119,770	41,050,969	19,428 664
1831	288,674,853	22,308 555	63¾	3.975,019	421¼	12,163,513	39,357,075	17,257,204
1832	286,832 525	18,027,940	75½	4,722,759	461	11,500,630	43,786,255	17,398 392
1833	303,656,837	17,363 882	70½	4,704,024	496¼	12,451,060	46,337,210	18 486.400
1834	326,875,425	24,461,963	76¼	5,211,015	555½	14,127,352	51,069,140	20,513 585
1835	363.702,963	32,779,734	83	5,706,589	557½	15,181,431	52,333,278	22,128.304
1836	406.959.057	31.739,763	88	6,120,366	637½	17,183,167	58,578,442	24,632,058
1837	407,286,783	39,722,031	103¼	6,955 942	531¼	12,727.989	51.130,290	20,597,123
1838	507,850,577	30,644,469	114½	7,431,869	690	15,554,733	64,812 528	24 147,726
1839	389 396,559	38,738,238	105½	6,858,193	731¼	16,378,445	67,917,021	24 550 376
1840	592.488,010	38,673,229	118¼	7,101,308	790½	16,302,220	73,152.251	24 668 618
1841	487,992,355	37,673 585	123	7,266.968	751	14,985,810	69 798,131	23,499,478
1842	531,750,086	45,251,302	137	7,771,464	734	12,887,220	68,684 891	21,674.598
1843	673,193,116	39,619,979	140¼	7.193,971	918½	15,168,464	82,189.599	23 447 971
1844	646,111,304	47,222,541	138½	6,988,504	1046½	17.612,146	91,039,574	25 805 348
1845	721,523,712	42.916,384	135	6,963,235	1091½	18,029,808		26,119,331
1846	467,748,624	65,930,704		7,873,727		16,600,678		25,600,693

CHAPTER VII.

THE MANUFACTURING INTEREST.—(*Continued.*)

*The Manufacture of Woollens.—Change of Fabric caused by the
Mixture of Coarse with Fine Wools.—Numbers employed.—Change
of Locality.—Capital invested.—Annual Productions.—Comparison
of Home and Foreign Trade.—Table of Woollen Goods exported
from* 1815 *to* 1844.

*The Manufacture of Linen.—Distribution of the Trade.—Number
of Persons employed.—Capital invested.—Annual Productions.—
Comparison of Home and Foreign Trade.—Table of Imports of
Flax and Exports of Linen from* 1834 *to* 1846.

*The Manufacture of Silk.—Notice of Mr Huskisson's Alteration in
Duties in* 1824, *and Progress of the Silk Trade since that Time.
—Quantity imported and smuggled into this Country.—Amount of
Capital invested.—Annual Productions.—Comparison of Home
and Foreign Trade.—Table of Imports of Raw Silk and Exports
of Manufactured goods from* 1820 *to* 1846.

*Summary of Manufactures.—The Amount of their Annual Pro-
ductions. — Comparison of the Home and Foreign Trade in the
Consumption and Distribution of these.*

IT was customary down to the sixteenth century for our merchants to carry large quantities of English wool to Flanders, whence
were brought back woollen cloths and foreign productions for our
consumption. From a very early period, however, the manufacture
of wool was an object of the especial protection of the Government;
and, until within a few years, this production of our own soil was
the great staple of the manufacturing interest.

The force of circumstances has compelled it to yield precedence
to its more successful rival; and its ancient glory is somewhat
obscured, not only by the competition of cotton, but by the increasing coarseness of the fabric, so that our finest woollens no

longer command a preference in other countries, and even our own consumption is made up of a very inferior quality to that which prevailed in the earlier stages of its history.

This has somewhat damaged the foreign trade in fine goods, but at the same time it has opened up a wide field for mixtures of every variety, and done great service to both the foreign and the home trade in this particular branch. The caprice of fashion, in respect of these mixtures, has in this instance not only adapted itself to our necessities, but also greatly encouraged the growth of wool both at home and in our colonies. Long may it continue to prevail and to flourish.

For this great alteration in the manufacture we are, however, indebted to our neighbours the French, who were the first to discover the value of our long wools, and to adapt them to their present use. Up to 1825 the exportation of British wool was prohibited, but as soon as the French manufacturers were able to procure the combing wool of England, they produced a great variety of new stuffs, not "superior to any that we had ever produced in this country," but of a different texture, fabric, and pattern; and our manufacturers, stimulated by their example, have been able to copy, if not to improve on their discoveries.

This is sufficient to account for the fact, that since 1825, although the quantities of foreign wool imported have fluctuated greatly in particular years; yet, on the average of twenty-one years from 1824 to 1845, the consumption has not increased above sixty per cent., while the wool imported from our colonies has increased in the same period from about half a million of pounds to thirty-one millions of pounds; and, collaterally with this, wool of British growth has increased from 6*d.* to its former value of 1*s.* 4*d.* per lb. Some have contended that the reduction of duty on foreign wool, which took place in December, 1824, at the same time that British wool was allowed to be exported, was the principal cause of this change in the fabric; but the facts we have given do not warrant any such conclusion. The ingenuity of the French, in the first instance, and the great influx of Colonial wools at low prices, have enabled our manufacturers to produce a great variety of articles,

which have supplanted the finer fabrics made from foreign wool;
and whatever increase has taken place in the consumption of foreign
wool is purely ascribable to the facilities of mixing it with the
coarser wools of this country. The falling off in the manufacture
of superfine cloths, both of the home and foreign trade, is conclusive
on this head.

As regards the amount of employment which this branch of trade
gives rise to, much difference of opinion appears to exist. Dr Campbell, in his "Political Survey of Great Britain," 1774, estimated the
number at 1,000,000. The manufacturers at the bar of the House
of Lords in 1800, stated the number to be not less than 1,500,000.
Mr Stevenson, whom Mr M'Culloch considers to be one of the few
writers on statistics to whom deference is due, estimates the present
number at 480,000, or perhaps 500,000, and Mr M'Culloch himself
states it at 300,000. Our own estimate is that given in the returns
of the Census; viz., for Great Britain, 167,296 (see Appendix,
p. 147), being rather more than one-half the lowest estimate; and for
Ireland, 77,650 (see Appendix, pp. 151 and 152); making together
244,946 in the United Kingdom.

That there was much exaggeration in the estimates of Dr
Campbell in 1774, and the manufacturers in 1800, none can doubt;
but it would be difficult to find a better illustration of the tendency
of machinery to supplant human labour than the history of the
woollen trade. Up nearly to the close of the war even the steam-
engine had made but little progress in the West of England, and the
mills in operation along the Bottoms of Gloucestershire, and in the
towns of Bradford, Trowbridge, Westbury, Melksham, Chippen-
ham, and Frome, gave employment to large numbers of the population, earning good wages. What has been their condition for
many years past? With very few exceptions the manufacturers
in this part of the kingdom have failed, and three-fourths of the
population in many towns are on the poor-rates. We much
doubt if the whole number now employed in the woollen trade in
Yorkshire is equal to that which before the introduction of this
machinery found employment in Gloucestershire, Wiltshire, and
Somersetshire.

Mr Porter, Mr M'Culloch, and many other writers, point in a tone of triumph to the increase in population, and enlargement of the towns of Leeds, Bradford, Halifax, and Huddersfield, when, in truth, this enlargement proceeds from no other cause than the decay of the same trades in other localities, and the concentration in large towns of the labour of the population, which had a much more fertilizing influence on society when it was spread over a greater extent of surface.

The total number of woollen and worsted mills in the United Kingdom in 1839 was returned by the Commissioners as follows:— England, 1,494; Wales, 161; Scotland, 117; Ireland, 38— total, 1810. And estimating these on the same scale as those engaged in the cotton trade, we arrive at the conclusion that the amount of capital actually employed in this branch of manufactures is as follows:—

Capital invested in 1,800 mills, producing an annual rental of about 360,000*l.*, which, at six per cent., would represent - - £6,000,000
Capital invested in machinery, about two-thirds the value of that employed in the manufacture of cotton - - - - 4,500,000
Capital employed in the purchase of the raw material, and stock in trade, the credit on the sale of the manufactured goods being much longer than on cotton - - - - - 4,000,000
Capital employed in the payment of wages, for the same reason - 2,000,000

Total of capital employed - - - - - £16,500,000

Mr M'Culloch and Mr Stevenson differ much in their estimate of the amount of manufactured goods annually produced; the several items are thus given by each:—

	Mr M'Culloch.	Mr Stevenson.
Raw material 110,000,000 lb. of British wool, at 1*s.* 3*d.* per lb., and 50,000,000 lb. foreign, at 2*s.* per lb. - - -	£11,875,000	6,000,000
Wages - - - - - - - -	7,000,000	9,600,000
Oil, dye-stuffs, soap, &c. - - - - -	1,100,000	
Profits, sums to replace, wear and tear, interest of capital, &c.	4,025,000	2,400,000
	£24,000,000	18,000,000

Our estimate rather exceeds that of Mr M'Culloch, and the several items are differently distributed; thus—

RAW MATERIAL.

Foreign wool, the average of twenty-one years, from

1825 to 1845 - - - - -	34,816,000 at 2s. 6d.	£4,351,625
Colonial wool, average of the last five years, about -	25,000,000 at 1s. 6d.	1,875,000
British wools, according to Mr Porter - -	145,000,000 at 1s. 3d.	9,062,500
		£15,289,125
Oil, dye-stuffs, soap, &c. - - - - - - -		1,500,000
Wages of 244,946 persons, returned in the Census, at 24l. a year - -		5,878,704
Manufacturers' profits, ten per cent. - - - - - -		2,266,782
Wear and tear, and interest on capital, ten per cent. - - -		2,266,782
Total value of manufactured goods - - - -		£26,108,073

Having ascertained the amount of goods produced, we have further to consider in what manner they are disposed of. From the table with which this article concludes it will be seen, that with the exception of woollens mixed with cottons and stuffs, woollen or worsted, every other branch of our foreign trade has not only made no progress for the last thirty years, but has fallen off in an extraordinary degree. The export of cloths of all sorts, hitherto the most important branch of this trade, has declined from 638,369 pieces in 1815, to 161,675 in 1842, and to 317,073 in 1844. Napped coatings and duffels have nearly disappeared from the list. Kerseymeres, which formerly were the boast of the West of England, is only one-third, and flannels about one-fourth, what they were in 1815. A glance at the table will show that the falling off has not taken place suddenly, from any failure in the supply of the raw material, or from any increase of duties discouraging the production; but, on the contrary, in the face of duties repealed, and increased facilities, the foreign demand has greatly diminished. The fact is, the manufacture of the fabrics, which now form the great bulk of our exports, namely, mixtures of cotton with wool, require no extraordinary machinery, nor any great degree of skill or ingenuity, to make them, and therefore they are made by all countries as well as ourselves.

Goods of such qualities as these are not calculated to sustain the reputation of past years, or to challenge the competition of other countries in the manufacture of woollens. Compare the progress of the French exports with that of our own, and you have a solution of our present position in this trade in an instant.

AN ACCOUNT of the QUANTITIES of BRITISH MANUFACTURED WOOLLEN GOODS EXPORTED in each Year from 1815 to 1844.

Years.	Cloths of all sorts.	Napped Coatings, Duffels, &c.	Kerseymeres.	Baizes of all sorts.	Stuffs, Woollen or Worsted.	Flannels.	Blankets and Blanketing.	Carpets and Carpeting.	Woollens mixed with Cotton.	Hosiery.	Sundries unenumerated.	Total Declared Value.
	Pieces.	Pieces.	Pieces.	Pieces.	Pieces.	Yards.	Yards.	Yards.	Yards.	Dozens.	£	£
1815	638,369	88,598	92,691	69,687	593,308	7,056,271	3,397,187	793,793	926,264	202,906	265,210	9,381,426
1816	467,222	90,481	91,183	50,038	585,842	3,592,331	1,934,469	820,038	764,435	119,465	182,461	7,842,768
1817	478,378	93,329	83,493	61,174	683,448	2,814,101	2,305,565	642,586	851,874	100,385	147,373	7,173,735
1818	446,872	78,525	104,468	58,578	937,944	4,621,860	2,706,904	1,144,330	824,848	161,217	170,497	8,140,767
1819	340,044	60,374	71,613	39,796	717,581	3,622,761	1,777,719	620,630	495,557	101,473	82,909	5,984,130
1820	288,700	59,644	78,944	37,183	828,901	2,569,105	1,288,409	526,124	407,716	59,960	39,337	5,586,139
1821	375,464	69,622	91,402	41,610	1,022,842	3,504,851	1,424,238	764,922	627,800	107,779	38,986	6,462,866
1822	420,497	67,757	95,570	43,447	1,078,428	4,503,612	1,926,711	884,922	1,120,326	136,597	47,042	6,488,167
1823	356,027	54,223	94,344	41,539	1,150,183	4,311,997	2,131,632	778,426	918,469	106,420	44,619	5,636,586
1824	407,720	51,585	108,012	47,105	1,242,403	3,105,961	1,990,041	848,842	1,393,443	113,123	43,861	6,043,051
1825	384,880	45,268	126,448	47,100	1,138,808	2,959,594	2,162,884	889,324	1,793,301	106,498	45,335	6,185,648
1826	328,559	41,800	86,038	36,862	1,125,318	2,423,120	1,082,382	903,597	531,517	71,922	37,223	4,966,879
1827	371,965	51,690	122,049	47,574	1,258,667	2,518,887	1,899,600	1,195,939	846,768	148,117	43,559	5,245,649
1828	335,042	40,646	84,524	49,567	1,310,853	2,589,766	2,097,542	1,197,947	981,152	159,463	48,314	5,069,741
1829	363,075	16,186	33,465	52,777	1,307,558	1,572,920	1,839,961	811,538	1,074,077	91,285	41,948	4,587,603
1830	383,269	22,377	34,714	49,164	1,252,512	1,613,099	2,176,391	672,869	1,099,518	111,146	54,038	4,728,666
1831	436,143	13,892	29,650	30,259	1,487,404	1,572,558	2,546,328	678,656	1,000,004	143,774	64,648	5,232,013
1832	396,661	23,453	40,984	34,874	1,800,714	2,304,750	1,681,840	690,042	1,334,072	152,810	55,443	5,254,478
1833	597,189	19,543	31,795	45,036	1,690,559	2,055,072	3,128,106	667,377	1,605,036	232,766	78,286	6,294,432
1834	521,214	22,868	23,891	43,338	1,298,775	1,821,394	2,537,772	606,912	1,723,069	173,073	75,841	5,736,870
1835	619,886	20,083	29,203	47,854	1,673,069	2,067,620	3,122,341	938,848	1,778,389	207,014	110,686	6,840,511
1836	720,587	22,814	29,610	45,555	1,406,000	2,190,008	4,333,876	1,008,013	1,467,927	163,182	142,533	7,639,353
1837	387,787	23,605	22,930	43,477	1,041,636	1,685,457	2,431,683	753,764	1,051,972	74,947	92,617	4,655,977
1838	587,903	26,847	36,428	41,813	1,358,984	1,779,525	2,558,806	727,539	1,846,231	109,758	123,835	5,791,069
1839	392,854	25,025	32,572	24,877	1,665,596	1,727,025	3,148,846	906,489	2,388,282	175,023	258,379	6,271,645
1840	215,746	16,091	27,122	36,044	1,718,617	1,613,477	2,162,653	758,639	3,628,874	96,946	164,034	5,927,853
1841	213,125	11,491	22,131	37,160	2,007,366	1,820,244	2,187,329	809,315	5,015,087	135,909	163,900	5,748,673
1842	161,673	8,433	22,467		1,979,492	1,619,496	1,392,591	763,762	6,950,010	137,062	152,629	5,185,045
1843	241,160	5,273	29,263	21,130	2,443,371	1,719,699	1,765,970	747,346	11,199,975	147,507	192,966	6,790,232
1844	317,073	4,616	28,041	22,780	2,492,217	1,993,896	3,860,690	724,326	20,661,259	284,390	156,093	8,294,836
1845	317,791	4,773	24,673	23,588	2,212,906	2,405,311	2,479,478	1,006,970	23,881,017	174,061	178,995	7,693,117
1846	.											6,834,298

From the foregoing table, it is clear, that to the extent of two-thirds we are dependent on the home trade for the consumption of what is produced; and considering the very little progress we have made in the export trade, it is difficult to understand the policy that has opened the home market to the competition of the cheaper labour and finer wools of other countries.

The Linen Manufacture.

The next in importance is the manufacture of linen, which, as compared with other branches, made but little progress, until within a very few years. It is now distributed as follows :—

England and Wales.—The principal seat of this manufacture is the West Riding of Yorkshire, and the mill of Messrs Marshall, at Leeds, is not only the largest in the world, but for perfection of machinery may be said to rival every other in any branch of trade whatever. It is also carried on to a small extent in Lancashire. The whole number of persons employed is only 19,148.

Scotland.—In this country the manufacture took root much earlier, and has been prosecuted with greater success than in England. Dundee, Aberdeen, and Dunfermline, are the chief places in which it is carried on to any great extent. The whole number of persons employed is 48,600. The wages of the hand-loom weaver are in general very low, seldom exceeding from 5*s.* to 8*s.* per week.

Ireland.—The woollen trade of Ireland, which had made some progress, was crushed by William III, and the linen manufacture established in its stead.

Mr M'Culloch appears to agree with Mr Young and Mr Wakefield, in the opinion that the extension of this manufacture in the north of Ireland, has been prejudicial rather than advantageous to that country. We quote Mr M'Culloch's words that, " it certainly contributed to that morbid increase of population, and that minute division of the land, which are the bane of Ireland, and which are carried to the greatest extent where the manufacture is and was most difficult. The manufacturers too, being not only spinners and weavers, but also little farmers, had their attention diverted from their proper business, and were neither sufficiently industrious nor inventive. As might be expected, their earnings were generally very low, and but few amongst them were ever able to emerge to a more elevated sphere. The introduction of the mill system, however, into Ireland, has nearly annihilated their former one, and the manufacture has consequently disappeared from several parts of the country, leaving those who were partially dependent on it for subsistence in a very depressed state."

We think that most of our readers will differ from these gentlemen as to the effect of the linen manufacture on the population of the north of Ireland; but as regards the operation of the mill system, as it is called, we apprehend there can be no doubt whatever, for it has had precisely the effect here described on every other branch of trade in which it has been introduced.

The number of flax and linen factories in the United Kingdom in 1839 was 415, affording employment to 12,897 males, and 30,594 females. A table at page 147 in the Appendix gives the whole number employed in 1841 thus—

England and Wales, and Isles in the British Seas	19,148
Scotland	48,600
	67,648
Add proportion of fabric not specified	17,465
Total of Great Britain	85,213
Ireland. See Appendix, page 149	135,303
Total of the United Kingdom	220,516

The capital invested in this business, if estimated on the same scale as that employed in the cotton manufacture, would not exceed 6,000,000*l.*, or 7,000,000*l.* Dr Colquhoun makes the annual productions of the linen manufacture to amount to 15,000,000*l.*—Mr M'Culloch to 10,000,000*l.* When, however, we consider that in 1824, now twenty-three years ago, the Linen Board in Ireland reported it to amount to 2,580,709*l.* 4*s.* 9*d.*, and that since that period the mill system has taken root, and greatly increased the production; with the extraordinary extension of this trade in Scotland, we are inclined to think that they exceed Mr M'Culloch's estimate, and may be stated thus:—

Ireland	£5,000,000
England	3,000,000
Scotland	4,000,000
	£12,000,000.

The following table will show the imports of flax, and the exportation of manufactured linens from 1834 to 1846.

FOREIGN FLAX IMPORTED.		LINEN EXPORTED.				Total declared Value, including small Wares.
		By the Yard.	Declared Value.	LINEN YARN.		
Years.	£	Millions of Yards.	£	Millions of lb.	£	£
1834	794,272	67¾	2,357,991	1½	136,312	2,579,658
1835	742,765	77¾	2,893,139	2½	216,635	3,208,778
1836	1,511.428	82	3,238.031	4½	318,772	3,645,097
1837	933,654	58¼	2,063,425	8¼	479,307	2,606,752
1838	1,615,905	77	2,717,979	14¾	746,163	3,566 435
1839	1.216,811	85¼	3,292,220	16¼	818,485	4,233,452
1840	1,256,322	89¼	3,194,827	17½	822,876	4,128,964
1841	1,338,213	90¼	3,200,467	25	972.466	4,320,021
1842	1,130,312	69	2,217,373	29¼	1,025,551	3,372,300
1843	1,422;992	84	2,615,566	23¼	898,829	3,702,052
1844	1,583,328	91¼	2,801,609	25¾	1,050 676	4,075.476
1845	1 418 323				1,060,566	4.096,936
1846	1,146,743				875,556	3,713,940

The home consumption of linen must consequently be about two-thirds of the whole quantity produced.

Mr M'Culloch remarks that the exportation of yarns has been decreasing for a year or two past, from the circumstance of the French and other foreigners having greatly extended the use of spinning machinery in their own countries. A great portion of the linens exported are sent on consignment to agents in foreign countries for sale, and are sold by them on a credit of six to twelve months.

The Silk Manufacture.

The experiment of Mr Huskisson on the silk trade in 1824 is often referred to as a signal triumph of free-trade principles.

The members of the League have quoted him continually in their debates, and claimed the honourable gentleman as a disciple of their school; and Sir Robert Peel, in the late debate on the Corn Laws.

endeavoured to impress on the country the history of the experiment in justification of his removal of all protection from agriculture A more fallacious conclusion it would be difficult to imagine. Let us, therefore, trace its history.

From 1815 to 1825 the manufacture of cotton goods had made most extraordinary strides. Not only were great improvements taking place almost daily in the fineness of the fabrics produced, but the art of printing cottons was carried to a degree of perfection hitherto unknown; and the very low price at which these could be produced enabled them not only to compete successfully with silk, but almost to extinguish the manufacture of that article altogether

With such a competition there was nothing extraordinary in the fact that the manufacturers of silk goods were in a constant state of trouble and embarrassment. But to add to these difficulties the government of that day laid on heavy import duties, not for the protection of any particular interest, but for revenue; viz., on—

	s.	d.	
Foreign Organzine Silk	14	7½	per lb.
Raw Silk from Bengal	4	0	„
„ from other places.	5	7½	„

Even, as Mr M'Culloch very properly remarks, "had the manufacture been otherwise in a flourishing condition, such exorbitant duties on the raw material were enough to have destroyed it." On the 8th of March, 1824, Mr Huskisson therefore proposed to reduce them as follows:—

	s.	d.	
Foreign thrown, to	7	6	per lb.
„ in 1826, to	5	0	
Raw Silk	0	3	

Foreign manufactured silks were up to this time prohibited, but a taste for the costly productions of France prevailed then, as it does at this hour, among the more wealthy classes; and notwithstanding the peril and risk attending his trade at that period the smuggler evaded the Coast Guard, and found opportunities of supplying the market with any amount of goods required. And even in 1810, when the smugglers' difficulties were rendered much greater by war, the quantity of contraband silks introduced increased to such an extent that an association was formed among the manufacturers to prevent smuggling. Again, in 1818 and 1819 the silk weavers of Spitalfields and Coventry petitioned Parliament against this illegal competition.

In this state of things, Mr Huskisson foresaw that if the silk trade was to be continued in this country, it must be relieved of those enormous duties on the raw material which absorbed the capital of the manufacturer, increased the cost of the production not only to the extent of the duty paid, but to nearly as much more in respect of the loss on the waste of so costly an article, and thus raised the cost of manufactured goods to such an extent as to place them out of the reach of any but the upper classes. These remarks apply with equal force to organzine or thrown silks, for so long as the duty on the raw material prevented manufactured silk goods from competing with muslins and cottons, protection to the throwster, high as it was, was utterly valueless.

But it is said that he threw open the trade to the competition of the foreigner at the same time, and that in consequence our manufacturers have been stimulated to greater exertion, and have succeeded in beating him. Mr Huskisson removed the prohibition, it is true, but he put on in its place a protecting duty of 30 per cent. ad valorem.

Whether this duty has answered the purpose for which it was imposed or not is quite another thing. It certainly was intended as a protection for our silk trade to the extent of 30 per cent., but the ingenuity and address of the smugglers have triumphed over all obstacles, and, since the year 1824 they have carried on their trade with more success than ever. These persons no longer run the risk of encountering in bodily strife the opposition of the Coast Guard, but, having first made their arrangements with the officers of the Custom-house, they send their packages through the Custom-house itself, and these are delivered with all the regularity of a regular trade to houses of the first eminence in the city, whose principals have figured as free traders on the boards of Covent Garden Theatre, and in the Court of Exchequer as freebooters on the revenue. The extent to which this has been carried on is shown in the following table, and it is incredible to suppose that it could have been done without the connivance of some of the officials of her Majesty's Government. The Commissioners of Customs are, or ought to be, men of business; and it is rather too much to conceive that the importation of one-half the silk goods for the last ten years should have been carried on in defiance of their regulations; and yet, if any reliance can be placed on the following statement, such is the fact:—

An Account of Silk on which Duties have been paid, and also of the Quantities Smuggled from France into England in the several years from 1827 to 1843.

Years.	Exported from France to England.	Entered at Custom Houses in England.	Quantity Shipped more than Entered.
	lb.	lb.	lb.
1827	224,880	104,040	120,840
1828	335,051	156,216	178,835
1829	211,842	115,918	95,924
1830	289,034	119,826	169,208
1831	303,642	149,187	154,455
1832	312,877	146,665	166,212
1833	351,085	148,196	202,889
1834	317,508	175,562	141,946
1835	298,780	168,772	130,008
1836	283,646	179,977	103,669
1837	268,164	166,723	101,441
1838	393,085	244,626	148,459
1839	505,236	255,245	249,991
1840	625,317	267,477	357,840
1841	624,269	254,120	370,149
1842	503,278	250,306	252,972
1843	484,438	276,256	208,182
	6,332,132	3,179,112	3,152,003

It is certainly something new to tell us that the greater the quantity of French silks imported and smuggled, the more our manufacturers are stimulated to competition. If such an argument be good for anything, this stimulant ought to have operated in like manner before 1825, and the sooner the remaining protection of 15 per cent. is taken off the better.

Had the importation of French silks declined, or the trade of the smuggler become extinguished by the competition of our own manufacturers, there might have been something in the argument;

but until both of these events have occurred, the extension of the manufacture in this country must be traced to its real cause, the removal of duties on the raw material which affected the production of the article and the progress of the trade.

Such is the history of the alterations proposed by Mr Huskisson, which have been the subject of much misrepresentation. His policy in respect of trade was one to which all may readily subscribe, for it was nothing more than this, that, compatibly with the protection of our home interests, every restriction ought to be removed, and every facility given to promote our intercourse with other nations.

As regards the silk trade, his first step was to abolish the book of prices, which had become to a great extent obsolete, and, where acted upon, only served to embroil both master and man; and when Macclesfield and afterwards Manchester set this book at nought, it was high time that Spitalfields should surrender what then existed to their prejudice. He at the same time relieved the manufacturers of duties on the raw material, which had become extremely onerous both to them and the consumer.

The instant, however, these revenue duties were taken off, the manufacturers began to make silks at a great reduction in price, and this has proceeded at such an extraordinary rate, that at the present moment the cheapest silks and the highest-priced cottons and muslins are of about the same value.

We certainly have not yet arrived at the point of time anticipated by Mr Huskisson when silk should prevail as an article of general wear among the humbler classes of society, but it would not much surprise us if the manufacture of cheap silks, and fabrics consisting of silk mixed with other materials, were to become a very important branch of trade, and the manufacturers of this article should for the future be able to carry on a successful competition with those of cotton, and recover much of the ground lost up to the year 1824.

Many of our leading men in and out of Parliament ascribe the improvement which has taken place in the silk manufacture solely to the removal of the prohibition against the importation of foreign silks, and the consequent stimulus which they say has been thereby given to our manufacturers to produce articles in competition with the French. A sufficient and a much more natural cause is to be found in the removal of the duties we have referred to, which puts us on the same footing as the foreigner in all respects but one—the price of labour; and to this and to nothing else is to be attributed our success in the manufacture of silks. The substituting a duty of 30 per cent. in the place of prohibition has certainly not checked the demand for French silks, or the trade of the smuggler, but, on the contrary, has increased both, for a reference to the foregoing table will prove that these have been, up to a late period, much more extensive and thriving than ever.

The reduction of the duty to 15 per cent. will probably put an end to the smuggler's nefarious trade, and at the same time compel some of those large free-trade houses who have already received the attentions of her Majesty's Attorney-General to carry on their trade in silk goods on a more equitable and honourable footing in competition with persons in the same trade. It will also test the ability of our manufacturers to compete with those of France, and we shall rejoice at their success, inasmuch as it will pave the way for that perfect freedom of trade in manufactured goods which in 1849 is to prevail in respect of agricultural productions.

The number of silk mills in the United Kingdom, in 1839, was 291. These differ in several respects from those engaged in other branches of the textile fabrics. There are a few large establishments in Lancashire, Cheshire, and Derbyshire, but the great bulk are comparatively small concerns, and spread over different parts of the kingdom. Mr Porter says that, with the exception of the preliminary branch—throwing, it has been found impracticable to apply machinery to the production of the finer kinds of silk goods. More depends, therefore, on individual effort to produce any improvement; and as the necessaries of life are much cheaper in France than England, it gives the French a decided advantage over us in this particular branch.

For these reasons, the number of persons employed in the mills is comparatively small. In 1839 it only amounted to 10,863 males, and 23,370 females. The returns in the census for 1811 give the whole number employed in the trade as 83,773. (See Appendix, p. 147.)

The amount of capital invested does not exceed 4,000,000*l.*, and the value of the goods produced may be estimated at about 10,000,000*l.*

It will be seen, on reference to the annexed Table of Imports and Exports, that our exports to all countries are more than counterbalanced by the imports from France, and that the home consumption has since 1820 amounted to 10,000,000*l.* more than the entire production of the silk trade in this country.

A duty for the protection of an interest is as distinct from that of a duty for revenue as any two things possibly can be. For instance, if the Chancellor of the Exchequer could dispense with the revenue derived from malt and spirits, he would find that the increase in the consumption would far exceed not only his most sanguine expectations, but would throw into the shade that which has taken place in the articles of coffee, silk, wool, and lard, which gentlemen so often refer to in illustration of their arguments when speaking on the subject of free trade. On the contrary, let him continue the present high duties, and open the ports to the importation of beer and spirits, and in six months every brewery and distillery in the land would be closed.

The continuance of these duties is, however, necessary to maintain the good faith and pay the consequent taxation of the country, and it would be just as absurd to suppose that the heavily-taxed grower of barley in this country could compete with the untaxed and half-civilized farmer of other countries, as to have expected that the manufacturers of silk goods in the year 1824, with such heavy duties on the raw material, could compete with either the manufacturers of cotton, or the cheaper and comparatively untaxed labour of other countries in respect of silk.

Were France to concede, what she never will concede, that our cheap cottons should compete with and extinguish her silk trade, we might perhaps be able to supply her with both silks and cottons; but as this is much too extravagant a proposition to be entertained by either the French or English people, we will only further remark that we are utterly at a loss to conceive what advantage can accrue to us in opening up so rich a preserve of native industry to the competition of the foreigner, or what this foreigner can give us as an equivalent for it; and we belong not to that party who would incur the responsibility of making such an experiment on the credulity and common sense of mankind.

IMPORTS of RAW WASTE, THROWN SILK, and EXPORTS of SILK GOODS from 1820 to 1845.

Years.	Raw and Waste.	Thrown.	Total.	Exports to all Countries.
	lb.	lb.	lb.	£
1820	1,717,682	309,953	2,027,635	371,755
1821	1,969,160	360,248	2,329,808	374,473
1822	2,058,685	382,878	2,441,563	381,703
1823	2,104,257	363,864	2,468,121	351,409
1824	3,547,777	463,271	4,011,048	442 596
1825	3,044,416	559,642	3,604,058	296,736
1826	1,964,188	289,325	2,253,513	168,801
1827	3 759,138	454,015	4,213,153	236,344
1828	4,162,550	385,262	4,547,812	255,870
1829	2,719,962	172,239	2,892,201	267,931
1830	4,256 982	436,535	4,693,517	521 010
1831	3,798,090	514,240	4,312,330	578,874
1832	4,643,315	329,732	4,373,247	529,990
1833	4,493,176	268,367	4,761,543	737,404
1834	4 356,683	165,768	4.522,451	636,419
1835	5,533,880	254,578	5.788,458	972,031
1836	5,764,222	294,201	6,058,423	917,822
1837	4,387,561	211,298	4,598.859	503,673
1838	4,548,121	242,135	4,790,256	777,280
1839	4,437,301	228,643	4,665,944	868,118
1840	4,531,115	288,147	4,819,262	792 648
1841	4,490,620	266,651	4,757.171	788,894
1842	5.281,059	363,524	5,644,583	590.189
1843	5,037,784	333,602	5,371,386	667.952
1844	5,679 706	405,927	6,085,633	736,455
1845	5,816,296	511.832	6,328,128	766 405
1846	5,285,672	431,681	5,717,353	837,577

The duty of 30 per cent. received on 3,173,676 lb. of silk goods imported from 1827 to 1843 amounted to 19s. 9d. per pound. Estimating the entire quantity both duty paid and smuggled, viz. 6,332,132 lb. at the same rate (see page 87), the value of French silks imported during this period was 20,843,268l., or 10,717,186l. more than the amount of all the silks exported by us to all countries.

We have thus reviewed the past and present circumstances of the four principal branches of the manufacturing interest of this country, which furnish employment to a large proportion of the whole number engaged in it. Of the others it is unnecessary to speak in detail, as the table in the Appendix, page 147, will give the several numbers, showing their individual and relative importance.

Our estimate of the whole may be shortly restated thus:—

	Number of Persons Employed.	Capital Employed.	Amount of Annual Productions.	Home Trade.	Foreign Trade.
		£	£	£	£
Cotton Manufacture:	377,622	24,500,000	45,000,000	20,000,000	25,000,000
Woollen ditto					
Great Britain 167,296					
Ireland . 77,650					
	244,946	16,500,000	26,000,000	18,000,000	8,000,000
Linen					
Great Britain 85,213					
Ireland . 135 303					
	220,516	7,000,000	12,000,000	8,000,000	4,000,000
Silk	83,773	4,000,000	10,000,000	9,300,000	700,000
Hose	50,955	1,000,000	2,500,000 }	4,300,000	1,200,000
Lace	35,347	2,000.000	3,000,000 }		
Hardware and Cutlery, including Brass, Copper, Iron, Steel, Tin, and Pewter Manufactures . . .			18,000,000	11,000,000	7,000,000
Leather	427,747	23,000,000	13,000,000	12,500,000	500,000
Paper Furniture, Books, Printing, &c. . .			14,000,000	13,500,000	500,000
China, Glass, Earthenware, &c. . .			5,000,000	4,000,000	1,000,000
Jewellery, Plate, &c. .			3,300,000	3,000,000	300,000
Miscellaneous . . .			35,384,292	25,000,000	10,384 292
Total . . .	1,440,906	78,000,000	187,184,292	118,600,000	58,584,292

This statement, of course, can be only a probable approximation to the annual value of the productions of the Manufacturing Interest of this country. It is, however, important, as showing the relative value of the home as compared with the foreign trade, the former being two-thirds and consequently double the latter.

To arrive at a just conclusion as to the addition which the Manufacturing Interest makes annually to the common stock of the community, it will be necessary that from this amount of 187 millions we deduct the value of the raw material used in our manufactures, which in round numbers may be estimated at fifty millions; thus:—

	£
Cotton	10,000,000
Wool	15,000,000
Flax	4,000,000
Silk	4,000 000
Dye stuffs, oils, and all other articles used in manufactures	5,000,000
Metals of all kinds	6,000,000
Coals	6,000,000
Total	50,000,000

This would leave 137,000,000*l.* for the labour of those employed (1,440,906), and for the support of those deriving their subsistence from or dependent on those employed (6,650,715), being together 8,091,621 persons. (See Appendix, page 152.) It also includes the manufacturer's profits, the wear and tear of machinery, and tools, and the interest of capital.

Having the assistance of machinery, the productions of this interest are of course much greater than the Agricultural, as compared with the capital and numbers employed by each, and this comes in confirmation of our conclusion as regards the degree of support which the Manufacturing Interest gives to the population.

Before we dismiss this branch of our subject, there is one fact arising out of the manufacturing system as at present carried on which requires especial notice. In the table given in this work of the value of all goods exported from 1801 to 1846, it will be seen that the real as compared with the official value has varied at different periods in a most remarkable manner; thus—

Years.	Official Value.	Real Value.	Increase or Decrease on the Real as compared with the Official Value.		
	£	£			
1801	24,927,684	39,730,659	Increase,	60	per Cent.
1805	23,376,941	38,077,144	,,	65	,,
1810	34,061,901	48,438,680	,,	41	,,
1815	42,875,996	51,603,028	,,	21	,,
1820	38,395,625	36,424,652	Decrease,	6	,,
1825	47,166,020	38,877,388	,,	20	,,
1830	61,140,864	38,271,597	,,	38	,,
1835	78,376,731	47,372,270	,,	40	,,
1840	102,714,060	51,406,430	,,	50	,,
1846	134,385,829	59,837,660	,,	56	,,

Now, if we were to estimate the 134,000,000*l.* exported in 1846 at the same rate as the 25,000,000*l.* in 1801, the real value would be 214,000,000*l.* ; but, producing only about 60,000,000*l.*, it would appear to prove that the articles manufactured and exported at the present time are depreciated in value to the extent of 154,000,000*l.*, or, as compared with 1801, 270 per cent. ; but this is not exactly so.

The reduced price of the raw material will certainly account for a portion, although a very small one, of this 154,000,000*l.* As we have already seen, the whole value of the raw materials used in our factories in any one year during the last twenty, would not reach to more than one-third of this amount. To what, then, are we to attribute this extraordinary fact? We answer, simply and solely to the extension of our mechanical power.

It is not that the manufacturer does not realize a profit on his goods,—the very reverse is the truth. He never was in a more palmy condition or made larger profits than during this period of apparent depreciation ; but the whole system has undergone a great revolution.

In the best days of the late Sir Robert Peel it was usual to estimate profits in the cotton trade at probably twenty times the present rate ; but then the quantity produced was comparatively small and wages proportionably high ; whereas at the present time the manufacturers calculate their profits by the fractional parts of a farthing, and counterbalance any deficiency in the rate of profit by producing every year of their existence almost enough to cover the entire circumference of the earth.

There would be great cause for triumph at such a result, if all classes in the community shared the profits equally with the manufacturer : but, unfortunately, just in proportion as the mill owner acquires great wealth, the condition of the operative outside the walls of the mill verges to one of extreme destitution.

An acre of land, if cultivated, must pay a tithe of its productions to support the religion of the State, and an equal contribution with any other property in respect of the poor, county, and church-rates ; but mechanical power may exercise its productive faculty ad infinitum, with but a trifling reference or liability to either the one or the other. The building may be rated at 200*l.*, 500*l.*, or 1,000*l.* a year, but it has a power within it, which, as compared with landed property rated at the same amount, will produce a hundred fold as great a return: a principle in legislation as deteriorating in its operation on the masses as it is unjust to individuals.

This is rendered every year more and more apparent by the fact that periods of stagnation are more frequent than ever, and the working classes, to check the operation of this system, have now combined for a ten hours bill. They are well aware that when trade is brisk they will be able to dictate the price of labour to their masters, and that in times of depression their condition could not be worse than it is at present. It will in all probability compel the manufacturers to keep larger stocks, and to equalize the labour of their factories by a more constant employment of those engaged, and thus raise not only the scale of wages, but also the rate of profits.

It is the first blow that has been effectively struck at the overwhelming preponderance of mechanical power, but it will not be the last.

The manufacturers may "fret and chafe under the infliction," to use the language of Sir James Graham, but they will have to submit; and the time is not far distant when this hitherto irresponsible power of production will be exercised only in the proportion that it may contribute to the taxation of the country and the necessities of the State.

CHAPTER VIII.

THE MINING INTEREST.

Its Antiquity.—Coal.— Iron.— Tin.—Lead. — Salt. — Summary of Persons employed.—Capital embarked.—Annual Productions.— Comparison of Home and Foreign Trade.

THE Mining Interest of this country is one of great antiquity, and is separate and distinct from the manufacturing, or any other. It existed for centuries before the manufacturing interest acquired any degree of importance, and, as some of our writers assure us that our present stock of coal is likely to hold out for at least 2,000 years more, it is not improbable that the mines of this country may be an inexhaustible source of wealth, long after the manufacture of the textile fabrics shall again have shifted its locality, and set out upon its travels to other countries.

Coal.—Our coal mines date from the thirteenth century; and the present annual cousumption is estimated at about 38,000,000 tons. According to Mr M'Culloch, it is thus distributed:—

		Tons.
Domestic consumption and small manufactures		20,000,000
Railway carriages, steamers, &c.		1,200,000
		21,200,000

MANUFACTURES.	Tons.	
Production of pig and bar iron	9,125,000	
Cotton manufacture	1,000,000	
Woollen, linen, silk, &c.	1,000,000	
Copper, smelting, brass manufactures	1,000,000	
Salt works	375,000	
Lime works	700,000	
Total consumed in manufactures		13,200,000

EXPORTS.	Tons.	
To Ireland	1,500,000	
To colonies and foreign parts	2,500,000	
		4 000,000
		38,400,000

The export trade is scarcely worthy of notice, and it will be seen from the above list that the quantity consumed in manufactures is only one-third. We believe this to be much overrated; but whether the calculation be true or not, there is very little doubt that the domestic consumption as here stated is equal to one half of the whole.

Estimated at an average of 10s. per ton, the annual produce of our coal mines would amount to 19,200,000l., but when so large a proportion of the whole is carried coastwise, as well as by canals and railroads ramifying in all directions throughout the kingdom, we should say this estimate is much too low, and, provided the quantity stated be correct, we entertain no doubt that the cost to the consumer falls very little short of 25,000,000l. annually.

The number of persons returned in the census as working in coal mines was 115,883 males and 2,350 females (see Appendix, p. 163). Other considerations, however, of vast importance attach not only to the coal trade, but to the mining interest generally ; and among others is the great amount of shipping it gives employment to. The north country trade alone employs 1,500 vessels, and above 15,000 seamen and boys, thus acting as an excellent nursery for seamen, and constituting a powerful arm of defence in the time of war.

Iron.—There is, it is said, authentic evidence to show that iron works were established by the Romans in the Forest of Dean, in Gloucestershire, and in other parts of the kingdom. Owing, however, to complaints of the destruction of timber for the smelting of iron, it made but little progress, until Lord Dudley, in 1619, discovered a process and obtained a patent for smelting iron ore with pit coal.

The manufacture was distributed in 1840 as follows :—

	Furnaces.		Tons.
South Wales	163	producing	505,000
Staffordshire	151	,,	427.650
Shropshire	31	,,	82,750
Yorkshire	32	,,	56,000
Derbyshire	18	,,	31,000
North Wales	15	,,	26,500
Forest of Dean	4	,,	15,500
Scotland	70	,,	241,000
Various, including Northumberland	6	,,	11,000
Total	490		1,396,400

The manufacture in Scotland, in 1846, was carried on at the rate of about 500,000 tons per annum; and assuming that the same rate of increase took place in the districts above-mentioned, the total make for the United Kingdom would be about 1,750,000 tons.

The number of persons working in the iron mines is returned in the census as 10,949 (see Appendix, page 163), and in the manufacture of iron, 30,342 (see Appendix, page 149). The latter are very properly classed as manufacturers, although closely allied to the mining interest.

Mr M'Culloch estimates the annual production of iron to be worth about 14,000,000*l.*, but we think this is much over-rated. In years of great excitement and railway speculation, the price is unnaturally forced up, and the production probably much increased; but at other times it is not unusual to deduct 25 or 30 per cent. from the quantities here stated for reduced make, and the prices average 25 per cent. under those on which this estimate is formed. These deductions would, in ordinary times, make the annual value about 8,000,000*l.*; and this is more in accordance with the profits returned under the income tax. The foreign trade in 1846 amounted to about 500,000 tons of all sorts, leaving for the consumption of the home trade the remaining 1,000,000 or 1,250,000 tons; being about two-thirds of the whole.

The United States of America, in 1844, took one-fifth of the whole quantity exported; but the reader will find, at page 57, a statement of their own progress in the manufacture of iron, not calculated to induce a hope that this branch of our trade with them will be either extended or continued.

Tin.—The tin mines of Cornwall are the most ancient of all. Herodotus mentions the " Cassiterides, or Tin Islands," to which the Phœnicians traded, which are generally supposed to mean those of Britain.

The number of persons actually working in the mines is very mall, only 6,101 in all. (See Appendix, page 163.) In addition to these, the manufacture of tin gives employment to 1,320 tin manufacturers (see Appendix, page 151), and 9,657 tin-plate workers, dealers, &c. (See Appendix, page 159.)

The quantity annually produced is about 4,500 tons, which at 70*l.* per ton amounts to 315,000*l.*, of which the export trade takes about one-third, and the home trade two-thirds. Until 1817, the China market took about 800 tons annually, but since the restoration of the island of Borneo to the Dutch, its mines have been so productive, that they now not only supply the markets of India and China, but send a large quantity to the Continent of Europe.

Mr Porter states that, inasmuch as our production of this metal is greater than our consumption, it would be absurd to suppose that any foreign produce could enter injuriously into competition with that of our own mines. A conclusion, we submit, that the history of no one article in commerce will justify. America may send us iron, and Borneo tin, if the price of their labour is less than ours; and the price of labour is governed not only by supply and demand, but by the amount of taxation, which enters into every element of which it is composed.

Copper.—The ores of copper and tin being frequently mixed, it follows that these mines are also of a very ancient date; but it was not till the beginning of the eighteenth century, that they acquired any great degree of importance. The annual produce is thus distributed:—Cornwall, 11,000 tons; Devon, 500; other parts of England, 260; Anglesey, 750; other parts of Wales, 150; Ireland, 1,400;—total, 14,060; which, at 100*l.* per ton, would produce 1,406,000*l.* The export trade takes about one-half, and the remainder is consumed at home. The number of persons actually employed in the mines in Great Britain is 15,407; in addition to which there are copper manufacturers, 2,140; and copper-smiths, 1,319. (See Appendix, pages 155 and 148.)

Mr M'Culloch estimates the numbers employed in and on the copper and tin mines at 45,000; but the numbers we have given are the only ones that appear in the returns of the census.

Lead.—The working of mines of this valuable mineral is also said to date from the time of the Romans. The total annual produce is estimated at 50,000 tons, which, at 20*l.* per ton, would be worth 1,000,000*l.* About one-fifth of this is exported, and the remainder taken for home consumption. It gives employment to 11,419 persons. (See Appendix, page 163.)

Salt.—Mr M'Culloch estimates the production of our salt mines and works at 537,000 tons per annum, of which 200,000 tons are consumed at home, and 337,000 tons exported. Value, at 15s. per ton, about 400,000l.

SUMMARY of the MINING INTEREST of the UNITED KINGDOM.

	Number of Persons Employed.	Amount of Annual Productions.	Home Trade.	Foreign Trade.
		£	£	£
Coal	118,233	25,000,000	23,500,000	1,500,000
Iron	10,949	8,000,000	5,500,000	2,500,000
Tin (exclusive of tin plates)	6,101	315,000	210,000	105,000
Copper	15,407	1,406 000	706,000	700,000
Lead	11,419	1,000,000	800,000	200,000
Salt	268	400,000	195,000	205,000
Manganese	275			
Minerals not specified .	34,269			
	196 921	36,121,000	30,911,000	5,210,000

It is difficult to form any estimate of the probable amount of capital embarked in this interest, but the assessment to the Property and Income Tax in 1842-3 was as follows:—

	£	s.	d.
Profits of mines	2,081,387	1	5
„ of iron works	550,435	5	6
„ of quarries.	240,483	9	6
	2,872,305	16	5

which, reckoning the profits at 10 per cent., would make the capital employed in the Mining Interest amount to 28,723,000l.

CHAPTER IX.

THE SHIPPING AND COLONIAL INTERESTS.
FOREIGN COMMERCE.

Notice of Commerce previous to the Rise of the Manufacturing Interest.

The Shipping Interest.—Navigation Laws.—Origin and Intention of them.—Reciprocity Treaties.—Reduction of Protective Duties on Whale Oil, and its Effect on the Whale Fisheries.—Mistake of Sir Robert Peel as to the Cause of the Advance in Value of Lard.—Coasting Trade.—Foreign Trade.—Colonial Trade.—Capital invested in Shipping.—Annual Profits.

The Colonial Interests.—The Political Importance of our Colonies.—Opinions of Mr M'Culloch and Mr Porter.—List of our Colonies.—Shipping.—Exports.

The Foreign Trade.—Comparative Tables of the Imports and Exports of England, France, and the United States from 1801 to 1844.—Exports of Great Britain to all Countries in 1844.—Official and Declared Value of the Exports and Imports of Great Britain from 1801 to 1846.

SHIPS, COLONIES, and COMMERCE, have long been considered the outward symbols of the greatness and power of the British empire. Long before Manchester and Birmingham had emerged from comparative obscurity as towns, or acquired any degree of importance either in trade or population, our mercantile fleets had circumnavigated the world, and the enterprise of our merchants had led them to traffic at all the ports and in all the productions of the most distant countries.

Like the Venetians and the Dutch in times of old, they waited not for the labours of the spindle and the loom, but made our cities the depôts for the merchandise of the world ; and, in bartering the productions of one quarter of the globe for those of another, they acquired great wealth for themselves, and at the same time extended and consolidated the power of the nation.

It was this spirit of enterprise that first gave to Britain the dominion of the seas. It was this which enabled her to plant in the Western Hemisphere the germ of a great and mighty nation that bids fair to powerfully influence, if not to control, the destinies of the world for ages yet to come. It was this which enabled a handful of merchant adventurers, who first were humble suppliants for a mercantile residence in Hindostan, to obtain and to hold possession of more than a million of square miles of the richest portion of the earth, and gave to the British Crown absolute dominion over a hundred and twenty millions of souls. It was this same spirit which planted the language, institutions, and interests of Britain in every portion of the globe, until it presents a combination of power and wealth without a parallel in the history of the world. As mainly instrumental in producing these mighty results, we must first speak of

The Shipping Interest.

The policy which governed this country in respect of its shipping for about 160 years originated with the Protectorate of Cromwell, and was afterwards perfected by the 12th Charles II, chap. 18. This act provided, that no merchandise of either Asia, Africa, or America should be imported into Great Britain in any but English built ships, navigated by an English commander, and having at least three-fourths of their crew English. Besides this exclusive right secured to British shipping, higher duties were levied on goods imported in foreign ships from Europe than if imported under the English flag.

To provide for and sustain this mighty arm of defence, which alone can render our insular position impregnable, it was also considered necessary that a well-ordered and extensive mercantile navy should co-exist, for without it that of the nation would soon be paralyzed; and not only during the late war, but in the most perilous times of our history, the recognition of this principle has done the state much service.

Were no other considerations to be attended to but that of cheapness, a nation's honour might become a matter of bargain or sale, and its independence would fall before the first aggressor. Our ancestors therefore considered a mercantile navy something more " than the mere tools with which the merchants work," as Mr Porter expresses it, and they wisely concluded that both " the means and the end of commerce " should be subservient to the security of the country.

In consequence of the Americans, immediately after obtaining their independence, having enacted navigation laws, the exact counterpart of our own, the first concession of reciprocal duties was made to them in 1815, and afterwards to nearly all nations, in virtue of the reciprocity acts passed in the 4th and 5th of George IV.

It is not within the object of the present work to discuss the political considerations which belong to such a matter, but there were many which at that time induced the Earl of Liverpool's Government to make this concession, which only, however, affected the principle of the navigation laws to a certain extent.

The preponderance of English shipping at the close of the war over that of all other nations, gave to our shipowners precedence and possession of the trade which a twenty years' war had conferred in like manner on our manufacturers, and left them little to fear on the score of competition.

Furthermore, the Americans, up to this time, had been harassed and humbled by the expenses of the war just concluded. They had made no progress in manufactures, and very little in any thing else; and it was at this conjuncture of their affairs, when our exports at that moment exceeded in value any thing they have ever done since, and our merchants and manufacturers promised to themselves a rich harvest of trade, that this concession was made to them. In fact, it was to counteract the operation of their own law, which, if the expectations of our merchants had been realised, would have affected our shipping much more seriously than our own regulations could have affected theirs.

A great depreciation in the value of British shipping, however, immediately took place, and a large portion of the capital invested in this interest at that period was wholly lost.

That our shipping has increased since is nothing very remarkable.

There has been an increase of 75 per cent. in our own population, and of 300 per cent. in that of America. The consumption and productions of our colonies have been greatly extended, and the commerce of our merchants with the South American States, and the opening of the East India and China trades have all tended to one end—the increase of our shipping. It must also be remembered that a very large proportion of our trade is carried on with countries either lying at a great distance, or having no commercial marine to compete with us, so that the actual value of the concession made to other countries by the reciprocity acts is not of the importance which some would imagine.

The only effect that we can legitimately trace to these treaties is, that they have prematurely called into existence the latent energies of other countries; and although for some years after the commencement of this reciprocity system they made little or no progress, yet they have latterly mended their pace, and in the race of competition are now in some instances enabled to beat us out of the field in respect to trades hitherto peculiarly our own. Take, for instance, that of the whale fisheries. Up to 1824 a bounty was given, but in that year discontinued. A protecting duty of 39*l.* 18*s.* per tun on sperm oil was substituted from that time down to 1830, when it was reduced to 15*l.* per tun. By the last alteration the duty is to cease altogether in 1848, and the markets of England for the sale of sperm oil to be opened to the foreigner.

The result may be told in a few words. In the year 1820 it found employment for 137 vessels, averaging about 350 tuns each, or 48,000 tons of shipping, with 4,000 men; and the annual import of sperm and black whale oil was estimated at from 500,000*l.* to 600,000*l.* The price of the article to the public during this period varied from 50*l.* to 70*l.* per tun. The protection to the English fisherman being taken away, he knew that he could no longer compete with the American, whose outfit was so much cheaper than his own, and therefore withdrew from the trade. *In the year 1845 not a single ship cleared out for this fishery, and it may be said to be all but extinct.* THE AMERICANS, *on the other hand, have increased the number of their ships to* 720, *giving employment to* 20,000 *men.*

Our colonists of New Zealand and Van Diemen's Land have adopted the trade which the mother country has been compelled to abandon, and have prosecuted it with some considerable degree of success; but Great Britain is now principally supplied with spermaceti and black whale oil from the United States of America, and *as a consequence* the prices for many years past have ranged from 20 to 25 per cent. above those of the preceding years.

It will be in the recollection of the public, that in the debate on the Corn Laws last session, Sir Robert Peel laid great stress on the fact of lard having increased in price since the reduction of duty. Now, what is the real state of the case ? The slightest inquiry of any one conversant with the trade in this article would have satisfied Sir Robert that his reduction of the duty on lard had nothing whatever to do with the advance in its value. This was solely owing to the discovery of a process for extracting oil from it, which is now used in our spinning factories to a great extent, in consequence of the extravagant price of spermaceti oil; and this would have taken place, had no reduction of the duty ever been made. This practice of ascribing effects to causes which have no relationship whatever to them, may deceive the multitude, and suit party purposes, but it is unworthy of the statesman or the politician.

The number of vessels in the British empire in 1844 consisted of 31,320, amounting to 3,637,231 tons, and giving employment to 216,350 men. From the number of times which each vessel enters and clears in the course of the year, it is impossible to ascertain with any degree of accuracy what proportion in point of numbers are engaged in the coasting and the foreign trade respectively, but it will be seen that the foreign trade conducted in British vessels is about one-fourth of the whole; thus:—

ENTERED INWARDS.		ENTERED OUTWARDS.	
	Tons.		Tons.
Coasting trade	10,964,707	Coasting trade	11,694,861
Foreign	3,647,463	Foreign	3,852,822
	14,612,170		15,547,683

Of the trade here described as foreign, more than one-third of the whole is carried on with our colonies. The colonial shipping consists of 7,304 vessels, amounting to 592,839 tons, and employing 40,659 men. This is about one-fourth of the whole Shipping Interest of the British empire, and is altogether independent of a large amount of shipping belonging to the United Kingdom, employed in the same trade. We are not aware of any return distinguishing the entries of colonial ships from those of the United Kingdom; but it will be seen, on referring to pages 170 and 171 in the Appendix, that for the year 1844 the colonial trade gave employment to more than one-third in tonnage of the ships that entered inwards and cleared outwards during that year; thus—

	Ships.	Tonnage.	Crews.
Entered Inwards from all parts during the year	19,687	3,647,463	195,728
Of which, from British Dependencies . .	4.202	1,377,848	61,311
Entered Outwards for all parts during the year .	19,788	3,582,222	212,924
Of which, for British Dependencies . .	4,854	1,562,251	77,534

The capital invested in the Shipping Interest of Great Britain and her colonies may be estimated in round numbers at 10*l.* per ton, which, on 3,637,231 tons, would amount to 36,372,310*l.*; and if we average the profits at the rate of 10 per cent., it gives about 3,637,231*l.* as the aggregate annual profit derived by this all-important branch of our national industry.

Repeal or suspend the navigation laws, and give the foreigner free access to our colonial and coasting trade, and it will be something new in the history of the world, if the same degree of competition which has driven us out of the whale fisheries should not be carried into every branch of our Shipping Interest. What the equivalent may be for this very extraordinary speculation we have yet to learn.

The Colonial Interest.

When we consider the vast extent of the dependencies of Great Britain, and that they embrace every climate, and possess every natural advantage which the great Creator has bestowed on the human race, our interests would appear to be unbounded, and the space for the exertion of our population unlimited.

In the East, the West, the North, and the South, our colonies are at once the evidence of our power and our wealth, and the possession of such mighty means, and at the same time the often recurring complaints of our own people, would seem to imply either an utter disregard of their importance, or the most absolute deficiency of ability to apply them for the general benefit of the commonwealth.

Men but little acquainted with either the history or the requirements of their country, but who nevertheless have been returned to Parliament as the representatives of the people, have talked of the baneful influence of this country over her colonies, and contributed to the mischievous delusion that they are a source of weakness instead of strength, and that their mismanagement was a sufficient justification for their separation from the parent state.

It would be more easy to account for such opinions than to justify them. That many grievous errors have been committed in our colonial policy none can doubt, but more sound principles of government begin to prevail, and the time may not be far distant when our colonies will be considered and treated as integral parts of one great and mighty kingdom.

In the East we have founded an empire of great extent, and almost boundless resources. Mr Porter estimates that India alone " pours into the lap of Britain" three millions annually, but this we consider a very limited view of a very important fact. The dividends on East India Stock charged on the land revenues of India amount to 630,000*l.* per annum. The yearly revenue of India is 18,000,000*l.*, and a large proportion of this is paid to natives of Great Britain employed in its government. Her trade with us is now about 8,000,000*l.* a year.   Coupling these, therefore, with the extraordinary fortunes made by individuals, and regularly transmitted home to increase our wealth and employ our artisans, we cannot help estimating the benefits which this country derives from her territorial and commercial connexion with India at not less than *ten millions* per annum.

Independently of this, the contiguity of India to the most populous nation on the face of the earth, and the means it affords us to influence and promote our interests in China, would seem to give to this acquisition a degree of importance which, either in a political or commercial sense, is incalculable.

In the West, we have also an interest not so magnificent in its commercial prospects as regards the future, but the preservation of which is probably of more political importance than our empire of the East.   It would be a folly to disguise from ourselves the truth, that a great and mighty nation, an offshoot from ourselves, is fast rising to maturity, and may soon be in a condition to dispute with us the empire of the seas and the trade of the world.

The hope so beautifully expressed by the late Right Honourable George Canning, "that the mother and daughter might stand, united, a match for the world in arms," is not justified by the experience of the past, and cannot be relied upon with any degree of safety for the future, for our rival interests have on all occasions had the effect of forcing us into the most deadly contests, and that in the most perilous times of our existence.

America will belie the truth of history if, when she shall have accumulated great wealth, and the arts and sciences shall have struck their roots deep in her institutions, she fails to become aristocratic, fond of distinctions and honours, and, as a natural consequence of her progress in civilization, to clothe herself in the imperial purple, put a royal diadem on her head, and set herself down among the nations of the earth as the Queen of the Western World.

To counteract this influence, and to oppose to it a formidable barrier by raising up another nation great and powerful at her own door, even if not embued with British feelings, and sensibly alive to the value and importance of British connexion, we imagine to be a duty on this country paramount to all others.

Every encouragement should therefore be given to induce emigration in the first instance to the Canadas and our possessions in that quarter, and the emigration of our people to this or any other dependency of the British Crown, instead of being left to provide for itself, or as a matter of profit in the hands of unprincipled speculators, ought to be one of anxious solicitude on the part of the mother country. Independently of the misery and ruin which any failure necessarily entails on the poor emigrants themselves, it is sure to react on this country by preventing great numbers from adopting it as a remedy for the evils of their present condition.

If our own population therefore is excessive—if the Malthusian theory is correct, and population increases faster than food, let them go forth, but let them go, as did the Greeks and Romans of old, with their institutions, their altars, and their gods.

The facilities which steam navigation is every year placing within our reach are such as to give us a command of means for as frequent a communication with these parts as one hundred years ago existed between London and Edinburgh, and with such facilities, and such a mass of wealth, as exists at the present time in this country, there ought to be no want of employment for our people, and no complaining in our streets.

The magnificent harbour of Halifax, and the numerous other ports, by which we can always keep in check and if necessary interfere with the trade of all the Atlantic cities in America, ought to be secured and maintained at any expense whatever; for in our hands they are a guarantee of peace, while in the hands of the Americans they would be certain to lead to the subjugation of all our interests in that part of the globe.

The Sugar Islands of the West Indies are the next in importance, and whether we consider the value of their own productions, or the amount of our exports, they may be considered a mine of wealth, for the loss of which nothing would compensate us.

Our possessions at the Cape of Good Hope, in the Mediterranean, in Australia, and the different other places set forth in the annexed list, are all so many points of offence and defence for the protection, the security, and the promotion of our interests.

Against this array of what has hitherto been considered the most important parts of our political system, the same antagonistic principle of no protection is, however, in full operation. Mr M'Culloch says that "the advantages supposed peculiarly to belong to the colony trade are in a great degree imaginary." "The surplus derived from India is quite trifling indeed." "Canada is a costly and worthless possession," "and our trade a forced and factitious one." "The Canadians would be better employed in cultivating the earth than in supplying us with timber, because it interferes with our trade in the Baltic, and prevents the Russians, Prussians, Norwegians, and Swedes from taking more of our manufactures." "Our West Indian Colonies, because they supply articles on which a great revenue is raised, are only on a par with China and Virginia."

Mr Porter reiterates the same arguments in nearly the same language, and in addition says that he is at a loss for words to describe adequately our folly in supporting such a policy, and "that occasion is sometimes taken by the advocates of the protective system to point out the actual and comparative magnitude of our colonial trade in proof of the practical wisdom of their doctrine."

This is precisely the fact, and we know not what can so well represent the value of a thing as its "actual and comparative magnitude." Against Mr M'Culloch's estimate of India "as quite trifling indeed," we say that it "pours into the lap of Britain" ten millions annually. In opposition to his opinion that Canada is a costly and worthless possession, we contend that, with the facilities of steam communication, it may be made a field of profit for the exertions of our surplus population for ages yet to come, and coupled with our other possessions in that quarter, its political importance is above all price.

With a balance of trade already in favour of the Baltic, and which will be fearfully increased when, as Mr Porter anticipates, we shall have become " habitually and increasingly " importers of foreign grain, the Russians, Prussians, &c., &c., want no additional inducement to take our manufactures, nor any timber trade to rectify exchanges already so much against us.

And as to our West Indian Islands, with what degree of fairness or honesty can our connexion with these be compared to that with China and Virginia. Until very recently their ports were closed against all manufacturers but our own, and the benefits were reciprocal. Both parties prospered by their mutual dependence on each other; but what security can we have that our interests will be regarded with equal favour by countries who owe to us no allegiance. Mr M'Culloch and Mr Porter both admit that " there are grave doubts whether, after the sugar duties are equalized, our planters can sustain the competition of the planters of Cuba or Brazil, who command the services of slaves." At the best, therefore, we are only exchanging a certainty for an uncertainty. Should the prices of sugar rise in Brazil and Cuba with the increased demand for our markets and the discouragement of its growth by our own planters, it will only serve as another illustration of the free-trade principle in respect of every article on which it has been tried; and it is not only possible, but extremely probable, that we shall ruin our planters without enriching our manufacturers.

We say nothing of the contradiction implied in giving 20,000,000*l.* to purchase the liberty of our own slaves, and then giving encouragement to the slave-grown productions of other countries, in respect of articles we can grow in sufficient abundance for our wants. The advocates of the new light are men whose ideas take a wider range, and while they are almost unable to imagine the extent to which the prosperity of the country may be carried under the operation of the free-trade system, they are not unwilling in the furtherance of their object to sacrifice the most noble and exalted act of philanthropy ever chronicled in the history of nations, and at the same time every other consideration, national, political, and moral.

We know of no authority for the amount of British capital invested in British colonies. But when it is considered that these dependencies embrace a vast population, and that they carry on an extensive trade not only with ourselves, but with all the world; that they give employment to more than one-third of the shipping employed in the foreign trade, and absorb one-fourth of the whole exports of the United Kingdom, their "actual and comparative importance" can be no longer matter of doubt. Some authors estimate the fee simple and annual produce at about one-half that of the United Kingdom; thus:—

	Fee Simple.	Annual Produce.
	£	£
Great Britain - - - -	3,769,500,000	514,823,059
Dependencies in Europe - - -	27,115,094	2,146,198
Settlements in North America - -	62,100,466	17,620,629
Ditto in the West Indies - -	131,052,424	22,196,674
Empire in India - - - -	1,611,977,354	313,200,000
Possessions in the Indian Ocean - -	27,500,781	4,201,332
In Africa and its Coasts - - -	6,114,308	1,057,065
In Australia - - - -	7,000,000	2,100,000
	5,642,360,427	877,344,957

Whether this is a close approximation to the truth or not, it is impossible to say, but at all events it is sufficient to show that the Colonial Interest is of such vast magnitude, that any event that shall separate Britain from her foreign possessions will not only lead to the dismemberment of the empire, but furnish materials to some future Gibbon for another work on the decline and fall of nations.

Of the total exports and imports of our colonies to and from all parts, there is no official account published, nor is there any separate one of the colonial produce imported into this country, from which it can be ascertained by any but the Custom-house authorities. They have, however, been estimated as follows:—

	£
Total exports from the colonies to all parts, about	30,000,000
Of which to Great Britain	15,000,000
Total imports into the colonies from all parts, about	26,000,000
Of which from Great Britain in 1844	16,903,587

LIST OF COLONIES BELONGING TO THE BRITISH EMPIRE.

COLONIES.	Date of Acquisition.	POPULATION. Whites.	POPULATION. Coloured.	COLONIES.	Date of Acquisition.	POPULATION. Whites.	POPULATION. Coloured.
EUROPE.							
Gibraltar -	1704	15,008				787,957	97,443,724
Malta -	1800	105,456		**N. AMERICA.**			
Gozo -	1800	16,472		Canada, Lr.	1759	690,932	261
Corfu -	1814	75,334		„ Upper	1759	481,888	4,167
Cephalonia -	1809	64,636		New Brunswick -	1630	156,162	
Zanté -	1809	40,899		Novia Scotia	1623	178,237	
Santa Maura	1810	17,450		Cape Breton	1758	27,000	
Ithaca -	1810	10,623		Prince Edward's Ild.	1763	47,033	
Cerigo -	1810	9,447		Newfoundld.	1583	74,405	
Paxo -	1814	4,966		Hudsn's Bay Territory	1670	4,066	4,867
Heligoland -	1807	2,200					
ASIA.							
Bengal -	1696	25,000	40,000,000				
Agra -	1803	3,000	32,000,000				
Ultra Gangetic territory -	1825	500	1,000,000	**S. AMERICA.**			
Madras -	1639	10,000	15,000,000	Brit. Guiana			
Bombay -	1661	10,000	8,000,000	Demerara	1803	3,006	71,877
Ceylon {	1796 and 1815	9,121	1,232,704	Essequibo	1803		
				Berbice -	1803	570	20,971
Penang -	1786	500	33,000	Honduras -	1650	235	7,700
Sincapore -	1819	2,000	20,000	Falkland I.			
				Soledad, W. Falkld.	1765		
AUSTRALIA.							
New South Wales, E. Australia -	1787	128,718					
Van Diemn's Land -	1803	57,420		**WEST INDIA ISLANDS.**			
Swan River, West Australia -	1829	4,350		Jamaica -	1655	37,152	336,253
So. Australia	1835	17,366		The Cayman	1655		
Norfolk Ild.	1787	1,500		Trinidad -	1797	3,621	35,707
New Zealnd.	1839	3,000		Tobago -	1763	306	12,894
				Grenada -	1783	3,804	17,190
AFRICA.				St Vincent -	1783	1,301	25,821
Cape of Good Hope -	1806	68,300	98,108	Barbadoes -	1625	15,959	86,646
Mauritius -	1810	81,967	53,230	St Lucia -	1803	983	13,196
Seychelles -	1810			Dominica -	1783	720	17,940
St Helena -	1651	2,500	2,236	St Kitt's -	1623	10,435	12,047
Ascension -				Montserrat -	1632	289	6,830
Sierra Leone	1787	175	4,446	Antigua -	1632	1,980	33,432
The Gambia {	1631 and 1816	49		Barbuda -	1632	50	1,540
				Nevis -	1628	500	9,500
Cape Coast Castle -	1661			Anguilla -	1650	365	3,301
Acera	1661			Tortola and Virgin I. -	1666	730	7,000
Dix Cove -				New Providence -	1628	2,000	6,000
Annamaboe				The Bahamas	1628	2,000	10,000
Fernando Po	1827			St George & the Bermudas -	1611	4,000	5,000
Aden, Red Sea Mouth	1838						
		787,957	97,443,724	Total -		1,828,686	98,193,864

To this must be added the population of those states in India possessing civil independence but no military force, about 30,000,000, making a total population of more than *one hundred and thirty millions of souls.*

The Foreign Trade.

We believe that there are not two opinions as to the great importance of the foreign trade of this country. This is derived, however, not so much from any actual profit we receive from the trade itself as from the collateral advantages which belong to it, and for which all nations fiercely compete with each other. Were we to estimate that our merchants made a profit of 10 per cent. on the amount of our exports and imports, this would not be more than about 15 millions a year. When, however, we consider the immense losses that are frequently sustained, as in 1836 with the Americans, this is certainly much above, rather than under the average of profit received from it.

This trade is, however, the means by which we annually exchange about 60 millions of the manufacturing and mineral productions of this country for those of others; and if we deduct this from the Manufacturing Interest, and consider it as represented by the foreign trade, it may be said to amount to about one-seventh of the whole trade of the country.

In another sense its importance is still much greater than any that can be estimated as a matter of profit; and so long as the principle which governs it makes this foreign trade subservient to the protection and defence of the country, its extension is an evidence of our increasing strength; but if this principle is to be surrendered, it is possible that, with a very enlarged trade carried on in the vessels of other nations, we may some day make the discovery that, by inverting the policy of our ancestors, we have sacrificed *both* " the means and the end of commerce."

To enable the reader to understand the full bearing of this important matter it is necessary that we direct his attention to what constitutes the foreign trade of this country, which will be found in the table on the opposite page. Following this we have given similar tables of the Import and Export trade of the three most important nations now competing with each other for the possession of it.

It will be seen from the first of these tables, that the Colonies of which Mr M'Culloch and others speak so slightingly, take no inconsiderable portion of the manufactures shipped from this country, and of the cotton goods in particular, they take nearly one-half the whole quantity exported.

STATEMENT OF THE EXPORTS OF FOREIGN COUNTRIES IN THE YEAR 1844.

COUNTRIES.	Cottons.	Woollens.	Linen.	Silk.	Sundries.	Total Exports.
COLONIES.	£	£	£	£	£	£
East India Co.'s Territories & Ceylon	4,793,192	438,643	53,642	—	2,410,189	7,695,666
British North American Colonies	702,229	536,397	135,664	} 109,191	{ 1,709,187	3,083,477
British West Indies	637,963	78,690	217,072		{ 1,517,752	2,451,477
Gibraltar	723,927	118,923	75,815	—	130,902	1,049,567
New So. Wales, Van Diemen's Land, and Swan River	135,985	60,758	30,110	}	{ 517,629	744,482
New Zealand and South Sea Islands	5,033	4,886	—	} 49,867	{ 37,593	47,512
Western Coast of Africa	195,030	7,119	—		256,265	458,414
Cape of Good Hope	93,730	47,333	16,346	}	{ 266,742	424,151
Mauritius	109,525	14,457	8,197	—	153,471	285,650
Malta	85,223	20,599	—	—	94,187	206,009
Ionian Islands	90,652	4,133	—	—	29,143	123,928
St Helena	1,458	743	783	—	18,022	21,006
Isles of Guernsey, Jersey, Alderney, and Man	53,618	51,359	22,904	—	261,879	389,760
	7,627,565	1,384,040	560,533	*	7,402,961	16,975,099
FOREIGN COUNTRIES.						
Russia	1,383,795	57,385	—	—	687,746	2,128,926
Sweden	53,081	20,813	—	—	34,581	108,475
Norway	64,027	22,538	—	—	66,259	152,824
Denmark	46,865	1,778	—	—	238,036	286,679
Prussia	12,016	1,569	—	—	491,799	505,384
Germany	3,109,328	1,031,573	441,087	—	1,569,540	6,151,528
Holland	1,584,161	408,761	161,203	—	977,845	3,131,970
Belgium	387,002	220,461	52,837	—	810,951	1,471,251
France	215,065	187,890	675,898	159,680	1,577,406	2,656,259
Portugal, Proper	788,181	}	{ 20,063	— }	{	1,153,847
„ Azores	38,775	} 186,039	—	— }	{ 195,623	56,839
„ Madeira	13,741	}	—	— }		31,736
Spain and the Balearic Islands	13,134	} 85,122	{ 193,811	— }	{ 235,143	{ 509,207
„ Canaries	28,318	}		— }		{ 46,321
Italy and the Italian Islands	1,359,525	331,996	134,485	—	743,234	2,569,240
Turkey and Continental Greece	1,992,296	85,320	10,616	—	203,172	2,291,404
Morea and Greek Islands	7,121	3,066	—	—	18,014	28,201
Syria and Palestine	563,572	3,438	—	—	10,818	577,828
Egypt (Ports in the Mediterranean)	287,528	4,600	—	—	109,973	402,101
Tripoli, Barbary, and Morocco	6,212	—	—	—	11.528	17,740
African Ports on the Red Sea	—	—	—	—	2.277	2,277
Ascension Island	104	—	—	—	2,100	2,204
Cape Verd Islands	692	76	—	—	1,219	1.987
Arabia	139	86	—	—	10,784	11,009
Hong Kong	1,271,790	—	—	—	—	} 2,305,617
China	303,857	565,428	7,882	—	156,660	}
Sumatra, Java, and other Islands of the Indian Seas	283,934	11,126	5,091	—	76,717	376,918
Philippine Islands	75,427	3,272	3,218	—	10,600	92 517
Hayti	107,127	—	47,420	—	19.910	174,457
Cuba and other Foreign West Indies	405,767	77,245	275,814	—	240,648	999,474
United States of America	1,052,908	2,444,789	938,392	189,698	3,501,990	7,938,079
Mexico	195,457	92,524	142,593	}	{ 63,521	494,095
Texas	1,759	—	—		2,147	3,906
Columbia	134,848	28,697	—		101,143	264.688
Brazil	1,361,658	288,924	170,296	} 117,594	592,660	2,413,538
States of the Rio de la Plata	411,115	184.957	31.097		156,795	784 564
Chili	361,923	206 341	69,699		169,870	806,633
Peru	250,573	263,248	37,197	}	{ 107,362	658,380
Falkland Islands	—	—	—	—	93	93
All other Places	—	—	† 39,138	110,425	—	—
TOTAL	18,172,871	6,819,062	3,419,099	‡736,455	13,198,161	41,609,190
Total Exports to all Countries						58,584,292

* † ‡ Amounts included in Sundries.

IMPORT TRADE OF ENGLAND, FRANCE, AND THE
UNITED STATES.

COMPARATIVE TABLE of the IMPORTS of FOREIGN and COLONIAL MERCHAN-
DISE into ENGLAND, FRANCE, and the UNITED STATES, in each year from
1801 to 1844.

YEARS.	ENGLAND.	FRANCE.	AMERICA.
	£	£	£
1801	31,786,262	16,609,167	23,200,731
1802	29,826.210	18,597,986	15,902.777
1803	26,622,696	17,195.986	13,462,313
1804	27,819,552	17,616,681	17.708,333
1805	28.561,270	19,676,230	25,125,000
1806	26,899,658	19,073,481	26,978,416
1807	26,734,425	15,728,104	28,869 765
1808	26,795,540	12,804,756	11,872,916
1809	31,750,557	11 469 964	12,375,000
1810	39,301,612	13,466,536	17,791,666
1811	26,510 186	11,942,464	11,125,000
1812	26,163,431	8,319,480	16,047,916
1813	Records destroyed by fire	10 043,420	4,584.375
1814	33,755,264	9,558,236	2,701,041
1815	32.987,396	7.936,648	17,308,349
1816	27,431,604	10,462,766	32,354,729
1817	30,834,299	13,592,010	20,574.661
1818	36,885,182	14,276,558	25,364,583
1819	30,776,810	12,368,931	18,155,552
1820	32,438,650	14,525,575	15,510,416
1821	30,792,760	15,777,694	13,038,592
1822	30 500,094	17,047,168	17,341,988
1823	35 798,707	14,473,129	16,162,347
1824	37,552,935	18 194,464	16,781,043
1825	44,137 482	21,344,896	20,070 849
1826	37,686,113	22 589,144	17,703,016
1827	44,887,774	22,632,169	16 559.180
1828	45 028.805	24,307,172	18,439,546
1829	43 981,317	24,654,136	15,519,276
1830	46,245,241	25,533,537	14,766,025
1831	49,713,889	20,513,022	21,498.140
1832	44,586,741	26,114,893	21,047,764
1833	45,952 551	27,731,030	22,524,648
1834	49,362 811	28.807,773	26,358.610
1835	48,911,542	30,429,067	31,228,279
1836	57,023,867	36,223,014	39,579,174
1837	54,737,301	32.311,718	29.372,753
1838	61,268,320	37.482.179	23,689.042
1839	62,004,000	37,878,857	33 769,202
1840	67,432,964	42 091,440	22,321,149
1841	64,377,962	44,856,969	26,655.453
1842	65,204.729	45,681,328	20,867,101
1843	70,093.353	47,476,366	18,596 020
1844	85,441,555	47,717,635	22,590,632
1845	75,281,958		

EXPORT TRADE OF ENGLAND, FRANCE, AND THE UNITED STATES.

COMPARATIVE TABLE of the EXPORTS of MERCHANDISE, the PRODUCE and MANUFACTURE, of ENGLAND, FRANCE, and the UNITED STATES, and of the FOREIGN and COLONIAL PRODUCE in each year, from 1801 to 1844.

	ENGLAND.		FRANCE.	UNITED STATES.	
	Foreign and Colonial.	British and Irish Produce and Manufactures.		Produce, &c. of United States.	Produce of Foreign Countries.
	£	£	£	£	£
1801	10 336,966	39,730,659	12,177,240	9,890,250	9,717,233
1802	12,677,431	45.102,330	12,973,046	7,647,539	7,458,†19
1803	8,032,643	36,127,787	13 835,118	8 792,908	2,832,098
1804	8,938,741	37.135.746	15,181,252	8,639,057	7,548,248
1805	7,643,120	38,077,144	14,985,375	8,830,625	11,078,964
1806	7,717,555	40,874,983	18,198,434	8,594,526	12,559.006
1807	7,624,312	37,245,877	15.022,963	10,145 747	12,425,741
1808	5,776,775	37,275,102	13,232,196	1,965,322	2,707,794
1809	12,750,358	47,371,393	13 273,824	6.542,854	4,332,818
1810	9,357.435	48,438,680	14.601,340	8,826,390	5,08 ,519
1811	6,117,720	32 890,712	13,116,232	9,436 258	3,338,081
1812	9,533,065	41,716.964	16 745.848	6,256,689	1,769,817
1813	Records destroyed by Fire.		14,170,292	5,220,031	593,301
1814	19,365,981	45,494,219	13,842 116	1,412,973	39,243
1815	15,748,554	51,603,028	15.908,174	9,578 000	1,381,531
1816	13,480,780	41,657.873	18,528,842	13,496,228	3,570,532
1817	10,292,684	41,761,132	15,791,494	14 231,979	4,032,931
1818	10,859,817	46,603,249	17,968 261	15,386,341	4,047,227
1819	9,904,813	35,208,321	16,619,177	10,620,174	3,992,840
1820	10,555,912	36,424,652	18,196,727	10,767,425	4,768,339
1821	9 629,689	36,659,630	16 190,583	9,098,310	4,446.351
1822	9,227,589	36 958,964	15,406,748	10,390,433	4,642,957
1823	8,603,904	35,458 048	15,638,177	9.824,042	5,738 254
1824	10,204,785	38 396,300	17,621,676	10,551,979	5,278,575
1825	9,169,494	38,877,388	26.691,764	13,946,822	6,789 717
1826	10,076,286	31,536,723	22,420,340	11,053,273	5,112,419
1827	9.830,728	37,181,335	24,096,071	11,275 352	4,875 653
1828	9,946.545	36,812,756	24,396,905	10,556,181	4,498,953
1829	10,622,402	35,842,623	24,312,746	11,604,206	3.470 515
1830	8,550,437	38,271,597	22,906,562	12.387,923	4,997,391
1831	10,745,071	37.164,372	24 726,796	12,766,052	4,173,651
1832	11,044,869	36.450,594	27,851,285	13,153,639	5,008,223
1833	9,833,753	39,667,347	30,652,652	14,649,519	4,129,736
1834	11,562,036	41,649,191	28,588 201	16,880,033	4 856,835
1835	12,797,724	47,372,270	33,376,545	21,081,052	4.271,770
1836	12,391,711	53,368,571	38,431,390	22,274,308	4,530,491
1837	13,233 622	42 069,245	30,323,898	19,909,252	4,553,116
1838	12,711,318	50,060,970	38,236,306	20,207,046	2,594,331
1839	12,795,990	53,233,580	40 133,271	21,569,560	3.644,692
1840	13,774,306	51,406,430	40,436,901	23,724,257	3,789.648
1841	14,723 151	51,634,623	42,614,304	22,163,066	3,222,725
1842	13,584,158	47,381,023	37,610,036	19,368,750	2,441,986
1843	13,956,113	52,278,449	39,678,488	16,207,038	1,365,145
1844	14,397,246	58,584,292	45,871,526	20,773,995	2,392,680
1845	16,280,870	60,111,081			

The progress which France and the United States have made, as compared with ourselves, will be seen on reference to pages 116 and 117, from which we extract the following figures, as the result of a thirty years' trade since the close of the war:—

IMPORTS.

Average of five Years.	England.	France.	America.
	£	£	£
1816 to 1820	31,273,309	13,045,168	22,391,982
1840 to 1844	70,510,112	45,564,747	22,206,071
Increase -	120 per cent.	250 per cent.	Nil.

EXPORTS.

1816 to 1820	40,211,045	17,420,900	12,900,429
1840 to 1844	52,256,963	41,242,251	20,448,221
Increase -	30 per cent.	143 per cent.	62½ per cent.

The repeal of our Corn and Navigation Laws may give additional facilities to those countries to extend their operations; but the above figures, we contend, clearly demonstrate that there is nothing in their present circumstances that can make it a matter of interest with them to reciprocate or adopt a similar course of policy.

The whole of the evidence given before the Navigation Committee goes to establish the fact, that the Baltic and the United States can successfully compete with us in both the building and manning of ships; and it was elicited from S. Browning, Esq., that at "Lloyd's," first-class Americans are insured for 4s. 9d. per cent. less than English ships of the same class.

The same gentleman, in answer to other questions, said, " My opinion is, that, owing to the repeal of the Corn Laws, *we shall lower the price in this country of corn and provisions so much* that we shall place foreigners at a great disadvantage in competing with us." Again, " *before the Navigation Laws were repealed it would be quite necessary to reduce the duty upon all materials used in the construction of ships, such as timber, copper ore, and all foreign copper sheeting for smelting, foreign ores and stamps upon marine instruments of all kinds, insurance policy and light duties.*"

In other words, with food at extreme low prices, and in the utter absenceof all taxation, duties, and dues, our ship-builders could pos- sibly compete with those of America and the Baltic. No doubt they could, but how the taxation of the country is to be paid, and who is to provide this food for the people at extreme low prices, so that the ship-builders may reduce the wages of the workmen to the level of other countries, are problems which neither Mr Browning nor any other witness examined by the committee has been able to solve.

Inasmuch, however, as we are neither the cheapest in point of taxation, nor consequently of food, it follows that our compe- tition with these countries for the carrying trade will be conducted with everything in favour of our rivals.

The fact of the exports from the United States being principally cotton and other raw produce, will account for the employment of a larger proportion of her shipping than her imports; but although she has not been able to keep pace with either France or England in respect to her imports, she has, like France, far surpassed us in her export trade, which has doubled itself in amount since 1815, notwithstanding cotton has undergone a greater reduction in value than almost any other article of merchandise.

From the foregoing facts we draw the following conclusions: that France and other continental nations are carrying on a suc- cessful competition with us in manufactures; that the United States are manufacturing more extensively, or require, from the nature of their employments, less of foreign productions than other nations, or it would be evidenced by a greater increase in their imports; and consequently that neither the one nor the other has anything to give us as an equivalent for opening up the home markets of Great Britain to their competition.

We now present a table of the Official and Declared Value of the Imports and Exports of this country since 1801, in illustration of our remarks at pages 93 and 94; and whether we regard the amount of our Imports so much in excess of our Exports or the slow progress of our Exports as compared with those of France and the United States, there is in this table much that requires the investigation and serious consideration of our rulers.

FOREIGN TRADE OF THE UNITED KINGDOM.

STATEMENT of the AMOUNT of the FOREIGN and COLONIAL TRADE of the UNITED KINGDOM, in each year from 1801 to 1846.

Years.	Official Value.			Real or Declared Value of British and Irish Produce and Manufactures Exported.		
	Imports of Foreign and Colonial Merchandise.	Exports of Foreign and Colonial Merchandise.	Exports of British and Irish Produce and Manufactures.	Europe.	Other Places.	TOTAL.
	£	£	£	£	£	£
1801	31,786,262	10,336,966	24.927,684	--	—	39,730 659
1802	29,826,210	12,677,431	25,632.549	—	—	45,102,330
1803	26,622,696	8,032,643	20,467,531	—	—	36.127,787
1804	27,819,552	8,938.741	22,687,309	—	—	37,135,746
1805	28,561,270	7,643,120	23,376,941	13,625.676	24,451.468	38,077,144
1806	26,899,658	7,717,555	25,861,879	11,363 635	29,511.348	40,874,983
1807	26,734,425	7,624,312	23,391,214	9,002,237	28,243,640	37 245,877
1808	26,795,540	5,776 775	24,611,215	9,016.033	28,259,069	37.275,102
1809	31,750,557	12,750,358	33,542,274	15,849,449	31,521,944	47,371,393
1810	39,301,612	9,357,435	34,061,901	15,627.806	32,810,874	48,438,680
1811	26 510,186	6,117,720	22,681,400	12,834,680	20,056,032	32 890 712
1812	26,163,431	9,533,065	29,508,508	—	—	41,716,964
1813	Records destroyed by fire.			—	—	—
1814	33,755,264	19,365,981	34,207,253	26,869,591	18,624.628	45,494,219
1815	32,987,396	15,748,554	42.875,996	20,736,244	30,866,784	51.603,028
1816	27,431.604	13,480,780	35,717,070	18,653,555	23,004,318	41,657,873
1817	30,834,299	10,292,684	40,111,427	19,093,574	22,667,558	41,761,132
1818	36,885,182	10,859,817	42,700,521	19 439,382	27,163.867	46,603,249
1819	30,776,810	9,904 813	33,534,176	16,790,652	18,417,669	35,208 321
1820	32,438,650	10,555.912	38.395,625	18,429,503	17,995,149	36,424,652
1821	30,792,760	10,629,689	40,831,744	15,903,442	20,756,188	36,659,630
1822	30,500,094	9,227,589	44,236,533	16,601,562	20,367,402	36,968 964
1823	35,798,707	8,603,904	43,804,372	14,857,128	20,600 920	35,458,048
1824	37,552.935	10,204,785	48,735,551	15.698.940	24,697,360	38,396,300
1825	44,137,482	9,169,494	47,166,020	14,646,358	24,231,030	38 877.388
1826	37,686,113	10,076,286	40.965,735	13,893,270	17,643,453	31,536,723
1827	44,887,774	9,830,728	52,219,280	14,478,964	22,702,371	37,181,335
1828	45,028,805	9,946,545	52,797,455	13,775,870	23,036,886	36,812 756
1829	43,981,317	10,622,402	56,213,041	14,545,474	21,297,149	35,842,623
1830	46,245,241	8,550,437	61,140,864	15,610,638	22,660,959	38,271,597
1831	49,713,889	10,745,071	60,683,933	13,550,440	23,613,932	37,164,372
1832	44,586,741	11,044,869	65,026,702	15.584 006	20,866,588	36,450,594
1833	45,952,551	9,833,753	69,989,339	15,011.789	24,055,558	39,667 347
1834	49,362.811	11,562,036	73,831,550	18,007,033	23,642 158	41 649,191
1835	48,911,542	12,797.724	78,376 731	18,464,433	28,907.837	47,372,270
1836	57,023.867	12,391.711	85.229.837	19,011,066	34.357.505	53,368.571
1837	54.737,301	13,233,622	72,548,047	19.071,303	22 999,441	42,067 245
1838	61,268,320	12,711.318	92,459,231	21,711,295	28 349,675	50,060,970
1839	62,004,000	12,795,990	97,402,726	20,414 520	32.819 060	53.233,580
1840	67,432,964	13,774,306	102,705,060	21,491,245	29,915,185	51,406.430
1841	64,377,962	14,723,151	102,183,517	22 854,540	28,780,083	47,381,023
1842	65,204.729	13,584,158	100,260,101	23,909,344	23,471,679	52,278.449
1843	70,093,353	13,956,113	117,877,278	24,971,457	27,306,992	58 584,292
1844	85,441,555	14,397,246	131,564.503	25.621,185	39,953 107	60,111,081
1845	75,281,958	16,280,870	134,599,116			
1846						

The rates by which the official value is computed were fixed in 1694, and consequently measure the *quantities* of all articles imported and exported. The real value is that which the merchant declares at the time of shipment. See remarks in explanation at pages 93 and 94.

CHAPTER X.

CONCLUSION.

Review of the whole Subject.

THE object of the present inquiry has been to ascertain and define the sources of the greatness, power, and wealth of Britain; and it has been conducted on the assumption that a knowledge of such facts ought to form the basis of all legislation affecting the circumstances of a people.

In the execution of this task we have had to encounter assertions as vague as they are contradictory. Men holding high official situations have not hesitated, in order to give a colour to a theory, to do an injustice to a principle, and, in their zeal to work out a particular result, have confounded classes essentially distinct.

Another difficulty we have had to contend with has arisen from the fact that many of our public writers, men of enlarged minds and great powers of mental vision, both as regards the past and the future, have been apt to take in too large a breadth of the political horizon in their views, and in doing so, have not unfrequently overlooked the most important objects within reach, for something very indistinct in the extreme distance, losing sight at the same time of their relative proportions, and actually mistaking effects for causes, and causes for effects.

Thus it is we have been gravely told, that for a long agricultural prosperity we have been mainly dependent on an interest not one-third so large as the agricultural interest itself, whether we speak of numbers, capital, or annual productions; and that for the payment of forty-six millions of taxation, the average amount annually raised by taxes from 1793 to 1815, to say nothing of 589 millions of our present debt borrowed during the same period, we are indebted to the same interest, although it has never paid more than one-fourth of this amount.

To negative these assertions, made without the slightest attempt at demonstration, we have traced, in the present work, the degree of dependence of every other class of which society is composed on one or the other of these two great interests, and pointed out the difference in their respective circumstances. Their numbers, locality, capital, and annual productions, all lead to the inevitable conclusion that the means which support twenty-two millions of the population, and which pay three-fourths of the entire taxation of the state, are drawn from the several classes in the community who are dependent on and supported by the productions of the soil of the United Kingdom.

To tell us, therefore, "that the spindle and the loom have been the moving powers of our armies and our fleets" may serve to round a period, but it is to assert that which has not the slightest foundation in fact.

To arrive at the truth in such a case we must return to first principles, although in the present enlightened and speculative age a reference to them may be considered somewhat vulgar. The simple rules of arithmetic must still decide the question, and figures continue to represent the actual and relative importance of an interest.

With men who deny the authority of figures, and who, in opposition to a demonstration however perfect, will set up some crude and ill-digested opinions of their own, it is of course useless to enter into discussion, but we nevertheless will place these on record, and rely with confidence that but a short time can elapse before their truth will be recognised and firmly established in the minds of a deliberate and thinking people.

If this, then, is the basis of our political power, it follows that the whole question resolves itself into one of taxation, and the capability of the two interests to sustain it. Exemptions from sharing this burden have been claimed on all hands. The manufacturer has insisted on the removal of all duties on the raw material, as opposed in his opinion, to the true principles of political economy, and this has been granted to such an extent that we look in vain through the account of the revenue for any item worthy of notice representing the raw material of the manufacturing interest. Not content with their exemption in this instance, they now claim to eat the bread of foreign growth free from any tax, in the place of that which bears the whole burden of the taxation of this country, knowing full well, as Sir Robert Peel stated in 1839, that low prices of food invariably produce low wages.

> "Look over the whole world, and you will find that low prices of food lead to low rates of wages, and that where there is a low rate of wages, there is a great degradation in the character of the working classes. Look at the Hindoos or the Sicilians in their respective countries: food is cheap, but the rate of wages is also extremely low, and hence there are not, in Asia or Europe, more miserable and degraded races."

The merchant and the ship-owner, as represented before the Navigation Committee by Mr Browning and Mr Houghton, put in claims for the repeal of the Navigation Laws and the removal of all duties on the materials for the building and the sailing of ships, in order that, by reducing wages, they may compete with other countries, or, failing in this, may employ foreign ships to carry their goods without regard to the ultimate security of the nation, or the sacrifice of its most important interests.

The working classes are clamorous for the reduction of indirect taxation, and complain that the hand of the government is distinctly visible in every man's dish. On every side, therefore, we have proposals for a further reduction of duties, which puts out of the question all probability that even in the hour of need we can look for any further assistance from that quarter.

To tax capital is always a doubtful and very injurious mode of proceeding; for capital is the most evanescent of all things. Make the tax both heavy and permanent, and it will seek for employment to your detriment in every portion of Europe—in every quarter of the globe.

What course, then, is open to us? It would be useless to call on the Manufacturing Interest to pay fifty millions a year, when they have never yet paid fifteen millions. It would be equally unjust to ask the Landed Interest to continue the payment of this enormous amount when you bring in competition with their productions those of countries who pay no part of our taxation; and yet this is the course of legislation at the present time, which a fatal blindness to every principle of political justice is fast hastening to its consummation.

There is certainly one solution of the difficulty; but this is so much opposed to the prejudices of mankind, that we should look in vain for its adoption. It is this. If the foreign market is of that importance as compared with the home market (which we deny), and the cheap grain of other countries is necessary to enable our manufacturers to extend their productions, we ought to put an export duty on our manufactured articles, so that by this process either the manufacturer or the foreigner would be made to contribute their fair proportion to our national burdens.

The improvements in manufactures, by reducing the price and bringing them within the reach of larger numbers, we admit, facilitates the circulation of particular articles, and gives rise to an increased consumption. But it is contended by the manufacturers themselves that, without an abundance of food and low prices, these improvements cannot proceed. To all of this we oppose a fact within the knowledge and experience of every one, that the wonderful progress which manufactures have made in point of quantity during the last forty years, affords the best possible evidence of food having been both cheap and abundant enough to have ensured their success. To take the grain of the foreigner without reference to the taxation paid by our own, and to supply him with goods which—inasmuch as to the extent of nine-tenths they are the production of mechanical power,—supersede the labour of the people, and to the same extent, neither as regards the raw material nor the manufactured one, pay anything directly or indirectly to the taxation of the state, is not just in principle, and cannot be engrafted on our system without danger to the public interests.

Since, then, taxation is the primary cause of our not being able to compete with other countries, it will be necessary if free trade is to prevail that we revise the whole system, and by equalizing the burdens on land, to spread them, over the entire surface of society, and make all classes contribute according to the amount of their their production. To the manufacturing interest we would hold out the right hand of fellowship to forward, promote, and extend the commerce of Britain, but on the condition that they pay their just proportion of the taxation necessary to support the state and provide employment or the means of emigration for the people.

On all sides there is not a tittle of evidence that it is either the interest or intention of other countries to imitate our example and to admit us to an equality in their markets. The idea that America will take our manufactures in barter for corn is a fallacy which the painful experience of the present year too palpably exposes, and even if she would, the first year of plenty would demonstrate the absurdity of her being able to compete with the Baltic in the growth or supply of grain.

Mr Cobden may extend his missionary labours for the propagation of his free-trade principles to every capital in Europe, and be received with open arms and hospitality by the rulers of all, for the benefits he has conferred on their people by giving them access to our own markets, but the first instance of any government who has any standing in manufactures being induced by him to follow our example will afford better evidence of the value of his doctrines than all the speeches he has uttered since the commencement of his agitation for this object.

But independently of this, we contend not only that the manufacturing interest owes its present importance to the sustaining power of the agricultural, but also that its future progress is wholly dependent on the latter. The prosperity of the agricultural interest is, therefore, an essential ingredient in that of the manufacturing, and without the power of consumption which "all other classes" derive from the successful prosecution of agriculture, the foreign trade for the sale of the productions of our manufacturing industry would be but as dust in the balance.

The cultivation of the soil and its increased production is therefore the root and not the branch—it is the primary cause and not the effect—and the awful condition of the starving masses in Ireland, and the suffering of the working classes in the manufacturing districts, are the best illustrations of the absurdity of the converse proposition. Our armies are formed of men drawn from agricultural pursuits, and our fleets are manned by others of the same origin, and the power that has moved both the one and the other, and the spindle and the loom into the bargain, has been the successful cultivation of the soil of the United Kingdom.

In support of these conclusions, we cannot help transcribing the address of Mr Huskisson to his constituents at Chichester. It is a faithful epitome not only of his own opinions, but of those of Mr Canning, the Earl of Liverpool, and all the great men that preceded him. For soundness of judgment and vigour of intellect their administration of the affairs of this country will bear a comparison with any in the best days of English history, and this chronicle of the political principle which governed them ought to be read and understood of all men.

" The history of this country proves that cheapness produced by foreign import is the sure forerunner of scarcity; and a steady home supply is the only safe foundation of steady moderate prices. During upwards of one hundred years to 1765, when the import of foreign corn was sustained by very high duties, our own growth of corn was ample for our own consumption in ordinary seasons, redundant in abundant seasons, and in bad seasons occasioned no apprehension of, or actual want. The price of corn seldom varied more than a few shillings per quarter; if there was no inordinate gain to the farmer, there was no starvation to the consumer; prices instead of rising from year to year, gradually diminished; whereas, since 1765 the supply has been unsteady and precarious, our dependence on foreign supplies gradually increasing till the war came, when by the foreign supply being interrupted, the country became dependent on its rivals and its enemies for the food of its people. In the first eighteen years of this war, we were forced to pay sixty millions of money to nations, every one of which has, in the course of that war, been our enemy, for a scanty and inadequate supply of foreign corn; and when for this purpose we parted with all our gold and even our silver currency, combined Europe shut its ports against us, and America co-operating, first laid an embargo, and then went to war. Shall I then be deterred from using my honest endeavours in Parliament to prevent the recurrence of such sufferings? I admit that if unlimited foreign import, which the war had suspended, were now again allowed, bread might be a little, though a very little, cheaper than it now is, for a year or two; but what would follow? The small farmer would be ruined; improvement would stand still; inferior lands now producing corn would return to a state of waste; the home consumption and brisk demands for all the various articles of the retail dealer would rapidly decline, to the great injury of our towns, especially those which are not connected with manufactures or commerce: farming servants, and all the trades which depend on agriculture, would be thrown out of work, and wages would fall even more rapidly than the price of corn. The great farmers and large capitalists might for a time bear up against foreign import, and should they do so, will command extravagant prices to repay themselves; but in the mean time the poorer, but not less industrious small farmers, will have been ruined. To protect the small farmers is ultimately to protect the people.

"It is the first and paramount law of every state to provide for its own safety and defence; we will never listen to a theory which, by withdrawing protection from the colonial trade, would render insecure those possessions on which essentially depends the power of Great Britain, to retain that high station in the rank of nations which she owes to her commercial and colonial ascendancy; and least of all shall we listen to the representation of states which evince boundless jealousy of our navigation in peace, and of our maritime ascendancy in case of war; and who tell us distinctly that they are steadily looking to the ulterior object, of one day disputing with us the dominion of the seas."

A short time, we imagine, will be sufficient to demonstrate that this is the true policy of our country, for the foundation whereon the prosperity of all has been hitherto based, has been the well-being of that class which in all times and seasons provides food for the people.

Circumstances of a political and even a scientific character may cause the manufactures of a country to change their locality and make again the tour of the world, but agriculture is immoveably fixed to the soil, and our rulers will ever find that its prosperity constitutes one of their heaviest responsibilities.

There are, doubtless, many other considerations of great importance arising out of or affecting "the occupations of the people," but such are not within the object of the present work, and therefore we forbear to do more than cursorily touch upon them in conclusion.

The currency question, from its intricacy, would appear to have baffled all the calculations of our most experienced statesmen, and the practical results of Sir Robert Peel's measure of 1844, which was considered by its author to be a concentration of all previous experience on the subject, have only involved us in greater difficulties than ever. If, as some suppose, the presence or absence of three or four millions of the precious metals, more or less, can influence the value of our national securities to the extent of 100 millions, paralyze labour, and stop production, such a state of things necessarily implies that our statesmen must be lamentably deficient in the practical knowledge necessary to a right understanding of the true principles which ought to govern the currency.

To eradicate these evils, and take from our national dealings the elements of mistrust and dishonesty;—to equalize taxation and make all interests in the state contribute their fair proportion to the support of its institutions;—to protect the native industry of the people by just and equitable laws, that shall yield to every man his meat in due season as the reward of his labour;—to raise the sinking artisan, by making that which has supplanted his labour minister to his wants;—to open up our vast colonial possessions to the enterprise and energy of the sons and daughters of Britain, so that they may go forth and plant in every quarter of the globe our religion, language, institutions, and interests, extending and consolidating our power, and at the same time making the country from whence they emanate to be the glory of all lands,—are doubtless among the most important duties which devolve on those entrusted with the Government of this country. To correct also the social misery which afflicts Ireland, and to raise her from her present degraded and desperate condition to one more compatible with the welfare of her people and our own security, is not less a matter of justice than one of imperious necessity.

With what degree of ability these duties have been hitherto discharged is not within our province to inquire, as we have carefully avoided all reference to political considerations except such as have incidentally and unavoidably arisen out of the subject matter of this inquiry, satisfied that whatever deficiencies experience may discover in the political principles of a minister or a party, the resources and energy of our constitution are sufficient to correct them.

To work out these great results, however, for the good of the people, and at the same time to give increased stability to existing institutions, is an object worthy of the loftiest ambition, and the minister that shall succeed in engrafting them on our political system will raise a monument to perpetuate his memory more enduring than the mightiest work of art, and in the page of history will stand out as a beacon to direct future statesmen

" To be just and fear not."

He will have based the government of a great and mighty nation on the eternal principles of truth and justice, and with such a government " the period to Britain's fame can be only the end of time."

APPENDIX.

AUTHORITIES.

In the compilation of the Tables which form the Appendix to the present Work, the following authorities have been taken :—

FOR ALL MATTERS relating to the NUMBERS and OCCUPATIONS of the SEVERAL CLASSES—

The Returns of the Census of 1841.

POOR and COUNTY RATES—ENGLAND and WALES—

A Return from the Poor Law Commissioners, dated Feb. 13th, 1846, made up to Lady-day, 1845.

POOR RELIEF—SCOTLAND—

Two Returns moved for by Mr Ellice, and ordered to be printed June 20th, 1843.

POOR RATES—IRELAND—
COUNTY CESS— ,, } The 11th Annual Report of the Poor Law Commissioners.

LAND TAX—ENGLAND and WALES—

A Return from the Commissioners of Stamps and Taxes, dated July 29th, 1844, made up to the 25th March, 1843.

LAND TAX—SCOTLAND—

The Act of 1797, Geo. III, cap. v, which fixes the amount for the whole kingdom at the sum given in the Summary (page 95 in the Appendix).

TITHES—
PROPERTY TAX on LAND,
,, ,, on DWELLING HOUSES,
,, ,, on other PROPERTY— } A Return of real Property moved for by Mr Villiers, and ordered to be printed March 6, 1845.

HIGHWAY RATES and CHURCH RATES—

A Return relative to Local Taxation ordered to be reprinted Feb. 3, 1846, being No. 562 of 1839.

TURNPIKE TRUSTS—

A Return of the Income and Expenditure from Jan. 1 to Dec. 31, 1843, ordered to be printed Aug. 5, 1845.

CRIMINALS—

A Return from the Secretary of State's Office, dated April 4, 1846.

ENGAGED IN	MALES.		FEMALES.		TOTAL.
	20 years of age and upwards.	Under 20 years of age.	20 years of age and upwards.	Under 20 years of age.	
AGRICULTURE:					
Farmers and Graziers	1,321	31	106	—	1458
Agricultural Labourers	10,977	1,813	59	12	12,861
Gardeners, Nurserymen, and Florists	557	40	17	—	614
	12,855	1,884	182	12	14,933
MANUFACTURES:					
Lace Dealers	15	—	5	—	20
Lace Makers	18	9	1,880	695	2,602
Straw-Plait Dealers	98	1	21	5	125
Straw-Plait Manufacturers	83	63	1,032	575	1,753
Straw Bonnet and Hat Makers	92	12	510	255	858
Miscellaneous	405	31	30	4	470
	711	116	3,478	1,523	5,828
ALL OTHER CLASSES:					
Employed in Retail Trade or in Handicraft, as Masters or Workmen	6,574	876	886	169	8,505
Labourers	1,658	294	404	13	2,369
Military and Naval	45	1	—	—	46
Professional Persons	353	—	—	—	353
Other Educated Persons following miscellaneous Pursuits	227	14	162	11	414
Persons engaged in the Government Civil Service	42	3	5	—	50
Parochial, Town, and Church Officers	83	—	12	—	95
Domestic Servants	766	635	2,069	1,223	4,693
Persons returned as Independent	454	19	1,154	93	1,720
Almspeople, Pensioners, Paupers, Lunatics, and Prisoners	654	137	360	141	1,292
RESIDUE OF POPULATION:					
Consisting of the Wives, Children, and others dependent on all Classes	1,822	21,976	21,049	22,791	67,638
Total of all other Classes	12,678	23,955	26,101	24,441	87,175

Divide "ALL OTHER CLASSES" between the AGRICULTURISTS and the MANUFACTURERS in the proportion which these respectively bear to each other, and the numbers engaged in, and dependent on, each interest will stand thus :—

Engaged in Agriculture	14,933	
Dependent on „	62,703	
AGRICULTURE—Total		77,636
Engaged in Manufactures	5,828	
Dependent on „	24,472	
MANUFACTURES—Total		30,300
Total of the County		107,935

TAXATION.

		Paid by the	
		LAND.	MANUFACTURERS.
		£	£
Paid exclusively by the Landed Interest :			
Land Tax		28,433	
Tithes		7,182	
Property Tax—on Land, assessed at	£377,994	11,024	
Paid in the Proportion of 5-7ths by the Landed Interest, and 2-7ths by the Manufacturers :			
Poor and County Rates	£53,907	38,505	15,402
Highway Rates	9,099	6,500	2,599
Church „	4,426	3,162	1,264
Turnpike Trusts	9,289	6,635	2,654
Property Tax—on Dwelling Houses, assessed at	132,296	2,755	1,102
„ on other Property „	none	—	—
		104,196	23,021
Total of Taxation of the County		£127,217	

ENGAGED IN	MALES.		FEMALES.		TOTAL.
	20 years of age and upwards.	Under 20 years of age.	20 years of age and upwards.	Under 20 years of age.	
Agriculture :					
Farmers and Graziers - - - -	1,728	32	116	—	1,876
Agricultural Labourers - - - -	13,997	3,005	1,329	318	18,649
Gardeners, Nurserymen, and Florists - - -	682	31	11	—	724
	16,407	3,068	1,456	318	21,249
Manufactures:					
Carpet Weavers - - - -	16	1	—	—	17
Cotton Spinners and Weavers - - -	8	—	11	4	23
Hemp Manufacturers - - - -	32	5	12	1	50
Paper Makers - - - - -	75	13	5	2	95
Silk Manufacture - - - -	2	—	—	—	2
Silk Weavers and Workers - - -	80	21	65	35	201
Spinners - - - - -	1	2	85	19	107
Straw-Plait Makers - - - -	4	—	24	7	35
Weavers - - - - -	162	12	38	10	222
Wool Manufacture - - - -	13	1	46	—	60
Miscellaneous - - - -	764	77	79	9	929
	1,157	132	365	87	1,741
All other Classes:					
Employed in Retail Trade or in Handicraft, as Masters or Workmen - - - - -	11,676	1,313	1,494	255	14,738
Labourers - - - - - -	3,504	443	1,147	36	5,130
Military and Naval - - - - -	1,477	149	—	—	1,626
Professional Persons - - - - -	563	—	—	—	563
Other Educated Persons following miscellaneous Pursuits	578	61	339	26	1,004
Persons engaged in the Government Civil Service -	88	2	19	—	109
Parochial, Town, and Church Officers - - -	158	—	21	1	180
Domestic Servants - - - - -	2,217	1,171	5,047	3,103	11,538
Persons returned as Independent - - - -	1,473	49	3,104	153	4,779
Almspeople, Pensioners, Paupers, Lunatics, and Prisoners	786	508	696	434	2,424
Residue of Population :					
Consisting of the Wives, Children, and others dependent on all Classes - - - - -	2,958	30,300	30,740	32,068	96,066
Total of all other Classes - -	25,478	33,996	42,607	36,076	138,157

Divide "**all other classes**" between the Agriculturists and the Manufacturers in the proportion which these respectively bear to each other, and the numbers engaged in, and dependent on, each interest will stand thus:—

Engaged in Agriculture - - -	21,249	
Dependent on ,, - - - -	127,675	
Agriculture—Total - - -		148,944
Engaged in Manufactures - - -	1,741	
Dependent on ,, - - -	10,462	
Manufactures—Total - - -		12,203
Total of the County - - -		161,147

TAXATION.

	Paid by the	
	Land.	Manufacturers.
Paid exclusively by the Landed Interest :	£	£
Land Tax - - - - - - - -	40,197	
Tithes - - - - - - - - -	29,866	
Property Tax—on Land, assessed at - - - £594,903	17,351	
Paid in the Proportion of 12-13ths by the Landed Interest, and 1-13th by the Manufacturers :		
Poor and County Rates - - - - £98,331	90,767	7,564
Highway Rates - - - - - - 12,694	11,718	976
Church ,, - - - - - - 5,790	5,345	445
Turnpike Trusts - - - - - - 12,249	11,307	942
Property Tax—on Dwelling Houses, assessed at - - 310,104	8,349	695
,, on other Property ,, - 62,468	1,681	140
	216,581	10.763
Total of Taxation of the County - - - £227,343		

ENGAGED IN	MALES.		FEMALES.		TOTAL.
	20 years of age and upwards.	Under 20 years of age.	20 years of age and upwards.	Under 20 years of age.	
AGRICULTURE:					
Farmers and Graziers	2,256	40	169	—	2,465
Agricultural Labourers	15,681	2,702	341	136	18,860
Gardeners, Nurserymen, and Florists	545	20	6	1	572
	18,482	2,762	516	137	21,897
MANUFACTURES:					
Chair Makers	398	62	7	1	468
Lace Dealers and Makers	61	45	3,454	903	4,463
Paper Makers	274	22	29	8	333
Silk Manufacture	28	36	29	51	144
Straw-Plait Dealers and Manufacturers	51	133	689	589	1,460
Miscellaneous	818	91	38	18	965
	1,630	389	4,246	1,568	7,833
ALL OTHER CLASSES:					
Employed in Retail Trade or in Handicraft, as Masters or Workmen	9,558	1,033	1,064	176	11,831
Labourers	2,345	244	552	23	3,214
Military and Naval	236	13	—	—	249
Professional Persons	485	—	—	—	485
Other Educated Persons following miscellaneous Pursuits	371	21	237	14	643
Persons engaged in the Government Civil Service	65	1	8	1	75
Parochial, Town, and Church Officers	132	—	13	—	145
Domestic Servants	1,830	1,248	3,702	1,870	8,650
Persons returned as Independent	928	32	2,018	106	3,084
Almspeople, Pensioners, Paupers, Lunatics, and Prisoners	616	366	598	266	1,846
RESIDUE OF POPULATION:					
Consisting of the Wives, Children, and others dependent on all Classes	2,782	30,868	30,205	32,176	96,031
Total of all other Classes	19,348	33,876	38,397	34,632	96,253

Divide "ALL OTHER CLASSES" between the AGRICULTURISTS and the MANUFACTURERS in the proportion which these respectively bear to each other, and the numbers engaged in, and dependent on, each interest will stand thus:—

Engaged in Agriculture	21,897	
Dependent on	92,989	
AGRICULTURE—Total		114,886
Engaged in Manufactures	7,833	
Dependent on	33,264	
MANUFACTURES—Total		41,097
Total of the County		155,983

TAXATION.

		Paid by the	
		LAND.	MANUFACTURERS.
Paid exclusively by the Landed Interest:		£	£
Land Tax		46,818	
Tithes		16,807	
Property Tax—on Land, assessed at £579,736		17,434	
Paid in the Proportion of 11-15ths by the Landed Interest, and 4-15ths by the Manufacturers:			
Poor and County Rates	£94,260	69,124	25,136
Highway Rates	17,567	12,877	4,684
Church „	7,954	5,930	2,024
Turnpike Trusts	13,488	9,892	3,596
Property Tax—on Dwelling Houses, assessed at	211,580	5,726	444
„ on other Property „	18,574	397	144
		185,005	36,028
Total of Taxation of the County		£221,033	

ENGAGED IN	MALES.		FEMALES.		TOTAL.
	20 years of age and upwards.	Under 20 years of age.	20 years of age and upwards.	Under 20 years of age.	
AGRICULTURE :					
Farmers and Graziers - - - -	3,136	29	176	—	3,341
Agricultural Labourers - - - -	15,990	2,068	619	239	18,916
Gardeners, Nurserymen, and Florists -	612	24	25	—	661
	19,738	2,121	820	239	22,918
MANUFACTURES :					
There is no leading Branch of Manufacture carried on in this County. The largest Number engaged in any one Branch is that of the					
Brick and Tile Makers - - - -	196	18	—	—	214
Miscellaneous - - - - -	479	43	63	3	588
	675	61	3	3	802
ALL OTHER CLASSES :					
Employed in Retail Trade or in Handicraft, as Masters or Workmen - - - - -	11,049	1,140	1,476	277	13,942
Labourers - - - - -	2,462	244	847	25	3,578
Military and Naval - - - -	488	25	—	—	513
Professional Persons - - - -	497	—	—	—	497
Other Educated Persons following miscellaneous Psursuits	531	57	328	27	943
Persons engaged in the Government Civil Service -	58	1	3	—	62
Parochial, Town, and Church Officers - -	124	2	17	—	143
Domestic Servants - - - - -	1,601	1,188	3,899	2,834	9,522
Persons returned as Independent - - -	1,071	78	2,544	133	3,826
Almspeople, Pensioners, Paupers, Lunatics, and Prisoners	461	304	421	302	1,488
RESIDUE OF POPULATION :					
Consisting of the Wives, Children, and others dependent on all Classes - - - - -	3,478	34,168	33,200	35,379	106,225
Total of all other Classes - - -	21,820	37,207	42,735	38,977	140,739

Divide "ALL OTHER CLASSES" between the AGRICULTURISTS and the MANUFACTURERS in the proportion which these respectively bear to each other, and the numbers engaged in, and dependent on, each interest will stand thus :—

Engaged in Agriculture - -	22,918	
Dependent on ,, - - -	135,981	
AGRICULTURE—Total -		158,899
Engaged in Manufactures - -	802	
Dependent on ,, - -	4,758	
MANUFACTURES—Total -		5,560
Total of the County - -	-	164,459

TAXATION.

	Paid by the	
	LAND.	MANUFACTURERS.
Paid exclusively by the Landed Interest :	£	£
Land Tax - - - - - -	32,462	
Tithes - - - - - - -	27,114	
Property Tax—on Land, assessed at - - - £774,657	22,594	
Paid in the Proportion of 15-16ths by the Landed Interest, and 1-16th by the Manufacturers :		
Poor and County Rates - - - - £93,877	88,010	5,867
Highway Rates - - - - - 20,850	19,547	1,303
Church ,, - - - - - 4,823	4,522	301
Turnpike Trusts - - - - - 15,159	14,212	947
Property Tax—on Dwelling Houses, assessed at - 267,273	7,308	487
,, on other Property, ,, - - 60,485	1,654	110
	217,423	9,015
Total of Taxation of the County - - - - - - £226,438		

ENGAGED IN	MALES.		FEMALES.		TOTAL.
	20 years of age and upwards.	Under 20 years of age.	20 years of age and upwards.	Under 20 years of age.	
AGRICULTURE:					
Farmers and Graziers - - - -	6,482	53	919	—	7,454
Agricultural Labourers - - - - -	14,795	2,675	542	443	18,455
Gardeners, Nurserymen, and Florists - - -	847	35	11	2	895
	22,124	2,763	1,472	445	26,804
MANUFACTURES:					
Cotton Manufacture (all branches) - - -	8,937	5,122	9,424	6,866	30,349
Silk Manufacture (all branches) - - -	4,530	2,924	3,812	3,948	15,214
Weavers (all branches) - - - -	2,120	760	625	539	4,044
Hatters and Hat Manufacture - - -	1,457	194	113	47	1,811
Printers (all branches) - - - -	476	174	56	80	786
Engineers, Machine and Engine Worker - -	553	71	7	8	639
Woollen and Woollen Cloth Manufacture (all branches)-	382	61	47	36	526
Salt Makers and Boilers, and Salt Proprietors -	472	20	—	—	492
Dyers (all branches) - - - -	567	143	13	13	736
Iron Founders and Moulders - - -	180	35	1	—	216
Nailers - - - - - -	170	24	2	—	196
Fustian Cutters - - - - -	104	37	27	27	195
Rope and Twine Makers - - - -	148	33	5	2	188
Tanners - - - - - -	141	13	1	—	155
Turners (all branches) - - - -	143	38	6	6	193
Miscellaneous - - - - -	2,029	341	145	38	2,553
	22,409	9,990	14,284	11,610	58,293
ALL OTHER CLASSES:					
Employed in Retail Trade or in Handicraft, as Masters or Workmen - - - -	26,671	4,098	3,521	731	35,021
Labourers (including miners) - - -	11,275	1,428	1,757	84	14,544
Military and Naval - - - -	2,866	239	—	—	3,105
Professional Persons - - - - -	868	—	—	—	868
Other Educated Persons following miscellaneous Pursuits	1,728	210	609	43	2,590
Persons engaged in the Government Civil Service	166	1	14	—	181
Parochial, Town, and Church Officers - -	396	5	22	—	423
Domestic Servants - - - - -	3,787	3,166	10,023	7,025	24,001
Persons returned as Independent - -	2,367	123	5,683	271	8,444
Almspeople, Pensioners, Paupers, Lunatics, and Prisoners	796	374	881	304	2,355
RESIDUE OF POPULATION:					
Consisting of the Wives, Children, and others dependent on all Classes - - - -	4,555	71,259	68,581	74,636	219,031
Total of all other Classes - - -	55,475	80,903	91,091	83,094	310,563

Divide " ALL OTHER CLASSES " between the AGRICULTURISTS and the MANUFACTURERS in the proportion which these respectively bear to each other, and the numbers engaged in, and dependent on, each interest will stand thus: —

```
                  Engaged in Agriculture    -    -    -    26,804
                  Dependent on        -      -    -    -    97,821
                        AGRICULTURE—Total    -    -        ——————    124,625

                  Engaged in Manufactures    -         58,293
                  Dependent on        -      -    -     212,742
                        MANUFACTURES—Total   -         ——————    271,035

                  Total of the County    -      -      -    395,660
```

TAXATION.

		Paid by the	
		LAND.	MANUFACTURERS.
Paid exclusively by the Landed Interest:		£	£
Land Tax - - - - - - - - -		27,476	
Tithes - - - - - - - - -		25,561	
Property Tax—on Land, assessed at - - - -£962,857		28,083	
Paid in the Proportion of 3-10ths by the Landed Interest, and 7-10ths by the Manufacturers:			
Poor and County Rates - - - - £113,880		34,164	79,716
Highway Rates - - - - - - 27,729		8,316	19,413
Church ,, - - - - - - 8,372		2,511	5,861
Turnpike Trusts - - - - - - 41,706		12,510	29,196
Property Tax—on Dwelling Houses, assessed at - - 780,102		6,825	15,927
,, on other Property ,, - - 146,978		1,284	3,002
		146,730	153,115

Total of Taxation of the County - - - - £299,845

(*For those engaged in Mines, see " Mining Interest."*)

ENGAGED IN	MALES. 20 years of age and upwards.	Under 20 years of age.	FEMALES. 20 years of age and upwards.	Under 20 years of age.	TOTAL.
AGRICULTURE :					
Farmers and Graziers - - - - -	7,668	128	405	—	8,201
Agricultural Labourers - - - -	14,279	2,752	795	177	18,003
Gardeners, Nurserymen, and Florists - - -	595	25	35	3	658
	22,542	2,905	1,235	180	26,862
MANUFACTURES :					
Tin Manufacture (all branches) - - -	657	301	118	146	1,222
Engine and Machine Makers - - - -	4	1	—	—	5
Engineer and Engine Workers - - - -	427	70	2	1	500
Woollen Manufacture (all branches) - - -	285	28	99	33	445
Ore Dressers - - - - -	37	69	117	204	427
Copper Manufacture (all branches) - - -	42	23	99	133	297
Clay Manufacture (all branches) - - -	150	39	23	33	225
Lead Manufacture (all branches) - - -	41	8	3	2	54
Miscellaneous - - - - -	1,174	243	363	96	1,876
	2,817	7,82	814	638	5,051
ALL OTHER CLASSES :					
Employed in Retail Trade or in Handicraft, as Masters or Workmen - - - - -	18,163	3,678	3,824	1,007	26,672
Labourers (including Miners) - - - -	20,270	6,134	2,402	1,519	30,325
Military and Naval - - - - -	3,609	312	—	—	3,921
Professional Persons - - - - -	844	—	—	—	844
Other Educated Persons following miscellaneous Pursuits	849	123	501	32	1,505
Persons engaged in the Government Civil Service -	404	6	22	1	433
Parochial, Town, and Church Officers - - -	135	3	24	—	162
Domestic Servants - - - - -	2,658	4,141	8,159	5,214	20,172
Persons returned as Independent - - -	2,033	76	6,768	200	9,077
Almspeople, Pensioners, Paupers, Lunatics, and Prisoners	1,182	347	1,495	347	3,371
RESIDUE OF POPULATION :					
Consisting of the Wives, Children, and others dependent on all Classes - - - - -	4,675	6,6075	68,569	73,565	212,884
Total of all other Classes - - -	54,822	80,895	91,764	81,885	309,366

Divide "ALL OTHER CLASSES" between the AGRICULTURISTS and the MANUFACTURERS in the proportion which these respectively bear to each other, and the numbers engaged in, and dependent on, each interest will stand thus:—

Engaged in Agriculture - - -	26,862	
Dependent on - - - - -	260,402	
AGRICULTURE—Total - -		287,264
Engaged in Manufactures - - -	5,051	
Dependent on - - - -	48,964	
MANUFACTURES—Total - -		54,015
Total of the County - - -		341,279

TAXATION.

	Paid by the LAND.	Paid by the MANUFACTURERS.
Paid exclusively by the Landed Interest :	£	£
Land Tax - - - - - - - -	30,477	
Tithes - - - - - - - - -	74,971	
Property Tax—on Land, assessed at - - £774,692	22,595	
Paid in the Proportion of 5-6ths by the Landed Interest, and 1-6th by the Manufacturers :		
Poor and County Rates - - - £95,710	79,759	15,951
Highway Rates - - - - - 29,679	24,733	4,946
Church „ - - - - - 5,365	4,471	894
Turnpike Trusts - - - - - 20,428	17,024	3,404
Property Tax—on Dwelling Houses, assessed at - 277,108	6,735	1,347
„ on other Property „ - 301,461	7,536	1,256
	268,301	27,798
Total of Taxation of the County - - -	£296,099	

(*For those engaged in Mines, see "Mining Interest."*)

ENGAGED IN	MALES.		FEMALES.		TOTAL.
	20 years of age and upwards.	Under 20 years of age.	20 years of age and upwards.	Under 20 years of age.	
AGRICULTURE:					
Farmers and Graziers - - - - -	4,796	26	432	—	5,254
Agricultural Labourers - - - -	7,574	1,075	1,073	357	10,079
Gardeners, Nurserymen, and Florists - -	243	20	14	1	278
	12,613	1,121	1,519	358	15,611
MANUFACTURES:					
Cotton Manufacture (all branches) - - -	1,499	433	1,075	599	3,606
Weavers (all branches) - - - -	1,511	267	216	110	2,104
Woollen and Woollen Cloth Manufacture (all branches)-	195	41	19	16	271
Printers (all branches) - - - -	188	74	1	—	263
Flax Manufacture (all branches) - - -	110	33	61	113	317
Dyers (all branches) - - - -	195	35	5	1	236
Engine and Machine Makers - - -	14	5	—	—	19
Engineers and Engine Workers - - -	130	14	1	—	145
Miscellaneous - - - - -	1,536	353	97	40	2,026
	5,378	1,255	1,475	879	8,987
ALL OTHER CLASSES:					
Employed in Retail Trade or in Handicraft, as Masters or Workmen - - - - -	11,591	2,404	2,636	435	17,066
Labourers (including miners) - - -	4,797	976	1,068	38	6,879
Military and Naval - - - - -	1,034	184	—	—	1,218
Professional Persons - - - -	497	—	—	—	497
Other Educated Persons following miscellaneous Pursuits	799	78	308	18	1,203
Persons engaged in the Government Civil Service -	132	3	7	1	143
Parochial, Town, and Church Officers - -	118	1	21	—	140
Domestic Servants - - - -	2,342	1,354	5,098	3,078	11,872
Persons returned as Independent - -	1,889	45	4,539	124	6,597
Almspeople, Pensioners, Paupers, Lunatics, and Prisoners	1,094	353	438	253	2,138
RESIDUE OF POPULATION;					
Consisting of the Wives, Children, and others dependent on all Classes - - - - -	2,918	33,320	33,595	35,854	105,687
Total of all other Classes - - -	27,211	38,718	47,710	39,801	153,440

Divide "ALL OTHER CLASSES" between the AGRICULTURISTS and the MANUFACTURERS in the proportion which these respectively bear to each other, and the numbers engaged in, and dependent on, each interest will stand thus:—

Engaged in Agriculture - - -	15,611	
Dependent on ,, - - -	97,379	
AGRICULTURE—Total - -		112,990
Engaged in Manufactures - -	8,987	
Dependent on ,, - - -	56,061	
MANUFACTURES—Total - -		65,048
Total of the County - - -		178,038

TAXATION.

		Paid by the	
		LAND.	MANUFACTURERS.
		£	£
Paid exclusively by the Landed Interest:			
Land Tax - - - - - -		3,727	
Tithes - - - - - -		10,265	
Property Tax—on Land, assessed at - -	£603,724	17,608	
Paid in the Proportion of 3-5ths by the Landed Interest, and 2-5ths by the Manufacturers:			
Poor and County Rates - - - -	£44,926	26,956	17,970
Highway Rates - - - -	11,869	7,123	4,746
Church ,, - - - -	2,389	1,433	956
Turnpike Trusts - - - -	15,507	9,303	6,204
Property Tax—on Dwelling Houses, assessed at -	220,549	3,860	2,572
,, on other Property ,, - -	86,061	1,506	1,004
		81,781	33,452
Total of Taxation of the County - - - -		£115,233	

(*For those engaged in Mines, see "Mining Interest."*)

ENGAGED IN	MALES.		FEMALES.		TOTAL.
	20 years of age and upwards.	Under 20 years of age.	20 years of age and upwards.	Under 20 years of age.	
Agriculture :					
Farmers and Graziers - - - -	6,182	53	756	—	6,991
Agricultural Labourers - - - -	10,019	1,447	188	122	11,776
Gardeners, Nurserymen, and Florists - -	514	42	10	—	566
	16,715	1,542	954	122	19,333
Manufactures :					
Cotton Manufactures (all branches) - -	2,173	1,412	2,411	2,525	8,521
Hose (Stocking) Manufacture (all branches) - -	3,689	540	1,027	530	5,786
Silk Manufacture (all branches) - - -	479	289	865	705	2,338
Lace ,, (all branches) - - -	544	165	796	447	1,952
Weavers (all branches) - - - -	683	198	188	104	1,173
Nail Makers - - - - - -	758	240	17	16	1,031
Pot Manufacture (all branches) - - -	441	172	26	50	689
Engine and Machine Makers - - -	83	21	1	—	105
Engineers and Engine Workers - - -	419	81	2	2	504
Iron Manufacture (all branches) - - -	410	98	3	2	513
Printers (Cotton and Calico) - - -	238	99	29	57	423
Brick and Tile Makers - - - -	303	114	1	1	419
Glove Manufacture (all branches) - -	107	15	156	102	380
Hatter and Hat Makers (all branches) - -	308	14	5	2	329
Woollen and Cloth Manufacture (all branches) -	230	51	25	14	320
Bleachers - - - - - -	103	111	20	64	298
Tape Manufacture (all branches) - -	110	41	66	47	264
Factory Workers - - - -	15	17	78	112	222
Dyers (all branches) - - - -	152	41	11	—	204
File Makers (all branches) - - -	86	42	—	—	128
Miscellaneous - - - - -	1,828	356	111	74	2,369
	13,159	4,117	5,838	4,854	27,968
All other Classes :					
Employed in Retail Trade or in Handicraft, as Masters or Workmen - - - - - -	18,222	2,638	2,321	526	23,707
Labourers (including miners) - - -	12,173	2,353	915	36	15,477
Military and Naval - - - - -	568	69	—	—	637
Professional Persons - - - -	692	—	—	—	692
Other Educated Persons following miscellaneous Pursuits	967	115	423	23	1,528
Persons engaged in the Government Civil Service -	99	1	10	—	110
Parochial, Town, and Church Officers - - -	192	2	12	—	206
Domestic Servants - - - - -	2,755	2.729	5,295	4,456	15,235
Persons returned as Independent - - -	1,454	37	3,541	161	5,193
Almspeople, Pensioners, Paupers, Lunatics, and Prisoners	636	207	556	186	1,585
Residue of Population :					
Consisting of the Wives, Children, and others dependent on all Classes - - - - - -	3,582	50,615	52,288	54,061	160,546
Total of all other Classes - - -	41,340	58,766	65,361	59,449	224,916

Divide "all other classes," between the Agriculturists and the Manufacturers in the proportion which these respectively bear to each other, and the numbers engaged in, and dependent on, each interest will stand thus :—

Engaged in Agriculture - - -   19,333
Dependent on ,, - - -   91,928
      Agriculture—Total - - -   111,261
Engaged in Manufactures - - -   27,968
Dependent on ,, - - -   132,988
      Manufactures—Total - -   160,956

     Total of the County - - -   272,217

TAXATION.

	Paid by the	
	Land.	Manufacturers.
Paid exclusively by the Landed Interest :	£	£
Land Tax - - - - - - -	23,403	
Tithes - - - - - - -	16,896	
Property Tax—on Land, assessed at - - - £845,681	24,665	
Paid in the Proportion of 2-5ths by the Landed Interest, and 3-5ths by the Manufacturers :		
Poor and County Rates - - - - - £83,229	33,292	49,936
Highway Rates - - - - - - 18,627	7,450	11.177
Church ,, - - - - - - 4,605	1,842	2,763
Turnpike Trusts - - - - - - 35,653	14,060	21,593
Property Tax—on Dwelling Houses, assessed at - - 328,488	3,872	5,708
,, on other Property ,, - 204,856	2,390	3,584
	127,870	94,761

     Total of Taxation of the County - - - - £222,631

(For those engaged in Mines, see "Mining Interest.")

ENGAGED IN	MALES.		FEMALES.		TOTAL.
	20 years of age and upwards.	Under 20 years of age.	20 years of age and upwards.	Under 20 years of age.	
AGRICULTURE:					
Farmers and Graziers - - -	11,187	324	521	—	12,032
Agricultural Labourers - - - -	31,667	7,481	1,178	728	41,054
Gardeners, Nurserymen, and Florists - -	1,351	62	22	1	1,436
	44,205	7,867	1,721	729	54,522
MANUFACTURES:					
Woollen and Cloth Manufacture (all branches) -	986	170	486	222	1,864
Lace Manufacture (all branches) - -	138	99	1,068	516	1,821
Glove Makers and Glovers - - -	73	6	492	192	763
Weavers (all branches) - - -	286	30	377	26	719
Rope and Cord Spinners and Manufacturers -	511	100	29	8	648
Silk Manufacture (all branches) - -	63	10	186	140	399
Cotton Manufacture (all branches) - -	9	2	358	29	398
Tanners - - - - -	366	30	1	—	397
Paper Manufacture (all branches) - -	232	26	58	18	334
Spinners - - - - -	2	—	238	33	273
Coach Makers (all branches) - -	209	40	—	—	249
Tinmen and Tin-plate Workers - -	183	52	2	—	237
Basket Makers - - - -	188	22	6	1	217
Hatters and Hat Makers - - -	173	20	20	2	215
Factory Workers - - - -	22	19	70	80	191
Sail Makers - - - -	138	34	—	—	172
Sail Cloth and Tarpaulin Makers - -	8	3	1	—	12
Lime Burners and Manufacturers - -	148	3	3	—	154
Miscellaneous - - - -	1,110	134	164	34	1,442
	4,845	800	3,559	1,301	10,505
ALL OTHER CLASSES:					
Employed in Retail Trade or in Handicraft, as Masters or Workmen - - - - }	40,367	8,091	8,081	2,426	58,965
Labourers - - - - -	7,691	705	3,248	124	11,768
Military and Naval - - - -	7,422	797	—	—	8,219
Professional Persons - - - -	1,814	—	—	—	1,814
Other Educated Persons following miscellaneous Pursuits	1,892	189	1,099	74	3,254
Persons engaged in the Government Civil Service -	561	4	35	2	602
Parochial, Town, and Church Officers - -	372	3	55	—	430
Domestic Servants - - -	6,567	6,411	18,122	10,755	41,855
Persons returned as Independent - - -	5,062	206	14,429	656	20,353
Almspeople, Pensioners, Paupers, Lunatics, and Prisoners	2,957	959	2,807	725	7,448
RESIDUE OF POPULATION:					
Consisting of the Wives, Children, and others dependent on all Classes - - - - }	8,296	94,689	105,759	104,981	313,725
Total of all other Classes - -	83,001	112,054	153,635	119,743	468,433

Divide "ALL OTHER CLASSES" between the AGRICULTURISTS and the MANUFACTURERS in the proportion which these respectively bear to each other, and the numbers engaged in, and dependent on, each interest will stand thus:—

Engaged in Agriculture - - -	54,522	
Dependent on ,, - -	392,759	
AGRICULTURE—Total -		447,281
Engaged in Manufactures - -	10,505	
Dependent on ,, -	75,674	
MANUFACTURES—Total -		86,179
Total of the County - - -		533,460

TAXATION.

	Paid by the	
	LAND.	MANUFACTURERS.
	£	£
Paid exclusively by the Landed Interest:		
Land Tax - - - - -	77,772	
Tithes - - - - -	115,509	
Property Tax—on Land, assessed at - - £1,556,180	33,721	
Paid in the Proportion of 5-6ths by the Landed Interest, and 1-6th by the Manufacturers:		
Poor and County Rates - - - - £218,532	182,111	36,421
Highway Rates - - - - - 37,356	31,130	6,226
Church ,, - - - - 17,021	14,184	2,837
Turnpike Trusts - - - - 75,651	63,043	12,608
Property Tax—on Dwelling Houses, assessed at - 766,745	18,803	3,560
,, on other Property ,, - 266,451	6,476	1,295
	542,749	62,947
Total of Taxation of the County - - - £605,696		

(For those engaged in Mines, see "Mining Interest.")

ENGAGED IN	MALES.		FEMALES.		TOTAL.
	20 years of age and upwards.	Under 20 years of age.	20 years of age and upwards.	Under 20 years of age.	
AGRICULTURE :					
Farmers and Graziers - - - -	2,701	33	120	—	2,854
Agricultural Labourers - - - -	13,043	2,060	592	181	15,876
Gardeners, Nurserymen, and Florists - -	438	15	9	—	462
	16,182	2,108	721	181	19,192
MANUFACTURES :					
Flax Manufacture (all branches) - - -	186	53	67	57	363
Woollen and Woollen Cloth Manufacture (all branches) -	139	37	104	39	319
Weavers (all branches) - - - -	193	30	69	17	309
Spinners - - - - - - -	5	3	221	69	298
Glovers and Glove Makers - - - -	23	2	116	91	232
Rope, Twine, and Cord Spinners and Makers - -	100	19	75	18	212
Button Makers - - - - - -	2	—	149	54	205
Silk Manufacture (all branches) - - -	13	9	69	68	159
Sail and Sail Cloth and Tarpaulin Weavers and Makers -	84	17	35	8	144
Miscellaneous - - - - -	648	100	174	39	961
	1,393	270	1079	460	3,202
ALL OTHER CLASSES :					
Employed in Retail Trade or in Handicraft, as Masters or Workmen - - - - - -	12,257	1,837	1,742	421	16,257
Labourers - - - - - -	3,009	412	896	65	4,382
Military and Naval - - - - -	1,324	134	—	—	1,458
Professional Persons - - - -	636	—	—	—	636
Other Educated Persons following miscellaneous Pursuits	388	46	337	25	796
Persons engaged in the Government Civil Service -	325	4	10	—	339
Parochial, Town, and Church Officers - - -	91	—	15	—	106
Domestic Servants - - - - -	1,565	837	4,821	2,307	9,530
Persons returned as Independent - - -	1,390	48	3,969	182	5,589
Almspeople, Pensioners, Paupers, Lunatics, and Prisoners	818	326	928	302	2,374
RESIDUE OF POPULATION :					
Consisting of the Wives, Children, and others dependent on all Classes - - - -	3,330	34,828	35,687	37,337	111,182
Total of all other Classes - -	25,133	38,472	48,405	40,639	152.649

Divide "ALL OTHER CLASSES," between the AGRICULTURISTS and MANUFACTURERS in the proportion which these respectively bear to each other, and the numbers engaged in, and dependent on, each interest will stand thus:—

Engaged in Agriculture - - -	19,192	
Dependent on ,, - - -	130,823	
AGRICULTURE—Total - -		150,015
Engaged in Manufactures - - -	3,202	
Dependent on ,, - - -	21,826	
MANUFACTURES—Total - -		25,028
Total of the County - - -		175,043

TAXATION.

	Paid by the	
	LAND.	MANUFACTURERS.
Paid exclusively by the Landed Interest :	£	£
Land Tax - - - - - - - - -	32,026	
Tithes - - - - - - - - -	56,971	
Property Tax—on Land, assessed at - - - £613,507	17,893	
Paid in the Proportion of 6-7ths by the Landed Interest, and 1-7th by the Manufacturers :		
Poor and County Rates - - - - £94,011	80,581	13,430
Highway Rates - - - - - 12,251	10,501	1,750
Church ,, - - - - - 8,671	7,433	1,238
Turnpike Trusts - - - - - 26,274	22,521	3,753
Property Tax—on Dwelling Houses, assessed at - 231,204	5,780	963
,, on other Property ,, - 72,366	1,809	301
	235,515	21,435

Total of Taxation of the County . . . £256,950

ENGAGED IN	MALES.		FEMALES.		TOTAL.
	20 years of age and upwards.	Under 20 years of age.	20 years of age and upwards.	Under 20 years of age.	
AGRICULTURE:					
Farmers and Graziers	3,274	46	218	—	3,538
Agricultural Labourers	7,886	1,203	726	274	10,089
Gardeners, Nurserymen, and Florists	690	35	10	—	735
	11,850	1,284	954	274	14,362
MANUFACTURES:					
Engineers and Engine Workers	1,117	195	—	—	1,312
Engine and Machine Makers	228	93	—	—	321
Iron Manufacture (all branches)	657	296	—	2	955
Glass and Glass Bottle Manufacture (all branches)	672	183	2	1	858
Woollen and Woollen Cloth Manufacture (all branches)	346	86	70	100	602
Weavers	521	44	23	8	596
Potters and Pot Makers	389	103	20	4	516
Rope and Cord Makers	303	121	2	1	427
Brick and Tile Makers	341	39	3	3	386
Carpet Makers and Weavers	313	63	7	2	385
Anchor Smiths and Chain Makers	315	62	—	—	377
Nail and Nail Makers	257	48	1	—	306
Sail and Sail Cloth and Tarpaulin Makers	209	84	5	1	299
Chemist Manufacture	234	24	4	—	262
Factory Workers	100	29	55	61	245
Linen Manufacture (all branches)	155	15	14	6	190
Hatters and Hat Makers	103	7	17	5	132
Paper Manufacture (all branches)	192	18	16	9	235
Miscellaneous	1,472	279	193	89	2,033
	7,924	1,789	432	292	10,437
ALL OTHER CLASSES:					
Employed in Retail Trade or in Handicraft, as Masters or Workmen	25,767	6,026	2,626	323	34,742
Labourers	21,403	5,305	803	69	27,580
Military and Naval	4,782	472	—	—	5,254
Professional Persons	840	—	—	—	840
Other Educated Persons following miscellaneous Pursuits	1,351	170	347	16	1,884
Persons engaged in the Government Civil Service	255	4	12	—	271
Parochial, Town, and Church Officers	278	1	21	—	300
Domestic Servants	1,776	1,081	6,542	5,712	15,111
Persons returned as Independent	1,627	40	6,331	233	8,231
Almspeople, Pensioners, Paupers, Lunatics, and Prisoners	748	248	835	212	2,043
RESIDUE OF POPULATION:					
Consisting of the Wives, Children, and others dependent on all Classes	3,912	61,158	68,802	69,357	203,229
Total of all other Classes	62,739	74,505	86,319	75,922	9,485

Divide "ALL OTHER CLASSES" between the AGRICULTURISTS and the MANUFACTURERS in the proportion which these respectively bear to each other, and the numbers engaged in, and dependent on, each interest will stand thus:—

Engaged in Agriculture	14,362	
Dependent on ,,	173,443	
AGRICULTURE—Total		187,805
Engaged in Manufactures	10,437	
Dependent on ,,	126,042	
MANUFACTURES—Total		136,479
Total of the County		324,284

TAXATION.

	Paid by the	
	LAND.	MANUFACTURERS.
	£	£
Paid exclusively by the Landed Interest:		
Land Tax	10,444	
Tithes	34,262	
Property Tax—on Land, assessed at £538,781	15,714	
Paid in the Proportion of 4-7ths by the Landed Interest, and 3-7ths by the Manufacturers:		
Poor and County Rates £111,026	63,446	47,586
Highway Rates 20,864	11,920	8,944
Church ,, 6,101	3,484	2,617
Turnpike Trusts 30,323	17,328	12,995
Property Tax—on Dwelling Houses, assessed at 429,287	7,152	5,368
,, on other Property ,, 700,917	11,680	8,763
	175,424	86,273
Total of Taxation of the County		£261,697

(For those engaged in Mines, see "Mining Interest.")

ESSEX—County of. [England.

ENGAGED IN.	MALES.		FEMALES.		TOTAL.
	20 years of age and upwards.	Under 20 years of age.	20 years of age and upwards.	Under 20 years of age.	
AGRICULTURE:					
Farmers and Graziers - - - -	4,575	120	415	—	5,110
Agricultural Labourers - - - -	36,272	6,541	1,074	321	44,208
Gardeners, Nurserymen and Florists - -	1,677	99	22	—	1,798
	42,524	6.760	1,511	321	51,116
MANUFACTURES:					
Silk Manufacture (all branches) - - -	507	139	493	447	1,586
Brick and Tile Makers - - - -	431	79	7	5	522
Coach Makers (all branches) - - -	201	26	2	—	229
Engine and Machine Makers - - -	15	—	—	—	15
Engineer and Engine Workers - - -	105	12	—	—	117
Straw-Plait Manufacture (all branches) -	8	4	281	138	431
Weavers - - - - - -	114	17	49	26	206
Basket Makers - - - - -	146	8	6	1	161
Miscellaneous - - - - -	861	103	129	66	1,159
	2,388	388	967	683	4,426
ALL OTHER CLASSES:					
Employed in Retail Trade or in Handicraft, as Masters or as Workmen - - - - -	22,058	2,595	2,493	548	27,694
Labourers - - - - - -	6,540	1,007	1,851	119	9,517
Military and Naval - - - -	2,650	450	—	—	3,100
Professional Persons - - - -	1,113	—	—	—	1,113
Other Educated Persons following miscellaneous Pursuits	925	89	786	31	1,831
Persons engaged in the Government Civil Service -	267	6	13	—	286
Parochial, Town, and Church Officers - -	407	7	30	—	444
Domestic Servants - - - -	3,478	1,850	8,699	6,229	20,256
Persons returned as Independent - - -	1,915	104	5,071	313	7,403
Almspeople, Pensioners, Paupers, Lunatics, and Prisoners	1,283	733	1,081	680	3,777
RESIDUE OF POPULATION:					
Consisting of the Wives, Children, and others dependent on all Classes - - - - - -	5,566	67,255	69,043	72,152	214,016
Total of all other Classes - -	46,202	74,096	89,067	80,072	289,437

Divide "ALL OTHER CLASSES" between the AGRICULTURISTS and the MANUFACTURERS in the proportion which these respectively bear to each other, and the numbers engaged in, and dependent on, each interest will stand thus :—

Engaged in Agriculture	-	-	-	51,116
Dependent on ,,	-	-	-	266,373
AGRICULTURE—Total	-	-		317,489
Engaged in Manufactures	-	-	-	4.426
Dependent on ,,	-	-	-	23,064
MANUFACTURES—Total	-	-		27,490
Total of the County	-	-	-	344,979

TAXATION.

	Paid by the	
	LAND.	MANUFACTURERS.
Paid exclusively by the Landed Interest.	£	£
Land Tax - - - - - - -	88 647	
Tithes - - - - - - -	106,793	
Property Tax—on Land, assessed at - - £1,289,645	37,614	
Paid in the Proportion of 12-13ths by the Landed Interest, and 1-13th by the Manufacturers.		
Poor and County Rates - - - - £212,776	196,486	16,290
Highway Rates - - - - - 31,669	29,233	2,436
Church ,, - - - - - 16,075	14,739	1,236
Turnpike Trusts - - - - - 32,906	30,375	2,531
Property Tax—on Dwelling Houses, assessed at - 517,446	13,855	1,237
,, on other Property ,, - 297,040	7,997	666
	525,739	24,396
Total of Taxation of the County - - - - £550,135		

ENGAGED IN	MALES.		FEMALES.		TOTAL.
	20 years of age and upwards.	Under 20 years of age.	20 years of age and upwards.	Under 20 years of age.	
AGRICULTURE :					
Farmers and Graziers	4,577	57	319	—	4,953
Agricultural Labourers	19,949	2,878	1,578	320	24,725
Gardeners, Nurserymen, and Florists	1,449	83	53	7	1,592
	25,975	3,018	1,950	327	31,270
MANUFACTURES :					
Woollen and Cloth Manufacture (all branches)	2,192	568	2,118	654	5,532
Weavers (all branches)	833	53	165	25	1,076
Hatters and Hat Manufacturers (all branches)	858	67	49	10	984
Engineers and Engine Workers	656	81	—	1	738
Engine and Machine Makers	74	9	2	—	85
Engine Turner	1	—	—	—	1
Cotton Manufacture (all branches)	64	60	278	384	786
Iron Manufacture (all branches)	438	83	10	—	531
Pin Manufacture (all branches)	125	30	251	118	524
Coach Makers (all branches)	323	40	3	—	366
Nail Makers	241	43	5	—	289
Basket Makers	217	32	19	20	288
Tin-plate worker and Tinman	221	39	14	9	283
Boiler Makers	233	45	—	—	278
Brick and Tile Makers	193	38	4	2	237
Pipe Makers	70	22	109	33	234
Turners	152	28	2	—	182
Chair Makers	157	14	6	—	177
Dyers	144	9	19	1	173
Potters	124	28	14	7	173
Rope and Twine Spinners	122	24	9	4	159
Spinner	30	4	99	16	149
Lace Manufactures (all branches)	43	4	56	44	147
Tanners	123	5	1	—	129
Glass Manufacture (all branches)	106	21	1	—	128
Paper Makers and Stainers	108	1	8	4	121
Silk Manufacture (all branches)	16	5	48	44	113
Miscellaneous	1,312	143	188	57	1,700
	9,176	1,496	3,478	1,433	15,583
ALL OTHER CLASSES :					
Employed in Retail Trade or in Handicraft, as Masters or Workmen	35,956	4,421	7,633	1,423	49,433
Labourers	14,734	2,590	4,022	257	21,603
Military and Naval	2,786	151	—	—	2,937
Professional Persons	1,539	—	—	—	1,539
Other Educated Persons following miscellaneous Pursuits	2,354	316	1,121	66	3,857
Persons engaged in the Government Civil Service	379	6	19	—	404
Parochial, Town, and Church Officers	628	7	97	—	732
Domestic Servants	4,736	2,976	15,462	7,920	31,094
Persons returned as Independent	3,862	232	11,164	744	16,002
Almspeople, Pensioners, Paupers, Lunatics, and Prisoners	1,577	833	1,651	786	4,847
RESIDUE OF POPULATION :					
Consisting of the Wives, Children, and others dependent on all Classes	6,311	79,512	80,838	85,421	252,082
Total of all other Classes	74,862	91,044	122,007	96,617	384,530

Divide " ALL OTHER CLASSES " between the AGRICULTURISTS and the MANUFACTURERS in the proportion which these respectively bear to each other, and the numbers engaged in, and dependent on, each interest will stand thus :—

Engaged in Agriculture	31,270	
Dependent on ,,	256,638	
AGRICULTURE—Total		287,908
Engaged in Manufactures	15,583	
Dependent on ,,	127,892	
MANUFACTURES—Total		143,475
Total of the County		431,383

TAXATION.

		Paid by the	
		LAND.	MANUFACTURERS.
Paid exclusively by the Landed Interest :		£	£
Land Tax		46,657	
Tithes		39,990	
Property Tax—on Land, assessed at	£1,121,124	32,699	
Paid in the Proportion of 2-3rds by the Landed Interest, and 1-3rd by the Manufacturers :			
Poor and County Rates	£194,249	129,500	64,749
Highway Rates	29,758	19,839	9,919
Church ,,	12,275	8,184	4,091
Turnpike Trusts	62,487	41,658	20,829
Property Tax—on Dwelling Houses, assessed at	839,689	16,327	8,163
,, on other Property ,,	113,701	2,211	1,105
		337,065	108,856
Total of Taxation of the County		£445,921	

(For those engaged in Mines, see "Mining Interest.")

ENGAGED IN	MALES.		FEMALES.		TOTAL.
	20 Years of age and upwards.	Under 20 years of age.	20 Years of age and upwards.	Under 20 years of age.	
Agriculture:					
Farmers and Graziers - - - - -	3,194	27	292	—	3,513
Agricultural Labourers - - - - -	10,664	1,474	603	90	12,831
Gardeners, Nurserymen, and Florists - -	257	11	4	—	272
	14.115	1,512	899	90	16,616
Manufactures:					
Glovers and Glove Makers - - - -	41	4	102	18	165
Nailers - - - - - - -	75	14	2	1	92
Brick and Tile Makers - - - - -	66	13	1	—	80
Weavers - - - - - - -	55	4	—	—	59
Basket Makers - - - - - -	45	5	2	—	52
Tanners - - - - - - -	47	3	—	—	50
Turners - - - - - - -	39	5	—	—	44
Miscellaneous - - - - - -	314	25	51	5	395
	682	73	158	24	937
All other Classes:					
Employed in Retail Trade or in Handicraft, as Masters or Workmen - - - - -	8,121	1,111	937	159	10,328
Labourers - - - - - -	2,134	220	667	31	3,052
Military and Naval - - - - -	152	1	—	—	153
Professional Persons - - - - -	499	—	—	—	499
Other Educated Persons following miscellaneous Pursuits	284	3!	182	13	510
Persons engaged in the Government Civil Service -	52	—	1	—	53
Parochial, Town, and Church Officers -	89	—	14	—	103
Domestic Servants - - - - -	2,272	2,312	3,617	2,992	11,193
Persons returned as Independent - - -	981	53	2,135	107	3,276
Almspeople, Pensioners, Paupers, Lunatics, and Prisoners	395	203	265	173	1,036
Residue of Population:					
Consisting of the Wives, Children, and others dependent on all Classes - - - - -	2,135	19,557	23,208	21,222	66,122
Total of all other Classes - -	17,114	23.488	31,026	24,697	96,325

Divide "all other classes" between the Agriculturists and the Manufacturers in the proportion which these respectively bear to each other, and the numbers engaged in, and dependent on, each interest will stand thus :—

Engaged in Agriculture	-	-	16,616
Dependent on ,,	-		91,184
	Agriculture—Total	-	107,800
Engaged in Manufactures	-		937
Dependent on ,,	-	-	5,141
	Manufactures—Total	-	6,078
	Total of the County	-	113,878

TAXATION.

		Paid by the	
		Land.	Manufacturers.
Paid exclusively by the Landed Interest :		£	£
Land Tax - - - - - - - -		20,106	
Tithes - - - - - - - - -		32,306	
Property Tax—on Land, assessed at - -	£629,981	18,374	
Paid in the Proportion of 18-19ths by the Landed Interest, and 1-19th by the Manufacturers :			
Poor and County Rates - - -	£55,442	52,998	2,944
Highway Rates - - - -	13,138	12,447	691
Church ,, - - - - -	4,928	4,668	259
Turnpike Trusts - - - -	21,795	20,648	1,147
Property Tax—on Dwelling Houses, assessed at -	128,572	3,553	197
,, on other Property ,, -	46,766	1,293	71
		166,393	5,309
Total of Taxation of the County - - -		£171,702	

ENGAGED IN	MALES.		FEMALES.		TOTAL.
	20 years of age and upwards.	Under 20 years of age.	20 years of age and upwards.	Under 20 years of age.	
AGRICULTURE:					
Farmers and Graziers - - - -	1,628	22	130	—	1,780
Agricultural Labourers - - - - - -	14,110	3,066	297	68	17,541
Gardeners, Nurserymen, and Florists - -	776	38	10	—	824
	16,514	3,126	437	68	20,145
MANUFACTURES:					
Straw-Plait Workers (all branches) - - -	97	239	2,840	1,575	4,751
Straw-Plait Dealers - - - -	81	8	21	9	119
Silk Manufacture (all branches) - -	71	175	85	169	500
Paper Makers - - - - -	193	29	29	5	256
Paper Stainers - - - -	—	1	—	—	1
Brick and Tile Makers - - - -	107	17	—	—	124
Coach Makers (all branches) - - -	64	16	—	—	80
Type Founders - - - - -	35	25	—	—	60
Engineers and Engine Workers - -	52	3	—	—	55
Engine and Machine Maker - - -	1	—	—	—	1
Weavers - - - - - -	42	11	—	1	54
Canvas Makers and Weavers - - -	46	5	—	—	51
Miscellaneous - - - -	449	34	37	7	527
	1,238	563	3,012	1,766	6,579
ALL OTHER CLASSES:					
Employed in Retail Trade or in Handicraft, as Masters or Workmen - - - - -	10,666	1,217	1,509	210	13,602
Labourers - - - - - -	3,689	625	879	25	5,218
Military and Naval - - - -	390	38	—	—	428
Professional Persons - - - -	499	—	—	—	499
Other Educated Persons following miscellaneous Pursuits	504	34	365	16	919
Persons engaged in the Government Civil Service -	110	3	8	—	121
Parochial, Town, and Church Officers - -	141	1	24	—	166
Domestic Servants - - - - -	2,257	1,228	4,426	2,282	10,193
Persons returned as Independent - -	1,117	38	2,420	121	3,696
Almspeople, Pensioners, Paupers, Lunatics, and Prisoners	737	335	606	349	2,027
RESIDUE OF POPULATION:					
Consisting of the Wives, Children, and others dependent on all Classes - - - - -	2,323	30,229	29,384	31,678	93,614
Total of all other Classes - - -	22,433	33,748	39,621	34,681	130,483

Divide " ALL OTHER CLASSES " between the AGRICULTURISTS and the MANUFACTURERS in the proportion which these respectively bear to each other, and the numbers engaged in, and dependent on, each interest will stand thus :—

```
          Engaged in Agriculture    -      -      -   20,145
          Dependent on     ,,     -      -      -   98,361
                                                   ————————
                 AGRICULTURE—Total   -      -            118,506

          Engaged in Manufactures   -      -      -    6,579
          Dependent on    ,, -      -      -   32,122
                                                   ————————
                 MANUFACTURES—Total   -      -           38,701


                 Total of the County   -      -      -   157,207
```

TAXATION.

	Paid by the	
	LAND.	MANUFACTURERS.
Paid exclusively by the Landed Interest:	£	£
Land Tax - - - - - -	41,783	
Tithes - - - - -	56,136	
Property Tax—on Land, assessed at - - - £438,225	12,781	
Paid in the Proportion of 3-4ths by the Landed Interest, and 1-4th by the Manufacturers :		
Poor and County Rates - - - - £86,281	64,711	21,570
Highway Rates - - - - 11,862	8,897	2,965
Church ,, - - - - - 9,393	7,045	2,348
Turnpike Trusts - - - - 21,676	16,257	5,419
Property Tax—on Dwelling Houses, assessed at - 340,267	7,443	2,481
,, on other Property ,, - - 71,301	1,559	520
	216,612	35,303
Total of Taxation of the County - - - £251,915		

ENGAGED IN	MALES.		FEMALES.		TOTAL.
	20 years of age and upwards.	Under 20 years of age.	20 years of age and upwards.	Under 20 years of age.	
Agriculture:					
Farmers and Graziers - - - - -	1,027	22	72	—	1,121
Agricultural Labourers - - - -	6,004	866	183	59	7,112
Gardeners, Nurserymen, and Florists -	206	13	28	—	247
	7,237	901	283	59	8,480
Manufactures:					
Brick and Tile Makers - - - -	175	27	—	—	202
Paper Makers - - - - -	29	2	14	7	52
Lace Makers - - - - -	3	—	33	9	45
Coach Makers (all branches) - - -	37	10	—	—	47
Basket Makers - - - - -	24	4	—	—	28
Miscellaneous - - - - -	181	17	19	1	218
	449	60	66	17	592
All other Classes:					
Employed in Retail Trade or in Handicraft, as Masters or Workmen - - - - -	3,755	483	443	92	4,773
Labourers - - - - -	807	67	282	5	1,161
Military and Naval - - - -	184	6	—	—	190
Professional Persons - - - -	233	—	—	—	233
Other Educated Persons following miscellaneous Pursuits	103	9	129	14	255
Persons engaged in the Government Civil Service -	19	—	2	—	21
Parochial, Town, and Church Officers - - -	33	—	4	—	37
Domestic Servants - - - -	559	471	1,359	1,135	3,524
Persons returned as Independent - -	301	17	797	42	1,157
Almspeople, Pensioners, Paupers, Lunatics, and Prisoners	179	100	165	57	501
Residue of Population:					
Consisting of the Wives, Children, and others dependent on all Classes - - - -	1,138	11,961	11,956	12,570	37,625
Total of all other Classes - -	7,311	13,114	15,137	13,915	49,477

Divide "All other classes" between the Agriculturists and the Manufacturers in the proportion which these respectively bear to each other, and the numbers engaged in, and dependent on, each Interest will stand thus:—

Engaged in Agriculture	-	-	-	8,480	
Dependent on ,,	-	-	-	46,249	
Agriculture—Total	-	-			54,729
Engaged in Manufactures	-	-	-	592	
Dependent on ,,	-	-	-	3,228	
Manufactures—Total	-	-			3,820
Total of the County	-	-	-		58,549

TAXATION.

	Paid by the	
	Land.	Manufacturers.
Paid exclusively by the Landed Interest :	£	£
Land Tax - - - - - - -	15,278	
Tithes - - - - - - -	7,842	
Property Tax—on Land, assessed at - £312,082	9,107	
Paid in the Proportion of 14-15ths by the Landed Interest, and 1-15th by the Manufacturers :		
Poor and County Rates - - - £36 076	33,671	2,405
Highway Rates - - - - 6,226	5,811	415
Church ,, - - - - 2,596	2,423	172
Turnpike Trusts - - - - 8,726	8,145	581
Property Tax—on Dwelling Houses, assessed at - 71,852	1,955	140
,, on other Property ,, - 17,749	483	34
	84,715	3,747
Total of Taxation of the County - - - -	£88,462	

ENGAGED IN	MALES.		FEMALES.		TOTAL.
	20 years of age and upwards.	Under 20 years of age.	20 years of age and upwards.	Under 20 years of age.	
AGRICULTURE:					
Farmers and Graziers - - - -	5,123	57	297	—	5,477
Agricultural Labourers - - - -	33,504	5,502	521	84	39,611
Gardeners, Nurserymen, and Florists - -	2,337	113	44	3	2,497
	40,964	5,672	862	87	47,585
MANUFACTURES:					
Paper Makers (all branches) - - -	539	75	244	76	934
„ Stainers - - - - -	11	1	—	—	12
Engine and Machine Makers - - -	19	3	—	—	22
Engineers and Engine Workers - - - -	562	60	4	1	627
Brick and Tile Makers - - - -	531	75	5	1	612
Rope and Cord Spinners and Makers - -	411	40	8	3	462
Coach Makers (all branches) . - -	235	29	1	—	265
Basket Makers - - - - -	195	9	8	—	212
Sail Makers - - - - -	170	21	1	—	192
Tanners - - - - - -	167	8	—	—	175
Printers (all branches) - - - -	112	19	7	2	140
Tin Plate Workers and Tinmen . - -	120	18	1	—	139
Iron Manufacturers (all branches) - - -	122	15	—	—	137
Hatters - - - - - -	112	2	18	2	134
Turners - - - - - -	118	14	2	—	134
Boiler Makers - - - - -	110	10	—	—	120
Pipe Makers - - - - -	86	21	7	—	114
Weavers (all branches) - - - -	83	6	15	1	105
Miscellaneous - - - - -	970	85	138	36	1,229
	4,673	511	459	122	5,765
ALL OTHER CLASSES:					
Employed in Retail Trade or in Handicraft, as Masters or Workmen - - - - -	39,511	4,463	5,263	686	49,923
Labourers - - - - - -	14,198	1,516	4,469	110	20,293
Military and Naval - - - - -	16,864	3,717	—	—	20,581
Professional Persons - - - -	1,855	—	—	—	1,855
Other Educated Persons following miscellaneous Pursuits	2,377	160	1,313	77	3,927
Persons engaged in the Government Civil Service -	1,071	25	15	1	1,112
Parochial, Town, and Church Officers - -	687	9	66	—	36 762
Domestic Servants - - - -	5,935	2,581	18,309	9,567	18,392
Persons returned as Independent - - -	5,156	164	12,718	591	1 ,629
Almspeople, Pensioners, Paupers, Lunatics, and Prisoners	7,013	1,901	2,621	1,512	3,047
RESIDUE OF POPULATION:					
Consisting of the Wives, Children, and others dependent on all Classes - - - - -	7,026	104,502	106,634	110,304	328,466
Total of all other Classes - - -	101,693	119,038	151,408	122,848	494,987

Divide "ALL OTHER CLASSES" between the AGRICULTURISTS and the MANUFACTURERS in the proportion which these respectively bear to each other, and the numbers engaged in, and dependent on, each interest will stand thus :—

Engaged in Agriculture - - -	47,585	
Dependent on „ - - - -	441,499	
AGRICULTURE—Total -		489,084
Engaged in Manufactures - -	5,765	
Dependent on „ - -	53,488	
MANUFACTURES—Total -		59,253
Total of the County - - -		548,337

TAXATION.

	Paid by the	
	LAND.	MANUFACTURERS.
Paid exclusively by the Landed Interest :	£	£
Land Tax - - - - - - -	80,495	
Tithes - - - - - - -	114,349	
Property Tax—on Land, assessed at - - - £1,327,490	38,718	
Paid in the Proportion of 8-9ths by the Landed Interest, and 1-9th by the Manufacturers :		
Poor and County Rates - - - - £258,166	231,481	26,685
Highway Rates - - - - 48,634	43,230	5,404
Church „ - - - - - 26,201	23,290	2,911
Turnpike Trusts - - - - - 56,727	50,424	6,303
Property Tax—on Dwelling Houses, assessed at - 1,372,881	35,593	4,449
„ on other property „ - - 207,234	5,373	671
	622,953	46,423
Total of Taxation of the County - - - £669,376		

LANCASTER – County of. [England.

ENGAGED IN	MALES.		FEMALES.		TOTAL.
	20 years of age and upwards.	Under 20 years of age.	20 years of age and upwards.	Under 20 years of age.	
AGRICULTURE:					
Farmers and Graziers	14,740	139	1,767	—	16,646
Agricultural Labourers	24,761	5,194	442	188	30,585
Gardeners, Nurserymen, and Florists	2,195	121	22	—	2,338
	41,696	5,454	2,231	188	49,569
MANUFACTURES:					
Cotton Manufacture (all branches)	45,920	24,363	45,271	34,119	149,673
Weavers (all branches)	21,190	5,197	8,787	5,125	40,299
Silk Manufacture (all branches)	5,748	1,427	5,209	2,949	15,333
Woollen and Cloth Manufacture (all branches)	6,758	1,733	2,099	1,440	12,030
Printers (all branches) Cotton, Silk, &c. &c.	5,715	1,666	146	535	8,062
Factory Workers (branch not specified)	2,064	1,092	2,129	1,372	6,657
Engine and Machine Makers	1,682	376	—	—	2,058
Engineers and Engine Workers	3,810	663	12	20	4,505
Dyers (all branches)	4,720	1,489	72	25	6,306
Hatters and Hat Makers	4,078	672	562	234	5,546
Spinners (branch not specified)	1,725	289	1,107	701	3,822
Fustian Manufacture (all branches)	1,661	388	877	325	3,251
Bleachers (branch not specified)	1,868	487	142	97	2,594
Iron Manufacture (all branches)	1,945	479	16	8	2,448
Nailers and Nail Makers	1,283	504	25	13	1,825
Rope and Cord Spinners	1,174	493	36	14	1,717
Brick and Tile Makers	1,153	223	35	8	1,419
Glass Manufacture (all branches)	706	268	70	29	1,073
Flax Manufacture (all branches)	426	215	198	225	1,064
Tin Plate Workers and Tinmen	814	214	11	2	1,041
Coach Makers (all branches)	800	181	7	—	988
Linen Manufacture (all branches)	195	114	325	317	951
Block and Print Cutters	743	176	4	3	926
Moulders (branch not specified)	637	234	4	1	876
Boiler Makers	686	187	—	—	873
Fullers	638	170	2	—	810
Paper Manufacture (all branches)	388	121	100	68	677
„ Stainers	75	45	3	4	127
Turners	601	140	3	—	} 748
Turners (Brass)	2	2	—	—	}
Knitters	58	64	339	207	668
Worsted Manufacture	159	87	206	180	632
Small Ware Manufacture	320	55	116	67	558
Chair Makers	464	59	23	1	547
File Cutters and Makers	393	149	4	—	546
Sail Makers	358	112	1	2	} 539
Sail Cloth Manufacture	56	3	7	—	}
Potters	413	87	18	3	521
Pin Manufacture (all branches)	73	86	132	178	469
Roller Makers and Coverers	286	43	103	23	455
Basket Makers	356	60	18	4	438
Pattern Designers and Makers	353	77	4	2	436
Tanners	400	20	—	—	420
Bobbin Makers and Turners	264	133	2	4	403
Card (Machine) Makers	187	85	47	59	378
Pipe Makers	254	72	30	9	365
Brass Founders and Moulders	266	84	4	—	354
Brass Finishers and Workers	80	28	3	—	111
Reed Makers	285	43	9	2	339
Tool Makers	221	75	4	—	300
Colour Manufacture	222	1	1	1	275
Flannel Manufacture (all branches)	228	10	25	7	270
Copper Manufacture (all branches)	213	54	—	—	267
Grinders	216	47	1	2	266
Hinge Makers	143	68	—	2	213
Straw Plait Workers	14	14	112	65	205
Hat and Band Box Makers	6	—	113	74	193
Shuttle Makers	142	36	1	—	179
Comb Makers	131	27	11	4	173
Skinners	140	30	2	—	172
Fringe and Tassel Manufacture	60	6	62	38	166
Hoopers and Hoop Makers	131	14	1	—	146
Wire Workers	116	23	5	2	146
Anchor Smiths and Chain Makers	125	14	—	—	139
Quilt Makers	60	19	51	6	136
Soap Manufacture	124	10	1	1	136
Marble Masons	106	25	1	—	132
Thread Manufacture	27	4	59	28	118
Muslin Manufacture (all branches)	74	13	18	9	114
Wire Drawers	91	18	—	—	109
Gun and Pistol Makers	94	12	1	—	107
Slate Manufacture	96	11	—	—	107
Bolt Makers	81	21	1	—	103
Miscellaneous	1,525	249	224	81	2,079
	128,016	45,806	69,012	48,695	292,129

ENGAGED IN	MALES.		FEMALES.		TOTAL.
	20 years of age and upwards.	Under 20 years of age.	20 years of age and upwards.	Under 20 years of age.	
ALL OTHER CLASSES:					
Employed in Retail Trade or in Handicraft, as Masters or Workmen -	128,921	21,157	21,378	4,199	175,655
Labourers -	56,861	10,195	7,969	1,054	76,079
Military and Naval -	9,598	1,026	—	—	10,624
Professional Persons -	3,495	—	—	—	3,495
Other Educated Persons following miscellaneous Pursuits	10,078	1,578	2,012	136	13,804
Persons engaged in the Government Civil Service -	1,195	16	23	—	1,234
Parochial, Town, and Church Officers -	2,408	19	113	1	2,541
Domestic Servants -	8,375	3,371	40,887	20,365	72,998
Persons returned as Independent -	8,127	491	23,343	1,246	33,207
Almspeople, Pensioners, Paupers, Lunatics, and Prisoners	4,838	2,325	4,060	1,494	12,717
RESIDUE OF POPULATION:					
Consisting of the Wives, Children, and others dependent on all Classes -	21,992	297,294	287,085	316,631	923,002
Total of all other Classes -	255,888	337,472	386,870	345,126	1,325,356

Divide "ALL OTHER CLASSES" between the AGRICULTURISTS and the MANUFACTURERS in the proportion which these respectively bear to each other, and the numbers engaged in, and dependent on, each interest will stand thus:—

Engaged in Agriculture -	49,569	
Dependent on ,, -	192,265	
AGRICULTURE—Total -		241,834
Engaged in Manufactures -	292,129	
Dependent on ,, -	1,133,091	
MANUFACTURES—Total -		1,425,220
Total of the County -		1,667,054

TAXATION.

		Paid by the	
		LAND.	MANUFACTURERS.
		£	£
Paid exclusively by the Landed Interest:			
Land Tax -		19,406	
Tithes -		39,728	
Property Tax—on Land, assessed at - £1,636,416		47,728	
Paid in the proportion of 1-7th by the Landed Interest, and 6-7ths by the Manufacturers:			
Poor and County Rates - £530,490		75,784	454,706
Highway Rates - 73,870		10,552	63,318
Church ,, - 22,068		3,152	18,916
Turnpike Trusts - 121,885		17,412	104,473
Property Tax—on Dwelling Houses, assessed at - 4,777,536		19,906	119,438
,, on other Property ,, - 1,342,276		5,878	33,271
		239,546	794,122
Total of Taxation of the County -		£1,033,668	

ENGAGED IN	MALES.		FEMALES.		TOTAL.
	20 years of age and upwards.	Under 20 years of age.	20 years of age and upwards.	Under 20 years of age.	
Agriculture:					
Farmers and Graziers - - - -	3,358	26	285	—	3,669
Agricultural Labourers - - - -	11,259	1,353	133	25	12,770
Gardeners, Nurserymen, and Florists - -	604	38	10	1	653
	15,221	1,417	428	26	17,092
Manufactures:					
Hose (Stocking) Manufacture (all branches) -	8,753	1,328	2,059	775	12,915
,, Woollen (Stocking) Manufacture (all branches)	1,265	198	493	212	2,168
Lace Manufacture (all branches) - - -	369	95	688	385	1,537
Woollen and Cloth Manufacture (all branches) -	768	86	72	64	990
Brick and Tile Makers - - - -	348	100	1	1	450
Glovers and Glove Manufacture (all branches) -	91	6	212	130	439
Cotton Manufacture (all branches) - -	84	85	172	82	423
Worsted Manufacture (all branches) - -	59	25	174	77	335
Trimmers - - - - -	144	41	4	—	189
Needle Makers - - - - -	146	32	4	—	182
Factory Workers (branch not specified) -	15	46	57	56	174
Dyers (all branches) - - - -	151	11	10	1	173
Potters and Pot Manufacture (all branches) -	106	25	12	4	147
Weavers (all branches) - - -	115	15	13	2	145
Engine and Machine Makers - - -	36	5	1	—	42
Engineers and Engine Workers - - -	99	3	—	—	102
Brace Makers (all branches) - - -	32	8	69	27	136
Turners - - - - -	108	19	2	—	129
,, (Ivory) - - - -	1	—	—	—	1
Basket Makers - - - - -	101	17	3	—	121
Miscellaneous - - - - -	871	195	134	31	1,231
	13,662	2,340	4,180	1,847	22,029
All other Classes:					
Employed in Retail Trade or in Handicraft, as Masters or Workmen - - - - - }	14,402	2,143	2,501	479	19,525
Labourers - - - - -	2,511	361	784	20	3,676
Military and Naval - - - -	506	75	—	—	581
Professional Persons - - - -	734	—	—	—	734
Other Educated Persons following miscellaneous Pursuits	531	98	404	18	1,051
Persons engaged in the Government Civil Service -	79	1	3	—	83
Parochial, Town, and Church Officers - - -	173	—	20	—	193
Domestic Servants - - - - -	2,386	2,266	5,006	3,889	13,547
Persons returned as Independent - - -	1,278	34	2,952	113	4,377
Almspeople, Pensioners, Paupers, Lunatics, and Prisoners	753	418	609	354	2,134
Residue of Population:					
Consisting of the Wives, Children, and others dependent on all Classes - - - - - }	3,285	40,956	42,685	43,919	130,845
Total of all other Classes - -	26,638	46,352	54,964	48,792	176,746

Divide "all other classes" between the Agriculturists and the Manufacturers in the proportion which these respectively bear to each other, and the numbers engaged in, and dependent on, each interest will stand thus :—

Engaged in Agriculture - - -	17,092	
Dependent on ,, - - -	77,221	
Agriculture—Total - - -		94,313
Engaged in Manufactures - -	22,029	
Dependent on ,, - -	99,525	
Manufactures—Total -		121,554
Total of the County - -		215,867

TAXATION.

	Paid by the	
	Land.	Manufacturers.
Paid exclusively by the Landed Interest :	£	£
Land Tax - - - - - - -	34,238	
Tithes - - - - - - -	19,474	
Property Tax—on Land, assessed at - £899,063	25,931	
Paid in the Proportion of 4-9ths by the Landed Interest, and 5-9ths by the Manufacturers :		
Poor and County Rates - - - - £103,718	46,996	57,622
Highway Rates - - - - - 23,816	10,628	13,188
Church ,, - - - - - 5,898	2,620	3,278
Turnpike Trusts - - - - - 22,243	9,884	12,339
Property Tax—on Dwelling Houses, assessed at - 314,966	4,080	5,106
,, on other Property ,, - - 162,355	2,204	2,531
	155,155	94,064
Total of Taxation of the County - - - -	£249,219	

ENGAGED IN	MALES.		FEMALES.		TOTAL.
	20 years of age and upwards.	Under 20 years of age.	20 years of age and upwards.	Under 20 years of age.	
AGRICULTURE:					
Farmers and Graziers - - - - -	10,579	78	631	—	11,288
Agricultural Labourers - - - -	36,917	7,712	643	122	45,394
Gardeners, Nurserymen, and Florists - -	830	35	14	—	879
	48,326	7,825	1,288	122	57,561
MANUFACTURES:					
Brick and Tile Makers - - -	698	106	5	—	809
Rope and Cord Spinners and Makers -	239	39	3	—	281
Engine and Machine Makers - - -	109	19	1	—	129
Engineers and Engine Workers - - -	74	6	—	—	80
Coachmakers (all branches) - - -	120	49	3	—	172
Tanners - - - - - -	116	25	2	—	143
Nail Makers - - - - -	115	14	—	—	129
Basket Makers - - - - -	114	13	1	—	128
Weavers (branch not specified) - - -	103	4	1	—	108
Miscellaneous - - - - -	810	102	154	21	1,087
	2,498	377	170	21	3,066
ALL OTHER CLASSES:					
Employed in Retail Trade or in Handicraft, as Masters or Workmen - - - - -	24,240	4,126	3,135	573	32,074
Labourers - - - - -	4,276	271	1,567	33	6,147
Military and Naval - - - -	2,297	108	—	—	2,405
Professional Persons - - - -	1,431	—	—	—	1,431
Other Educated Persons following miscellaneous Pursuits	814	121	750	46	1,731
Persons engaged in the Government Civil Service - -	169	3	12	—	184
Parochial, Town, and Church Officers - -	234	3	33	1	271
Domestic Servants - - - -	3,025	2,646	10,460	10,403	26,534
Persons returned as Independent - - -	2,390	45	6,443	221	9,099
Almspeople, Pensioners, Paupers, Lunatics, and Prisoners	1,013	564	1,118	574	3,269
RESIDUE OF POPULATION:					
Consisting of the Wives, Children, and others dependent on all Classes - - - - -	6,113	68,849	71,837	72,031	218,830
Total of all other Classes - - -	46,002	76,736	95,355	83,882	301,975

Divide " ALL OTHER CLASSES " between the AGRICULTURISTS and the MANUFACTURERS in the proportion which these respectively bear to each other, and the numbers engaged in, and dependent on, each interest will stand thus :—

Engaged in Agriculture	-	-	57,561	
Dependent on ,,	-	-	286,704	
AGRICULTURE—Total	-	-		344,265
Engaged in Manufactures	-	-	3,066	
Dependent on ,,	-	-	15,271	
MANUFACTURES—Total	-	-		18,337
Total of the County	-	-	-	362,602

TAXATION.

	Paid by the	
	LAND.	MANUFACTURERS.
Paid exclusively by the Landed Interest :	£	£
Land Tax - - - - - - -	70,548	
Tithes - - - - - - -	44,877	
Property Tax—on Land, assessed at - - £2,340,624	68,268	
Paid in the Proportion of 19-20ths by the Landed Interest, and 1-20th by the Manufacturers :		
Poor and County Rates - - - £151,999	144,399	7,600
Highway Rates - - - - - 80,664	76,628	4,036
Church ,, - - - - - 12,698	12,059	639
Turnpike Trusts - - - - - 35,957	34,165	1,792
Property Tax—on Dwelling Houses, assessed at - 420,978	11,665	613
,, on other Property ,, - - 106,737	2,958	155
	465,567	14,835
Total of Taxation of the County - - - - £480,402		

ENGAGED IN	MALES.		FEMALES.		TOTAL.
	20 years of age and upwards.	Under 20 years of age.	20 years of age and upwards.	Under 20 years of age.	
Agriculture:					
Farmers and Graziers - - - - - -	1,118	32	55	—	1,205
Agricultural Labourers - - - - -	9,627	1,437	522	82	11,668
Gardeners, Nurserymen, and Florists - - -	4,761	185	275	70	5,291
	15,506	1,654	852	152	18,164
Manufactures:					
Silk Manufacture (all branches) - - - -	3,728	450	2,440	530	7,148
Weavers (branch not specified) - - -	3,241	369	1,148	203	4,961
Coach Makers (all branches) - - - -	3,408	327	68	8	3,811
Engineers and Engine Workers - - -	2,114	299	—	—	2,413
Engine and Machine Makers - - - -	193	22	5	—	220
Dyers (all branches) - - - - -	1,172	102	85	13	1,372
Hat Makers (all branches) - - - -	1,020	100	171	39	1,330
Brick and Tile Makers - - - -	1,068	204	23	13	1,308
Turners - - - - - -	1,059	145	29	4	1,237
,, (Brass) - - - -	75	14	1	—	90
Chair Makers - - - - -	937	147	85	10	1,179
Tin-plate Workers and Tinmen - - -	1,004	122	8	—	1,134
Cotton Manufacture (all branches) - - -	98	29	832	163	1,122
Gun Makers (all branches) - - - -	955	120	27	2	1,104
Paper Manufacture (all branches) - - -	791	264	37	10	1,102
Glass Manufacture (all branches) - - -	744	79	33	6	862
Rope and Cord Makers - - - -	614	132	60	5	811
Brass Finishers and Workers - - -	674	73	15	—	762
Brass Founders and Moulders - - -	607	80	—	6	693
Lace Manufacture (all branches) - - -	249	18	327	83	677
Sugar Bakers, Boilers, and Refiners - - -	604	22	3	—	629
Basket Makers - - - - -	488	34	43	6	571
Glovers and Glove Makers - - -	229	20	240	35	524
Wire Drawers and Workers - - - -	356	50	18	3	427
Iron Manufacture (all branches) - - -	381	36	5	—	422
Type Founders - - - - -	353	58	1	1	413
Pipe Makers - - - - - -	318	45	35	6	404
Copper Manufacture (all branches) - - -	311	78	8	—	397
Sail Makers - - - - - -	348	34	1	—	383
Sail Cloth and Tarpaulin Makers - - -	55	5	6	2	68
Trimming Makers - - - - -	136	21	146	66	369
Fringe Manufacturers - - - -	160	32	109	57	358
Carpet Manufacturers - - - -	271	49	19	2	341
Gold Beaters - - - - -	249	67	6	—	322
Gold Workers (all branches) - - -	141	16	29	14	200
Japanners - - - - - -	244	31	39	8	322
Comb Makers - - - - -	273	29	15	—	317
Wool Manufacture (all branches) - - -	232	21	46	6	305
Musical Instrument Makers - - -	236	30	3	—	269
Ivory Turners and Workers - - -	229	30	3	1	263
Boiler Makers - - - - -	213	45	—	—	258
Straw-Plait Manufacture - - - -	81	9	132	19	241
Brace Makers - - - - -	52	10	120	19	201
Skin Dressers - - - - -	167	14	12	4	197
Pewterers - - - - - -	175	8	11	—	194
Willow Weavers and Workers - - -	104	20	49	20	193
Soap Boilers - - - - -	176	8	3	1	188
Organ Builders - - - - -	153	25	2	—	180
Crape Manufacturers - - - -	40	23	71	32	166
Card Makers - - - - -	105	27	18	8	158
Mat Makers - - - - -	116	10	25	2	153
Pencil Makers - - - - -	116	22	9	2	149
Marble Masons - - - - -	126	14	4	—	144
Horse Hair Manufacturers and Weavers - -	105	11	17	1	134
Tool Dealers and Makers - - -	109	19	2	—	130
Tanners - - - - - -	111	14	1	—	126
Distillers - - - - - -	122	1	1	—	124
Hair Manufacturers and Weavers - - -	54	8	48	14	124
Button Makers - - - - -	85	11	21	4	121
Looking Glass Makers and Silverers - - -	105	6	6	—	117
Lamp Makers - - - - -	108	5	2	—	115
Tobacco Pipe Makers - - - -	74	15	14	2	105
Potters - - - - -	93	7	2	—	102
Floor Cloth Manufacturers - - -	85	11	1	—	97
Hot Pressers - - - - -	81	15	1	—	97
Spring Makers - - - - -	72	10	15	—	97
Moulders (branch not specified) - - -	80	11	1	1	93
Founders (branch not specified) - - -	80	10	1	—	91
Lint Makers and Dealers - - -	6	—	63	20	89
Pen Makers and Dealers - - -	57	6	23	1	87
Zinc Manufacturers and Workers - - -	73	12	1	—	86
Instrument Makers - - - -	68	9	7	—	84
Spinners (branch not specified) - - -	31	4	34	9	78
Miscellaneous - - - - -	2,505	221	453	97	3,276
	35,093	4,445	7,339	1,558	48,435

ENGAGED IN	MALES.		FEMALES.		TOTAL.
	20 years of age and upwards.	Under 20 years of age.	20 years of age and upwards.	Under 20 years of age.	
ALL OTHER CLASSES :					
Employed in Retail Trade or in Handicraft, as Masters or Workmen - - - - -	195,830	21,660	42,344	6,990	266,824
Labourers - - - - - -	53,472	5,958	22,171	639	82,240
Military and Naval - - - -	13,289	868	—	—	14,157
Professional Persons - - - - - -	10,389	—	—	—	10,389
Other Educated Persons following miscellaneous Pursuits	21,465	2,892	5,029	286	29,672
Persons engaged in the Government Civil Service -	2,119	41	15	—	2,175
Parochial, Town, and Church Officers - -	5,200	171	387	4	5,762
Domestic Servants - - - - -	31,975	9,331	86,870	28,555	156,731
Persons returned as Independent - - -	22,260	960	50,707	2,442	76,369
Almspeople, Pensioners, Paupers, Lunatics, and Prisoners	8,378	3,171	9,910	2,624	24,083
RESIDUE OF POPULATION :					
Consisting of the Wives, Children, and others dependent on all Classes - - - - -	19,699	253,199	289,943	278,794	841,635
Total of all other Classes - - -	384,076	298,251	507,376	320,334	1,510,037

The Metropolis being the representative of every other interest in the Kingdom, the same rule of dividing " ALL OTHER CLASSES " and the Taxation of the County between the AGRICULTURISTS and MANUFACTURERS in the proportion which those resident in the County bear to each other will not apply in the instance of Middlesex.

We therefore adopt the result given in the Summary of the proportion which each bears to the other in the whole population of the three Kingdoms, irrespective of the Metropolis, and this gives 2-3rds to the Agriculturists, and 1-3rd to the Manufacturers:—

Engaged in Agriculture - - -	18,164	
Dependent on ,, - - -	1,006,692	
AGRICULTURE—Total - -		1,024,856
Engaged in Manufactures - -	48,435	
Dependent on ,, - -	503,345	
MANUFACTURES—Total - -		551,780
Total of the County - - -		1,576,636

TAXATION.

		Paid by the	
		LAND.	MANUFACTURERS.
		£	£
Paid exclusively by the Landed Interest :			
Land Tax - - - - - -		236,249	
Tithes - - - - - -		54,698	
Property Tax—on Land, assessed at - -	£387,861	11,312	
Paid in the Proportion of 2-3rds by the Landed Interest, and 1-3rd by the Manufacturers :			
Poor and County Rates - - -	£758,160	505,440	252,720
Highway Rates - - - -	33,055	22,037	11,018
Church ,, - - - -	94,287	62,858	31,429
Turnpike Trusts - - - -	74,818	49,879	24,939
Property Tax—on Dwelling Houses, assessed at	9,223,475	179,346	89,672
,, on other Property ,, -	1,724,514	33,530	16,768
		1,155,349	426,546
Total of Taxation of the County - - -		£1,581,895	

ENGAGED IN	MALES.		FEMALES.		TOTAL.
	20 years of age and upwards.	Under 20 years of age.	20 years of age and upwards.	Under 20 years of age.	
Agriculture:					
Farmers and Graziers - - - -	2,263	56	278	—	2,597
Agricultural Labourers - - - -	4,472	1,172	126	83	5,853
Gardeners, Nurserymen, and Florists - -	222	11	2	—	235
	6,957	1,239	406	83	8,685
Manufactures:					
Iron Manufacture (all branches) - - -	2,491	532	19	12	3,054
Engineers and Engine Workers - - -	294	27	—	—	321
Engine and Machine Makers - - - -	48	5	1	—	54
Nail Makers - - - - -	125	26	2	—	153
Tin Manufacture (all branches) - - -	120	23	5	2	150
Coke Burners and Dealers - - - -	99	6	9	2	116
Brick and Tile Makers - - - - -	76	9	6	8	99
Weavers - - - - - -	66	17	—	—	83
Hoop Makers and Shavers - - - -	68	11	—	—	79
Paper Makers and Stainers - - - -	62	10	4	3	79
Miscellaneous - - - - -	426	62	40	7	535
	3,875	728	86	34	4,723
All other Classes:					
Employed in Retail Trade or in Handicraft, as Masters or Workmen - - - - - }	9,973	1,555	1,132	258	12,918
Labourers - - - - - - -	13,061	2,739	710	278	16,788
Military and Naval - - - -	914	83	—	—	997
Professional Persons - - - - -	431	—	—	—	431
Other Educated Persons following miscellaneous Pursuits	411	64	106	10	591
Persons engaged in the Government Civil Service - -	62	3	3	—	68
Parochial, Town, and Church Officers	79	—	8	—	87
Domestic Servants - - - - -	1,117	757	2,975	2,707	7,556
Persons returned as Independent - - -	676	36	1,759	151	2,622
Almspeople, Pensioners, Paupers, Lunatics, and Prisoners	303	120	207	107	737
Residue of Population:					
Consisting of the Wives, Children, and others dependent on all Classes - - - - - }	2,025	23,407	26,875	25,845	78,152
Total of all other Classes - - -	29,052	28,764	33,775	29,356	120,947

Divide "all other classes" between the Agriculturists and the Manufacturers in the proportion which these respectively bear to each other, and the numbers engaged in, and dependent on, each interest will stand thus :—

             Engaged in Agriculture - - - -   8,685
             Dependent on   ,,   -   78,344
                  Agriculture—Total   -   -   87,029

             Engaged in Manufactures   -   -   4,723
             Dependent on   ,,   -   -   42,603
                  Manufactures—Total   -   47,326

                  Total of the County   -   -   -   134,355

TAXATION.

		Paid by the	
		Land.	Manufacturers.
Paid exclusively by the Landed Interest :		£	£
Land Tax - - - - - -		9,612	
Tithes - - - - - -		18,103	
Property Tax—on Land, assessed at -	£290,334	8,468	
Paid in the Proportion of 5-8ths by the Landed Interest, and 3-8ths by the Manufacturers:			
Poor and County Rates - - - -	£44,598	27,810	16,788
Highway Rates - - - - -	7,881	4,925	2,956
Church ,, - - - - -	2,821	1,760	1,061
Turnpike Trusts - - - - -	14,498	9,060	5,438
Property Tax - on Dwelling Houses, assessed at -	158,420	2,885	1,735
,, on other Property ,, -	142,407	2,598	1,557
		84,591	29,535
Total of Taxation of the County - - - -		£114,126	

ENGAGED IN	MALES.		FEMALES.		TOTAL.
	20 years of age and upwards.	Under 20 years of age.	20 years of age and upwards.	Under 20 years of age.	
AGRICULTURE:					
Farmers and Graziers - - - - -	6,960	73	414	—	7 447
Agricultural Labourers - - - -	34,592	5,784	735	164	41,275
Gardeners, Nurserymen, and Florists - -	1,534	67	39	3	1,643
	43,086	5,924	1,188	167	50,365
MANUFACTURES:					
Weavers - - - - - -	1,735	117	817	177	2,846
Silk Manufacture (all branches) - - -	621	74	686	360	1,741
Brick and Tile Makers - - - -	462	59	—	—	521
Woollen and Cloth Manufacture (all branches) -	352	64	20	13	449
Rope and Cord Spinners and Makers - -	289	74	1	—	364
Coach Makers (all branches) - - - -	239	54	2	—	295
Factory Workers (branch not specified) - -	21	22	88	110	241
Dyers - - - - - - -	210	17	7	1	235
Basket Makers - - - - -	193	23	12	—	228
Braziers, Brass Workers and Tinkers - -	171	21	—	—	192
Worsted Manufacture (all branches) - -	134	6	33	10	183
Cotton Manufacture (all branches) - -	31	12	87	36	166
Glovers and Glove Makers - - -	93	6	43	14	156
Engineers and Engine Workers - - -	114	12	—	—	126
Engine and Machine Makers - - -	63	8	—	—	71
Turners - - - - - -	99	24	1	—	124
Miscellaneous - - - - -	1,099	164	244	75	1,582
	5,926	757	2,041	796	9,520
ALL OTHER CLASSES:					
Employed in Retail Trade or in Handicraft, as Masters or Workmen - - - - -	29,726	4,079	4,533	963	39,301
Labourers - - - - - -	5,537	760	1,929	65	8,291
Military and Naval - - - -	3,010	307	—	—	3,317
Professional Persons - - - -	1,552	—	—	—	1,552
Other Educated Persons following miscellaneous Pursuits	945	179	842	47	2,013
Persons engaged in the Government Civil Service -	271	3	24	1	299
Parochial, Town, and Church Officers -	472	7	56	1	536
Domestic Servants - - - - -	3,139	1,902	10,999	7,078	23,118
Persons returned as Independent - - -	2,556	69	7,432	301	10,358
Almspeople, Pensioners, Paupers, Lunatics, and Prisoners	1,594	789	1,739	718	4,840
RESIDUE OF POPULATION:					
Consisting of the Wives, Children, and others dependent on all Classes - - -	6,368	80,166	86,790	85,830	259,154
Total of all other Classes -	55,170	88,261	114,344	95,004	352,779

Divide "ALL OTHER CLASSES" between the AGRICULTURISTS and the MANUFACTURERS in the proportion which these respectively bear to each other, and the numbers engaged in, and dependent on, each interest will stand thus:—

Engaged in Agriculture - - -	50,365	
Dependent on ,, - - -	296,698	
AGRICULTURE—Total -		347,063
Engaged in Manufactures - -	9,520	
Dependent on ,, - -	56.081	
MANUFACTURES—Total -		65,601
Total of the County - -		412,664

TAXATION.

	Paid by the	
	LAND.	MANUFACTURERS.
Paid exclusively by the Landed Interest :	£	£
Land Tax - - - - - - -	81,819	
Tithes - - - - - - -	70,417	
Property Tax—on Land, assessed at - - £1,644,933	47,977	
Paid in the Proportion of 5-6ths by the Landed Interest, and 1-6th by the Manufacturers :		
Poor and County Rates - - - - £228,377	190,314	38,063
Highway Rates - - - - - 25,853	21,545	4,308
Church ,, - - - - - 15,108	12,590	2,518
Turnpike Trusts - - - - - 15,588	12,990	2,598
Property Tax—on Dwelling Houses, assessed at - 589,768	14,304	2,860
,, on other Property ,, - 92,669	2,252	450
	454,208	50,797
Total of Taxation of the County - - - - £505,005		

ENGAGED IN	MALES.		FEMALES.		TOTAL.
	20 years of age and upwards.	Under 20 years of age.	20 years of age and upwards.	Under 20 years of age.	
Agriculture :					
Farmers and Graziers - - - - -	3,069	41	205	—	3,315
Agricultural Labourers - - - - -	18,538	3,045	186	23	21,792
Gardeners, Nurserymen, and Florists - - -	586	26	12	—	624
	22,193	3,112	403	23	25,731
Manufactures :					
Boot and Shoe Makers - - -	5,237	1,215	355	214	7,021
Lace Makers - - - - - - -	25	13	1,854	839	2,731
Weavers - - - - - - -	235	45	17	9	306
Silk Manufacture (all branches) - - -	198	54	16	32	300
Brick and Tile Makers - - - -	177	20	—	—	197
Mat Makers - - - - - -	84	20	3	—	107
Coach Makers (all branches) - - - -	87	12	1	—	100
Woollen and Cloth Manufacture (all branches)	79	9	9	3	100
Miscellaneous - - - - - -	780	96	101	14	991
	6,902	1,484	2,356	1,111	11,853
All other Classes :					
Employed in Retail Trade or in Handicraft, as Masters or Workmen - - - - - }	11,817	1,509	1,439	241	15,006
Labourers - - - - - -	2,234	213	767	14	3,228
Military and Naval - - - - -	886	190	—	—	1,076
Professional Persons - - - - -	694	—	—	—	694
Other Educated Persons following miscellaneous Pursuits	448	57	336	24	865
Persons engaged in the Government Civil Service -	98	—	9	—	107
Parochial, Town, and Church Officers - - -	179	1	19	—	199
Domestic Servants - - - - -	1,675	1,048	4,556	3,289	10,568
Persons returned as Independent - - -	1,084	20	2,575	109	3,788
Almspeople, Pensioners, Paupers, Lunatics, and Prisoners	757	414	886	332	2,389
Residue of Population :					
Consisting of the Wives, Children, and others dependent on all Classes - - - - - }	3,423	38,542	40,907	40,852	123,724
Total of all other Classes - - -	23,295	41,994	51,494	44,861	161,644

Divide "**all other classes**" between the Agriculturers and the Manufacturers in the proportion which these respectively bear to each other, and the numbers engaged in, and dependent on, each interest will stand thus :—

Engaged in Agriculture - - -	25,731	
Dependent on ,, - - -	110,666	
Agriculture—Total - - -		136,397
Engaged in Manufactures - - -	11,853	
Dependent on ,, - - -	50,978	
Manufactures—Total - - -		62,831
Total of the County -		199,228

TAXATION.

		Paid by the	
		Land.	Manufacturers.
Paid exclusively by the Landed Interest :		£	£
Land Tax - - - - - - -		47,159	
Tithes - - - - - -		10,879	
Property Tax—on Land, assessed at - - -	£973,144	28,383	
Paid in the Proportion of 2-3rds by the Landed Interest, and 1-3rd by the Manufacturers :			
Poor and County Rates - - - -	£113,725	75,817	37,908
Highway Rates - - - - -	25,055	16,704	8,351
Church ,, - - - - -	8,612	5,742	2,870
Turnpike Trusts - - - - -	29,984	19,990	9,994
Property Tax—on Dwelling Houses, assessed at	263,516	5,124	2,561
,, on other Property ,, - -	15,440	300	150
		210,098	61,834
Total of Taxation of the County - - - -		£271,932	

ENGAGED IN	MALES.		FEMALES.		TOTAL.
	20 years of age and upwards.	Under 20 years of age.	20 years of age and upwards.	Under 20 years of age.	
AGRICULTURE:					
Farmers and Graziers - - - - -	2,817	26	222	—	3,065
Agricultural Labourers - - - -	10,669	1,817	883	290	13,659
Gardeners, Nurserymen, and Florists - - -	550	57	8	—	615
	14,036	1,900	1,113	290	17,339
MANUFACTURES:					
Engineers and Engine Workers - - -	566	173	—	—	739
Engine and Machine Makers - - - -	196	61	—	—	257
„ Turners - - - -	1	—	—	—	1
Iron Manufacture (all branches) - -	415	144	—	—	559
Glass Manufacture (all branches) - - -	374	95	16	3	488
Lead Manufacture - - - - -	253	118	5	1	377
Weavers (branch not specified) - - -	326	11	—	—	337
Potters and Pot Makers - - - -	244	61	17	9	331
Pottery Painters and Printers - - -	12	2	1	—	15
Brick and Tile Makers - - - -	212	61	2	2	277
Rope and Card Spinners and Makers - -	187	71	4	—	262
Tanners - - - - - - -	201	44	—	—	245
Hatters and Hat Makers - - - -	158	19	20	4	201
Glovers and Glove Makers - - - -	42	1	134	15	192
Coach Makers (all branches) - - -	137	41	1	—	179
Paper Makers, Rulers, and Stainers - - -	96	22	18	13	149
Flax Manufacture (all branches) - - -	101	9	10	14	134
Nailers and Nail Makers - - - -	100	19	—	—	119
Moulders (branch not specified) - - -	58	56	—	—	114
Spinners „ - - - -	5	—	84	25	114
Sail, Sail Cloth, and Tarpaulin Makers - -	87	24	—	—	111
Miscellaneous - - - - -	1,311	252	126	33	1,722
	5,082	1,284	438	119	6,923
ALL OTHER CLASSES:					
Employed in Retail Trade or in Handicraft, as Masters or Workmen - - - - -	22,369	4,485	3,119	402	30,375
Labourers - - - - -	11,382	3,206	982	45	15,615
Military and Naval - - - -	3,137	282	—	—	3,419
Professional Persons - - - -	747	—	—	—	747
Other Educated Persons following miscellaneous Pursuits	1,127	202	277	13	1,619
Persons engaged in the Government Civil Service -	290	1	4	—	295
Parochial, Town, and Church Officers - - -	371	10	31	—	412
Domestic Servants - - - -	1,265	497	7,346	4,810	13,918
Persons returned as Independent - - -	1,315	30	5,367	163	6,875
Almspeople, Pensioners, Paupers, Lunatics, and Prisoners	551	226	876	205	1,858
RESIDUE OF POPULATION:					
Consisting of the Wives, Children, and others dependent on all Classes - - - - -	2,950	44,545	52,481	50,907	150,883
Total of all other Classes - - -	45,504	53,484	70,483	56,545	226,016

Divide "ALL OTHER CLASSES" between the AGRICULTURISTS and the MANUFACTURERS in the proportion which these respectively bear to each other, and the numbers engaged in, and dependent on, each interest will stand thus :—

Engaged in Agriculture - - -	17,339	
Dependent on „ - - -	161,524	
AGRICULTURE—Total - - -		178,863
Engaged in Manufactures - - -	6,923	
Dependent on „ - - -	64,492	
MANUFACTURES—Total - -		71,415
Total of the County - - -		250,278

TAXATION.

		Paid by the	
		LAND.	MANUFACTURERS
Paid exclusively by the Landed Interest :		£	£
Land Tax - - - - - - -		13,460	
Tithes - - - - - - -		58,866	
Property Tax—on Land, assessed at - - -	£855,856		
Paid in the Proportion of 5-7ths by the Landed Interest, and 2-7ths by the Manufacturers :			
Poor and County Rates - - - -	£84,402	60,285	24,117
Highway Rates - - - - -	15,484	11,060	4,424
Church „ - - - - -	4,396	3,210	1,186
Turnpike Trusts - - - -	17,285	12,345	4,940
Property Tax—on Dwelling Houses, assessed at -	431,877	8,995	3,601
„ on other Property „ -	274,700	5,720	2,292
		173,941	30,560
Total Taxation of the County - - - -		£204,501	

(*For those engaged in Mines, see* "*Mining Interest.*")

ENGAGED IN	MALES.		FEMALES.		TOTAL.
	20 years of age and upwards.	Under 20 years of age.	20 years of age and upwards.	Under 20 years of age.	
Agriculture:					
Farmers and Graziers - - - - -	3,444	49	294	—	3,787
Agricultural Labourers - - - -	12,769	2,923	220	14	15,926
Gardeners, Nurserymen, and Florists - -	595	34	15	1	645
	16,808	3,006	529	15	20,358
Manufactures:					
Hose (Stocking) Manufacture (all branches) -	9,383	1,550	1,809	671	13,413
Lace Manufacture (all branches) - - -	3,528	455	2 763	1,139	7,885
Cotton Manufacture (all branches) - -	439	197	456	332	1,424
Factory Workers (branch not specified) -	164	89	206	141	600
Brick and Tile Makers - - - -	335	87	3	—	425
Bleachers - - - - -	231	85	5	3	324
Silk Manufacture (all branches) - - -	241	52	10	3	306
Engineers and Engine Workers - - -	66	41	128	69	304
Engine and Machine Makers - - -	184	19	—	—	203
Hatters and Hat Makers - - - -	113	19	—	—	132
Brass Founders and Moulders - - -	110	10	36	21	177
Braziers, Brass Workers, and Tinkers - -	128	37	3	—	168
Needle Makers - - - - -	135	29	3	—	167
Turners - - - - - -	126	33	—	—	159
Coach Makers (all branches) - - -	111	20	—	—	131
Weavers - - - - - -	113	7	5	1	126
Spinners (branch not specified) - - -	1	2	109	11	123
Rope and Cord Makers, and Spinners - -	96	18	6	—	120
Chair Makers - - - - -	93	19	4	—	116
Basket Makers - - - - -	97	13	2	—	112
Miscellaneous	971	156	135	33	1,295
	16,665	2,938	5,683	2,424	27,710
All other Classes:					
Employed in Retail Trade or in Handicraft, as Masters or Workmen - - - - - }	17,116	2,947	3,076	524	23,663
Labourers - - - - - -	3,855	541	1,020	44	5,460
Military and Naval - - - -	1,107	63	—	—	1,170
Professional Persons - - - -	664	—	—	—	664
Other Educated Persons following miscellaneous Pursuits	740	121	420	21	1,302
Persons engaged in the Government Civil Service -	91	—	4	—	95
Parochial, Town, and Church Officers - -	218	—	16	—	234
Domestic Servants - - - - -	1,617	1,188	5,715	4,763	13,283
Persons returned as Independent - - -	1,325	22	3,383	88	4,818
Almspeople, Pensioners, Paupers, Lunatics, and Prisoners	723	373	589	238	1,923
Residue of Population:					
Consisting of the Wives, Children, and others dependent on all Classes - - - }	3,241	46,385	48,685	50,919	149,230
Total of all other Classes - - -	30,697	51,640	62,908	56,597	201,842

Divide "ALL OTHER CLASSES" between the AGRICULTURISTS and the MANUFACTURERS in the proportion which these respectively bear to each other, and the numbers engaged in, and dependent on, each interest, will stand thus :—

Engaged in Agriculture - - -	20,358		
Dependent on ,, - - -	85,486		
AGRICULTURE—Total - -		105,844	
Engaged in Manufactures - - -	27,710		
Dependent on - - -	116,356		
MANUFACTURERS—Total - -		144,066	
Total of the County - - -		249,910	

TAXATION.

		Paid by the	
		Land.	Manufacturers.
		£	£
Paid exclusively by the Landed Interest:			
Land Tax - - - - - - -		26,733	
Tithes - - - - - - -		12,469	
Property Tax—on Land, assessed at - - -	£707,756		
Paid in the Proportion of 2-5ths by the Landed Interest, and 3-5ths by the Manufacturers:			
Poor and County Rates - - - -	£87,770	35,108	52,662
Highway Rates - - - - -	23,091	9,236	13,855
Church ,, - - - - -	4,311	1,724	2,587
Turnpike Trusts - - - - -	14,959	5,982	8,977
Property Tax—on Dwelling Houses, assessed at -	380,744	4,442	6,663
,, on other Property ,, -	53,867	628	943
		96,322	85,687

Total of Taxation of the County - - - £182,009

(*For those engaged in Mines, see "Mining Interest."*)

ENGAGED IN	MALES.		FEMALES.		TOTAL.
	20 years of age and upwards.	Under 20 years of age.	20 years of age and upwards.	Under 20 years of age.	
AGRICULTURE;					
Farmers and Graziers - - - -	2,178	23	164	—	2,365
Agricultural Labourers - - - -	14,483	2,350	870	206	17,909
Gardeners, Nurserymen, and Florists - -	486	22	6	1	515
	17,147	2,395	1,040	207	20,789
MANUFACTURES :					
Lace Makers - - - - -	1	3	452	108	564
Weavers (all branches) - - - -	297	24	11	1	333
Woollen and Woollen Cloth Manufacture -	165	12	17	3	197
Chair Makers - - - - -	128	14	4	—	146
Brick and Tile Makers - - -	120	10	3	—	133
Coachmakers (all branches) - - -	109	14	—	—	123
Plush Manufacture - - - -	103	13	—	—	116
Glovers and Glove Makers - - -	87	1	140	53	281
Miscellaneous - - - - -	653	75	60	33	821
	1,663	166	687	198	2,714
ALL OTHER CLASSES :					
Employed in Retail Trade or in Handicraft, as Masters or Workmen - - - - -	11,637	1,438	1,344	236	14,655
Labourers - - - - -	2,636	376	825	41	3,878
Military and Naval - - - -	340	16	—	—	356
Professional Persons - - - -	661	—	—	—	661
Other Educated Persons, following miscellaneous Pursuits	508	53	326	23	910
Persons engaged in the Government Civil Service -	89	3	6	—	98
Parochial, Town, and Church Officers - -	160	1	13	—	174
Domestic Servants - - - -	1,635	716	4.210	3,012	9,573
Persons returned as Independent - -	1,338	62	2,336	121	3,857
Almspeople, Pensioners, Paupers, Lunatics, and Prisoners	628	351	573	368	1,920
RESIDUE OF POPULATION :					
Consisting of the Wives, Children, and others dependent on all Classes - - - - -	4,069	32,353	32,117	33,519	102,058
Total of all other Classes - - -	23,701	35,369	41,750	37,320	138,140

Divide " ALL OTHER CLASSES" between the AGRICULTURISTS and the MANUFACTURES in the proportion which these respectively bear to each other, and the numbers engaged in, and dependent on, each interest will stand thus :—

Engaged in Agriculture - - -	20,789	
Dependent on ,, - -	122,189	
AGRICULTURE—Total - -		142,978
Engaged in Manufactures - - -	2,714	
Dependent on ,, -	15,951	
MANUFACTURES—Total - -		18,665
Total of the County - - -		161,643

TAXATION.

	Paid by the	
	LAND.	MANUFACTURERS.
Paid exclusively by the Landed Interest :	£	£
Land Tax - - - - - - -	38,127	
Tithes - - - - - - -	22,193	
Property Tax—on Land, assessed at - - £602,395	17,569	
Paid in the Proportion of 8-9ths by the Landed Interest, and 1-9th by the Manufacturers :		
Poor and County Rates - - - £91,065	79,836	11,229
Highway Rates - - - - - 13,246	11,774	1,472
Church ,, - - - - - 6,069	5,385	674
Turnpike Trusts - - - - 18,797	16,709	2,088
Property Tax—on Dwelling Houses, assessed at - 285,849	7,411	926
,, on other Property ,, - - 137,176	3,556	444
	202,560	16,833
Total of Taxation of the County - - - - £219,393		

ENGAGED IN	MALES.		FEMALES.		TOTAL.
	20 years of age and upwards.	Under 20 years of age.	20 years of age and upwards.	Under 20 years of age.	
Agriculture:					
Farmers and Graziers - - - - -	567	2	47	—	616
Agricultural Labourers - - - -	2,169	420	39	1	2,629
Gardeners, Nurserymen, and Florists - -	64	6	1	—	71
	2,800	428	87	1	3,316
Manufactures:					
There is no leading branch of Manufacture carried on in this County					
Miscellaneous - - - - -	118	7	14	15	154
	118	7	14	15	154
All other Classes:					
Employed in Retail Trade or in Handicraft, as Masters or Workmen - - - - -	1,423	185	165	28	1,801
Labourers - - - - - - -	301	12	116	1	430
Military and Naval - - - -	25	—	—	—	25
Professional Persons - - - - -	90	—	—	—	90
Other educated Persons following Miscellaneous Pursuits	38	—	50	—	90
Persons engaged in the Government Civil Service -	7	—	1	2	8
Parochial, Town, and Church Officers - -	11	—	3	—	14
Domestic Servants - - - - -	242	165	564	464	1,435
Persons returned as Independent - - -	112	1	297	6	416
Almspeople, Pensioners, Paupers, Lunatics, and Prisoners	65	42	121	31	259
Residue of Population:					
Consisting of the Wives, Children, and others dependent on all Classes - - - - -	420	4,230	4,339	4,27 5	13,264
Total of all other Classes - - -	2,734	4,635	5,656	4,807	17,832

Divide " all other classes " between the Agriculturists and the Manufacturers in the proportion which these respectively bear to each other, and the numbers engaged in, and dependent on, each interest will stand thus—

Engaged in Agriculture	-	-	-	3,316	
Dependent on ,,	-	-	-	17,041	
Agriculture—Total	-		-		20,357
Engaged in Manufactures	-	-		154	
Dependent on ,,	.	-		791	
Manufactures—Total	-				945
Total of the County	-	-			21,302

TAXATION.

	Paid by the	
	Land.	Manufacturers.
Paid exclusively by the Landed Interest:	£	£
Land Tax - - - - - - -	5,473	
Tithes - - - - - - - -	3,518	
Property Tax—on Land, assessed at - £130,935	3,818	
Paid in the Proportion of 21-22ndths by the Landed Interest: and 1-22ndth by the Manufacturers:		
Poor and County Rates - - - £9,763	9,320	443
Highway Rates - - - - - 4,694	4,481	213
Church ,, - - - - - 874	839	35
Turnpike Trusts - - - - 3,319	3,169	150
Property Tax—on Dwelling Houses, asscssed at - 21,632	602	28
,, on other Property ,, - 4,420	123	5
	31,343	874
Total of Taxation of the County - - - £32,217		

ENGAGED IN	MALES.		FEMALES.		TOTAL.
	20 years of age and upwards.	Under 20 years of age.	20 years of age and upwards.	Under 20 years of age.	
AGRICULTURE:					
Farmers and Graziers - - - -	4,487	43	494	—	5,024
Agricultural Labourers - - -	17,075	4,929	297	60	22,361
Gardeners, Nurserymen, and Florists - -	584	23	11	—	618
	22,146	4,995	802	60	28,003
MANUFACTURES:					
Nail Manufacture (all branches) - -	846	128	222	78	1,274
Iron Manufacture (all branches) - - -	699	347	4	10	1,060
Brick and Tile Makers - - -	386	68	9	13	476
Engineers and Engine Workers - - -	315	58	—	3	376
Engine and Machine Makers - - -	38	13	—	—	51
Factory Workers (branch not specified) - -	30	64	109	114	317
Potters - - - - - -	112	18	48	27	205
China Painters and Stainers - - -	74	11	50	27	162
Weavers (branch not specified) - - -	132	5	14	6	157
Thread Manufacture (all branches) -	20	30	19	54	123
Hatters and Hat Makers - - -	94	4	12	—	110
Flax Manufacture (all branches - - -	43	26	12	22	103
Coach Makers (all branches) - -	80	22	—	—	102
Tanners - - - - -	95	4	2	—	101
Miscellaneous - - - -	969	175	179	88	1,411
	3,933	973	680	442	6,028
ALL OTHER CLASSES:					
Employed in Retail Trade or in Handicraft, as Masters or Workmen - - - - -	17,253	2,950	1,916	338	22,457
Labourers - - - - -	9,939	2,677	994	318	13,928
Military and Naval - - - -	655	57	—	—	712
Professional Persons - - - -	744	-	—	—	744
Other educated Persons following miscellaneous Pursuits	878	100	394	16	1,388
Persons engaged in the Government Civil Service -	129	—	17	1	147
Parochial, Town, and Church Officers - -	200	1	32	—	233
Domestic Servants - - - -	2,096	1,133	7.636	6,616	17,481
Persons returned as Independent - -	1,447	56	3,686	127	5,316
Almspeople, Pensioners, Paupers, Lunatics, and Prisoners	708	397	636	316	2,057
RESIDUE OF POPULATION:					
Consisting of the Wives, Children, and others dependent on all Classes - - - -	3,617	42,277	48,270	46,390	140,554
Total of all other Classes - - -	37,666	49,648	63,581	54,122	205,017

Divide "ALL OTHER CLASSES" between the AGRICULTURISTS and the MANUFACTURERS in the proportion which these respectively bear to each other, and the numbers engaged in, and dependent on, each interest will stand thus:—

Engaged in Agriculture - - -	28,003	
Dependent on ,, - - - -	168,702	
AGRICULTURE—Total - -		196,705
Engaged in Manufactures - - -	6,028	
Dependent on ,, - - -	36,315	
MANUFACTURES—Total -		42,343
Total of the County - -		239,048

TAXATION.

	Paid by the	
	LAND.	MANUFACTURERS.
Paid exclusively by the Landed Interest:	£	£
Land Tax - - - - - - -	28,684	
Tithes - - - - - - -	31,366	
Property Tax—on Land, assessed at - - £1,050,131	30,628	
Paid in the Proportion of 9-11ths by the Landed Interest, and 2-11ths by the Manufacturers:		
Poor and County Rates - - - - £95,684	78,288	17,396
Highway Rates - - - - - 12,362	10,116	2,246
Church ,, - - - - - 8,595	7,033	1,562
Turnpike Trusts - - - - 26,885	21,997	4,888
Property Tax—on Dwelling Houses, assessed at - 254,353	6,070	1,348
,, on other Property ,, - - 170,845	4,076	906
	218,258	28,346
Total of Taxation of the County - - -	£246,604	

(*For those engaged in Mines, see "Mining Interest."*)

ENGAGED IN	MALES. 20 years of age and upwards.	Under 20 years of age.	FEMALES. 20 years of age and upwards.	Under 20 years of age.	TOTAL.
AGRICULTURE:					
Farmers and Graziers	8,196	84	407	—	8,687
Agricultural Labourers	26,949	5,693	1,382	314	34,338
Gardeners, Nurserymen, and Florists	1,340	68	33	1	1,442
	36,485	5,845	1,822	315	44,467
MANUFACTURES:					
Glovers and Glove Makers	614	170	1,365	707	2,856
Woollen and Cloth Manufacture	998	248	604	177	2,027
Weavers (all branches)	904	79	433	105	1,521
Silk Manufacture (all branches)	92	87	451	390	1,020
Lace Manufacture (all branches)	178	136	125	116	555
Coach Makers	263	53	2	—	318
Brick and Tile Makers	216	20	4	5	245
Tanners	227	16	2	—	245
Brass Founders and Moulders, Braziers and Brass Workers, and Tinkers	205	32	—	—	237
Stocking Makers	5	2	158	62	227
Rope, Cord, and Twine Makers	151	37	23	5	216
Knitters	1	—	183	29	213
Basket Makers	167	19	16	—	202
Spinners (branch not specified)	10	2	145	16	173
Cotton Manufacture (all branches)	31	66	51	11	159
Flax Manufacture (all branches)	87	11	29	24	151
Factory Workers (branch not specified)	23	33	26	62	144
Paper Makers and Stainers	107	10	11	4	132
Tool Makers	117	14	—	—	131
Miscellaneous	1,480	202	325	116	2,123
	5,876	1,237	3,953	1,829	12,895
ALL OTHER CLASSES:					
Employed in Retail Trade or in Handicraft, as Masters or Workmen	31,738	4,618	5,952	1,328	43,636
Labourers	13,561	2,932	3,723	258	20,474
Military and Naval	1,428	118	—	—	1,546
Professional Persons	1,616	—	—	—	1,616
Other Educated Persons following miscellaneous Pursuits	1,845	189	1,013	60	3,107
Persons engaged in the Government Civil Service	254	2	24	—	280
Parochial, Town, and Church Officers	350	2	46		398
Domestic Servants	3,527	1,987	14,875	8,636	29,025
Persons returned as Independent	3,958	163	10,340	446	14,907
Almspeople, Pensioners, Paupers, Lunatics, and Prisoners	1,827	1,030	2,063	776	5,696
RESIDUE OF POPULATION:					
Consisting of the Wives, Children, and others dependent on all Classes	7,536	81,283	82,999	86,117	257,935
Total of all other Classes	67,640	92,324	121,035	97,621	378,620

Divide "ALL OTHER CLASSES," between the AGRICULTURISTS and the MANUFACTURERS in the proportion which these respectively bear to each other, and the numbers engaged in, and dependent on, each interest will stand thus :—

Engaged in Agriculture	44,467	
Dependent on	293,507	
AGRICULTURE—Total		337,974
Engaged in Manufactures	12,895	
Dependent on	85,113	
MANUFACTURES—Total		98,008
Total of the County		435,982

TAXATION.

		Paid by the LAND. £	MANUFACTURERS £
Paid exclusively by the Landed Interest.			
Land Tax		69,902	
Tithes		59,812	
Property Tax—on Land, assessed at	£1,715,497	50,035	
Paid in the Proportion of 7-9ths by the Landed Interest, and 2-9ths by the Manufacturers.			
Poor and County Rates	£203,622	158,374	45,248
Highway Rates	37,889	33,471	4,418
Church ,,	16,780	13,052	3,728
Turnpike Trusts	57,288	44,558	12,730
Property Tax—on Dwelling Houses, assessed at	1,025,297	23,243	6,640
,, on other Property ,,	250,952	5,693	1,626
		458,140	74,390
Total of Taxation of the County		£532,530	

(*For those engaged in Mines, see "Mining Interest."*)

ENGAGED IN	MALES.		FEMALES.		TOTAL.
	20 years of age and upwards.	Under 20 years of age.	20 years of age and upwards.	Under 20 years of age	
AGRICULTURE :					
Farmers and Graziers	3,420	47	147	—	3,614
Agricultural Labourers	24,898	4,948	514	175	30,535
Gardeners, Nurserymen, and Florists	1,320	61	11	—	1,392
	29,638	5,056	672	175	35,541
MANUFACTURES :					
Brick and Tile Makers	334	25	4	—	363
Coachmakers (all branches)	206	58	2	1	267
Rope and Cord Spinners	241	18	2	2	263
Lace Makers -	86	8	82	30	206
Silk Manufacture (all branches)	21	9	114	59	203
Paper Makers	102	26	32	11	171
Engineers and Engine Workers	138	12	—	—	150
Engine and Machine Makers	15	2	—	—	17
Tanners -	118	6	2	—	126
Miscellaneous	1,299	156	140	51	1,646
	2,560	320	378	154	3,412
ALL OTHER CLASSES :					
Employed in Retail Trade or in Handicraft, as Masters or Workmen	26,241	3,186	3,896	731	34,054
Labourers	9,235	1,176	2,207	97	12,715
Military and Naval	7,158	1,082	—	—	8,240
Professional Persons	1,158	—	—	—	1,158
Other Educated Persons following miscellaneous pursuits	1,364	161	790	44	2,359
Persons engaged in the Government Civil Service -	669	5	17	—	691
Parochial, Town, and Church Officers	421	3	54	—	478
Domestic Servants	3,692	1,589	11,403	6,014	22,698
Persons returned as Independent	2,989	161	8,175	437	11,762
Almspeople, Pensioners, Paupers, Lunatics, and Prisoners	3,616	1,208	1,510	874	7,208
RESIDUE OF POPULATION :					
Consisting of the Wives, Children, and others dependent on all Classes	5,234	67,122	70,611	71,721	214,688
Total of all other Classes	61,777	75,693	98,663	79,918	316,051

Divide "ALL OTHER CLASSES" between the AGRICULTURISTS and the MANUFACTURERS in the proportion which these respectively bear to each other, and the numbers engaged in, and dependent on, each interest will stand thus :—

Engaged in Agriculture	35,541	
Dependent on ,,	288,368	
AGRICULTURE—Total		323,909
Engaged in Manufactures	3,412	
Dependent on ,,	27,683	
MANUFACTURES—Total		31,095
Total of the County		355,064

TAXATION.

		Paid by the	
		LAND.	MANUFACTURERS.
Paid exclusively by the Landed Interest :		£	£
Land Tax		52,596	
Tithes -		114,169	
Property Tax - on Land, assessed at	£777,636	22,681	
Paid in the Proportion of 10-11ths by the Landed Interest, and 1-11th by the Manufacturers :			
Poor and County Rates	£179,195	162,905	16,290
Highway Rates	20,714	18,831	1,883
Church ,,	9,628	8,753	875
Turnpike Trusts	24,611	22,374	2,237
Property Tax—on Dwelling Houses, assessed at	730,959	19,390	1,929
,, on other Property ,,	152,852	4,053	405
		415,762	23,619
Total of Taxation of the County		£439,371	

ENGAGED IN	MALES.		FEMALES.		TOTAL.
	20 years of age and upwards.	Under 20 years of age.	20 years of age and upwards.	Under 20 years of age.	
AGRICULTURE:					
Farmers and Graziers -	5,791	39	685	—	6,515
Agricultural Labourers	17,484	3,847	194	43	21,568
Gardeners, Nurserymen, and Florists	989	38	10	—	1,037
	24,264	3,924	889	43	29,120
MANUFACTURES:					
Pottery Manufacture (all branches) -	7,690	3,757	3,397	2,981	17,825
Iron and Steel Manufacture (all branches)	4,744	1,607	70	26	6,447
Lock and Key Smiths and Bell Hangers	3,278	959	25	6	4,268
Nailers and Nail Makers	2,462	395	771	364	3,992
Silk Manufacture (all branches)	546	353	548	578	2,025
Brick and Tile Makers	1,304	323	69	81	1,777
Engineers and Engine Workers	1,503	243	5	1	1,752
Engine and Machine Makers -	257	48	2	—	307
Cotton Manufacture (all branches)	193	108	481	361	1,143
Glass Manufacture (all branches)	678	224	25	9	936
Gun and Pistol Makers (all branches)	613	112	1	3	729
Hatters and Hat Makers	572	48	61	29	710
Bit Makers	477	170	11	4	662
Moulders (branch not specified) -	468	180	1	3	652
Brass Founders, Braziers, and Brass Workers -	487	137	8	1	633
Tin-Plate Workers and Tinmen	420	160	15	17	612
Screw Makers	291	44	87	74	496
Japanners	207	105	77	85	474
Coach Makers (all branches)	397	72	4	1	474
Tape Manufacture (all branches)	222	53	132	39	446
Crate Makers	347	86	5	1	439
Chain Makers	284	99	6	8	397
Hinge Makers	307	79	7	1	394
Platers	269	66	3	—	338
Factory Workers (branch not specified)	185	85	13	27	310
Boiler Makers	250	41	—	—	291
Weavers	189	18	39	8	254
Rope and Cord Spinners and Makers	172	37	8	—	217
Buckle Makers	147	34	27	8	216
File Makers	157	46	2	2	207
Turners -	169	32	—	—	201
Miscellaneous	2,557	484	419	165	3,625
	31,842	10,205	6,319	4,883	53,249
ALL OTHER CLASSES:					
Employed in Retail Trade or in Handicraft, as Masters or Workmen	32,361	5,207	3,822	942	42,332
Labourers	26,799	6,172	1,722	224	34,917
Military and Naval	1,657	174	—	—	1,831
Professional Persons	954	—	—	—	954
Other Educated Persons following miscellaneous Pursuits	2,157	263	749	38	3,207
Persons engaged in the Government Civil Service	207	3	28	—	238
Parochial, Town, and Church Officers	338	6	32	—	376
Domestic Servants	2,778	1,473	9,642	9,438	23,331
Persons returned as Independent	2,271	75	5,594	233	8,173
Almspeople, Pensioners, Paupers, Lunatics, and Prisoners	1,461	611	1,048	549	3,669
RESIDUE OF POPULATION:					
Consisting of the Wives, Children, and others dependent on all Classes	6,719	96,964	98,988	106,436	309,107
Total of all other Classes -	77,702	110,948	121,625	117,860	428,135

Divide "ALL OTHER CLASSES" between the AGRICULTURISTS and the MANUFACTURERS in the proportion which these respectively bear to each other, and the numbers engaged in, and dependent on, each interest will stand thus:—

Engaged in Agriculture -	29,120	
Dependent on ,, -	151,360	
AGRICULTURE—Total -		180,480
Engaged in Manufactures -	53,249	
Dependent on ,, -	276,775	
MANUFACTURES—Total -		330,024
Total of the County -		510,504

TAXATION.

		Paid by the	
		LAND.	MANUFACTURERS.
Paid exclusively by the Landed Interest:		£	£
Land Tax -		26,140	
Tithes -		33,074	
Property Tax—on Land, assessed at -	£1,104,150	32,204	
Paid in the Proportion of 4-11ths by the Landed Interest, and 7-11th by the Manufacturers:			
Poor and County Rates -	£172,965	62,896	110,069
Highway Rates -	23,908	8,692	15,216
Church ,, -	12,614	4,584	8,030
Turnpike Trusts -	59,027	21,464	37,563
Property Tax—on Dwelling Houses, assessed at -	818,993	8,684	15,193
,, on other Property ,, -	518,410	5,496	9,624
		203,234	195,695

Total of Taxation of the County -   £398,929

(For those engaged in Mines, see "Mining Interest.")

ENGAGED IN	MALES.		FEMALES.		TOTAL.
	20 years of age and upwards.	Under 20 years of age.	20 years of age and upwards.	Under 20 years of age.	
AGRICULTURE :					
Farmers and Graziers - - - -	4,957	44	381	—	5,382
Agricultural Labourers - - - -	31,700	4,952	567	132	37,351
Gardeners, Nurserymen, and Florists - -	1,059	57	9	—	1,125
	37,716	5,053	957	132	43,858
MANUFACTURES :					
Silk Manufacture (all branches) - - -	216	89	240	329	874
Brick and Tile Makers - - - -	350	42	5	—	397
Weavers (branch not specified) - - - -	233	29	61	9	332
Coach Makers (all branches) - - -	197	53	2	—	252
Basket Makers and Sellers - - - -	142	14	13	6	175
Glovers and Glove Makers - - - -	84	3	61	7	155
Rope and Cord Spinners - - - -	125	27	2	1	155
Brass Finishers and Workers, Brass Founders, and Braziers and Tinkers - - -	114	16	4	—	134
Iron Manufacture (all branches) - -	110	21	—	—	131
Woollen Manufacture (all branches) - - -	86	3	20	10	119
Miscellaneous - - - - -	807	103	209	59	1,178
	2,464	400	617	421	3,902
ALL OTHER CLASSES :					
Employed in Retail Trade or in Handicraft, as Masters or Workmen - - - -	21,476	2,988	2,608	598	27,670
Labourers - - - - -	3,235	488	1,445	44	5,212
Military and Naval - - - - -	1,779	148	—	—	1,927
Professional Persons - - - -	1,159	—	—	—	1,159
Other Educated Persons following miscellaneous Pursuits	652	81	656	47	1,436
Persons engaged in the Government Civil Service -	249	4	12	—	265
Parochial, Town, and Church Officers - -	257	4	35	—	296
Domestic Servants - - - - -	2,330	1,225	8,350	5,912	17,817
Persons returned as Independent - - -	2,007	76	5,157	259	7,499
Almspeople, Pensioners, Paupers, Lunatics, and Prisoners	1,332	636	1,331	602	3,901
RESIDUE OF POPULATION :					
Consisting of the Wives, Children, and others dependent on all Classes - - - -	4,951	63,397	65,553	66,230	200,131
Total of all other Classes -	39,427	69,047	85,147	73,692	267,313

Divide " ALL OTHER CLASSES " between the AGRICULTURISTS and the MANUFACTURERS in the proportion which these respectively bear to each other, and the numbers engaged in, and dependent on, each interest will stand thus : —

Engaged in Agriculture - - -	43,858	
Dependent on ,, - - -	245,474	
AGRICULTURE—Total - -		289,332
Engaged in Manufactures - -	3,902	
Dependent on ,, - - -	21,839	
MANUFACTURES—Total - -		25,741
Total of the County - - -		315,073

TAXATION.

	Paid by the	
	LAND.	MANUFACTURERS.
Paid exclusively by the Landed Interest :	£	£
Land Tax - - - - - - - -	72,499	
Tithes - - - - - - - -	65,714	
Property Tax—on Land, assessed at - - £1,147,535	33,469	
Paid in the Proportion of 11-12ths by the Landed Interest, and 1-12ths by the Manufacturers :		
Poor and County Rates - - - - - £173,829	159,344	14,485
Highway Rates - - - - - - 26,304	24,112	2,192
Church ,, - - - - - - 14,443	13,240	1,203
Turnpike Trusts - - - - - - 9,983	9,151	832
Property Tax—on Dwelling Houses, assessed at - - 479,407	12,817	1,165
,, on other Property ,, - - - 90,883	2,430	220
	392,776	20,097
Total of Taxation of the County - - - £412,873		

ENGAGED IN	MALES.		FEMALES.		TOTAL.
	20 years of age and upwards.	Under 20 years of age.	20 years of age and upwards.	Under 20 years of age.	
Agriculture:					
Farmers and Graziers - - - -	1,892	27	111	—	2,030
Agricultural Labourers - - - -	15,865	3,140	207	70	19,282
Gardeners, Nurserymen, and Florists - -	3,734	176	118	12	4,040
	21,491	3,343	436	82	25,352
Manufactures:					
Hatters and Hat Manufacturers - - -	1,565	117	368	89	2,139
Engineers and Engine Workers - - -	1,308	172	1	—	1,481
Engine and Machine Makers - - -	82	6	—	—	88
,, Turners - - - - -	1	—	—	—	1
Tanners - - - - - -	797	73	7	—	877
Coach Makers (all branches) - - - -	711	81	8	—	800
Chair Makers - - - - -	431	69	53	15	568
Paper Makers (all branches) - - - -	253	51	26	9	339
Brick and Tile Makers - - - -	430	62	2	—	494
Brass Finishers and Workers, Brass Founders, and Braziers and Tinkers - - - - }	359	52	4	—	415
Rope and Cord Spinners and Makers - -	284	57	32	—	373
Turners - - - - - -	298	46	7	—	351
Glass Manufacture (all branches) - - -	294	31	2	—	327
Dyers - - - - - -	284	28	14	—	326
Tin Plate Workers and Tinmen - - -	274	29	—	1	304
Basket Makers - - - - -	232	39	19	2	292
Silk Manufacture (all branches) - - -	147	19	47	19	232
Iron Manufacture (all branches) - - -	202	21	2	—	225
Potters - - - - - -	181	34	1	1	217
Glovers and Glove Makers - - - -	86	5	93	18	202
Miscellaneous - - - - -	3,527	465	521	154	4,667
	11,746	1,457	1,207	308	14,718
All other Classes:					
Employed in Retail Trade or in Handicraft, as Masters or Workmen - - - - - }	60,517	6,419	11,282	1,453	79,671
Labourers - - - - - -	21,852	2,509	7,473	245	32,079
Military and Naval - - - - -	3,599	518	—	—	4,117
Professional Persons - - - -	2,386	—	—	—	2,386
Other Educated Persons following miscellaneous Pursuits	6,939	903	1,926	103	9,871
Persons engaged in the Government Civil Service -	841	17	10	—	868
Parochial, Town, and Church Officers - -	1,565	9	117	4	1,695
Domestic Servants - - - -	6,737	2,625	24,168	10,672	44,202
Persons returned as Independent - - -	7,310	293	16,250	677	24,530
Almspeople, Pensioners, Paupers, Lunatics, and Prisoners	2,880	2,240	3,162	1,935	10,217
Residue of Population;					
Consisting of the Wives, Children, and others dependent on all Classes - - - - - }	6,906	103,137	112,024	110,905	332,972
Total of all other Classes - - -	121,532	118,670	176,412	125,994	542,608

Divide "All other classes" between the Agriculturists and the Manufacturers in the proportion which these respectively bear to each other, and the numbers engaged in, and dependent on, each interest will stand thus:—

Engaged in Agriculture	-	-	25,352	
Dependent on ,,	-	-	478,720	
Agriculture—Total	-	-		504,072
Engaged in Manufactures	-	-	14,718	
Dependent on ,,	-	-	63,888	
Manufactures—Total	-	-		78,606
Total of the County	-	-		582,678

TAXATION.

		Paid by the	
		Land.	Manufacturers.
		£	£
Paid exclusively by the Landed Interest:			
Land Tax - - - - - -	-	65,110	
Tithes - - - - - -	-	43,692	
Property Tax—on Land, assessed at - -	£433,504	12,643	
Paid in the Proportion of 11-13ths by the Landed Interest, and 2-13ths by the Manufacturers:			
Poor and County Rates - - - -	£299,718	253,608	46,110
Highway Rates - - - - -	29,430	24,810	4,620
Church ,, - - - - -	19,772	18,251	1,521
Turnpike Trusts - - - -	56,951	48,191	8,760
Property Tax—on Dwelling Houses, assessed at -	2,158,725	53,276	9,686
,, on other Property ,, -	346,838	8,560	1,556
		528,141	72,253
Total of Taxation of the County - - -		£600,394	

ENGAGED IN	MALES.		FEMALES.		TOTAL.
	20 years of age and upwards.	Under 20 years of age.	20 years of age and upwards.	Under 20 years of age.	
AGRICULTURE :					
Farmers and Graziers - - - -	3,805	31	206	—	4,042
Agricultural Labourers - - - -	24,845	5,264	323	90	30,522
Gardeners, Nurserymen, and Florists - -	1,069	58	16	1	1,144
	29,719	5,353	545	91	35,708
MANUFACTURES :					
There is no leading branch of Manufactures carried on in this County. The largest numbers employed in any one branch are the—					
Brick and Tile Makers - - - -	299	47	1	—	347
Coach Makers (all branches) - - -	147	28	1	—	176
Miscellaneous - - - - -	1,178	129	101	20	1,428
	1,624	204	103	20	1,951
ALL OTHER CLASSES :					
Employed in Retail Trade or in Handicraft, as Masters or Workmen - - - - - -	21,122	2,579	2,774	708	27,183
Labourers - - - - - -	7,242	796	2,052	59	10,149
Military and Naval - - - - -	2,498	232	—	—	2,730
Professional Persons - - - -	1,002	—	—	—	1,002
Other Educated Persons following miscellaneous Pursuits	1,042	107	693	57	1,899
Persons engaged in the Government Civil Service -	612	8	9	—	629
Parochial, Town, and Church Officers - - -	313	2	51	1	367
Domestic Servants - - - - -	3,499	1,361	10,829	6,519	22,208
Persons returned as Independent - - -	2,580	117	5,922	296	8,915
Almspeople, Pensioners, Paupers, Lunatics, and Prisoners	1,319	1,016	990	912	4,237
RESIDUE OF POPULATION :					
Consisting of the Wives, Children, and others dependent on all Classes - - - - -	4,169	59,100	56,949	62,557	182,775
Total of all other Classes - -	45,398	65,318	80,269	71,109	262,094

Divide "ALL OTHER CLASSES" between the AGRICULTURISTS and the MANUFACTURERS in the proportion which these respectively bear to each other, and the numbers engaged in, and dependent on, each interest will stand thus :—

Engaged in Agriculture - - -	35,708	
Dependent on ,, - - -	248,516	
AGRICULTURE—Total - -		284,224
Engaged in Manufactures - - -	1,951	
Dependent on ,, - - -	13,578	
MANUFACTURES—Total - -		15,529
Total of the County - - -		299,753

TAXATION.

	Paid by the	
	LAND.	MANUFACTURERS.
Paid exclusively by the Landed Interest :	£	£
Land Tax - - - - - - -	58,399	
Tithes - - - - - - -	88,509	
Property Tax—on Land, assessed at - - £855,373	24,948	
Paid in the Proportion of 19-20ths by the Landed Interest, and 1-20ths by the Manufacturers :		
Poor and County Rates - - - £174,984	166,235	8,749
Highway Rates - - - - - - 25,053	23,801	1,252
Church ,, - - - - - - 9,192	8,733	459
Turnpike Trusts - - - - - 36,526	34,700	1,826
Property Tax—on Dwelling Houses, assessed at - 697,771	19,341	1,010
,, on other Property ,, - - 123,855	3,427	185
	428,093	13,481
Total of Taxation of the County - - -	£441,574	

ENGAGED IN	MALES.		FEMALES.		TOTAL.
	20 years of age and upwards.	Under 20 years of age.	20 years of age and upwards.	Under 20 years of age.	
Agriculture :					
Farmers and Graziers - - - -	3,461	45	293	—	3,799
Agricultural Labourers - - -	15,914	3,009	328	33	19,284
Gardeners, Nurserymen, and Florists -	1,105	46	5	—	1,156
	20,480	3,100	626	33	24,239
Manufactures :					
Ribbon Manufacture (all branches) - -	2,914	441	2,298	611	6,264
Weavers (all branches) - -	1,947	326	1,250	356	3,879
Brass Founders and Moulders, Finishers, and Workers -	2,504	845	32	7	3,388
Braziers and Tinkers - - -	226	44	5	3	278
Button Manufacture (all branches) - -	1,323	432	699	459	2,913
Silk Manufacture (all branches) - -	419	106	1,914	464	2,903
Gun and Pistol Makers (all branches) - -	1,708	401	47	9	2,165
Glass Manufacture (all branches) - -	668	264	57	21	1,010
Platers - - - - -	740	146	13	3	902
Needle Manufacture (all branches) - -	348	138	156	88	730
Brick and Tile Makers - - - -	600	120	8	1	729
Japanners and Lacquerers - - -	283	98	199	70	650
Wire Drawers and Workers - - -	467	132	21	7	627
Iron Manufacture (all branches) - -	438	111	7	4	560
Founders (branch not specified) - - -	338	174	5	—	517
Nailers and Nail Makers - - -	302	127	64	23	516
Coach Makers (all branches) - -	447	53	11	—	511
Hatters and Hat Makers - - -	384	24	38	4	450
Tool Makers (all branches) - - -	385	61	2	1	449
Engineers and Engine Workers - -	387	51	5	2	445
Engine and Machine Makers, and Engine Turners	253	45	5	1	304
Screw Makers - - - -	106	30	248	87	471
Turners - - - - -	326	76	5	1	408
Spoon Makers - - - -	210	68	53	21	352
Pen (Steel) Makers - - -	37	41	125	104	307
Dyers (all branches) - - -	229	33	23	1	286
Tin Plate Workers and Tinmen - - -	222	60	4	—	286
Lamp Makers - - - -	190	59	7	—	256
Comb Makers - - - -	197	17	13	7	234
Miscellaneous - - - -	3,759	742	804	356	5,661
	22,357	5,265	8,118	2,711	38,451
All other Classes :					
Employed in Retail Trade or in Handicraft, as Masters or Workmen - - -	36,122	5,448	6,535	1,391	49,496
Labourers - - - -	8,553	927	2,232	92	11,804
Military and Naval - - - -	1,443	117	—	—	1,560
Professional Persons - - -	1,077	—	—	—	1,077
Other Educated Persons following miscellaneous Pursuits	2,681	358	932	60	4,031
Persons engaged in the Government Civil Service -	193	3	13	—	209
Parochial, Town, and Church Officers - -	617	4	40	—	661
Domestic Servants - - - -	3,089	1,578	10,962	8,296	23,925
Persons returned as Independent - -	2,267	87	6,354	268	8,976
Almspeople, Pensioners, Paupers, Lunatics, and Prisoners	1,289	623	1,148	439	3,499
Residue of Population :					
Consisting of the Wives, Children, and others dependent on all Classes - - -	4,708	73,322	76,116	79,641	233,787
Total of all other Classes - - -	62,039	82,467	104,332	90,187	339,025

Divide "all other classes" between the Agriculturists and the Manufacturers in the proportion which these respectively bear to each other, and the numbers engaged in, and dependent on, each interest will stand thus :—

Engaged in Agriculture -   -   -   24,239
Dependent on ,, -   -   -   131,083
             Agriculture—Total -   -   -   155,322
Engaged in Manufactures -   -   -   38,451
Dependent on ,, -   -   -   207,942
             Manufactures—Total -   -   246,393

         Total of the County -   -   -   401,715

TAXATION.

	Paid by the	
	Land.	Manufacturers.
Paid exclusively by the Landed Interest :	£	£
Land Tax - - - - - -	39,106	
Tithes - - - - - -	32,261	
Property Tax—on Land, assessed at - £905,868	26,421	
Paid in the Proportion of 4-10ths by the Landed Interest, and 6-10ths by the Manufacturers :		
Poor and County Rates - - - £170,412	68,164	102,248
Highway Rates - - - 36,353	14,540	21,813
Church ,, - - - 9,824	3,928	5,896
Turnpike Trusts - - - 28,011	11,204	16,807
Property Tax—on Dwelling Houses, assessed at 1,122,126	13,088	19,640
,, on other Property, ,, - - 336,495	3,716	5,571
	212,428	171,975

         Total of Taxation of the County -   -   -   -   £384,405

(For those engaged in Mines, see "Mining Interest.")

ENGAGED IN	MALES.		FEMALES.		TOTAL.
	20 years of age and upwards.	Under 20 years of age.	20 years of age and upwards.	Under 20 years of age.	
AGRICULTURE:					
Farmers and Graziers - - - -	2,293	12	173	—	2,478
Agricultural Labourers - - - -	3,085	708	122	60	3,975
Gardeners, Nurserymen, and Florists -	103	8	2	—	113
	5,481	728	297	60	6,566
MANUFACTURES:					
Weavers (all branches) - - -	544	122	27	2	695
Woollen and Cloth Manufacture (all branches) -	220	56	90	51	417
Bobbin Makers - - - - -	168	98	16	2	284
Flax Manufacture (all branches) - - -	56	37	75	80	248
Worsted Manufacture (all branches) - - -	9	11	55	33	108
Miscellaneous - - - - -	721	151	118	26	1,016
	1,718	475	381	194	2,768
ALL OTHER CLASSES:					
Employed in Retail Trade or in Handicraft, as Masters or Workmen - - - -	3,541	677	686	99	5,003
Labourers - - - - - -	763	87	420	7	1,277
Military and Naval - - - - -	76	5	—	—	81
Professional Persons - - - - -	206	—	—	—	206
Other Educated Persons following miscellaneous Pursuits	264	21	119	3	407
Persons engaged in the Government Civil Service -	25	1	4	—	30
Parochial, Town, and Church Officers - -	34	—	12	—	46
Domestic Servants - - - - -	734	404	1,832	1,359	4,329
Persons returned as Independent - - -	749	20	1,444	62	2,275
Almspeople, Pensioners, Paupers, Lunatics, and Prisoners	164	128	254	129	675
RESIDUE OF POPULATION:					
Consisting of the Wives, Children, and others dependent on all Classes - - - -	1,219	10,694	9,746	11,132	32,791
Total of all other Classes - -	7,775	12,037	14,517	12,791	47,120

Divide "ALL OTHER CLASSES" between the AGRICULTURISTS and the MANUFACTURERS in the proportion which these respectively bear to each other, and the numbers engaged in, and dependent on, each interest will stand thus:—

Engaged in Agriculture - - -	6,566	
Dependent on ,, - - -	33,147	
AGRICULTURE—Total - -		39,713
Engaged in Manufactures - - -	2,768	
Dependent on ,, - - -	13,973	
MANUFACTURES—Total -		16,741
Total of the County - - -		56,454

TAXATION.

	Paid by the	
	LAND.	MANUFACTURERS.
Paid exclusively by the Landed Interest:	£	£
Land Tax - - - - - - - -	3,030	
Tithes - - - - - - - -	4,999	
Property Tax—on Land, assessed at - - -£269,417	7,857	
Paid in the Proportion of 5-7ths by the Landed Interest, and 2-7ths by the Manufacturers:		
Poor and County Rates - - - - - £21,538	15,384	6,154
Highway Rates - - - - - - 3,510	2,508	1,002
Church ,, - - - - - 1,033	739	294
Turnpike Trusts - - - - - - 6,070	3,468	2,602
Property Tax—on Dwelling Houses, assessed at - 52,056	1,124	444
,, on other Property ,, - - 13,028	271	108
	39,380	10,604
Total of Taxation of the County - - - -	£49,984	

ENGAGED IN	MALES.		FEMALES.		TOTAL.
	20 years of age and upwards.	Under 20 years of age.	20 years of age and upwards.	Under 20 years of age.	
AGRICULTURE :					
Farmers and Graziers - - - -	4,149	133	174	—	4,456
Agricultural Labourers - - - -	22,965	5,133	2,308	693	31,099
Gardeners, Nurserymen, and Florists - - -	773	36	20	6	835
	27,887	5,302	2,502	699	36,390
MANUFACTURES:					
Woollen and Woollen Cloth Manufacture (all branches) -	1,509	416	1,310	409	3,644
Weavers (all branches) - - - -	1,407	118	608	86	2,219
Silk Manufacture (all branches) - - - - -	28	25	153	123	329
Lace Makers - - - - - -	—	—	167	81	248
Spinners (branch not specified) - - - -	89	4	131	18	242
Brick and Tile Makers - - - -	171	32	3	—	206
Miscellaneous - - - -	1,244	191	273	111	1,819
	4,448	786	2,645	828	8,707
ALL OTHER CLASSES:					
Employed in Retail Trade or in Handicraft, as Masters or Workmen - - - - -	14,875	2,137	1,917	391	19,320
Labourers - - - - - - -	6,919	1,096	1,121	116	9,252
Military and Naval - - - - -	442	39	—	—	481
Professional Persons - - - - -	798	—	—	—	798
Other Educated Persons following miscellaneous Pursuits	584	100	445	25	1,154
Persons engaged in the Government Civil Service -	137	2	8	—	147
Parochial, Town, and Church Officers - - -	317	—	35	—	352
Domestic Servants - - - - -	1,869	848	6,329	4,050	13,096
Persons returned as Independent - - - -	1,665	100	4,031	200	5,996
Almspeople, Pensioners, Paupers, Lunatics, and Prisoners	1,515	658	1,828	658	4,659
RESIDUE OF POPULATION :					
Consisting of the Wives, Children, and others dependent on all Classes - - - - -	5,443	50,284	49,427	53,227	158,381
Total of all other Classes - -	34,564	55,264	65,141	58,667	213,636

Divide "ALL OTHER CLASSES" between the AGRICULTURISTS and the MANUFACTURERS in the proportion which these respectively bear to each other, and the numbers engaged in, and dependent on, each interest will stand thus:—

Engaged in Agriculture -	36,390	
Dependent on ,, - - - -	172,389	
AGRICULTURE—Total - -		208,779
Engaged in Manufactures - -	8,707	
Dependent on ,, - - -	41,247	
MANUFACTURES—Total - -		49,954
Total of the County - -		258,733

TAXATION.

	Paid by the	
	LAND.	MANUFACTURERS.
Paid exclusively by the Landed Interest :	£	£
Land Tax - - - - - - - -	50,987	
Tithes - - - - - - - - -	78,830	
Property Tax—on Land, assessed at - - £1,021,706	29,799	
Paid in the Proportion of 4-5ths by the Landed Interest, and 1-5th by the Manufacturers :		
Poor and County Rates - - - - - £167,249	133,800	33,449
Highway Rates - - - - - - - 20,135	16,108	4,027
Church ,, - - - - - - - 7,544	6,035	1,509
Turnpike Trusts - - - - - - - 31,331	25,065	6,266
Property Tax—on Dwelling Houses, assessed at - - 291,185	6,794	1,698
,, on other Property ,, - - 111,667	2,605	651
	344,023	47,600
Total of Taxation of the County - - - £391,623		

ENGAGED IN.	MALES.		FEMALES.		TOTAL.
	20 years of age and upwards.	Under 20 years of age.	20 years of age and upwards.	Under 20 years of age.	
AGRICULTURE :					
Farmers and Graziers	2,991	42	323	—	3,356
Agricultural Labourers	13,577	2,904	1,820	942	19,243
Gardeners, Nurserymen, and Florists	849	64	33	4	950
	17,417	3,010	2,176	946	23,549
MANUFACTURES :					
Nailers and Nail Makers	3,034	871	1,482	839	6,226
Glovers and Glove Makers	642	55	898	253	1,848
Carpet and Rug Manufacture	964	329	24	109	1,426
Iron Manufacture (all branches)	903	273	3	1	1,180
Needle Manufacture (all branches)	549	166	307	140	1,162
Weavers (all branches)	927	184	12	30	1,153
Brick and Tile Makers	311	44	26	18	399
Glass Manufacture (all branches)	312	75	1	—	388
Chain Makers	253	70	15	11	349
Woollen Manufacture (all branches)	160	22	79	58	319
Engineers and Engine Workers	215	37	—	—	252
Engine and Machine Makers	45	4	—	—	49
Factory Workers (branch not specified)	49	17	50	54	170
Fish Hook Makers	76	37	36	11	160
Tanners	147	5	6	—	158
Miscellaneous	1,881	319	318	126	2,644
	10,468	2,508	3,257	1,650	17,883
ALL OTHER CLASSES :					
Employed in Retail Trade or in Handicraft, as Masters or Workmen	16,257	2,142	2,287	458	21,144
Labourers	6,506	1,146	1,289	79	9,020
Military and Naval	1,028	88	—	—	1,116
Professional Persons	648	—	—	—	648
Other Educated Persons following miscellaneous Pursuits	931	115	517	52	1,615
Persons engaged in the Government Civil Service	122	—	7	1	130
Parochial, Town, and Church Officers	210	—	23	—	233
Domestic Servants	1,727	851	4,911	3,542	11,031
Persons returned as Independent	1,469	51	3,572	139	5,231
Almspeople, Pensioners, Paupers, Lunatics, and Prisoners	681	318	642	294	1,935
RESIDUE OF POPULATION :					
Consisting of the Wives, Children, and others dependent on all Classes	3,543	43,437	45,404	47,417	139,801
Total of all other Classes	33,122	48,148	58,652	51,982	191,904

Divide " ALL OTHER CLASSES" between the AGRICULTURISTS and the MANUFACTURERS in the proportion which these respectively bear to each other, and the numbers engaged in, and dependent on, each interest will stand thus :—

Engaged in Agriculture	23,549	
Dependent on ,,	109,074	
AGRICULTURE—Total		132,623
Engaged in Manufactures	17,883	
Dependent on ,,	82,830	
MANUFACTURES—Total		100,713
Total of the County		233,336

TAXATION.

		Paid by the	
		LAND.	MANUFACTURERS.
Paid exclusively by the Landed Interest :		£	£
Land Tax		32,411	
Tithes		28,934	
Property Tax—on Land, assessed at -	£716,497	20,897	
Paid in the Proportion of 5-9ths by the Landed Interest, and 4-9ths by the Manufacturers :			
Poor and County Rates	£101,311	56,287	45,024
Highway Rates	15,359	6,979	6,380
Church ,,	8,800	4,892	3,908
Turnpike Trusts	33,860	18,812	15,048
Property Tax—on Dwelling Houses, assessed at	514,734	8,341	6,672
,, on other Property ,,	101,306	1,642	1,312
		96,953	78,344
Total of Taxation of the County		£175,297	

(For those engaged in Mines, see "Mining Interest.")

ENGAGED IN	MALES. 20 years of age and upwards.	Under 20 years of age.	FEMALES. 20 years of age and upwards.	Under 20 years of age.	TOTAL.
Aɢʀɪᴄᴜʟᴛᴜʀᴇ:					
Farmers and Graziers - - - - -	4,165	39	271	—	4,475
Agricultural Labourers - - - -	13,824	4,110	324	120	18,378
Gardeners, Nurserymen, and Florists - - -	593	26	32	2	653
	18,582	4,175	627	122	23,506
Mᴀɴᴜꜰᴀᴄᴛᴜʀᴇs:					
Brick and Tile Makers - - -	355	44	6	1	406
Cotton Manufacture (all branches) - - -	99	31	63	57	250
Engineer and Engine Workers - - • -	190	45	—	—	235
Engine and Machine Makers - - -	62	16	—	—	78
Rope and Cord Spinners and Makers - -	147	18	2	—	167
Weavers (branch not specified) - - -	126	17	18	5	166
Tanners - - - - - •	121	23	—	—	144
Spinners (branch not specified) - - -	1	1	104	20	126
Hatters and Hat Makers - - -	97	5	8	4	114
Miscellaneous - - • - - -	1,215	170	107	21	1,513
	2,413	370	308	108	3,199
Aʟʟ ᴏᴛʜᴇʀ Cʟᴀssᴇs:					
Employed in Retail Trade or in Handicraft, as Masters or Workmen - - - - -	16,421	2,849	2,496	332	22,098
Labourers - - - - - -	3,818	221	1,214	51	5,304
Military and Naval - - - -	2,981	338	—	—	3,319
Professional Persons - - - - -	660	—	—	—	660
Other Educated Persons following miscellaneous Pursuits	965	188	378	19	1,550
Persons engaged in the Government Civil Service	273	3	9	—	285
Parochial, Town, and Church Officers - - -	170	2	21	—	193
Domestic Servants - - - - -	1,320	728	5,917	5,110	13,075
Persons returned as Independent - - -	1,850	40	4,042	106	6,038
Almspeople, Pensioners, Paupers, Lunatics, and Prisoners	650	232	688	147	1,717
Rᴇsɪᴅᴜᴇ ᴏꜰ Pᴏᴘᴜʟᴀᴛɪᴏɴ:					
Consisting of the Wives, Children, and others dependent on all Classes - - -	2,856	33,918	39,935	37,283	113,992
Total of all other Classes - - -	31,964	38,519	54,700	43,048	168,231

Divide "ᴀʟʟ ᴏᴛʜᴇʀ ᴄʟᴀssᴇs" between the Aɢʀɪᴄᴜʟᴛᴜʀɪsᴛs and the Mᴀɴᴜꜰᴀᴄᴛᴜʀᴇʀs in the proportion which these respectively bear to each other, and the numbers engaged in, and dependent on, each interest will stand thus:—

Engaged in Agriculture - - - £23,506
Dependent on ,, - - • - 148,079
     Aɢʀɪᴄᴜʟᴛᴜʀᴇ—Total - - ———— 171,585

Engaged in Manufactures - - - 3,199
Dependent on ,, - - - 20,152
     Mᴀɴᴜꜰᴀᴄᴛᴜʀᴇs—Total - - ———— 23,351

     Total of the East Riding - - - 194,936

CITY AND AINSTY.

ENGAGED IN	MALES. 20 years of age and upwards.	Under 20 years of age.	FEMALES. 20 years of age and upwards.	Under 20 years of age.	TOTAL.
Aɢʀɪᴄᴜʟᴛᴜʀᴇ:					
Farmers and Graziers - - - -	449	4	42	—	495
Agricultural Labourers - - - -	1,180	284	49	6	1,519
Gardeners, Nurserymen, and Florists - - -	159	6	—	—	165
	1,788	294	91	6	2,179
Mᴀɴᴜꜰᴀᴄᴛᴜʀᴇs:					
Coach Makers (all branches) - - - -	84	30	1	—	115
Comb Makers (all branches) - - - -	101	5	1	—	107
Linen Manufacture (all branches) - -	59	6	10	11	86
Brick and Tile Makers - - - -	61	8	—	—	69
Glass Manufacture (all branches) - - -	52	3	—	—	55
Engineers and Engine Workers - - -	39	9	—	—	48
Engine and Machine Makers - - -	6	2	—	—	8
Weavers (all branches) - - - -	42	3	—	—	45
Braziers, Brass Workers, and Tinkers -	29	7	1	—	37
Brass Founders - - - - -	1	—	—	—	1
Flax Manufacture - - - -	28		3	2	33
Miscellaneous - - - - -	383	40	60	19	502
	885	113	76	32	1,106

ENGAGED IN	MALES.		FEMALES.		TOTAL.
	20 years of age and upwards.	Under 20 years of age.	20 years of age and upwards.	Under 20 years of age.	
ALL OTHER CLASSES :					
Employed in Retail Trade or in Handicraft, as Masters or Workmen	4,297	788	695	108	5,888
Labourers	933	59	210	—	1,202
Military and Naval	230	18	—	—	248
Professional Persons	227	—	—	—	227
Other Educated Persons following miscellaneous Pursuits	310	50	86	7	453
Persons engaged in the Government Civil Service	24	—	—	—	24
Parochial, Town, and Church Officers	37	1	9	—	47
Domestic Servants	471	131	1,681	1,062	3,345
Persons returned as Independent	389	9	1,155	43	1,596
Almspeople, Pensioners, Paupers, Lunatics, and Prisoners	356	11	134	12	513
RESIDUE OF POPULATION :					
Consisting of the Wives, Children, and others dependent on all Classes	452	6,304	7,730	7,007	21,493
Total of all other Classes	7,726	7,371	11,700	8,239	35,036

Divide "ALL OTHER CLASSES" between the AGRICULTURISTS and the MANUFACTURERS in the proportion which these respectively bear to each other, and the numbers engaged in, and dependent on, each interest will stand thus :—

Engaged in Agriculture	2,179	
Dependent on ,,	23,241	
AGRICULTURE—Total		25,420
Engaged in Manufactures	1,106	
Dependent on ,,	11,795	
MANUFACTURES—Total		12,901
Total of the City and Ainsty		38,321

NORTH RIDING.

ENGAGED IN	MALES.		FEMALES.		TOTAL.
	20 years of age and upwards.	Under 20 years of age.	20 years of age and upwards.	Under 20 years of age.	
AGRICULTURE :					
Farmers and Graziers	7,265	68	613	—	7,946
Agricultural Labourers	13,982	3,984	1,343	443	19,752
Gardeners, Nurserymen, and Florists	446	27	6	—	479
	21,693	4,079	1,962	443	28,177
MANUFACTURES :					
Linen Manufacture (all branches)	462	60	24	14	560
Weavers (all branches)	418	17	7	—	442
Brick and Tile Makers	316	32	10	1	359
Potters and Pot Makers	160	50	45	43	298
Woollen and Cloth Manufacture (all branches)	201	22	4	4	231
Alum Works	184	31	—	—	215
Rope and Cord Spinners and Makers	114	21	16	3	154
Flax Manufacture (all branches)	69	12	24	14	119
Tanners	88	12	1	—	101
Miscellaneous	972	163	222	24	1,381
	2,984	420	353	103	3,860
ALL OTHER CLASSES :					
Employed in Retail Trade or in Handicraft, as Masters or Workmen	14,679	2,915	1,922	249	19,765
Labourers	3,386	305	857	8	4,556
Military and Naval	1,307	96	—	—	1,403
Professional Persons	711	—	—	—	711
Other Educated Persons following miscellaneous Pursuits	736	68	310	14	1,128
Persons engaged in the Government Civil Service	162	3	9	—	174
Parochial, Town, and Church Officers	103	—	22	—	125
Domestic Servants	1,601	1,013	6,036	5,127	13,777
Persons returned as Independent	1,962	46	4,270	111	6,389
Almspeople, Pensioners, Paupers, Lunatics, and Prisoners	526	180	654	155	1,515
RESIDUE OF POPULATION :					
Consisting of the Wives, Children, and others dependent on all Classes	4,332	37,180	41,668	39,362	122,542
Total of all other Classes	29,505	41,806	55,748	45,026	172,085

Divide "ALL OTHER CLASSES" between the AGRICULTURISTS and the MANUFACTURERS in the proportion which these respectively bear to each other, and the numbers engaged in, and dependent on, each interest will stand thus:—

Engaged in Agriculture	28,177	
Dependent on ,,	151,352	
AGRICULTURE—Total		179,529
Engaged in Manufactures	3,860	
Dependent on ,,	20,733	
MANUFACTURES—Total		24,593
Total of the North Riding		204,122

WEST RIDING.

ENGAGED IN	MALES.		FEMALES.		TOTAL.
	20 years of age and upwards.	Under 20 years of age.	20 years of age an upwards	Under 20 years of age.	
AGRICULTURE :					
Farmers and Graziers	15,327	164	1,247	—	16,738
Agricultural Labourers	24,615	4,941	613	152	30,321
Gardeners, Nurserymen, and Florists	2,038	163	33	4	2,238
	41,980	5,268	1,893	156	49,297
MANUFACTURES :					
Woollen and Cloth Manufacture	35,632	9,378	5,140	4,300	54,450
Worsted Manufacture (all branches)	5,604	2,515	5,445	5,776	19,340
Cotton Manufacture (all branches)	4,306	2,510	4,570	3,940	15,326
Weavers (all branches)	8,634	1,526	2,795	1,612	14,567
Stuff Manufacture (all branches)	2,921	458	2,020	1,141	6,540
Factory Workers (branch not specified)	1,563	1,456	1,347	2,135	6,501
Flax Manufacture (all branches)	1,376	1,162	1,229	2,257	6,024
Linen Manufacture (all branches)	2,590	459	431	363	3,843
Fancy Goods Manufacture	2,572	366	354	197	3,489
Dyers (all branches)	2,457	540	44	11	3,052
File Makers	2,033	712	81	28	2,854
Iron Manufacture (all branches)	1,653	531	20	4	2,208
Engineers and Engine Workers	1,596	272	6	19	1,893
Engine and Machine Makers	891	281	13	3	1,188
Grinders	1,350	515	10	4	1,879
Spinners (branch not specified)	217	188	363	773	1,541
Card Makers	596	171	399	288	1,454
Nail Makers and Nailers	925	238	68	31	1,262
Potters	696	210	71	62	1,039
Scissor Makers	647	150	101	47	945
Silk Manufacture (all branches)	385	120	172	191	868
Brick and Tile Makers	655	159	8	—	822
Moulders (branch not specified)	496	242	4	—	742
Haft and Scale Makers	599	105	17	2	723
Tool Makers (all branches)	557	121	3	—	681
Wire Drawers and Workers	524	69	21	25	639
Razor Makers	462	116	—	3	581
Fork Makers (all branches)	388	138	32	10	568
White Metal Smiths and Workers	449	106	4	5	564
Carpet Manufacture (all branches)	412	91	22	12	537
Paper Manufacture (all branches)	302	124	61	20	507
Hatters and Hat Makers	390	48	44	6	488
Rope and Cord Spinners and Makers	399	66	7	9	481
Turners	383	88	6	—	477
Miscellaneous	7,124	1,513	892	482	10,011
	91,784	26,744	25,800	23,756	168,084
ALL OTHER CLASSES :					
Employed in Retail Trade or in Handicraft, as Masters or Workmen	87,822	15,145	11,269	2,126	116,362
Labourers	29,389	6,952	4,007	333	40,681
Military and Naval	4,818	307	—	—	5,125
Professional Persons	2,283	—	—	—	2,283
Other Educated Persons following miscellaneous Pursuits	4,474	593	1,331	74	6,472
Persons engaged in the Government Civil Service	388	14	16	4	422
Parochial, Town, and Church Officers	846	10	90	—	946
Domestic Servants	5,179	2,627	19,090	15,504	42,400
Persons returned as Independent	5,282	251	15,432	585	21,550
Almspeople, Pensioners, Paupers, Lunatics, and Prisoners	2,959	999	2,468	724	7,150
RESIDUE OF POPULATION :					
Consisting of the Wives, Children, and others dependent on all Classes	14,080	223,949	216,383	238,917	693,329
Total of all other Classes	157,520	250,847	270,086	258,267	936,720

Divide " ALL OTHER CLASSES " between the AGRICULTURISTS and the MANUFACTURERS in the proportion which these respectively bear to each other, and the numbers engaged in, and dependent on, each interest will stand thus:—

Engaged in Agriculture	49,297	
Dependent on ,,	212,426	
AGRICULTURE—Total		261,723
Engaged in Manufactures	168,084	
Dependent on ,,	724,294	
MANUFACTURES—Total		892,378
Total of the West Riding		1,154,101

YORK—County of.

POPULATION.

	AGRICULTURAL.	MANUFACTURING.
EAST RIDING	171,585	23,351
CITY AND AINSTY	25,420	12,901
NORTH RIDING	179,529	24,593
WEST RIDING	261,723	892,378
	658,257	958,223

Total of Population of the County -   1,591,480

TAXATION.

		Paid by the	
		LAND.	MANUFACTURERS.
		£	£
Paid exclusively by the Landed Interest :			
Land Tax		88,405	
Tithes		77,491	
Property Tax—on Land, assessed at	£3,989,936	116,373	
Paid in the Proportion of 2-5ths by the Landed Interest, and 3-5ths by the Manufacturers :			
Poor and County Rates	£574,883	229,952	344,831
Highway Rates	190,186	76,074	114,112
Church ,,	24,690	9,876	14,814
Turnpike Trusts	153,134	61,252	91,882
Property Tax—on Dwelling Houses, assessed at	2,707,513	31,586	47,383
,, on other Property ,,	797,579	9,304	13,958
		418,044	626,980

Total of Taxation of the County -   £1,045,024

(For those engaged in Mines, see " Mining Interest.")

COUNTIES.	AGRICULTURE.			MANUFACTURES.			TOTAL OF THE COUNTY.
	Engaged in :	Dependent on :	TOTAL.	Engaged in :	Dependent on :	TOTAL.	
BEDFORD	14,933	62,703	77,636	5,828	24,472	30,300	107,936
BERKS	21,249	127,695	148,944	1,741	10,462	12,203	161,147
BUCKS	21,897	92,989	114,886	7,833	33,264	41,097	155,983
CAMBRIDGE	22,918	135,981	158,899	802	4,758	5,560	164,459
*CHESTER	26,804	97,821	124,625	58,293	212,742	271,035	395,660
CORNWALL	26,862	260,402	287,264	5,051	48,964	54,015	341,279
CUMBERLAND	15,611	97,379	112,990	8,987	56,061	65,048	178,038
*DERBY	19,333	91,928	111,261	27,968	132,988	160,956	272,217
DEVON	54,522	392,759	447,281	10,505	75,674	86,179	533,460
DORSET	19,192	130,823	150,015	3,202	21,826	25,028	175,043
DURHAM	14,362	173,443	187,805	10,437	126,042	136,479	324,284
ESSEX	51,116	266,373	317,489	4,426	23,064	27,490	344,979
GLOUCESTER	31,270	256,638	287,908	15,583	127,892	143,475	431,383
HEREFORD	16,616	91,184	107,800	937	5,141	6,078	143,878
HERTFORD	20,145	98,361	118,506	6,579	32,122	38,701	157,207
HUNTINGDON	8,480	46,249	54,729	592	3,228	3,820	58,549
KENT	47,585	441,499	489,084	5,765	53,488	59,253	548,337
*LANCASTER	49,569	192,265	241,834	292,129	1,133,091	1,425,220	1,667,054
*LEICESTER	17,092	77,221	94,313	22,029	99,525	121,554	215,867
LINCOLN	57,561	286,704	344,265	3,066	15,271	18,337	362,602
MIDDLESEX	18,164	1,006,692	1,024,856	48,435	503,345	551,780	1,576,636
MONMOUTH	8,685	78,344	87,029	4,723	42,603	47,326	134,355
NORFOLK	50,365	296,698	347,063	9,520	56,081	65,601	412,664
NORTHAMPTON	25,731	110,666	136,397	11,853	50,978	62,831	199,228
NORTHUMBERLAND	17,339	161,524	178,863	6,923	64,492	71,415	250,278
*NOTTINGHAM	20,358	85,486	105,844	27,710	116,356	144,066	249,910
OXFORD	20,789	122,189	142,978	2,714	15,951	18,665	161,643
RUTLAND	3,316	17,041	20,357	154	791	945	21,302
SALOP	28,003	168,702	196,705	6,028	36,315	42,343	239,048
SOMERSET	44,467	293,507	337,974	12,895	85,113	98,008	435,982
SOUTHAMPTON	35,541	288,368	323,909	3,412	27,683	31,095	355,004
*STAFFORD	29,120	151,360	180,480	53,249	276,775	330,024	510,504
SUFFOLK	43,858	245,474	289,332	3,902	21,839	25,741	315,073
SURREY	25,352	478,720	504,072	14,718	63,886	78,606	582,678
SUSSEX	35,708	248,516	284,224	1,951	13,578	15,529	299,753
*WARWICK	24,239	131,083	155,322	38,451	207,942	246,393	401,715
WESTMORELAND	6,556	33,147	39,713	2,768	13,973	16,741	56,454
WILTS	36,390	172,389	208,779	8,707	41,247	49,954	258,733
WORCESTER	23,549	109,074	132,623	17,883	82,830	100,713	233,336
YORK (EAST RIDING)	23,506	148,079	171,585	3,199	20,152	23,351	194,936
YORK (CITY AND AINSTY)	2,179	23,241	25,420	1,106	11,795	12,901	38,321
YORK (NORTH RIDING)	28,177	151,352	179,529	3,860	20,733	24,593	204,122
*YORK (WEST RIDING)	49,297	212,426	261,723	168,084	724,294	892,378	1,154,101
TRAVELLING on the night of the Census	—	—	—	—	—	—	5,016
	1,157,816	8,154,495	9,312,311	943,998	4,738,829	5,682,827	15,000,154

* It will be seen from the above Table that the Agricultural Interest preponderates in 35 Counties, and Divisions of Counties, and the Manufacturing Interest in 7 Counties, and 1 Division of the County of York, marked thus.*

COUNTIES.	Paid by the Landed Interest and those dependent on it.	Paid by the Manufacturing Interest and those dependent on it.	Total Taxation of the County.
	£	£	£
BEDFORD	104,196	23,021	127,217
BERKS	216,581	10,763	227,343
BUCKS	185,005	36,028	221,033
CAMBRIDGE	217,423	9,015	226,438
CHESTER	146,730	153,115	299,845
CORNWALL	268,301	27,798	296,099
CUMBERLAND	81,781	33,452	115,233
DERBY	127,870	94,761	222,631
DEVON	542,749	62,947	605,596
DORSET	235,515	21,435	256,950
DURHAM	175,424	86,273	261,697
ESSEX	525,739	24,396	550,135
GLOUCESTER	337,065	108,856	445,921
HEREFORD	166,393	5,309	171,702
HERTFORD	216,612	35,303	251,915
HUNTINGDON	84,715	3,747	88,462
KENT	622,953	46,423	669,376
LANCASTER	239,546	794,122	1,033,668
LEICESTER	155,155	94,064	249,219
LINCOLN	465,567	14,835	480,402
MIDDLESEX	1,155,349	426,546	1,581,895
MONMOUTH	84,591	29,535	114,126
NORFOLK	454,208	50,797	505,005
NORTHAMPTON	210,098	61,834	271,932
NORTHUMBERLAND	173,941	30,560	204,501
NOTTINGHAM	96,322	85,687	182,009
OXFORD	202,560	16,833	219,393
RUTLAND	31,343	874	32,217
SALOP	218,258	28,346	246,604
SOMERSET	458,140	74,390	532,530
SOUTHAMPTON	415,752	23,619	439,371
STAFFORD	203,234	195,695	398,929
SUFFOLK	392,776	20,097	412,873
SURREY	528,141	72,253	600,394
SUSSEX	428,093	13,481	441,574
WARWICK	212,428	171,975	384,405
WESTMORELAND	39,380	10,604	49,984
WILTS	344,023	47,600	391,623
WORCESTER	96,953	78,344	175,297
YORKSHIRE	418,044	626,980	1,045,024
	11,278,954	3,751,713	15,030,667

Total of Direct and Local Taxation paid by the Landed Interest - - £11,278,954

,,   ,,   Manufacturing   -   3,751,713

Total of Direct and Local Taxation of England   -   -   -   15,030,667

ENGAGED IN	MALES.		FEMALES.		TOTAL.
	20 years of age and upwards.	Under 20 years of age.	20 years of age and upwards.	Under 20 years of age.	
Agriculture:					
Farmers and Graziers - - - -	2,068	19	261	—	2,348
Agricultural Labourers - - - - -	3,706	1,222	227	144	5,299
Gardeners, Nurserymen, and Florists - -	69	4	—	—	73
	5,843	1,245	488	144	7,720
Manufactures: There is no leading branch of Manufacture carried on in this County. The largest number employed in any one branch is					
Weavers (all branches) - - - -	137	10	2	—	149
Smelters (branch not specified) - -	41	4	1	—	46
Nailers and Nail Makers - - -	27	11	1	1	40
Miscellaneous - - - -	203	28	66	6	303
	408	53	70	7	538
All other Classes:					
Employed in Retail Trade or in Handicraft, as Masters or Workmen - - - -	2,680	339	426	117	3,562
Labourers - - - - - -	1,123	135	70	8	1,336
Military and Naval - - - -	3,816	24	—	—	410
Professional Persons - - - -	142	—	—	—	142
Other Educated Persons following miscellaneous Pursuits	58	8	24	2	92
Persons engaged in the Government Civil Service -	41	2	5	1	49
Parochial, Town, and Church Officers - -	31	—	—	—	31
Domestic Servants - - - -	233	237	1,446	1,070	2,986
Persons returned as Independent - -	166	9	887	32	1,094
Almspeople, Pensioners, Paupers, Lunatics, and Prisoners	137	40	501	40	718
Residue of Population:					
Consisting of the Wives, Children, and others dependent on all Classes - - -	1,179	9,860	10,857	10,317	32,213
Total of all other Classes - -	6,176	10,654	14,216	11,587	42,633

Divide " all other classes " between the Agriculturists and the Manufacturers in the proportion which these respectively bear to each other, and the numbers engaged in, and dependent on, each interest will stand thus :—

Engaged in Agriculture   -   -   - 7,720
Dependent on   ,,   -   - 39,856

     Agriculture—Total   -   -   47,576

Engaged in Manufactures   -   -   - 538
Dependent on   ,,   -   -   - 2,777

     Manufactures—Total   -   3,315

     Total of the County   -   -   -   - 50,899

TAXATION.

	Paid by the	
	Land.	Manufacturers.
	£	£
Paid exclusively by the Landed Interest:		
Land Tax - - - - - -	1,535	
Tithes - - - - -	15,114	
Property Tax—on Land, assessed at - - £129,063	3,764	
Paid in the Proportion of 14-15ths by the Landed Interest, and 1-15th by the Manufacturers:		
Poor and County Rates - - - - 21,476	20,045	1,431
Highway Rates - - - - 2,447	2,284	163
Church ,, - - - - - 1,980	1,848	132
Turnpike Trusts - - - - 6,392	5,966	426
Property Tax—on Dwelling Houses, assessed at - 15,231	405	29
,, on other Property ,, - 21,029	373	40
	51,334	2,221

     Total of Taxation of the County   -   -   -   - £53,555

(For those engaged in Mines, see "Mining Interest.")

ENGAGED IN	MALES.		FEMALES.		TOTAL.
	20 years of age and upwards.	Under 20 years of age.	20 years of age and upwards.	Under 20 years of age.	
AGRICULTURE:					
Farmers and Graziers	1,941	6	160	—	2,107
Agricultural Labourers	2,358	949	64	39	3,410
Gardeners, Nurserymen, and Florists	69	2	1	—	72
	4,368	957	225	39	5,589
MANUFACTURES:					
Iron Manufacture (all branches)	414	84	17	6	521
Weavers (all branches)	101	11	—	—	112
Coke Burners	56	5	8	13	82
Nailers and Nail Makers	46	5	—	—	51
Miscellaneous	225	31	44	8	308
	842	136	69	27	1,074
ALL OTHER CLASSES:					
Employed in Retail Trade or in Handicraft, as Masters or Workmen	3,608	636	404	67	4,715
Labourers	4,102	899	270	147	5,418
Military and Naval	221	43	—	—	264
Professional Persons	206	—	—	—	206
Other Educated Persons following miscellaneous Pursuits	126	13	31	3	173
Persons engaged in the Government Civil Service	20	—	—	—	20
Parochial, Town, and Church Officers	40	—	5	—	45
Domestic Servants	321	185	1,700	1,500	3,706
Persons returned as Independent	382	16	850	57	1,305
Almspeople, Pensioners, Paupers, Lunatics, and Prisoners	139	41	175	38	393
RESIDUE OF POPULATION:					
Consisting of the Wives, Children, and others dependent on all Classes	1,261	9,517	11,343	10,574	32,695
Total of all other Classes	10,426	11,350	14,778	12,386	48,940

Divide "ALL OTHER CLASSES" between the AGRICULTURISTS and the MANUFACTURERS in the proportion which these respectively bear to each other, and the numbers engaged in, and dependent on, each interest will stand thus:—

Engaged in Agriculture	5,589	
Dependent on ,,	41,052	
AGRICULTURE—Total		46,641
Engaged in Manufactures	1,074	
Dependent on ,,	7,888	
MANUFACTURES—Total		8,962
Total of the County		55,603

TAXATION.

	Paid by the	
	LAND.	MANUFACTURERS.
Paid exclusively by the Landed Interest :	£	£
Land Tax	2,954	
Tithes	12,558	
Property Tax—on Land, assessed at £139,224	4,060	
Paid in the Proportion of 5-6ths by the Landed Interest, and 1-6th by the Manufacturers :		
Poor and County Rates £24,887	20,740	4,147
Highway Rates 2,787	2,323	464
Church ,, 922	762	153
Turnpike Trusts	—	—
Property Tax—on Dwelling Houses, assessed at 31,401	763	153
,, on other Property ,, 27,847	668	133
	44,834	5,050
Total of Taxation of the County	£49,884	

ENGAGED IN	MALES.		FEMALES.		TOTAL.
	20 years of age and upwards.	Under 20 years of age.	20 years of age and upwards.	Under 20 years of age.	
AGRICULTURE :					
Farmers and Graziers - - - -	3,072	24	371	—	3,467
Agricultural Labourers - - - -	3,560	1,687	129	102	5,478
Gardeners, Nurserymen, and Florists - -	50	—	1	—	51
	6,682	1,711	501	102	8,996
MANUFACTURES :					
Weavers (all branches) - - - -	258	11	2	1	272
Spinners (branch not specified) - - -	16	2	159	10	187
Woollen Manufacture (all branches) - -	54	12	58	14	138
Hatters and Hat Makers - - -	112	2	3	—	117
Miscellaneous - - - - -	159	13	96	17	285
	599	40	318	42	999
ALL OTHER CLASSES :					
Employed in Retail Trade or in Handicraft, as Masters or Workmen - - - - -	3,740	496	373	49	4,658
Labourers - - - - - -	1,384	102	105	5	1,596
Military and Naval - - - - -	360	38	—	—	398
Professional Persons - - - -	213	—	—	—	213
Other Educated Persons following miscellaneous Pursuits	117	6	18	2	143
Persons engaged in the Government Civil Service -	38	1	2	—	41
Parochial, Town, and Church Officers - - -	33	1	4	—	38
Domestic Servants - - - -	534	678	2,339	2,314	5,865
Persons returned as Independent - - -	385	46	1,699	63	2,193
Almspeople, Pensioners, Paupers, Lunatics, and Prisoners	222	19	413	11	665
RESIDUE OF POPULATION :					
Consisting of the Wives, Children, and others dependent on all Classes - - - - -	1,770	13,003	14,456	13,732	42,961
Total of all other Classes - - -	8,796	14,390	19,409	16,176	58,771

Divide "ALL OTHER CLASSES" between the AGRICULTURISTS and the MANUFACTURERS in the proportion which these respectively bear to each other, and the numbers engaged in, and dependent on, each interest will stand thus :—

Engaged in Agriculture - - -	8,996	
Dependent on ,, - - -	52,897	
AGRICULTURE—Total - -		61,893
Engaged in Manufactures - - -	999	
Dependent on ,, - -	5,874	
MANUFACTURES—Total - -		6,873
Total of the County - - -		68,766

TAXATION.

	Paid by the	
	LAND.	MANUFACTURERS.
Paid exclusively by the Landed Interest :	£	£
Land Tax - - - - - - - -	1,278	
Tithes - - - - - - - - -	13,086	
Property Tax—on Land, assessed at - - £159,948	4,665	
Paid in the Proportion of 8-9ths by the Landed Interest, and 1-9th by the Manufacturers :		
Poor and County Rates - - - - - £21,947	19,620	2,327
Highway Rates - - - - - - 3,449	3,066	383
Church ,, - - - - - - 882	784	98
Turnpike Trusts - - - - - - 2,006	1,784	222
Property Tax—on Dwelling Houses, assessed at - - 23,081	599	74
,, on other Property ,, - - 22,298	578	72
	45,460	3,176
Total of Taxation of the County - - - £48,636		

(*For those engaged in Mines, see "Mining Interest."*)

ENGAGED IN	MALES.		FEMALES.		TOTAL.
	20 years of age and upwards.	Under 20 years of age.	20 years of age and upwards.	Under 20 years of age.	
AGRICULTURE :					
Farmers and Graziers - - - -	4,817	26	660	—	5,503
Agricultural Labourers - - - -	5,787	2,568	384	197	8,936
Gardeners, Nurserymen, and Florists - -	67	2	3	—	72
	10,671	2,596	1,047	197	14,511
MANUFACTURES :					
Weavers (all branches) - - - -	293	32	21	2	348
Copper Manufacture (all branches) - -	229	28	—	—	257
Woollen Manufacture (all branches) - -	58	18	26	4	106
Miscellaneous - - - - -	503	75	124	10	712
	1,083	153	171	16	1,423
ALL OTHER CLASSES :					
Employed in Retail Trade or in Handicraft, as Masters or Workmen - - - - -	5,962	873	710	102	7,647
Labourers - - - - - -	2,615	425	365	24	3,429
Military and Naval - - - -	313	28	—	—	341
Professional Persons - - - - -	321	—	—	—	321
Other Educated Persons following miscellaneous Pursuits	277	27	69	11	384
Persons engaged in the Government Civil Service -	44	1	2	—	47
Parochial, Town, and Church Officers - -	60	1	8	—	69
Domestic Servants - - - - -	559	509	3,548	3,462	8,078
Persons returned as Independent - - -	586	72	2,807	137	3,602
Almspeople, Pensioners, Paupers, Lunatics, and Prisoners	235	105	558	133	1,031
RESIDUE OF POPULATION :					
Consisting of the Wives, Children, and others dependent on all Classes - - - - -	2,247	20,919	20,577	21,700	65,443
Total of all other Classes - - -	13,219	22,960	28,644	25,569	90,392

Divide " ALL OTHER CLASSES" between the AGRICULTURISTS and the MANUFACTURERS in the proportion which these respectively bear to each other, and the numbers engaged in, and dependent on, each interest will stand thus :—

Engaged in Agriculture - - -	14,511	
Dependent on ,, - - -	82,320	
AGRICULTURE—Total - -		96,831
Engaged in Manufactures - -	1,423	
Dependent on ,, - - -	8,072	
MANUFACTURES—Total - -		9,495
Total of the County - - -		106,326

TAXATION.

		Paid by the	
		LAND.	MANUFACTURERS.
Paid exclusively by the Landed Interest :		£	£
Land Tax - - - - - -		4,148	
Tithes - - - - - -		26,177	
Property Tax—on Land, assessed at - - £315,761		9,209	
Paid in the Proportion of 10-11ths by the Landed Interest, and 1-11th by the Manufacturers :			
Poor and County Rates - - - - £43,230		39,300	3,930
Highway Rates - - - - - 7,108		6,462	646
Church ,, - - - - 1,288		1,171	117
Turnpike Trusts - - - - 10,373		9,430	943
Property Tax—on Dwelling Houses, assessed at - 37,720		1,000	100
,, on other Property ,, - - 43,473		11,527	1,152
		108,424	6,888
Total of Taxation of the County - - - - £115,312			

(*For those engaged in Mines, see " Mining Interest."*)

ENGAGED IN	MALES.		FEMALES.		TOTAL.
	20 Years of age and upwards.	Under 20 years of age.	20 Years of age and upwards.	Under 20 years of age.	
Agriculture:					
Farmers and Graziers - - - - -	3,064	12	420	—	3,496
Agricultural Labourers - - - - -	4,708	1,428	44	15	6,195
Gardeners, Nurserymen, and Florists - -	107	11	3	1	122
	7,879	1,451	467	16	9,813
Manufactures:					
Weavers (branch not specified) - - -	190	12	2	—	204
Nailers - - - - - - -	44	7	1	—	52
Woollen Manufacture (all branches) - - -	28	6	3	—	37
Miscellaneous - - - - - -	320	47	47	7	421
	582	72	53	7	714
All other Classes:					
Employed in Retail Trade or in Handicraft, as Masters or Workmen	4,360	663	481	60	5,564
Labourers - - - - - -	4,482	1,231	83	3	5,799
Military and Naval - - - - -	747	76	—	—	823
Professional Persons - - - -	220	—	—	—	220
Other Educated Persons following miscellaneous Pursuits	147	20	30	3	200
Persons engaged in the Government Civil Service -	47	—	1	—	48
Parochial, Town, and Church Officers - -	35	3	2	—	40
Domestic Servants - - - - -	309	181	2,638	1,994	5,122
Persons returned as Independent - - -	377	24	1,800	80	2,281
Almspeople, Pensioners, Paupers, Lunatics, and Prisoners	120	29	243	9	401
Residue of Population:					
Consisting of the Wives, Children, and others dependent on all Classes - - - - -	1,466	15,110	16,760	16,732	50,068
Total of all other Classes - - -	12,310	17,337	22,038	18,881	70,566

Divide " ALL OTHER CLASSES " between the Agriculturists and the Manufacturers in the proportion which these respectively bear to each other, and the numbers engaged in, and dependent on, each interest will stand thus :—

Engaged in Agriculture - - -	9,813	
Dependent on ,, - - -	65,780	
AGRICULTURE—Total - -		75,593
Engaged in Manufactures - - -	714	
Dependent on ,, - - -	4,786	
MANUFACTURES—Total - -		5,500
Total of the County - -		81,093

TAXATION.

	Paid by the	
	Land.	Manufacturers.
Paid exclusively by the Landed Interest :	£	£
Land Tax - - - - - - - - -	2,272	
Tithes - - - - - - - - - - -	12,318	
Property Tax—on Land, assessed at - - £150,046	4,376	
Paid in the Proportion of 14-15ths by the Landed Interest, and 1-15th by the Manufacturers :		
Poor and County Rates - - - £29,812	27,825	1,987
Highway Rates - - - - - 2,661	2,484	177
Church ,, - - - - - 443	414	29
Turnpike Trusts - - - - - 2,892	2,700	192
Property Tax—on Dwelling Houses, assessed at - 32,979	897	64
,, on other Property ,, - - 68,018	1,851	132
	55,137	2,581
Total of Taxation of the County - - - -	£57,718	

(For those engaged in Mines, see " Mining Interest.")

ENGAGED IN	MALES.		FEMALES.		TOTAL.
	20 years of age and upwards.	Under 20 years of age.	20 years of age and upwards.	Under 20 years of age.	
AGRICULTURE:					
Farmers and Graziers - - - - -	3,022	13	432	—	3,467
Agricultural Labourers - - - -	5,758	1,937	48	24	7,767
Gardeners, Nurserymen, and Florists - -	194	10	3	—	207
	8,977	1,960	483	24	11,441
MANUFACTURES:					
Iron Manufacture (all branches) - - -	165	51	1	—	217
Woollen Manufacture (all branches) - -	116	35	18	5	174
Weavers (all branches) - - - -	134	21	5	—	160
Nailors and Nail Makers - - - -	114	32	1	—	147
Engineers and Engine Workers - - -	115	19	—	—	134
Engine and Machine Makers - - - -	3	—	—	—	3
Miscellaneous - - - - -	452	93	95	21	661
	1,099	251	120	26	1,496
ALL OTHER CLASSES:					
Employed in Retail Trade or in Handicraft, as Masters or Workmen - - - - -	5,267	846	616	109	6,838
Labourers - - - - - -	3,716	684	224	15	4,636
Military and Naval - - - -	66	8	—	—	74
Professional Persons - - - -	223	—	—	—	223
Other Educated Persons following miscellaneous Pursuits	252	18	70	5	345
Persons engaged in the Government Civil Service -	38	1	2	—	41
Parochial, Town, and Church Officers - - -	72	—	4	—	76
Domestic Servants - - - -	740	552	2,729	2,647	6,668
Persons returned as Independent - - -	481	31	1,374	82	1,968
Almspeople, Pensioners, Paupers, Lunatics, and Prisoners	201	85	568	77	931
RESIDUE OF POPULATION:					
Consisting of the Wives, Children, and others dependent on all Classes - - - - - -	2,093	16,777	17,779	17,477	54,126
Total of all other Classes - -	13,149	19,002	23,366	20,412	75,929

Divide "ALL OTHER CLASSES" between the AGRICULTURISTS and the MANUFACTURERS in the proportion which these respectively bear to each other, and the numbers engaged in, and dependent on, each interest will stand thus:—

Engaged in Agriculture - - - 11,441
Dependent on - - - - 67,149
AGRICULTURE—Total - - ——— 78,590

Engaged in Manufactures - - - 1,496
Dependent on - - - 8,780
MANUFACTURES—Total - - ——— 10,276

Total of the County - - - 86,866

TAXATION.

	Paid by the	
	LAND.	MANUFACTURERS.
Paid exclusively by the Landed Interest:	£	£
Land Tax - - - - - - -	6,717	
Tithes - - - - - -	17,966	
Property Tax—on Land, assessed at - - £284,345	8,293	
Paid in the Proportion of 7-8ths by the Landed Interest, and 1-8th by the Manufacturers:		
Poor and County Rates - - - - £41,827	36,599	5,228
Highway Rates - - - - - - 4,365	3,820	545
Church ,, - - - - - 1,603	1,403	200
Turnpike Trusts - - - - - 5,079	4,445	634
Property Tax—on Dwelling Houses, assessed at - 53,936	1,377	196
,, on other Property ,, - - 33,068	844	120
	81,464	6,923
Total of Taxation of the County - - - £88,387		

ENGAGED IN	MALES.		FEMALES.		TOTAL.
	20 years of age and upwards.	Under 20 years of age.	20 years of age and upwards.	Under 20 years of age.	
Agriculture:					
Farmers and Graziers - - - - -	1,499	13	259	—	1,771
Agricultural Labourers - - - - -	2,742	822	18	4	3,586
Gardeners, Nurserymen, and Florists - - -	130	4	—	—	134
	4,371	839	277	4	5,491
Manufactures:					
Lead Manufacture (all branches) - - -	259	21	4	1	285
Cotton Manufacture (all branches) - - -	63	45	59	79	246
Engineers and Engine Workers - - -	170	34	2	—	206
Engine and Machine Makers - - - -	17	3	1	—	21
Brick and Tile Makers - - - -	121	21	—	—	142
Nailers - - - - - -	62	22	2	—	86
Miscellaneous - - - - - -	465	98	38	8	609
	1,157	244	106	88	1,595
All other Classes:					
Employed in Retail Trade or in Handicraft, as Masters or Workmen - - - - - -	3,782	559	380	71	4,792
Labourers - - - - - -	4,754	807	126	14	5,701
Military and Naval - - - - - -	441	12	—	—	453
Professional Persons - - - -	170	—	—	—	170
Other Educated Persons following miscellaneous Pursuits	226	25	65	2	318
Persons engaged in the Government Civil Service -	25	—	3	—	28
Parochial, Town, and Church Officers - - -	44	—	3	—	47
Domestic Servants - - - - -	629	497	1,679	1,465	4,270
Persons returned as Independent - - -	265	16	913	58	1,252
Almspeople, Pensioners, Paupers, Lunatics, and Prisoners	143	2	248	2	395
Residue of Population:					
Consisting of the Wives, Children, and others dependent on all Classes - - - - -	1,480	13,326	13,738	13,863	42,407
Total of all other Classes - - -	11,959	15,244	17,155	15,475	59,833

Divide " all other classes" between the Agriculturists and the Manufacturers in the proportion which these respectively bear to each other, and the numbers engaged in, and dependent on, each interest will stand thus :—

Engaged in Agriculture - - -	5,491		
Dependent on ,, - - -	46,366		
Agriculture—Total - -		51,857	
Engaged in Manufactures - -	1,595		
Dependent on ,, - -	13,467		
Manufactures—Total -		15,062	
Total of the County - -		66,919	

TAXATION.

	Paid by the	
	Land.	Manufacturers.
Paid exclusively by the Landed Interest :	£	£
Land Tax - - - - - - -	2,246	
Tithes - - - - - - -	9,835	
Property Tax—on Land, assessed at - - - £193,505	5,643	
Paid in the Proportion of 7-9ths by the Landed Interest, and 2-9ths by the Manufacturers :		
Poor and County Rates - - - £26,123	20,319	5,804
Highway Rates - - - - - 2,827	2,199	628
Church ,, - - - - - 723	563	160
Turnpike Trusts - - - - 15,346	11,936	3,410
Property Tax—on Dwelling Houses, assessed at - 27,617	627	178
,, on other Property ,, - 53,348	1,211	344
	54,579	10,524
Total of Taxation of the County - - - - £65,103		

(*For those engaged in Mines, see " Mining Interest."*)

ENGAGED IN	MALES.		FEMALES.		TOTAL.
	20 years of age and upwards.	Under 20 years of age.	20 years of age and upwards.	Under 20 years of age.	
AGRICULTURE:					
Farmers and Graziers - - - -	2,957	26	208	—	3,191
Agricultural Labourers - - -	4,825	1,699	89	30	6,643
Gardeners, Nurserymen, and Florists -	233	17	1	1	252
	8,015	1,742	298	31	10,086
MANUFACTURES:					
Iron Manufacture (all branches) - - -	2,456	513	91	66	3,126
Copper Manufacture (all branches) -	1,137	273	6	5	1,421
Tin Manufacture (all branches) - - -	234	115	71	71	491
Tin Plate Workers and Tinmen -	88	29	—	—	117
Engineers and Engine Workers - - -	395	66	2	1	464
Engine and Machine Makers - - -	97	26	—	—	123
Weavers (all branches) - - - -	245	31	14	1	291
Spinners (branch not specified) - - -	8	—	150	29	187
Nailors - - - - - -	148	19	3	—	170
Coke Burners - - - - -	123	11	1	3	138
Potters - - - - - -	89	29	16	1	135
Woollen Manufacture (all branches) - -	88	9	16	6	119
Miscellaneous - - - - -	626	102	44	8	780
	5,734	1,223	414	191	7,562
ALL OTHER CLASSES:					
Employed in Retail Trade or in Handicraft, as Masters or Workmen - - - - -	12,076	2,193	1,689	419	16,377
Labourers - - - - -	14,881	3,526	795	167	19,369
Military and Naval - - - - -	1,501	225	—	—	1,726
Professional Persons - - - -	481	—	—	—	481
Other Educated Persons following miscellaneous Pursuits	572	85	132	4	793
Persons engaged in the Government Civil Service -	108	7	3	—	118
Parochial, Town, and Church Officers - - -	114	1	8	—	123
Domestic Servants - - - -	835	529	4,218	3,561	9,143
Persons returned as Independent - - -	808	87	2,943	233	4,071
Almspeople, Pensioners, Paupers, Lunatics, and Prisoners	251	102	407	94	854
RESIDUE OF POPULATION:					
Consisting of the Wives, Children, and others dependent on all Classes - - - - -	2,553	30,233	33,661	34,038	100,485
Total of all other Classes - - -	34,180	36,988	43,856	38,516	153,540

Divide " ALL OTHER CLASSES " between the AGRICULTURISTS and the MANUFACTURERS in the proportion which these respectively bear to each other, and the numbers engaged in, and dependent on, each interest will stand thus :—

Engaged in Agriculture - - -	10,086	
Dependent on ,, - - -	87,750	
AGRICULTURE—Total -		97,836
Engaged in Manufactures - - -	7,562	
Dependent on ,, - -	65,790	
MANUFACTURES—Total -		73,352
Total of the County - - -		171,188

TAXATION.

	Paid by the	
	LAND.	MANUFACTURERS.
Paid exclusively by the Landed Interest :	£	£
Land Tax - - - - - - - -	7,671	
Tithes - - - - - - - -	12,351	
Property Tax—on Land, assessed at - - - £258,470	7,538	
Paid in the Proportion of 7-12ths by the Landed Interest, and 5-12ths by the Manufacturers :		
Poor and County Rates - - - - - £60,057	35,034	25,023
Highway Rates - - - - - - 5,715	3,334	2,381
Church ,, - - - - - - 2,115	1,234	881
Turnpike Trusts - - - - - - 13,358	7,793	5,565
Property Tax—on Dwelling Houses, assessed at - 219,165	3,729	2,663
,, on other property ,, - - 139,762	2,378	1,698
	81,062	38,211
Total of Taxation of the County - - - - £119,273		

(For those engaged in Mines, see " Mining Interest.")

ENGAGED IN	MALES.		FEMALES.		TOTAL.
	20 years of age and upwards.	Under 20 years of age.	20 years of age and upwards.	Under 20 years of age.	
Agriculture:					
Farmers and Graziers - - - - -	2,110	11	246	—	2,367
Agricultural Labourers - - - -	2,324	856	58	24	3,262
Gardeners, Nurserymen, and Florists - -	46	1	1	—	48
	4,480	868	305	24	5,677
Manufactures:					
Weavers (all branches) - - - -	175	7	10	2	194
Spinners (branch not specified) - - - -	21	16	33	3	73
Woollen Manufacture (all branches) - - -	23	4	34	6	67
Miscellaneous - - - - -	142	14	51	1	208
	361	41	128	12	542
All other Classes:					
Employed in Retail Trade or in Handicraft, as Masters or Workmen - - - - - -	2,045	238	310	41	2,634
Labourers - - - - - - -	1,479	230	88	4	1,801
Military and Naval - - - - - -	149	22	—	—	171
Professional Persons - - - - -	102	—	—	—	102
Other Educated Persons following miscellaneous Pursuits	88	7	19	2	116
Persons engaged in the Government Civil Service -	17	—	2	—	19
Parochial, Town, and Church Officers - -	27	—	3	—	30
Domestic Servants - - - - -	237	156	1,433	1,197	3,023
Persons returned as Independent - - -	264	21	725	33	1,043
Almspeople, Pensioners, Paupers, Lunatics, and Prisoners	90	32	311	22	455
Residue of Population:					
Consisting of the Wives, Children, and others dependent on all Classes - - - - -	1,103	7,225	8,110	7,281	23,719
Total of all other Classes - - -	5,601	7,931	11,001	8,580	33,113

Divide "ALL OTHER CLASSES" between the AGRICULTURISTS and the MANUFACTURERS in the proportion which these respectively bear to each other, and the numbers engaged in, and dependent on, each interest will stand thus:—

Engaged in Agriculture - - -	5,677	
Dependent on „ - - - -	30,228	
AGRICULTURE—Total - -		35,905
Engaged in Manufactures - - -	542	
Dependent on „ - - -	2,885	
MANUFACTURES—Total - -		3,427
Total of the County - - -		39,332

TAXATION.

	Paid by the	
	Land.	Manufacturers.
Paid exclusively by the Landed Interest:	£	£
Land Tax - - - - - - -	2,423	
Tithes - - - - - - -	3,188	
Property Tax—on Land, assessed at - - £108,237	3,156	
Paid in the Proportion of 21-23rds by the Landed Interest, and 2-23rds by the Manufacturers:		
Poor and County Rates - - - - £17,284	15,781	1,503
Highway Rates - - - - - 648	592	56
Church „ - - - - - 236	215	21
Turnpike Trusts - - - - - 2,921	2,667	254
Property Tax—on Dwelling Houses, assessed at - 31,231	831	79
„ on other Property „ - 14,197	378	36
	29,231	1,949
Total of Taxation of the County - - - - £31,180		

ENGAGED IN	MALES.		FEMALES.		TOTAL.
	20 years of age and upwards.	Under 20 years of age.	20 years of age and upwards.	Under 20 years of age.	
AGRICULTURE:					
Farmers and Graziers - - - -	3,143	15	325	—	3,483
Agricultural Labourers - - - -	4,600	1,928	81	60	6,669
Gardeners, Nurserymen, and Florists - -	74	3	—	—	77
	7,817	1,946	406	60	10,229
MANUFACTURES:					
Weavers (branch not specified) - -	537	110	169	59	875
Woollen and Cloth Manufacture (all branches) -	527	111	192	36	866
Flannel Manufacture - - - -	228	37	59	26	350
Spinners (branch not specified) - -	141	20	153	6	320
Miscellaneous - - - - -	325	37	66	14	442
	1,758	315	639	141	2,853
ALL OTHER CLASSES:					
Employed in Retail Trade or in Handicraft, as Masters or Workmen - - - - -	3,593	500	525	79	4,697
Labourers - - - - -	1,052	51	154	9	1,266
Military and Naval - - - - -	157	15	—	—	172
Professional Persons - - - -	202	—	—	—	202
Other Educated Persons following miscellaneous Pursuits	155	14	31	1	201
Persons engaged in the Government Civil Service -	27	—	2	—	29
Parochial, Town, and Church Officers - - -	62	—	3	—	65
Domestic Servants - - - -	459	328	2,024	2,199	5,010
Persons returned as Independent - - -	391	23	727	36	1,177
Almspeople, Pensioners, Paupers, Lunatics, and Prisoners	239	148	413	64	864
RESIDUE OF POPULATION:					
Consisting of the Wives, Children, and others dependent on all Classes - - - - -	1,901	13,133	13,482	13,938	42,454
Total of all other Classes - - -	8,238	14,212	17,361	16,326	56,137

Divide " ALL OTHER CLASSES" between the AGRICULTURISTS and the MANUFACTURERS in the proportion which these respectively bear to each other, and the numbers engaged in, and dependent on, each interest will stand thus :—

Engaged in Agriculture - - -	10,229	
Dependent on ,, - - -	43,902	
AGRICULTURE—Total - -		54,131
Engaged in Manufactures - - -	2,853	
Dependent on ,, - - -	12,235	
MANUFACTURES—Total -		15,088
Total of the County - - -		69,219

TAXATION.

		Paid by the	
		LAND.	MANUFACTURERS.
Paid exclusively by the Landed Interest :		£	£
Land Tax - - - - - - -		5,805	
Tithes - - - - - - -		20,313	
Property Tax—on Land, assessed at - -	£258,067	7,526	
Paid in the Proportion of 7-9ths by the Landed Interest, and 2-9ths by the Manufacturers :			
Poor and County Rates - - - -	£39,756	30,922	8,834
Highway Rates - - - - -	2,557	1,989	5б8
Church ,, - - - - -	1,003	781	222
Turnpike Trusts - - - - -	11,297	8,787	2,510
Property Tax—on Dwelling Houses, assessed at -	54,091	1,227	350
,, on other Property ,, - -	28,928	656	187
		78,006	12,671
Total of Taxation of the County - - - -		£90,677	

ENGAGED IN	MALES.		FEMALES.		TOTAL.
	20 years of age and upwards.	Under 20 years of age.	20 years of age and upwards.	Under 20 years of age.	
Agriculture:					
Farmers and Graziers - - - -	2,632	22	339	—	2,993
Agricultural Labourers - - - -	5,003	1,300	66	15	6,384
Gardeners, Nurserymen, and Florists - -	85	5	3	—	93
	7,720	1,327	408	15	9,470
Manufactures:					
Weavers (all branches) - - -	126	11	3	—	140
Spinners (branch not specified) - - -	—	1	71	6	78
Stocking Knitters - - - -	—	—	40	—	40
Woollen and Cloth Manufacture (all branches) -	17	4	11	1	33
Miscellaneous - - - - -	243	29	29	1	302
	386	45	154	8	593
All other Classes:					
Employed in Retail Trade or in Handicraft, as Masters or Workmen - - - - -	5,408	946	789	147	7,290
Labourers - - - - - -	1,932	290	459	89	2,770
Military and Naval - - - -	864	48	—	—	912
Professional Persons - - - - - -	327	—	—	—	327
Other Educated Persons following miscellaneous Pursuits	163	26	83	2	274
Persons engaged in the Government Civil Service - -	81	1	1	—	83
Parochial, Town, and Church Officers - -	69	18	6	—	93
Domestic Servants - - - - -	745	668	3,642	2,360	7,415
Persons returned as Independent - - -	571	56	2,399	121	3,147
Almspeople, Pensioners, Paupers, Lunatics, and Prisoners	293	107	439	104	943
Residue of Population:					
Consisting of the Wives, Children, and others dependent on all Classes - - - - -	1,453	16,707	18,100	18,467	54,727
Total of all other Classes - - -	11,906	18,867	25,918	21,290	77,981

Divide " all other classes" between the Agriculturists and the Manufacturers in the proportion which these respectively bear to each other, and the numbers engaged in, and dependent on, each interest will stand thus :—

Engaged in Agriculture - - - -	9,470	
Dependent on ,, - - -	73,386	
Agriculture—Total - -		82,856
Engaged in Manufactures - - -	593	
Dependent on ,, - - -	4,595	
Manufactures—Total - -		5,188
Total of the County - - -		88,044

TAXATION.

		Paid by the	
		Land.	Manufacturers.
Paid exclusively by the Landed Interest :		£	£
Land Tax - - - - - -		2,902	
Tithes - - - - - -		24,438	
Property Tax—on Land, assessed at - -	£266,864	7,783	
Paid in the Proportion of 16-17ths by the Landed Interest, and 1-17th by the Manufacturers:			
Poor and County Rates - - -	£28,636	26,952	1,684
Highway Rates - - - - -	5,833	5,490	343
Church ,, - - - - -	1,682	1,583	99
Turnpike Trusts - - - - -	2,397	2,256	141
Property Tax—on Dwelling Houses, assessed at - -	57,731	1,584	99
,, on other Property ,, -	37,047	1,017	63
		74,105	2,429
Total of Taxation of the County - - -		£76,534	

ENGAGED IN	MALES.		FEMALES.		TOTAL.
	20 years of age and upwards.	Under 20 years of age.	20 years of age and upwards.	Under 20 years of age.	
AGRICULTURE:					
Farmers and Graziers - - - - -	1,482	3	99	—	1,584
Agricultural Labourers - - - -	2,076	759	92	81	3,008
Gardeners, Nurserymen, and Florists - -	17	—	—	—	17
	3,575	762	191	81	4,609
MANUFACTURES:					
There is no leading branch of Manufactures carried on in this County; the largest number employed in any one branch, is—					
Weavers (branch not specified) - - - -	27	2	2	—	31
Woollen Manufacture - - - -	2	4	9	4	19
Miscellaneous - - - - -	65	7	6	—	78
	94	13	17	4	128
ALL OTHER CLASSES:					
Employed in Retail Trade or in Handicraft, as Masters or Workmen - - - - -	1,460	202	153	27	1,842
Labourers - - - - - - -	218	14	74	—	306
Military and Naval - - - - -	13	1	—	—	14
Professional Persons - - - -	90	—	—	—	90
Other Educated Persons following miscellaneous Pursuits	36	3	11	1	51
Persons engaged in the Government Civil Service - -	6	—	2	—	8
Parochial, Town, and Church Officers - - -	21	—	4	—	25
Domestic Servants - - - - -	203	165	787	775	1,930
Persons returned as Independent - - -	276	15	534	20	845
Almspeople, Pensioners, Paupers, Lunatics, and Prisoners	36	27	95	22	180
RESIDUE OF POPULATION:					
Consisting of the Wives, Children, and others dependent on all Classes - - - - -	762	4,834	4,636	5,096	15,328
Total of all other Classes - - -	3,121	5,261	6,296	5,941	20,619

Divide " ALL OTHER CLASSES " between the AGRICULTURISTS and the MANUFACTURERS in the proportion which these respectively bear to each other, and the numbers engaged in, and dependent on, each interest will stand thus :—

Engaged in Agriculture - - - 4,609
Dependent on ,, - - - 20,062
    AGRICULTURE—Total - - ——— 24,671

Engaged in Manufactures - - - 128
Dependent on ,, - - - 557
    MANUFACTURES—Total - - ——— 685

Total of the County - - - 25,356

TAXATION.

	Paid by the	
	LAND.	MANUFACTURERS.
Paid exclusively by the Landed Interest :	£	£
Land Tax - - - - - - - -	2,653	
Tithes - - - - - - - -	6,039	
Property Tax—on Land, assessed at - - £107,647	3,139	
Paid in the Proportion of 36-37ths by the Landed Interest, and 1-37th by the Manufacturers :		
Poor and County Rates - - - - £13,034	12,682	352
Highway Rates - - - - - 1,980	1,927	53
Church ,, - - - - - 665	647	18
Turnpike Trusts - - - - - 2,187	2,128	59
Property Tax—on Dwelling Houses, assessed at - 14,863	422	11
,, on other Property ,, - 6,476	183	5
	29,820	498
Total of Taxation of the County - - - - £30,318		

WALES—SUMMARY OF POPULATION.

COUNTIES.	AGRICULTURE.			MANUFACTURES.			TOTAL OF THE COUNTY.
	Engaged in :	Dependent on :	TOTAL.	Engaged in :	Dependent on :	TOTAL.	
ANGLESEA - - -	7,720	39,856	47,576	538	2,777	3,315	50,891
BRECON - - -	5,589	41,052	46,641	1,074	7,888	8,962	55,603
CARDIGAN - - -	8,996	52,897	61,893	999	5,874	6,873	68,766
CARMARTHEN - - -	14,511	82,320	96,831	1,423	8,072	9,495	106,326
CARNARVON - -	9,813	65,780	75,593	714	4,786	5,500	81,093
DENBIGH - - -	11,441	67,149	78,599	1,496	8,780	10,276	88,866
FLINT - - -	5,491	46,366	51,857	1,595	13,467	15,062	66,919
GLAMORGAN - - -	10,086	87,750	97,836	7,562	65,790	73,352	171,188
MERIONETH - -	5,677	30,228	35,905	542	2,885	3,427	39,332
MONTGOMERY - - -	10,229	43,902	54,131	2,853	12,235	15,088	69,219
PEMBROKE - - -	9,470	73,386	82,855	593	4,595	5,188	88,044
RADNOR - - -	4,609	20,062	24,671	128	557	685	25,356
	103,632	650,748	754,380	19,517	137,706	157,223	911,603

Total of the Agricultural Interest - - - 734,380

„ Manufacturing Interest - - - - 157,223

Total of the Principality - - - 911,603

WALES—SUMMARY OF DIRECT AND LOCAL TAXATION.

COUNTIES.	Paid by the Landed Interest and those dependent on it.	Paid by the Manufacturing Interest and those dependent on it.	Total Taxation of the County.
	£	£	£
ANGLESEA	51,334	2,221	53,555
BRECON	44,834	5,050	49,884
CARDIGAN	45,460	3,176	48,636
CARMARTHEN	108,424	6,888	115,312
CARNARVON	55,137	2,581	57,718
DENBIGH	81,464	6,923	88,387
FLINT	54,579	10,524	65,103
GLAMORGAN	81,062	38,211	119,273
MERIONETH	29,231	1,949	31,180
MONTGOMERY	78,006	12,671	90,677
PEMBROKE	74,105	2,429	76,534
RADNOR	29,820	498	30,318
	733,456	93,121	826,577

Total of Direct and Local Taxation paid by the Landed Interest - -	£733,456
,, ,, Manufacturing - -	93,121
Total of Direct and Local Taxation of Wales - - -	£826,577

ENGAGED IN	MALES.		FEMALES.		TOTAL.
	20 years of age and upwards.	Under 20 years of age.	20 years of age and upwards.	Under 20 years of age.	
Agriculture:					
Farmers and Graziers - - - - -	8,052	39	586	—	8,677
Agricultural Labourers - - - -	9,134	5,896	517	427	15,974
Gardeners, Nurserymen, and Florists - -	496	77	—	—	573
	17,682	6,012	1,103	427	25,224
Manufactures:					
Linen Manufacture (all branches) - -	875	275	549	376	2,075
Cotton Manufacture (all branches) - -	252	73	608	512	1,445
Flax Manufacture (all branches) - -	314	284	430	386	1,414
Stocking Knitters and Weavers - -	12	1	1,290	27	1,330
Woollen and Cloth Manufacture (all branches) -	293	87	221	204	805
Spinners (branch not specified) - -	2	2	332	89	425
Weavers (branch not specified) - - -	273	34	71	29	407
Factory Workers (branch not specified) - -	81	36	93	105	315
Rope, Cord, and Twine Manufacture (all branches)	115	91	16	2	224
Lint Manufacture (all branches) - -	10	15	80	118	223
Comb Makers (all branches) - - -	58	127	14	21	220
Carpet Manufacture (all branches) - -	142	34	10	—	186
Paper Manufacture (all branches) - -	73	12	58	30	173
Iron Founders and Moulders - - -	118	35	—	—	153
Engineers and Engine Workers - - -	99	41	—	—	140
Engine and Machine Makers - - -	31	8	—	—	39
Miscellaneous - - - - -	803	248	209	73	1,333
	3,551	1,403	3,981	1,972	10,907
All other Classes:					
Employed in Retail Trade or in Handicraft, as Masters or Workmen - - - - - -	12,838	2,236	1,752	204	17,030
Labourers - - - - - -	2,965	170	407	17	3,559
Military and Naval - - - -	1,936	324	—	—	2,260
Professional Persons - - - -	735	—	—	—	735
Other Educated Persons following miscellaneous Pursuits	776	148	235	12	1,171
Persons engaged in the Government Civil Service	229	1	16	—	246
Parochial, Town, and Church Officers -	155	1	7	—	163
Domestic Servants - - - - -	838	496	7,727	5,650	14,711
Persons returned as Independent - -	1,027	47	5,593	170	6,837
Almspeople, Pensioners, Paupers, Lunatics, and Prisoners	660	88	1,112	87	1,947
Residue of Population:					
Consisting of the Wives, Children, and others dependent on all Classes - - - - -	2,466	33,042	36,178	35,911	107,597
Total of all other Classes - - -	24,625	36,553	53,027	42,051	156,256

Divide "**all other classes**" between the **Agriculturists** and the **Manufacturers** in the proportion which these respectively bear to each other, and the numbers engaged in, and dependent on, each interest will stand thus:—

Engaged in Agriculture - - -	25,224	
Dependent on ,, - - -	109,087	
Agriculture—Total - - -		134,311
Engaged in Manufactures - -	10,907	
Dependent on ,, - -	47,169	
Manufactures—Total -		58,076
Total of the County - -		192,387

TAXATION.

	Paid by the	
	Land.	Manufacturers.
Paid exclusively by the Landed Interest:	£	£
Land Tax - - - - - -	(*See Summary.*)	
Property Tax—on Land, assessed at - - - £423,388	12,348	
Paid in the Proportion of 5-7ths by the Landed Interest, and 2-7ths by the Manufacturers:		
Poor Relief - - - - - - £17,471	12,481	4,990
Highway Rates, ⎫		
Church ,, ⎬ No Return.		
Turnpike Trusts, ⎭		
Property Tax—on Dwelling Houses, assessed at - - 145,365	3,029	1,210
,, on other Property ,, - - 37,049	772	308
	28,630	6,508
Total of Taxation of the County - - -	£35,138	

ENGAGED IN	MALES.		FEMALES.		TOTAL.
	20 years of age and upwards.	Under 20 years of age.	20 years of age and upwards.	Under 20 years of age.	
AGRICULTURE:					
Farmers and Graziers	3,811	28	707	—	4,546
Agricultural Labourers	5,951	2,097	364	110	8,522
Gardeners, Nurserymen, and Florists	111	6	2	—	119
	9,873	2,131	1,073	110	13,187
MANUFACTURES:					
Weavers (all branches)	554	13	64	3	634
Woollen and Cloth Manufacture (all branches)	109	—	7	—	116
Spinners	1	—	142	12	155
Miscellaneous	356	37	50	1	444
	1,020	50	263	16	1,349
ALL OTHER CLASSES:					
Employed in Retail Trade or in Handicraft, as Masters or Workmen	3,953	405	446	41	4,845
Labourers	1,313	135	92	5	1,545
Military and Naval	1,841	188	—	—	2,029
Professional Persons	236	—	—	—	236
Other Educated Persons following Miscellaneous Pursuits	326	44	35	3	408
Persons engaged in the Government Civil Service	166	4	5	—	175
Parochial, Town, and Church Officers	68	—	1	—	69
Domestic Servants	625	523	2,827	2,096	6,071
Persons returned as Independent	319	23	1,006	53	1,401
Almspeople, Pensioners, Paupers, Lunatics, and Prisoners	426	18	588	7	1,039
RESIDUE OF POPULATION:					
Consisting of the Wives, Children, and others dependent on all Classes	3,163	20,969	20,033	20,852	65,017
Total of all other Classes	12,436	22,309	25,033	23,057	82,835

Divide "ALL OTHER CLASSES" between the AGRICULTURISTS and the MANUFACTURERS in the proportion which these respectively bear to each other, and the numbers engaged in, and dependent on, each interest will stand thus—

```
        Engaged in Agriculture          -   13,187
        Dependent on    ,,              -   75,148
                AGRICULTURE—Total   -          88,335

        Engaged in Manufactures         -    1,349
        Dependent on    ,,              -    7,687
                MANUFACTURES—Total  -           9,036

                Total of the County    -       97,371
```

TAXATION.

	Paid by the	
	LAND.	MANUFACTURERS.
	£	£
Paid exclusively by the Landed Interest:		
Land Tax	(See Summary.)	
Property Tax—on Land, assessed at £232,441	6,779	
Paid in the Proportion of 9-10ths by the Landed Interest, and 1-10th by the Manufacturers:		
Poor Relief £3,139	2,826	313
Highway Rates, Church ,, Turnpike Trusts, No Return.		
Property Tax—on Dwelling Houses, assessed at 25,361	666	73
,, on other Property ,, 4,471	117	30
	10,388	416
Total of Taxation of the County £10,804		

(*For those engaged in Mines, see "Mining Interest."*)

ENGAGED IN	MALES.		FEMALES.		TOTAL.
	20 years of age and upwards.	Under 20 years of age.	20 years of age and upwards.	Under 20 years of age.	
Agriculture:					
Farmers and Graziers - - - -	2,839	28	161	—	3,028
Agricultural Labourers - - -	5,665	1,869	234	61	7,829
Gardeners, Nurserymen, and Florists -	284	14	5	—	303
	8,788	1,911	400	61	11,160
Manufactures:					
Cotton Manufacture (all branches) - - -	5,201	1,633	1,377	664	8,875
Weavers (all branches) - - -	1,403	504	89	78	2,074
Muslin Embroiderers and Workers - - -	6	4	1,207	498	1,715
Muslin Manufacture (all branches) - -	144	46	58	22	270
Woollen and Cloth Manufacture (all branches) - -	346	74	110	67	597
Silk Manufacture (all branches) - -	434	85	23	8	550
Carpet and Rug Manufacture (all branches) -	431	60	18	6	515
Printers (Cotton, Carpet, and Muslin) -	263	90	3	5	361
Flax Manufacture (all branches) - - -	46	28	100	84	258
Spinners (branch not specified) - -	2	—	198	37	237
Engineers and Engine Workers - - - -	160	44	—	—	204
Engine and Machine Makers - -	7	—	—	—	7
Bleachers - - - - -	119	29	26	4	178
Brick and Tile Makers - - -	104	50	5	3	162
Thread Manufacture (all branches) - -	31	6	91	32	160
Nailers and Nail Makers - - -	123	12	—	—	135
Stocking Makers and Knitters - -	55	—	68	2	125
Snuff Box Maker - - - -	107	5	10	1	123
Linen Manufacture (all branches) - - -	63	4	32	17	116
Miscellaneous - - - -	747	176	116	35	1,074
	9,792	2,850	3,531	1,563	17,736
All other Classes:					
Employed in Retail Trade or in Handicraft, as Masters or Workmen - - - - -	9,155	1,919	3,411	916	15,401
Labourers - - - - -	4,917	859	400	13	6,189
Military and Naval - - - -	841	177	—	—	1,018
Professional Persons - - - -	459	—	—	—	459
Other Educated Persons following miscellaneous Pursuits	476	72	81	5	634
Persons engaged in the Government Civil Service -	80	2	—	—	82
Parochial, Town, and Church Officers -	78	—	3	1	82
Domestic Servants - - - -	839	511	4,071	3,059	8,480
Persons returned as Independent - - -	672	16	1,746	76	2,510
Almspeople, Pensioners, Paupers, Lunatics, and Prisoners	262	50	367	41	720
Residue of Population:					
Consisting of the Wives, Children, and others dependent on all Classes - - - - -	2,018	32,258	31,170	34,439	99,885
Total of all other Classes - - -	19,797	35,864	41,249	38,550	135,460

Divide "all other classes" between the Agriculturists and the Manufacturers in the proportion which these respectively bear to each other, and the numbers engaged in, and dependent on, each interest will stand thus :—

Engaged in Agriculture - - -	11,160	
Dependent on - - - -	52,316	
Agriculture—Total - -		63,476
Engaged in Manufactures - - -	17,736	
Dependent on - - - -	83,144	
Manufactures—Total - -		100,880
Total of the County - - -		164,356

TAXATION.

		Paid by the	
		Land.	Manufacturers.
		£	£
Paid exclusively by the Landed Interest:			
Land Tax - - - - - -		(*See Summary.*)	
Property Tax—on Land, assessed at - - -	£390,277	11,383	
Paid in the Proportion of 2-5ths by the Landed Interest, and 3-5ths by the Manufacturers:			
Poor Relief - - - - -	£11,639	4,656	6,983
Highway Rates, }			
Church ,, } No Return.			
Turnpike Trusts, }			
Property Tax—on Dwelling Houses, assessed at - -	86,429	1,008	1,512
,, on other Property ,, -	54,612	636	856
-		17,683	9,351
Total of Taxation of the County - - - -		£27,034	

(*For those engaged in Mines, see "Mining Interest.*")

ENGAGED IN	MALES.		FEMALES.		TOTAL.
	20 years of age and upwards.	Under 20 years of age.	20 years of age and upwards.	Under 20 years of age.	
Agriculture:					
Farmers and Graziers - - - -	2,301	10	242	—	2,553
Agricultural Labourers - - -	2,562	1,824	303	236	4,925
Gardeners, Nurserymen, and Florists - -	87	16	—	—	103
	4,950	1,850	545	236	7,581
Manufactures:					
Spinners (branch not specified) - - -	—	—	176	7	183
Weaver (all branches) - - - -	153	8	3	—	164
Miscellaneous - - - - -	159	22	79	1	261
	312	30	258	8	608
All other Classes:					
Employed in Retail Trade or in Handicraft, as Masters or Workmen - - - - -	2,807	425	375	21	3,628
Labourers - - - - -	485	12	116	2	615
Military and Naval - - - -	928	114	—	—	1,042
Professional Persons - - - -	196	—	—	—	196
Other Educated Persons following miscellaneous Pursuits	141	30	89	1	261
Persons engaged in the Government Civil Service -	57	1	5	—	63
Parochial, Town, and Church Officers - - -	33	—	1	—	34
Domestic Servants - - - - -	191	118	1,727	1,679	3,715
Persons returned as Independent - - -	238	14	1,288	41	1,581
Almspeople, Pensioners, Paupers, Lunatics, and Prisoners	197	9	349	18	573
Residue of Population:					
Consisting of the Wives, Children, and others dependent on all Classes - - - -	1,003	9,150	9,971	9,658	29,782
Total of all other Classes - - -	6,276	9,873	13,921	11,420	41,490

Divide "ALL OTHER CLASSES" between the AGRICULTURISTS and the MANUFACTURERS in the proportion which these respectively bear to each other, and the numbers engaged in, and dependent on, each interest will stand thus:—

Engaged in Agriculture - - -	7,581	
Dependent on ,, - - -	38,410	
AGRICULTURE—Total - -		45,991
Engaged in Manufactures - - -	608	
Dependent on ,, - - -	3,080	
MANUFACTURES—Total -		3,688
Total of the County - -		49,679

TAXATION.

	Paid by the	
	LAND.	MANUFACTURERS.
	£	£
Paid exclusively by the Landed Interest:		
Land Tax - - - - - - -	(See Summary.)	
Property Tax—on Land, assessed at - - - £110,608	3,226	
Paid in the Proportion of 12-13ths by the Landed Interest, and 1-13th by the Manufacturers:		
Poor Relief - - - - - £2,372	2,190	182
Highway Rates, }		
Church ,, } No Return.		
Turnpike Trusts, }		
Property Tax—on Dwelling Houses, assessed at - - 8,402	227	18
,, on other Property ,, - 5,327	133	12
	5,776	212
Total of Taxation of the County - - - - £5,988		

ENGAGED IN	MALES.		FEMALES.		TOTAL.
	20 years of age and upwards.	Under 20 years of age.	20 years of age and upwards.	Under 20 years of age.	
Agriculture:					
Farmers and Graziers - - - - - -	560	9	10	—	579
Agricultural Labourers - - - - -	3,443	1,117	623	318	5,501
Gardeners, Nurserymen, and Florists - - -	80	13	—	—	93
	4,083	1,139	633	318	6,173
Manufactures:					
Cotton Manufacture (all branches) - - -	88	13	22	5	128
Linen Manufacture - - - - - -	78	2	—	—	80
Paper Makers - - - - - -	37	2	23	7	69
Woollen Manufacture - - - - -	21	7	12	6	46
Weavers (branch not specified) - - -	32	—	—	—	32
Miscellaneous - - - - -	82	16	47	—	145
	338	40	104	18	500
All other Classes:					
Employed in Retail Trade or in Handicraft, as Masters or Workmen - - - - -	2,257	517	309	25	3,108
Labourers - - - - - -	360	30	49	—	439
Military and Naval - - - - -	294	42	—	—	336
Professional Persons - - - - -	135	—	—	—	135
Other Educated Persons following miscellaneous Pursuits	100	15	38	5	158
Persons engaged in the Government Civil Service -	20	2	2	—	24
Parochial, Town, and Church Officers - - -	22	—	1	—	23
Domestic Servants - - - -	258	148	1,253	765	2,424
Persons returned as Independent - - -	170	6	542	16	734
Almspeople, Pensioners, Paupers, Lunatics, and Prisoners	126	5	203	6	340
Residue of Population:					
Consisting of the Wives, Children, and others dependent on all Classes - - - - -	313	6,144	6,835	6,752	20,044
Total of all other Classes - - -	4,055	6,909	9,232	7,569	27,765

Divide " All other classes " between the Agriculturists and the Manufacturers in the proportion which these respectively bear to each other, and the numbers engaged in, and dependent on, each interest will stand thus :—

Engaged in Agriculture - - -	6,173	
Dependent on ,, - - - -	25,685	
Agriculture—Total - -		31,858
Engaged in Manufactures - - -	500	
Dependent on ,, - - -	2,080	
Manufactures—Total - -		2,580
Total of the County - - -		34,438

TAXATION.

		Paid by the	
		Land.	Manufacturers.
		£	£
Paid exclusively by the Landed Interest :			
Land Tax - - - - -		(See Summary.)	
Property Tax—on Land, assessed at - - - £237,041		6,913	
Paid in the Proportion of 12-13ths by the Landed Interest, and 1-13th by the Manufacturers :			
Poor Relief - - - - - £6,428		5,934	494
Highway Rates ⎫			
Church ,, ⎬ No Return.			
Turnpike Trusts ⎭			
Property Tax—on Dwelling Houses, assessed at - - 16,743		451	37
,, on other Property ,, - - 384			175
		13,308	706
Total of Taxation of the County - - - - £14,014			

	MALES.		FEMALES.		
ENGAGED IN	20 years of age and upwards.	Under 20 years of age.	20 years of age and upwards.	Under 20 years of age.	TOTAL.
AGRICULTURE:					
Farmers and Graziers - - - -	592	1	19	—	612
Agricultural Labourers - - -	442	291	16	15	764
Gardeners, Nurserymen, and Florists - -	40	3	—	—	43
	1,074	295	35	15	1,419
MANUFACTURES:					
Cotton Manufacture (all branches) - - -	120	69	100	68	357
Weavers (branch not specified) - - . -	79	2	11	19	111
Spinners (branch not specified) - - -	—	—	38	—	38
Miscellaneous - - - - -	84	11	3	1	99
	283	82	152	88	605
ALL OTHER CLASSES:					
Employed in Retail Trade or in Handicraft, as Masters or Workmen - - - - -	891	131	195	26	1,243
Labourers - - - - - -	127	7	22	—	156
Military and Naval - - - - -	460	38	—	—	498
Professional Persons - - - -	67	—	—	—	67
Other Educated Persons following miscellaneous Pursuits	63	21	7	1	92
Persons engaged in the Government Civil Service -	28	—	—	—	28
Parochial, Town, and Church Officers - -	7	—	—	—	7
Domestic Servants - - - - -	68	61	613	347	1,089
Persons returned as Independent - - -	136	3	360	12	511
Almspeople, Pensioners, Paupers, Lunatics, and Prisoners	42	1	24	—	67
RESIDUE OF POPULATION:					
Consisting of the Wives, Children, and others dependent on all Classes - - -	337	2,943	3,558	3,120	9,958
Total of all other Classes - -	2,226	3,205	4,779	3,506	13,716

Divide "ALL OTHER CLASSES" between the AGRICULTURISTS and the MANUFACTURERS in the proportion which these respectively bear to each other, and the numbers engaged in, and dependent on, each interest will stand thus:—

Engaged in Agriculture - - -	1,419	
Dependent on ,, - - -	9,617	
AGRICULTURE—Total - -		11,036
Engaged in Manufactures - - -	605	
Dependent on ,, - - -	4,099	
MANUFACTURES—Total - -		4,704
Total of the County - - -		15,740

TAXATION.

		Paid by the	
		LAND.	MANUFACTURERS.
		£	£
Paid exclusively by the Landed Interest :		(See Summary.)	
Land Tax - - - - -			
Property Tax—on Land, assessed at - - -	£20,597	600	
Paid in the Proportion of 5-7ths by the Landed Interest, and 2-7ths by the Manufacturers :			
Poor Relief - - - - -	£567	405	162
Highway Rates ⎫			
Church ,, ⎬ No Return.			
Turnpike Trusts ⎭		206	80
Property Tax—on Dwelling Houses, assessed at - -	9,835	206	80
,, on other Property ,, - -	728	15	6
		1,226	248
Total of Taxation of the County - - -	- £1,474		

ENGAGED IN	MALES.		FEMALES.		TOTAL.
	20 years of age and upwards.	Under 20 years of age.	20 years of age and upwards.	Under 20 years of age.	
Agriculture :					
Farmers and Graziers - - - - - -	1,768	3	144	—	1,915
Agricultural Labourers - - - - -	1,610	1,012	397	145	3,164
Gardeners, Nurserymen, and Florists - - -	33	2	1	1	37
	3,411	1,017	542	146	5,116
Manufactures :					
Hemp Spinners - - - - , - -	—	—	150	1	151
Spinners (branch not specified) - - -	—	—	99	3	102
Net Makers and Weavers - - - - -	2	1	51	15	69
Weavers (branch not specified) - - - -	57	3	1	—	61
Rope and Cord Makers - - - - -	31	29	—	—	60
Miscellaneous - - - - - -	58	2	9	—	69
	148	35	310	19	512
All other Classes :					
Employed in Retail Trade or in Handicraft, as Masters or Workmen - - - - - -	2,150	324	156	24	2,654
Labourers - - - - - -	313	34	71	4	422
Military and Naval - - - - - -	1,004	51	—	—	1,055
Professional Persons - - - - -	56	—	—	—	56
Other Educated Persons following miscellaneous Pursuits	112	19	19	3	153
Persons engaged in the Government Civil Service -	32	—	2	—	34
Parochial, Town, and Church Officers - - -	21	—	1	—	22
Domestic Servants - - - - -	136	102	1,006	691	1,935
Persons returned as Independent - - -	98	7	527	16	648
Almspeople, Pensioners, Paupers, Lunatics, and Prisoners	167	2	154	—	323
Residue of Population :					
Consisting of the Wives, Children, and others dependent on all Classes - - - - -	757	7,149	7,927	7,580	23,413
Total of all other Classes - - -	4,846	7,688	9,863	8,318	30,715

Divide "all other classes" between the Agriculturists and the Manufacturers in the proportion which these respectively bear to each other, and the numbers engaged in, and dependent on, each interest will stand thus :—

Engaged in Agriculture - - - -	5,116	
Dependent on ,, - - - -	27,921	
Agriculture—Total - - ———		33,037
Engaged in Manufactures - - -	512	
Dependent on ,, - - -	2,794	
Manufactures—Total - - ———		3,306
Total of the County - - - -		36,343

TAXATION.

		Paid by the	
		Land.	Manufacturers.
		£	£
Paid exclusively by the Landed Interest :		(*See Summary.*)	
Land Tax - - - - - - -			
Property Tax—on Land, assessed at - - - £57,981		1,691	—
Paid in the Proportion of 10-11ths by the Landed Interest, and 1-11th by the Manufacturers :			
Poor Relief			
Church Rates `}`			
Highway Rates `}` No Return. - - - £658		598	59
Turnpike Trusts			
Property Tax—on Dwelling Houses, assessed at - - 6,870		163	18
,, on other Property ,, - - 1,721		46	4
		2,498	81
Total of Taxation of the County - - - £2,579			

(*For those engaged in Mines, see "Mining Interest."*)

ENGAGED IN	MALES.		FEMALES.		TOTAL.
	20 years of age and upwards.	Under 20 years of age.	20 years of age and upwards.	Under 20 years of age.	
AGRICULTURE :					
Farmers and Graziers - - - -	113	6	7	—	126
Agricultural Labourers - - - -	581	166	12	12	771
Gardeners, Nurserymen, and Florists - -	46	8	1	—	55
	740	180	20	12	952
MANUFACTURES :					
Woollen and Cloth Manufacture (all branches)	559	183	86	120	948
Engineers and Engine Workers - - -	67	19	—	—	86
Cotton Weaver - - - - -	55	9	1	4	69
Glass and Glass Bottle Manufacture - - -	34	20	—	—	54
Miscellaneous - - - -	254	82	36	20	392
	969	313	123	144	1,549
ALL OTHER CLASSES :					
Employed in Retail Trade or in Handicraft, as Masters or Workmen - - - - -	1,180	242	156	17	1,595
Labourers - - - - -	1,032	191	35	16	1,274
Military and Naval - - -	106	1	—	—	107
Professional Persons - - - -	56	—	—	—	56
Other Educated Persons following miscellaneous Pursuits	88	17	9	—	114
Persons engaged in the Government Civil Service -	30	—	—	—	30
Parochial, Town, and Church Officers - -	14	—	—	—	14
Domestic Servants - - - -	65	35	293	281	674
Persons returned as Independent - -	72	1	311	4	387
Almspeople, Pensioners, Paupers, Lunatics, and Prisoners	19	—	13	1	34
RESIDUE OF POPULATION :					
Consisting of the Wives, Children, and others dependent on all Classes - - -	207	3,830	4,212	4,120	12,369
Total of all other Classes - - -	2,869	4,317	5,029	4,439	16,654

Divide "ALL OTHER CLASSES" between the AGRICULTURISTS and the MANUFACTURERS in the proportion which these respectively bear to each other, and the numbers engaged in, and dependent on, each interest will stand thus :—

Engaged in Agriculture - - -	952	
Dependent on ,, - - -	6,339	
AGRICULTURE—Total - -		7,291
Engaged in Manufactures - - -	1,549	
Dependent on ,, - - -	10,315	
MANUFACTURES—Total - -		11,864
Total of the County - - -		19,155

TAXATION.

	Paid by the	
	LAND.	MANUFACTURERS.
	£	£
Paid exclusively by the Landed Interest :		
Land Tax - - - - - -	(*See Summary.*)	—
Property Tax—on Land, assessed at - - - £35,249	1,028	
Paid in the Proportion of 2-5ths by the Landed Interest, and 3-5ths by the Manufacturers :		
Poor Relief - - - - - £1,061	424	637
Highway Rates ⎫		
Church ,, ⎬ No Return.		
Turnpike Trusts ⎭		
Property Tax—on Dwelling Houses, assessed at - 7,608	88	133
,, on other Property ,, - 10,066	116	177
	1,656	947
Total of Taxation of the County - - - - £2,603		

(*For those engaged in Mines, see "Mining Interest."*)

ENGAGED IN	MALES.		FEMALES.		TOTAL.
	20 years of age and upwards.	Under 20 years of age.	20 years of age and upwards.	Under 20 years of age.	
Agriculture:					
Farmers and Graziers - - - -	500	2	19	—	521
Agricultural Labourers - - -	1,468	367	81	25	1,941
Gardeners, Nurserymen, and Florists - -	128	9	2	2	141
	2,096	378	102	27	2,603
Manufactures:					
Cotton Manufacture (all branches) - -	805	641	710	903	3,059
Printers (Calico and Cotton) - - -	1,024	651	119	352	2,146
Weavers (all branches) - - -	360	247	176	263	1,046
Paper Makers - - - -	36	14	46	34	130
Dyers (all branches) - - - -	78	24	4	23	129
Block and Print Cutters - - -	83	25	—	—	108
Miscellaneous - - - -	456	151	130	62	799
	2,842	1,753	1,185	1,637	7,417
All other Classes:					
Employed in Retail Trade or in Handicraft, as Masters or Workmen	2,898	578	459	65	4,000
Labourers - - - - - -	2,392	312	93	20	2,817
Military and Naval - - -	434	20	—	—	454
Professional Persons - - -	154	—	—	—	154
Other Educated Persons following miscellaneous Pursuits	175	40	24	1	240
Persons engaged in the Government Civil Service -	37	1	6	—	44
Parochial, Town, and Church Officers - -	46	—	—	—	46
Domestic Servants - - - -	259	156	1,228	737	2,380
Persons returned as Independent - -	190	11	638	13	852
Almspeople, Pensioners, Paupers, Lunatics, and Prisoners	53	—	47	—	100
Residue of Population:					
Consisting of the Wives, Children, and others dependent on all Classes - - - -	310	7,413	7,725	7,741	23,189
Total of all other Classes - - -	6,948	8,531	10,220	8,577	34,276

Divide " all other classes " between the Agriculturists and the Manufacturers in the proportion which these respectively bear to each other, and the numbers engaged in, and dependent on, each interest will stand thus: —

Engaged in Agriculture - - -	2,603	
Dependent on ,, - - -	8,905	
Agriculture—Total - -		11,508
Engaged in Manufactures - -	7,417	
Dependent on ,, - - -	25,371	
Manufactures—Total - -		32,788
Total of the County - -		44,296

TAXATION.

	Paid by the	
	Land.	Manufacturers.
Paid exclusively by the Landed Interest:	£	£
Land Tax - - - - - -	(*See Summary.*)	
Property Tax—on Land, assessed at - - - £72,041	2,101	
Paid in the Proportion of 1-4th by the Landed Interest, and 3-4ths by the Manufacturers:		
Poor Relief - - - - - - £2,837	709	2,128
Highway Rates, ⎫		
Church ,, ⎬ No Return.		
Turnpike Trust, ⎭		
Property Tax—on Dwelling Houses, assessed at - - 61,321	447	1,341
,, on other Property ,, - - 7,390	54	161
	3,311	3,630

Total of Taxation of the County - - - - £6,941

(*For those engaged in Mines, see "Mining Interest."*)

ENGAGED IN	MALES.		FEMALES.		TOTAL.
	20 years of age and upwards.	Under 20 years of age.	20 years of age and upwards.	Under 20 years of age.	
AGRICULTURE:					
Farmers and Graziers	1,708	17	133	—	1,858
Agricultural Labourers	4,650	1,632	1,736	901	8,919
Gardeners, Nurserymen, and Florists	139	22	—	—	161
	6,497	1,671	1,869	901	10,938
MANUFACTURES:					
Cotton Manufacture (all branches)	727	177	193	92	1,189
Stocking Makers	253	89	30	3	375
Weavers (all branches)	257	37	4	—	298
Woollen and Woollen Cloth Manufacture (all branches)	134	32	36	21	223
Muslin Flowerers	—	1	98	76	175
Miscellaneous	408	57	77	5	547
	1,779	393	438	197	2,807
ALL OTHER CLASSES:					
Employed in Retail Trade or in Handicraft, as Masters or Workmen	4,425	993	871	133	6,422
Labourers	1,075	123	294	23	1,515
Military and Naval	177	18	—	—	195
Professional Persons	252	—	—	—	252
Other Educated Persons following miscellaneous Pursuits	316	43	80	6	445
Persons engaged in the Government Civil Service	42	—	8	—	50
Parochial, Town, and Church Officers	63	—	4	—	67
Domestic Servants	329	169	1,938	1,276	3,712
Persons returned as Independent	384	9	1,267	23	1,683
Almspeople, Pensioners, Paupers, Lunatics, and Prisoners	255	9	464	15	743
RESIDUE OF POPULATION:					
Consisting of the Wives, Children, and others dependent on all Classes	1,009	14,114	14,182	14,696	44,001
Total of all other Classes	8,327	15,478	19,108	16,172	59,085

Divide " ALL OTHER CLASSES" between the AGRICULTURISTS and the MANUFACTURERS in the proportion which these respectively bear to each other, and the numbers engaged in, and dependent on, each interest will stand thus:—

Engaged in Agriculture	10,938	
Dependent on ,,	47,019	
AGRICULTURE—Total		57,957
Engaged in Manufactures	2,807	
Dependent on ,,	12,066	
MANUFACTURES—Total		14,873
Total of the County		72,830

TAXATION.

		Paid by the	
		LAND.	MANUFACTURERS.
		£	£
Paid exclusively by the Landed Interest :			
Land Tax		(*See Summary.*)	
Property Tax—on Land, assessed at	£266,547	7,774	
Paid in the Proportion of 4-5ths by the Landed Interest, and 1-5th by the Manufacturers :			
Poor Relief	£8,134	6,507	1,627
Highway Rates }			
Church ,, } No Return.			
Turnpike Trusts }			
Property Tax—on Dwelling Houses, assessed at	46,131	1,076	269
,, on other Property ,,	7,072	165	41
		15,522	1,937
Total of Taxation of the County		£17,459	

(*For those engaged in Mines, see " Mining Interest."*)

ENGAGED IN	MALES.		FEMALES.		TOTAL.
	20 years of age and upwards.	Under 20 years of age.	20 years of age and upwards.	Under 20 years of age.	
AGRICULTURE:					
Farmers and Graziers	632	8	17	—	657
Agricultural Labourers	4,012	1,102	635	116	5,865
Gardeners, Nurserymen, and Florists	1,074	134	22	4	1,234
	5,718	1,244	674	120	7,756
MANUFACTURES:					
Paper Manufacture (all branches)	303	99	266	126	794
Coach Makers (all branches)	281	91	1	—	373
Brass Founders	203	167	—	—	370
Engineers and Engine Workers	260	88	—	—	348
Silk Manufacture (all branches)	132	28	49	55	264
Tin Plate Workers and Tinmen	167	83	3	—	253
Rope and Cord Spinners and Makers	141	102	8	1	252
Type Founders	149	97	—	—	246
Hair Manufacture (all branches)	128	35	51	29	243
Flax Manufacture (all branches)	60	14	88	70	232
Weavers (branch not specified)	204	16	5	—	225
Glass Manufacture (all branches)	127	70	4	—	201
Iron Manufacture (all branches)	149	32	3	1	185
Tanners	134	20	—	—	154
Chair Makers	141	10	—	—	151
Skinners	100	37	1	—	138
Stocking Manufacture (all branches)	83	10	38	4	135
Nailors	110	17	—	—	127
Potters	89	24	8	4	125
Linen Manufacture (all branches)	120	2	1	—	123
Turners	93	26	—	—	119
„ Ivory	3	—	—	—	3
Cotton Manufacture (all branches)	100	6	8	3	117
Dyers	90	21	5	1	117
Worsted Weavers	88	18	1	—	107
Miscellaneous	1,193	309	278	84	1,864
	4,648	1,422	818	378	7,266
ALL OTHER CLASSES:					
Employed in Retail Trade or in Handicraft, as Masters or Workmen	23,649	6,007	6,405	1,152	37,213
Labourers	6,365	749	1,863	149	9,126
Military and Naval	2,235	409	—	—	2,644
Professional Persons	2,492	—	—	—	2,492
Other Educated Persons following miscellaneous Pursuits	2,673	404	463	45	3,585
Persons engaged in the Government Civil Service	390	9	5	—	404
Parochial, Town, and Church Officers	553	4	35	1	593
Domestic Servants	1,881	575	12,426	5,782	20,664
Persons returned as Independent	1,442	104	6,752	336	8,634
Almspeople, Pensioners, Paupers, Lunatics, and Prisoners	984	429	1,809	316	3,538
RESIDUE OF POPULATION:					
Consisting of the Wives, Children, and others dependent on all Classes	1,140	37,192	41,516	41,691	121,539
Total of all other Classes	43,804	45,882	71,274	49,472	210,432

Divide " ALL OTHER CLASSES" between the AGRICULTURISTS and the MANUFACTURERS in the proportion which these respectively bear to each other, and the numbers engaged in, and dependent on, each interest will stand thus:—

Engaged in Agriculture	7,756	
Dependent on „	108,649	
AGRICULTURE—Total		116,405
Engaged in Manufactures	7,266	
Dependent on „	101,783	
MANUFACTURES—Total		109,049
Total of the County		225,454

TAXATION.

		Paid by the	
		LAND.	MANUFACTURERS.
		£	£
Paid exclusively by the Landed Interest:			
Land Tax		(See Summary,)	
Property Tax—on Land, assessed at	£239,189	6,976	
Paid in the Proportion of One-half by the Landed Interest, and One-half by the Manufacturers:			
Poor Relief	£33,090	16,545	16,545
Highway Rates, Church „, Turnpike Trusts, } No Return.			
Property Tax—on Dwelling Houses, assessed at	781,235	11,398	11,398
„ on other Property „	54,567	795	795
		35,714	28,738
Total of Taxation of the County		£64,452	

(*For those engaged in Mines, see " Mining Interest.")*

ENGAGED IN	MALES.		FEMALES.		TOTAL.
	20 years of age and upwards.	Under 20 years of age.	20 years of age and upwards.	Under 20 years of age.	
AGRICULTURE:					
Farmers and Graziers - - - -	1,390	1	92	—	1,483
Agricultural Labourers - - -	1,780	1,287	321	83	3,471
Gardeners, Nurserymen, and Florists -	112	14	—	—	126
	3,282	1,302	413	83	5,080
MANUFACTURES:					
Spinners (branch not specified) - -	1	—	91	2	94
Weavers (all branches) - - -	77	2	—	—	79
Woollen and Cloth Manufacture (all branches) -	42	2	10	—	54
Miscellaneous - - - -	101	16	18	—	135
	221	20	119	2	362
ALL OTHER CLASSES:					
Employed in Retail Trade or in Handicraft, as Masters or Workmen - - - -	2,465	452	259	9	3,185
Labourers - - - - -	484	8	244	3	739
Military and Naval - - - -	334	24	—	—	358
Professional Persons - - - -	106	—	—	—	106
Other Educated Persons following miscellaneous Pursuits	129	39	65	3	236
Persons engaged in the Government Civil Service -	52	—	2	—	54
Parochial, Town, and Church Officers - -	33	—	2	—	35
Domestic Servants - - - -	186	105	1,609	1,247	3,147
Persons returned as Independent - -	147	5	1,084	23	1,259
Almspeople, Pensioners, Paupers, Lunatics, and Prisoners	151	3	221	4	379
RESIDUE OF POPULATION;					
Consisting of the Wives, Children, and others dependent on all Classes - - - -	563	6,004	6,812	6,693	20,072
Total of all other Classes - - -	4,650	6,640	10,298	7,982	29,570

Divide "ALL OTHER CLASSES" between the AGRICULTURISTS and the MANUFACTURERS in the proportion which these respectively bear to each other, and the numbers engaged in, and dependent on, each interest will stand thus:—

Engaged in Agriculture	-	-	-	5,080
Dependent on „	-	-	-	27,604
AGRICULTURE—Total	-	-		32,684
Engaged in Manufactures	-	-	-	362
Dependent on „	-	-	-	1,966
MANUFACTURES—Total	-	-		2,328
Total of the County	-	-	-	35,012

TAXATION.

	Paid by the	
	LAND.	MANUFACTURERS.
	£	£
Paid exclusively by the Landed Interest:		
Land Tax - - - - - - -	(*See Summary.*)	
Property Tax—on Land, assessed at - - £84,082	2,452	
Paid in the Proportion of 14-15ths by the Landed Interest, and 1-15th by the Manufacturers :		
Poor Relief - - - - - £1,653	1,542	110
Highway Rates ⎫		
Church „ ⎬ No Returns.		
Turnpike Trusts ⎭		
Property Tax—on Dwelling Houses, assessed at - 7,350	200	14
„ on other Property „ - - 6,682	181	13
	4,385	137
Total of Taxation of the County - - - - £4,522		

ENGAGED IN	MALES. 20 years of age and upwards.	MALES. Under 20 years of age.	FEMALES. 20 years of age and upwards.	FEMALES. Under 20 years of age.	TOTAL.
Agriculture:					
Farmers and Graziers - - - - -	1,137	16	42	—	1,195
Agricultural Labourers - - - -	6,019	1,730	555	181	8,485
Gardeners, Nurserymen, and Florists	318	41	2	—	361
	7,474	1,787	599	181	10,041
Manufactures:					
Linen Manufacture (all branches) - - -	5,173	1,755	1,619	1,075	9,622
Flax Manufacture (all branches) - - -	775	257	712	657	2,401
Weavers (all branches) - - - -	1,319	424	304	203	2,250
Cotton Manufacture (all branches) - -	353	166	172	73	764
Yarn Manufacture (all branches) - - -	70	13	510	66	659
Spinners (branch not specified) - - -	21	12	325	246	604
Factory Workers (branch not specified) - -	104	22	314	85	525
Bleachers - - - - - -	125	12	160	154	451
Damask Manufacture - - - - -	148	54	6	—	208
Engineers and Engine Workers - - - -	156	45	—	—	201
Engine and Machine Makers - - -	41	13	4	—	58
Miscellaneous - - - - -	733	197	201	105	1,236
	9,018	2,970	4,327	2,664	18,979
All other Classes:					
Employed in Retail Trade or in Handicraft, as Masters or Workmen - - - - -	8,265	2,034	1,296	117	11,712
Labourers - - - - - -	2,797	661	424	153	4,035
Military and Naval - - - - -	1,372	214	—	—	1,586
Professional Persons - - - -	428	—	—	—	428
Other Educated Persons following miscellaneous Pursuits	457	126	122	10	715
Persons engaged in the Government Civil Service -	107	1	13	—	121
Parochial, Town, and Church Officers -	120	12	3	—	135
Domestic Servants - - - - -	489	259	2,914	1,846	5,508
Persons returned as Independent - - -	608	13	2,229	61	2,911
Almspeople, Pensioners, Paupers, Lunatics, and Prisoners	273	13	355	9	650
Residue of Population:					
Consisting of the Wives, Children, and others dependent on all Classes - - - - -	736	25,519	28,678	28,386	83,319
Total of all other Classes - - -	15,652	28,852	36,034	30,582	111,120

Divide "all other classes" between the Agriculturists and the Manufacturers in the proportion which these respectively bear to each other, and the numbers engaged in, and dependent on, each interest will stand thus:—

Engaged in Agriculture - - -	10,041	
Dependent on ,, - - -	38,447	
Agriculture—Total - -		48,488
Engaged in Manufactures - -	18,979	
Dependent on ,, - - -	72,673	
Manufactures—Total - -		91,652
Total of the County - - -		140,140

TAXATION.

		Paid by the LAND.	Paid by the MANUFACTURERS.
		£	£
Paid exclusively by the Landed Interest:			
Land Tax - - - - - -	-	(See Summary.)	
Property Tax—on Land, assessed at - - -	£381,572	11,129	
Paid in the Proportion of 5-14ths by the Landed Interest, and 9-14ths by the Manufacturers:			
Poor Relief - - - - -	£10,562	3,770	6,792
Highway Rates ⎫			
Church ,, ⎬ No Return.			
Turnpike Trusts ⎭			
Property Tax—on Dwelling Houses, assessed at -	74,654	775	1,402
,, on other Property ,, - -	52,696	545	991
		16,219	9,185
Total of Taxation of the County - - -		£25,404	

(For those engaged in Mines, see " Mining Interest.")

ENGAGED IN	MALES.		FEMALES.		TOTAL.
	20 years of age and upwards.	Under 20 years of age.	20 years of age and upwards.	Under 20 years of age.	
Agriculture :					
Farmers and Graziers - - - - -	1,665	14	92	—	1,771
Agricultural Labourers - - - -	5,193	2,072	483	157	7,905
Gardeners, Nurserymen, and Florists - -	380	20	2	—	402
	7,238	2,106	577	157	10,078
Manufactures:					
Linen and Flax Manufacture (all branches) - -	9,498	2,728	6,921	3,925	23,072
Weavers (all branches) - - - -	497	100	378	137	1,112
Yarn Manufacture (all branches) - -	110	16	400	29	555
Engine and Machine Makers - - -	259	93	1	—	353
Engineers and Engine Workers - - -	130	30	1	—	161
Canvass Manufacture (all branches) - - -	288	53	6	1	348
Factory Workers (branch not specified) - -	79	11	228	7	325
Bleachers - - - - -	152	65	50	24	291
Rope and Cord Spinners and Makers -	129	79	3	3	214
Cotton Manufacture (all branches) - - -	11	—	108	46	165
Lint Manufacture (all branches) - -	7	7	83	57	154
Spinners (branch not specified) - - -	20	14	63	19	116
Tin-Plate Workers and Tinmen - - -	88	27	1	—	116
Miscellaneous - - - - -	889	250	118	21	1,278
	12,157	3,473	8,361	4,269	28,260
All other Classes :					
Employed in Retail Trade or in Handicraft, as Masters or Workmen - - - - -	11,576	2,657	1,987	229	16,449
Labourers - - - - -	2,948	169	610	20	3,747
Military and Naval - - - -	630	323	—	—	1,953
Professional Persons - - - -	528	—	—	—	528
Other Educated Persons following miscellaneous Pursuits	802	221	170	9	1,202
Persons engaged in the Government Civil Service -	154	5	1	—	160
Parochial, Town, and Church Officers - - -	201	1	5	—	207
Domestic Servants - - -	593	385	4,401	3,317	8,696
Persons returned as Independent - -	636	26	2,849	88	3,599
Almspeople, Pensioners, Paupers, Lunatics, and Prisoners	456	40	405	27	928
Residue of Population :					
Consisting of the Wives, Children, and others dependent on all Classes - - - - -	1,180	29,895	32,225	31,413	94,713
Total of all other Classes - - -	20,704	33,722	42,653	35,103	132,182

Divide " all other classes " between the Agriculturists and the Manufacturers in the proportion which these respectively bear to each other, and the numbers engaged in, and dependent on, each interest will stand thus:—

Engaged in Agriculture - - -	10,078	
Dependent on ,, - - -	34,747	
AGRICULTURE—Total - -		44,825
Engaged in Manufactures - - -	28,260	
Dependent on ,, - - -	97,435	
MANUFACTURES—Total - -		125,695
Total of the County - - -		170,520

TAXATION.

		Paid by the	
		Land.	Manufacturers.
Paid exclusively by the Landed Interest :		£	£
Land Tax - - - - - - -		*(See Summary.)*	
Property Tax—on Land, assessed at - -	£312,200	9,105	
Paid in the Proportion of 1-4th by the Landed Interest, and 3-4ths by the Manufacturers :			
Poor Relief - - - - -	£18,494	4,623	13,871
Highway Rates ⎫			
Church ,, ⎬ No Return.			
Turnpike Trusts ⎭			
Property Tax—on Dwelling Houses, assessed at -	180,495	1,316	3,948
,, on other Property ,, - -	10,146	78	222
		15,122	18,041
Total of Taxation of the County - - -		£33,163	

ENGAGED IN	MALES.		FEMALES.		TOTAL.
	20 years of age and upwards.	Under 20 years of age.	20 years of age and upwards.	Under 20 years of age.	
Agriculture :					
Farmers and Graziers - - - - -	308	8	5	—	321
Agricultural Labourers - - - -	3,610	976	694	434	5,714
Gardeners, Nurserymen, and Florists - -	123	7	3	—	133
	4,041	991	702	434	6,168
Manufactures :					
There is no leading branch of Manufactures in this county.—The largest number employed in any one branch is					
Brick and Tile Makers - - - -	51	9	—	—	60
Weavers - - - - - - -	55	2	—	—	57
Miscellaneous - - - - -	208	26	14	—	248
	314	37	14	—	365
All other Classes :					
Employed in Retail Trade or in Handicraft, as Masters or Workmen - - - - -	2,312	558	313	16	3,199
Labourers - - - - - - -	487	123	108	34	752
Military and Naval - - - - -	363	50	—	—	413
Professional Persons - - - -	121	—	—	—	121
Other Educated Persons following miscellaneous pursuits	138	21	34	—	193
Persons engaged in the Government Civil Service - -	48	—	1	—	49
Parochial, Town, and Church Officers - -	27	—	3	—	30
Domestic Servants - - - - -	354	148	1,040	588	2,130
Persons returned as Independent - - - -	158	8	618	26	810
Almspeople, Pensioners, Paupers, Lunatics, and Prisoners	68	5	102	1	176
Residue of Population :					
Consisting of the Wives, Children, and others dependent on all Classes - - - - -	270	6,644	7,330	7,236	21,480
Total of all other Classes - -	4,346	7,557	9,549	7,901	29,353

Divide "ALL OTHER CLASSES" between the AGRICULTURISTS and the MANUFACTURERS in the proportion which these respectively bear to each other, and the numbers engaged in, and dependent on, each interest will stand thus :—

```
          Engaged in Agriculture    -      -        -     6,168
          Dependent on      ,,           -        -    27,714
                 AGRICULTURE—Total         -      ————      33,882

          Engaged in Manufactures    -      -      -       365
          Dependent on      ,,                 -       1,639
                 MANUFACTURES—Total      -      ————       2,004

                 Total of the County     -      -         35,886
```

TAXATION.

		Paid by the	
		LAND.	MANUFACTURERS.
Paid exclusively by the Landed Interest :		£	£
Land Tax - - - - - - -		(See Summary.)	
Property Tax—on Land, assessed at - - -	£221,713	6,466	
Paid in the Proportion of 15-16ths by the Landed Interest, and 1-16th by the Manufacturers :			
Poor Relief - - - - - - -	£4,958	4,649	309
Highway Rates ⎫			
Church　　,, ⎬ No Return.			
Turnpike Trusts ⎭			
Property Tax—on Dwelling Houses, assessed at - -	31,558	863	57
,,　　　 on other Property　　,, - - -	5,472	150	10
		12,128	376
Total of Taxation of the County		£12,504	

(*For those engaged in Mines, see* "*Mining Interest.*")

ENGAGED IN	MALES.		FEMALES.		TOTAL.
	20 years of age and upwards.	Under 20 years of age.	20 years of age and upwards.	Under 20 years of age.	
Agriculture:					
Farmers and Graziers - - - -	3,495	22	249	—	3,766
Agricultural Labourers - - - -	7,088	1,411	1,138	163	9,800
Gardeners, Nurserymen, and Florists - -	164	13	3	—	180
	10,747	1,446	1,390	163	13,746
Manufactures:					
Weavers (branch not specified) - - - -	261	15	198	15	489
Spinners (branch not specified) - - -	—	—	112	3	115
Woollen and Cloth Manufacture (all branches) - -	72	2	27	1	102
Hemp Manufacture (all branches) - - -	21	5	24	—	50
Miscellaneous - - - -	166	29	19	2	216
	520	51	380	21	972
All other Classes:					
Employed in Retail Trade or in Handicraft, as Masters or Workmen - - - - -	3,977	505	361	32	4,875
Labourers - - - - -	927	49	314	19	1,309
Military and Naval - - - - -	887	170	—	—	1,057
Professional Persons - - -	223	—	—	—	223
Other Educated Persons following miscellaneous Pursuits	336	62	56	4	458
Persons engaged in the Government-Civil Service -	96	3	3	—	102
Parochial, Town, and Church Officers - -	81	—	2	—	83
Domestic Servants - - - -	631	529	3,579	2,251	6,990
Persons returned as Independent - - -	337	18	1,645	44	2,044
Almspeople, Pensioners, Paupers, Lunatics, and Prisoners	559	7	626	28	1,220
Residue of Population:					
Consisting of the Wives, Children, and others dependent on all Classes - - - -	3,446	19,954	20,790	20,530	64,720
Total of all other Classes - -	11,500	21,297	27,376	22,908	83,081

Divide " all other classes" between the Agriculturists and the Manufacturers in the proportion which these respectively bear to each other, and the numbers engaged in, and dependent on, each interest will stand thus:—

```
          Engaged in Agriculture    -      -      -    13,746
          Dependent on      ,,      -      -      -    77,595
                AGRICULTURE—Total    -      -             ———————  91,341

          Engaged in Manufactures   -      -      -       972
          Dependent on      ,,      -      -      -     5,486
                MANUFACTURES—Total   -      -             ———————   6,458

              Total of the County    -      -      -               97,799
```

TAXATION.

	Paid by the	
	LAND.	MANUFACTURERS.
Paid exclusively by the Landed Interest :	£	£
Land Tax - - - - - - -	(*See Summary.*)	
Property Tax—on Land, assessed at - - -£161,499	4,710	
Paid in the Proportion of 14-15ths by the Landed Interest, and 1-15th by the Manufacturers :		
Poor Relief - - - - - - - £1,827	1,706	121
Highway Rates }		
Church ,, } No Return.		
Turnpike Trusts }		
Property Tax—on Dwelling Houses, assessed at - - 17,894	487	34
,, on other Property ,, - - 2,671	72	5
	6,975	160
Total of Taxation of the County - - -	£7,135	

ENGAGED IN	MALES.		FEMALES.		TOTAL.
	20 years of age and upwards.	Under 20 years of age.	20 years of age and upwards.	Under 20 years of age.	
Agriculture :					
Farmers and Graziers - - - -	1,234	1	97	—	1,332
Agricultural Labourers - - - -	2,615	1,345	350	109	4,419
Gardeners, Nurserymen, and Florists - -	81	14	2	—	97
	3,930	1,360	449	109	5,848
Manufactures :					
Linen Manufacture (all branches) - - -	676	144	255	40	1,115
Flax Manufacture - - - -	41	19	120	49	229
Stocking Knitters and Weavers - - - -	—	—	140	1	141
Weavers (all branches) - - - -	18	7	23	3	51
Miscellaneous - - - -	76	11	74	9	170
	811	181	612	102	1,706
All other Classes :					
Employed in Retail Trade or in Handicraft, as Masters or Workmen - - - - -	1,728	283	323	21	2,355
Labourers - - - - -	237	6	56	8	307
Military and Naval - - - - -	607	55	—	—	662
Professional Persons - - - -	93	—	—	—	93
Other Educated Persons following miscellaneous Pursuits	97	33	45	5	180
Persons engaged in the Government Civil Service -	42	—	2	—	44
Parochial, Town, and Church Officers - - -	19	—	1	—	20
Domestic Servants - - - -	135	65	1,381	1,233	2,814
Persons returned as Independent - - -	146	2	540	11	699
Almspeople, Pensioners, Paupers, Lunatics, and Prisoners	91	3	399	10	503
Residue of Population :					
Consisting of the Wives, Children, and others dependent on all Classes - - - - -	248	5,674	5,844	6,078	17,844
Total of all other Classes - -	3,443	6,121	8,591	7,366	25,521

Divide "ALL OTHER CLASSES" between the AGRICULTURISTS and the MANUFACTURERS in the proportion which these respectively bear to each other, and the numbers engaged in, and dependent on, each interest will stand thus :—

Engaged in Agriculture - - -	5,848	
Dependent on ,, - - -	19,758	
AGRICULTURE—Total - -		25,606
Engaged in Manufactures - - -	1,706	
Dependent on ,, - - -	5,763	
MANUFACTURES—Total -		7,469
Total of the County - - -		33,075

TAXATION.

		Paid by the	
		LAND.	MANUFACTURERS.
Paid exclusively by the Landed Interest :		£	£
Land Tax - - - - - -	-	(*See Summary.*)	
Property Tax—on Land, assessed at - - -	- £128,468	3,746	
Paid in the Proportion of 7-9ths by the Landed Interest, and 2-9ths by the Manufacturers :			
Poor Relief - - - - -	- £2,774	2,158	616
Highway Rates ⎫			
Church ,, ⎬ No Return.			
Turnpike Trusts ⎭			
Property Tax—on Dwelling Houses, assessed at -	- 2,014	45	13
,, on other Property ,, -	- 3,859	87	25
		6,036	654
Total of Taxation of the County - -	-	£6,690	

ENGAGED IN	MALES.		FEMALES.		TOTAL.
	20 years of age and upwards.	Under 20 years of age.	20 years of age and upwards.	Under 20 years of age.	
AGRICULTURE:					
Farmers and Graziers - - - - -	157	1	2	—	160
Agricultural Labourers - - - -	585	209	54	9	857
Gardeners, Nurserymen, and Florists - -	14	1	—	—	15
	756	211	56	9	1,032
MANUFACTURES:					
Cotton Manufacture (all branches) - - -	260	112	89	30	491
Woollen and Cloth Manufacture (all branches)	209	42	48	15	314
Linen Manufacture (all branches) - -	92	27	34	29	182
Miscellaneous - - - - -	40	3	41	10	94
	601	184	212	84	1,081
ALL OTHER CLASSES:					
Employed in Retail Trade or in Handicraft, as Masters or Workmen - - - - - -	487	109	108	13	717
Labourers - - - - - - -	92	9	22	6	129
Military and Naval - - - - -	4	—	—	—	4
Professional Persons - - - - -	33	—	—	—	33
Other Educated Persons following miscellaneous Pursuits	33	4	7	—	44
Persons engaged in the Government Civil Service -	5	—	—	—	5
Parochial, Town, and Church Officers - -	5	—	—	—	5
Domestic Servants - - - - -	33	20	204	154	411
Persons returned as Independent - - -	53	2	201	10	266
Almspeople, Pensioners, Paupers, Lunatics, and Prisoners	22	—	3	—	25
RESIDUE OF POPULATION:					
Consisting of the Wives, Children, and others dependent on all Classes - - -	43	1,490	1,831	1,647	5,011
Total of all other Classes - -	810	1,634	2,376	1,830	6,650

Divide " ALL OTHER CLASSES " between the AGRICULTURISTS and the MANUFACTURERS in the proportion which these respectively bear to each other, and the numbers engaged in, and dependent on, each interest will stand thus:—

Engaged in Agriculture - - -	1,032		
Dependent on ,, - - -	3,247		
AGRICULTURE—Total - -		4,279	
Engaged in Manufactures - -	1,081		
Dependent on ,, - - -	3,403		
MANUFACTURES—Total -		4,484	
Total of the County - - -		8,763	

TAXATION.

		Paid by the	
		LAND.	MANUFACTURERS.
		£	£
Paid exclusively by the Landed Interest:			
Land Tax - - - - - - -		(See Summary.)	
Property Tax—on Land, assessed at - - - £38,892		1,134	
Paid in the Proportion of One-half by the Landed Interest, and One-half by the Manufacturers:			
Poor Relief - - - - - £340		170	170
Highway Rates ⎫			
Church ,, ⎬ No Return.			
Turnpike Trusts ⎭			
Property Tax—on Dwelling Houses, assessed at - - 4,375		63	63
,, on other Property ,, - - 742		11	11
		1,388	244

Total of Taxation of the County - - - - £1,632

(For those engaged in Mines, see " Mining Interest.")

ENGAGED IN.	MALES.		FEMALES.		TOTAL.
	20 years of age and upwards.	Under 20 years of age.	20 years of age and upwards.	Under 20 years of age.	
Agriculture:					
Farmers and Graziers - - - -	1,046	5	72	—	1,123
Agricultural Labourers - - - -	2,864	709	379	55	4,007
Gardeners, Nurserymen, and Florists - -	116	16	4	—	126
	4,016	730	455	55	5,256
Manufactures:					
Cotton Manufacture (all branches)	158	22	50	12	242
Weavers (all branches) - - -	112	1	1	1	115
Spinners (branch not specified) - - -	1	—	80	—	81
Stocking Makers and Knitters - - -	52	10	5	1	68
Woollen and Cloth Manufacture (all branches) - -	44	3	4	1	52
Linen Spinners and Weavers - - -	48	—	2	—	50
Miscellaneous - - - - -	183	49	12	4	248
	598	85	154	19	856
All other Classes:					
Employed in Retail Trade or in Handicraft, as Masters or Workmen - - - - - -	2,220	408	479	62	3,169
Labourers - - - - - -	552	36	124	3	715
Military and Naval - - - -	179	14	—	—	193
Professional Persons - - - - -	122	—	—	—	122
Other Educated Persons following miscellaneous Pursuits	143	20	38	3	204
Persons engaged in the Government Civil Service	29	1	3	—	33
Parochial, Town, and Church Officers - -	26	—	1	—	27
Domestic Servants - - - - -	293	140	1,603	1,045	3,081
Persons returned as Independent - - -	310	5	838	22	1,175
Almspeople, Pensioners, Paupers, Lunatics, and Prisoners	96	9	200	4	309
Residue of Population:					
Consisting of the Wives, Children, and others dependent on all Classes - - - - -	731	8,096	8,496	8,656	25,979
Total of all other Classes - - -	4,701	8,729	11,782	9,795	35,007

Divide "ALL OTHER CLASSES" between the AGRICULTURISTS and the MANUFACTURERS in the proportion which these respectively bear to each other, and the numbers engaged in, and dependent on, each interest will stand thus :—

Engaged in Agriculture - - -	5,256	
Dependent on ,, - - -	30,105	
AGRICULTURE—Total - -		35,361
Engaged in Manufactures - -	856	
Dependent on ,, - - -	4,902	
MANUFACTURES—Total - -		5,758
Total of the County - - -		41,119

TAXATION.

	Paid by the	
	LAND.	MANUFACTURERS.
Paid exclusively by the Landed Interest :	£	£
Land Tax - - - - - - -	(*See Summary.*)	
Property Tax—on Land, assessed at - - - £182,926	5,355	
Paid in the Proportion of 6-7ths by the Landed Interest, and 1-7th by the Manufacturers :		
Poor Relief - - - - - - £4,289	3,677	612
Highway Rates ⎫		
Church ,, ⎬ No Return.		
Turnpike Trusts ⎭		
Property Tax—on Dwelling Houses, assessed at - - 9,444	236	39
,, on other Property ,, - - 1,431	36	6
	9,304	657
Total of Taxation of the County - - - £9,961		

ENGAGED IN	MALES. 20 years of age and upwards	MALES. Under 20 years of age.	FEMALES. 20 years of age and upwards.	FEMALES. Under 20 years of age.	TOTAL.
Agriculture :					
Farmers and Graziers - - - -	2,395	30	127	—	2,552
Agricultural Labourers - - -	7,126	2,109	422	372	10,029
Gardeners, Nurserymen, and Florists -	542	37	7	2	588
	10,063	2,176	556	374	13,169
Manufactures :					
Cotton Manufacture (all branches) - -	11,616	3,748	7,734	6,070	29,168
Weavers (all branches) - - -	3,545	850	1,916	1,690	8,001
Factory Workers (branch not specified) - -	697	369	1,994	682	3,742
Iron Manufacture (all branches) - - -	1,756	493	21	6	2,276
Engineers and Engine Workers - -	1,541	431	3	—	1,975
Engine and Machine Makers - - -	232	66	6	—	304
,, Turners - - - -	3	1	—	—	4
Printers (Cotton, Calico, &c.) - - -	870	309	81	150	1,410
,, Copperplate - - - -	20	12	1	—	33
Woollen and Cloth Manufacture (all branches) -	811	305	125	116	1,357
Dyers (all branches) - - - -	750	275	124	65	1,214
Silk Manufacture (all branches) - -	267	79	316	365	1,027
Muslin Embroiderers and Workers - -	6	2	576	171	755
,, Manufacture (all branches) -	159	22	109	33	323
Potters - - - - -	266	183	55	38	542
Yarn Manufacture (all branches) - - -	22	1	447	64	534
Rope and Cord Spinners and Maker - -	240	182	14	10	446
Moulders (branch not specified) - - -	245	190	2	—	437
Boiler Makers - - - -	328	107	—	—	435
Bleachers - - - - -	110	25	154	92	381
Nailers and Nail Makers - - - -	270	86	2	1	359
Brick and Tile Makers - - - -	257	75	7	2	341
Tin Plate Workers and Tinmen - -	224	91	5	—	320
Flax Manufacture (all branches) - - -	97	34	107	63	301
Lace Makers - - - - -	21	3	177	92	293
Turners - - - - -	226	60	4	1	291
Glass and Glass Bottle Manufacture - -	182	91	7	3	283
Hatters and Hat Makers - - -	183	32	46	13	274
Brass Founders and Moulders - - -	151	110	—	—	261
,, Workers - - - -	17	11	1	—	29
Spinners (branch not specified) - - -	26	4	144	73	247
Block and Print Cutters and Makers - -	190	46	1	—	237
Pattern Designers and Makers - - -	164	54	8	3	229
Carpet and Rug Manufacture (all branches) -	157	55	7	9	228
Miscellaneous - - - -	1,904	552	509	356	3,321
	27,553	8,954	14,703	10,168	61,378
All other Classes :					
Employed in Retail Trade or in Handicraft, as Masters or Workmen - - - - - }	35,554	7,831	9,075	2,283	54,743
Labourers - - - - -	21,100	4,372	1,338	126	26,936
Military and Naval - - - -	2,458	403	—	—	2,861
Professional Persons - - - -	1,244	—	—	—	1,244
Other Educated Persons following miscellaneous Pursuits	3,049	783	204	30	4,066
Persons engaged in the Government Civil Service -	310	10	8	—	328
Parochial, Town, and Church Officers -	677	7	29	1	714
Domestic Servants - - - -	1,781	879	10,680	7,370	20,710
Persons returned as Independent - - -	1,388	87	5,043	361	6,879
Almspeople, Pensioners, Paupers, Lunatics, and Prisoners	1,017	246	1,614	222	3,099
Residue of Population :					
Consisting of the Wives, Children, and others dependent on all Classes - - - - }	3,607	72,806	74,674	79,758	230,845
Total of all other Classes - -	72,185	87,424	102,665	90,151	352,425

Divide "ALL OTHER CLASSES" between the Agriculturists and the Manufacturers in the proportion which these respectively bear to each other, and the numbers engaged in, and dependent on, each interest will stand thus:—

Engaged in Agriculture - - -	13,169	
Dependent on ,, - - -	62,257	
Agriculture—Total - -		75,426
Engaged in Manufactures - -	61,378	
Dependent on ,, - -	290,168	
Manufactures—Total - -		351,546
Total of the County - - -		426,972

TAXATION,

		Paid by the	
		LAND.	MANUFACTURERS.
Paid exclusively by the Landed Interest :		£	£
Land Tax - - - - - -		(*See Summary.*)	
Property Tax—on Land, assessed at - - - £341,121		9,950	—
Paid in the Proportion of 1-6th by the Landed Interest, and 5-6ths by the Manufacturers :			
Poor Relief - - - - - £33,977		5,663	28,314
Highway Rates ⎫			
Church ,, ⎬ No Return.			
Turnpike Trusts ⎭			
Property Tax—on Dwelling Houses, assessed at - 902,992		4,389	21,948
,, on other Property ,, - 590,805		2,872	14,359
		22,874	64,621

Total of Taxation of the County   - - - £87,495

(*For those engaged in Mines, see " Mining Interest."*)

LINLITHGOW—County of.

	MALES.		FEMALES.		
ENGAGED IN	20 years of age and upwards.	Under 20 years of age.	20 years of age and upwards.	Under 20 years of age.	TOTAL.
AGRICULTURE :					
Farmers and Graziers - - - -	354	3	15	—	372
Agricultural Labourers - - -	1,423	438	107	39	2,007
Gardeners, Nurserymen, and Florists - -	61	16	—	—	77
	1,838	457	122	39	2,456
MANUFACTURES :					
Cotton Manufacture (all branches) - - -	363	109	120	57	649
Tambour Workers - - - -	—	2	184	30	216
Printers (Calico and Cotton) - - -	50	46	1	4	101
Weavers (all branches) - - - -	20	3	33	32	88
Miscellaneous - - - - -	195	34	78	4	311
	628	194	416	127	1,365
ALL OTHER CLASSES :					
Employed in Retail Trade or in Handicraft, as Masters ⎫ or Workmen - - - - - ⎬	1,945	359	328	41	2,673
Labourers - - - - - -	2,250	345	85	27	2,707
Military and Naval - - - - -	90	4	—	—	94
Professional Persons - - - -	78	—	—	—	78
Other Educated Persons following miscellaneous Pursuits	74	12	24	4	114
Persons engaged in the Government Civil Service -	32	1	—	—	33
Parochial, Town, and Church Officers - - -	42	9	1	—	52
Domestic Servants - - - -	170	122	609	486	1,387
Persons returned as Independent - - -	105	1	376	5	487
Almspeople, Pensioners, Paupers, Lunatics, and Prisoners	42	1	54	1	98
RESIDUE OF POPULATION :					
Consisting of the Wives, Children, and others dependent ⎫ on all Classes - - - - - ⎬	248	4,756	4,954	5,370	15,328
Total of all other Classes - -	5,076	5,610	6,431	5,934	23,051

Divide " ALL OTHER CLASSES " between the AGRICULTURISTS and the MANUFACTURERS in the proportion which these respectively bear to each other, and the numbers engaged in, and dependent on, each interest will stand thus :—

Engaged in Agriculture - - -	2,456		
Dependent on ,, - - -	14,817		
AGRICULTURE—Total - -		17,273	
Engaged in Manufactures - - -	1,365		
Dependent on ,, - - -	8,234		
MANUFACTURES—Total		9,599	
Total of the County - -		26,872	

TAXATION.

		Paid by the	
		LAND.	MANUFACTURERS.
Paid exclusively by the Landed Interest :		£	£
Land Tax - - - - - - -		(*See Summary.*)	
Property Tax—on Land, assessed at - - £82,841		2,416	—
Paid in the Proportion of 2-3rds by the Landed Interest, and 1-3rd by the Manufacturers :			
Poor Relief - - - - - £1,984		1,223	661
Highway Rates, ⎫			
Church ,, ⎬ No Return.			
Turnpike Trusts, ⎭			
Property Tax—on Dwelling Houses, assessed at - 21,149		411	205
,, on other Property ,, - 5,331		104	51
		4,154	917

Total of Taxation of the County   - - - £5,071

ENGAGED IN	MALES.		FEMALES.		TOTAL
	20 years of age and upwards.	Under 20 years of age.	20 years of age and upwards.	Under 20 years of age.	
AGRICULTURE :					
Farmers and Graziers - - - - -	386	—	7	—	393
Agricultural Labourers - - - - -	577	360	209	37	1,183
Gardeners, Nurserymen, and Florists - -	13	2	—	—	15
	976	362	216	37	1,591
MANUFACTURES :					
There is no leading branch of Manufacture carried on in this County. The largest number engaged in any one branch is that of the - - - - -					
Hand Loom Weavers - - - - - -	27	—	—	—	27
Miscellaneous - - - - - -	13	1	17	—	31
	40	1	17	—	58
ALL OTHER CLASSES :					
Employed in Retail Trade or in Handicraft, as Masters or Workmen - - - - -	577	101	43	3	724
Labourers - - - - - -	88	3	45	—	136
Military and Naval - - - -	138	6	—	—	144
Professional Persons - - - -	27	—	—	—	27
Other Educated Persons following miscellaneous Pursuits	28	8	3	1	40
Persons engaged in the Government Civil Service -	4	—	2	—	6
Parochial, Town, and Church Officers - - -	7	—	—	—	7
Domestic Servants - - - -	31	37	402	318	788
Persons returned as Independent - - - -	27	—	186	6	219
Almspeople, Pensioners, Paupers, Lunatics, and Prisoners	69	1	11	—	81
RESIDUE OF POPULATION :					
Consisting of the Wives, Children, and others dependent on all Classes - - - - -	186	1,521	2,035	1,654	5,396
Total of all other Classes - - -	1,182	1,677	2,727	1,982	7,568

Divide "ALL OTHER CLASSES" between the AGRICULTURISTS and the MANUFACTURERS in the proportion which these respectively bear to each other, and the numbers engaged in, and dependent on, each interest will stand thus :—

Engaged in Agriculture - - -	1,591	
Dependent on ,, - - -	7,302	
AGRICULTURE—Total - -		8,893
Engaged in Manufactures - - -	58	
Dependent on ,, - - -	266	
MANUFACTURES—Total - -		324
Total of the County - - -		9,217

TAXATION.

		Paid by the	
		LAND.	MANUFACTURERS.
		£	£
Paid exclusively by the Landed Interest :			
Land Tax - - - - - - -	-	*(See Summary.)*	
Property Tax—on Land, assessed at - -	£15,201	443	—
Paid in the Proportion of 27-28ths by the Landed Interest, and 1-28th by the Manufacturers :			
Poor Relief - - - - - -	£170	142	28
Highway Rates ⎫			
Church ,, ⎬ No Return.			
Turnpike Trusts ⎭			
Property Tax—on Dwelling Houses, assessed at - -	1,043	29	1
,, on other Property ,, - -	551	16	—
		630	29
Total of Taxation of the County - - -		- £659	

ENGAGED IN	MALES.		FEMALES.		TOTAL.
	20 years of age and upwards.	Under 20 years of age.	20 years of age and upwards.	Under 20 years of age.	
AGRICULTURE:					
Farmers and Graziers - - - -	3,656	14	343	—	4,013
Agricultural Labourers - - - -	1,119	761	286	63	2,229
Gardeners, Nurserymen, and Florists - -	9	—	—	—	9
	4,784	775	629	63	6,251
MANUFACTURES:					
Straw-Plait Manufacture (all branches) - -	10	—	1,030	286	1,326
Spinners (branch not specified) - - - -	—	—	211	3	214
Stocking Knitters and Makers - - -	2	—	171	5	178
Woollen Manufacture (all branches) - - -	45	—	71	—	116
Weavers (all branches) - - - -	91	—	—	—	91
Hemp Manufacture (all branches) - - -	1	—	49	—	50
Miscellaneous - - - - -	65	14	58	5	142
	214	14	1,590	299	2,117
ALL OTHER CLASSES:					
Employed in Retail Trade or in Handicraft, as Masters or Workmen - - - - -	1,926	290	264	30	2,510
Labourers - - - - - -	253	5	93	1	352
Military and Naval - - - -	3,017	156	—	—	3,173
Professional Persons - - - - -	165	—	—	—	165
Other Educated Persons following miscellaneous Pursuits	129	16	34	4	183
Persons engaged in the Government Civil Service -	55	—	—	—	53
Parochial, Town, and Church Officers - - -	25	—	1	—	26
Domestic Servants - - - -	154	350	2,150	1,169	3,823
Persons returned as Independent - - -	202	9	801	11	1,023
Almspeople, Pensioners, Paupers, Lunatics, and Prisoners	252	5	486	5	748
RESIDUE OF POPULATION:					
Consisting of the Wives, Children, and others dependent on all Classes - - - - -	1,551	12,694	14,041	12,355	40,641
Total of all other Classes - -	7,727	13,525	17,870	13,575	52,697

Divide "ALL OTHER CLASSES" between the AGRICULTURISTS and the MANUFACTURERS in the proportion which these respectively bear to each other, and the numbers engaged in, and dependent on, each interest will stand thus :—

Engaged in Agriculture - - - 6,251
Dependent on - - - - - 39,366
     AGRICULTURE—Total - - 45,617

Engaged in Manufactures - - 2,117
Dependent on - - - 13,331
     MANUFACTURES—Total - - 15,448

Total of the County - - - 61,065

TAXATION.

	Paid by the	
	LAND.	MANUFACTURERS.
	£	£
Paid exclusively by the Landed Interest:		
Land Tax - - - - - -	(See Summary.)	
Property Tax—on Land, assessed at - - - £38,887	1,134	—
Paid in the Proportion of 3-4ths by the Landed Interest, and 1-4th by the Manufacturers:		
Poor Relief - - - - - £689	517	172
Highway Rates ⎫		
Church ,, ⎬ No Return.		
Turnpike Trusts ⎭		
Property Tax—on Dwelling Houses, assessed at - - 3,137	69	22
,, on other Property ,, - - 762	17	5
	1,737	199
Total of Taxation of the County - - -	£1,936	

ENGAGED IN	MALES.		FEMALES.		TOTAL.
	20 Years of age and upwards.	Under 20 years of age.	20 Years of age and upwards.	Under 20 years of age.	
AGRICULTURE:					
Farmers and Graziers - - - -	245	3	4	—	252
Agricultural Labourers - - -	825	395	89	65	1,374
Gardeners, Nurserymen, and Florists - -	41	2	—	—	43
	1,111	400	93	65	1,669
MANUFACTURES:					
Cotton Manufacture (all branches) - - -	93	9	5	—	107
Woollen Manufacture (all branches) - -	21	13	4	2	40
Weavers (all branches) - - -	19	3	—	—	22
Spinners (branch not specified) - - -	—	—	18	—	18
Miscellaneous - - - - -	30	11	5	—	46
	163	36	32	2	233
ALL OTHER CLASSES:					
Employed in Retail Trade or in Handicraft, as Masters or Workmen - - - - -	588	99	76	8	771
Labourers - - - - -	221	26	21	18	286
Military and Naval - - - -	5	—	—	—	5
Professional Persons - - - -	53	—	—	—	53
Other Educated Persons following miscellaneous Pursuits	47	5	11	2	65
Persons engaged in the Government Civil Service -	7	—	1	—	8
Parochial, Town, and Church Officers - -	16	—	1	—	17
Domestic Servants - - - -	103	42	451	388	984
Persons returned as Independent - -	82	4	147	9	242
Almspeople, Pensioners, Paupers, Lunatics, and Prisoners	33	1	55	—	89
RESIDUE OF POPULATION:					
Consisting of the Wives, Children, and others dependent on all Classes - - - - -	134	1,945	1,895	2,103	6,077
Total of all other Classes - -	1,289	2,122	2,658	2,528	8,597

Divide "ALL OTHER CLASSES" between the AGRICULTURISTS and the MANUFACTURERS in the proportion which these respectively bear to each other, and the numbers engaged in, and dependent on, each interest will stand thus:—

Engaged in Agriculture - - -	1,669	
Dependent on ,, - - - -	7,544	
AGRICULTURE—Total - -		9,213
Engaged in Manufactures - - -	233	
Dependent on ,, - - - -	1,053	
MANUFACTURES—Total - -		1,286
Total of the County - -		10,499

TAXATION.

		Paid by the	
		LAND.	MANUFACTURERS.
Paid exclusively by the Landed Interest:		£	£
Land Tax - - - - - - -		*(See Summary.)*	
Property Tax—on Land, assessed at - - -	£67,675	1,973	—
Paid in the Proportion of 7-8ths by the Landed Interest, and 1-8th by the Manufacturers:			
Poor Relief - - - - - -	£1,370	1,200	170
Highway Rates }			
Church ,, } No Return.			
Turnpike Trusts }			
Property Tax—on Dwelling Houses, assessed at - -	6,247	160	22
,, on other Property ,, - -	888	22	3
		3,355	195
Total of Taxation of the County - - - -		£3,550	

ENGAGED IN	MALES.		FEMALES.		TOTAL.
	20 years of age and upwards.	Under 20 years of age.	20 years of age and upwards.	Under 20 years of age.	
Agriculture:					
Farmers and Graziers - - - - -	3,690	13	176	—	3,879
Agricultural Labourers - - - - -	7,489	3,534	729	228	11,980
Gardeners, Nurserymen, and Florists - - -	388	51	4	—	443
	11,567	3,598	909	228	16,302
Manufactures:					
Cotton Manufacture (all branches) - - -	1,701	755	765	577	3,798
Linen Manufacture (all branches) - - - -	1,358	269	814	302	2,743
Weavers (branch not specified) - - -	991	187	274	183	1,635
Factory Workers (branch not specified) - - -	48	13	361	80	502
Flax Manufacture (all branches) - - -	185	61	144	90	480
Woollen and Cloth Manufacture (all branches) - -	363	57	42	17	479
Spinners (branch not specified) - - - -	6	26	326	69	427
Bleachers - - - - -	113	24	61	37	235
Printers (Cotton and Calico) - - -	103	31	9	11	154
Printers (Silk) - .. - - -	1	—	—	—	1
Miscellaneous - - - - -	616	170	211	58	1,055
	5,485	1,593	3,007	1,424	11,509
All other Classes:					
Employed in Retail Trade or in Handicraft, as Masters or Workmen - - - - -	8,798	1,624	1,346	123	11,891
Labourers - - - - - -	2,203	131	284	6	2,624
Military and Naval - - - - -	448	47	—	—	495
Professional Persons - - - - -	558	—	—	—	558
Other Educated Persons following miscellaneous Pursuits	580	94	83	10	767
Persons engaged in the Government Civil Service -	135	1	6	—	142
Parochial, Town, and Church Officers - - -	146	—	4	—	150
Domestic Servants - - - - -	988	528	4,644	3,323	9,483
Persons returned as Independent - - -	711	22	2,333	81	3,147
Almspeople, Pensioners, Paupers, Lunatics, and Prisoners	403	11	510	20	944
Residue of Population:					
Consisting of the Wives, Children, and others dependent on all Classes - - - - -	2,279	23,066	28,887	25,146	79,378
Total of all other Classes - -	17,249	25,524	38,097	28,709	109,579

Divide "ALL OTHER CLASSES" between the AGRICULTURISTS and the MANUFACTURERS in the proportion which these respectively bear to each other, and the numbers engaged in, and dependent on, each interest will stand thus:—

Engaged in Agriculture - - -	16,302
Dependent on ,, - - - -	64,233
AGRICULTURE—Total - -	80,535
Engaged in Manufactures - - -	11,509
Dependent on ,, - - -	45,346
MANUFACTURES—Total - -	56,855
Total of the County - - -	137,390

TAXATION.

	Paid by the	
	Land.	Manufacturers.
Paid exclusively by the Landed Interest:	£	£
Land Tax - - - - - - -	(*See Summary.*)	
Property Tax—on Land, assessed at - - - £551,077	16,073	—
Paid in the Proportion of 3-5ths by the Landed Interest, and 2-5ths by the Manufacturers:		
Poor Relief - - - - - £11,164	6,700	4,464
Highway Rates ⎫		
Church ,, ⎬ No Return		
Turnpike Trusts ⎭		
Property Tax—on Dwelling Houses, assessed at - - 54,610	954	638
,, on other Property ,, - 7,479	142	76
	23,869	5,178
Total of Taxation of the County - - - - £29,047		

ENGAGED IN	MALES.		FEMALES.		TOTAL.
	20 years of age and upwards.	Under 20 years of age.	20 years of age and upwards.	Under 20 years of age.	
Agriculture:					
Farmers and Graziers - - - - -	1,054	18	56	—	1,128
Agricultural Labourers - - - -	3,432	753	167	58	4,410
Gardeners, Nurserymen, and Florists - -	304	22	2	—	328
	4,790	793	225	58	5,866
Manufactures:					
Cotton Manufacture (all branches) - - -	5,107	2,595	3,550	3,095	14,347
Silk Manufacture (all branches) - -	1,250	311	336	309	2,216
Weavers (all branches) - - - -	1,023	282	102	149	1,556
Bleachers - - - - -	187	108	605	338	1,238
Printers (Calico and Cotton) - -	660	293	44	136	1,133
,, Silk - - - -	3	—	—	—	3
Shawl Manufacture (all branches) - - -	99	4	449	283	835
Engineers and Engine Workers - - -	396	90	1	—	487
Engine and Machine Makers - - - -	54	20	—	—	74
Woollen and Cloth Manufacture (all branches) - -	210	71	50	43	374
Dyers (all branches) - - - -	261	84	6	3	354
Thread Manufacture (all branches) - -	22	8	176	141	347
Flax Manufacture (all branches) - - -	53	1	153	90	297
Canvass Manufacture (all branches) - -	213	39	8	6	266
Factory Workers (branch not specified) - -	70	35	74	86	265
Pattern Makers - - - - -	171	72	2	2	247
Muslin Embroiderers and Workers - - -	40	11	139	53	243
,, Manufacture (all branches) - -	20	10	63	25	118
Rope and Cord Spinners and Makers -	152	50	17	12	231
Miscellaneous - - - - -	1,516	499	335	61	2,411
	11,517	4,583	6,110	4,832	27,042
All other Classes:					
Employed in Retail Trade or in Handicraft, as Masters or Workmen - - - - - }	10,971	2,234	2,999	871	17,075
Labourers - - - - -	4,123	512	328	11	4,974
Military and Naval - - - - -	1,109	219	—	—	1,328
Professional Persons - - - -	396	—	—	—	396
Other Educated Persons following miscellaneous Pursuits	756	216	64	6	1,042
Persons engaged in the Government Civil Service -	160	4	—	—	164
Parochial, Town, and Church Officers - - -	238	2	8	—	248
Domestic Servants - - - - -	441	225	3,305	2,034	6,005
Persons returned as Independent - - -	423	20	1,974	100	2,517
Almspeople, Pensioners, Paupers, Lunatics, and Prisoners	346	68	404	65	883
Residue of Population:					
Consisting of the Wives, Children, and others dependent on all Classes - - - - - }	1,110	27,632	28,696	30,094	87,532
Total of all other Classes - -	20,073	31,132	37,778	33,181	122,164

Divide "ALL OTHER CLASSES" between the AGRICULTURISTS and the MANUFACTURERS in the proportion which these respectively bear to each other, and the numbers engaged in, and dependent on, each interest will stand thus :—

Engaged in Agriculture - - -	5,866	
Dependent on ,, - - -	21,776	
AGRICULTURE—Total -		27,642
Engaged in Manufactures - -	27,042	
Dependent on ,, - -	100,388	
MANUFACTURES—Total -		127,430
Total of the County - -		155,072

TAXATION.

		Paid by the	
		LAND.	MANUFACTURERS.
		£	£
Paid exclusively by the Landed Interest:			
Land Tax - - - - - - -		(*See Summary.*)	
Property Tax—on Land, assessed at - - - £152,923		4,460	—
Paid in the Proportion of 1-6th by the Landed Interest, and 5-6ths by the Manufacturers:			
Poor Relief - - - - - - £18,779		3,129	15,650
Highway Rates }			
Church ,, } No Return.			
Turnpike Trusts }			
Property Tax—on Dwelling Houses, assessed at - - 265,774		1,292	6,459
,, on other property ,, - 55,869		271	1,358
		9,152	23,467
Total of Taxation of the County - - - - £32,619			

ENGAGED IN	MALES.		FEMALES.		TOTAL.
	20 years of age and upwards.	Under 20 years of age.	20 years of age and upwards.	Under 20 years of age.	
Agriculture:					
Farmers and Graziers - - - -	2,169	18	153	—	2,340
Agricultural Labourers - - - -	5,822	1,007	858	139	7,826
Gardeners, Nurserymen, and Florists - -	109	6	—	—	115
	8,100	1,031	1,011	139	10,281
Manufactures:					
Weavers (all branches) - - - -	235	2	11	2	250
Woollen and Cloth Manufacture (all branches) -	137	—	18	1	156
Hemp Manufacture (all branches) - -	34	1	84	2	121
Spinners (branch not specified) - - -	—	—	75	—	75
Miscellaneous - - - - -	93	13	32	1	139
	499	16	220	6	741
All other Classes:					
Employed in Retail Trade or in Handicraft, as Masters or Workmen - - - -	3,191	290	179	10	3,670
Labourers - - - - - -	491	32	102	6	631
Military and Naval - - - -	1,784	116	—	—	1,900
Professional Persons - - - -	133	—	—	—	133
Other Educated Persons following miscellaneous Pursuits	250	42	32	2	326
Persons engaged in the Government Civil Service -	69	4	6	—	78
Parochial, Town, and Church Officers - -	71	—	—	—	71
Domestic Servants - - - - -	459	506	2,572	1,430	4,967
Persons returned as Independent - - -	153	5	802	23	983
Almspeople, Pensioners, Paupers, Lunatics, and Prisoners	322	5	408	7	741
Residue of Population:					
Consisting of the Wives, Children, and others dependent on all Classes - - -	3,084	16,145	18,873	16,061	54,163
Total of all other Classes - - -	10,007	17,143	22,974	17,539	67,663

Divide "ALL OTHER CLASSES" between the AGRICULTURISTS and the MANUFACTURERS in the proportion which these respectively bear to each other, and the numbers engaged in, and dependent on, each interest will stand thus:—

Engaged in Agriculture - - -	10,281	
Dependent on ,, - - -	63,115	
AGRICULTURE—Total - - -		73,396
Engaged in Manufactures - - -	741	
Dependent on ,, - - -	4,548	
MANUFACTURES—Total - -		5,289
Total of the County - - -		78,685

TAXATION.

		Paid by the	
		LAND.	MANUFACTURERS.
Paid exclusively by the Landed Interest:		£	£
Land Tax - - - - - -		(*See Summary.*)	
Property Tax—on Land, assessed at - - - £126,681		3,694	—
Paid in the Proportion of 14-15ths by the Landed Interest, and 1-15th by the Manufacturers:			
Poor Relief - - - - - £1,500		1,400	100
Highway Rates ⎫			
Church ,, ⎬ No Return.			
Turnpike Trusts ⎭			
Property Tax—on Dwelling Houses, assessed at - 7,072		193	13
,, on other Property ,, - 9,461		258	18
		5,545	131
Total of Taxation of the County - - - -		£5,676	

ENGAGED IN	MALES.		FEMALES.		TOTAL.
	20 years of age and upwards.	Under 20 years of age.	20 years of age and upwards.	Under 20 years of age	
AGRICULTURE:					
Farmers and Graziers - - - - -	664	14	20	—	698
Agricultural Labourers - - - -	3,402	985	807	440	5,634
Gardeners, Nurserymen, and Florists - -	179	18	1	—	198
	4,245	1,017	828	440	6,530
MANUFACTURES:					
Woollen and Cloth Manufacture (all branches) - -	625	244	204	244	1,317
Stocking Manufacture (all branches) - - -	623	262	47	32	964
Weavers (all branches) - - - -	105	13	5	2	125
Dyers (all branches) - - - - -	48	14	4	—	66
Miscellaneous - - - - -	230	52	42	22	346
	1,631	585	302	300	2,818
ALL OTHER CLASSES:					
Employed in Retail Trade or in Handicraft, as Masters or Workmen - - - -	3,240	736	562	90	4,628
Labourers - - - - - -	636	47	134	1	818
Military and Naval - - - - -	35	3	—	—	38
Professional Persons - - - - -	160	—	—	—	160
Other Educated Persons following miscellaneous Pursuits	178	45	51	5	279
Persons engaged in the Government Civil Service -	18	1	1	—	20
Parochial, Town, and Church Officers - - -	27	—	2	—	29
Domestic Servants - - - -	327	173	1,549	852	2,901
Persons returned as Independent - - -	286	8	784	24	1,102
Almspeople, Pensioners, Paupers, Lunatics, and Prisoners	119	20	331	24	494
RESIDUE OF POPULATION:					
Consisting of the Wives, Children, and others dependent on all Classes - - - -	360	8,059	8,702	9,087	26,208
Total of all other Classes - - -	5,386	9,092	12,116	10,083	36,677

Divide "ALL OTHER CLASSES" between the AGRICULTURISTS and the MANUFACTURERS in the proportion which these respectively bear to each other, and the numbers engaged in, and dependent on, each interest will stand thus:—

Engaged in Agriculture - - -	6,530		
Dependent on „ - - -	25,621		
AGRICULTURE—Total - -		32,151	
Engaged in Manufactures - - -	2,818		
Dependent on „ - -	11,056		
MANUFACTURES—Total - -		13,874	
Total of the County - - -		46,025	

TAXATION.

		Paid by the	
		LAND.	MANUFACTURERS.
Paid exclusively by the Landed Interest :		£	£
Land Tax - - - - - -	-	(See Summary.)	
Property Tax—on Land, assessed at - -	- £235,040	6,855	—
Paid in the Proportion of 5-7ths by the Landed Interest, and 2-7ths by the Manufacturers :			
Poor Relief - - - - -	- £8,458	6,040	2,418
Highway Rates }			
Church „ }No Return.			
Turnpike Trusts }			
Property Tax—on Dwelling Houses, assessed at -	48,684	1,015	405
„ on other Property „ - -	480	10	4
		13,920	2,827
Total of Taxation of the County - - - -	£16,747		

ENGAGED IN	MALES.		FEMALES.		TOTAL.
	20 years of age and upwards.	Under 20 years of age.	20 years of age and upwards.	Under 20 years of age.	
AGRICULTURE:					
Farmers and Graziers - - - - - -	90	2	1	—	93
Agricultural Labourers - - - - -	601	160	18	6	785
Gardeners, Nurserymen, and Florists - - -	21	3	—	—	24
	712	165	19	6	902
MANUFACTURES:					
Woollen and Cloth Manufacture (all branches) -	149	94	79	89	411
Weavers (all branches) - - - -	111	40	—	—	151
Stocking Makers and Weavers - - -	67	23	—	—	90
Miscellaneous - - - - -	53	20	8	—	81
	380	177	87	89	733
ALL OTHER CLASSES:					
Employed in Retail Trade or in Handicraft, as Masters or Workmen - - - - -	466	97	68	8	639
Labourers - - - - - -	123	23	4	—	150
Military and Naval - - - - -	4	—	—	—	4
Professional Persons - - - -	28	—	—	—	28
Other Educated Persons following miscellaneous Pursuits	36	1	8	—	45
Persons engaged in the Government Civil Service -	6	—	—	—	6
Parochial, Town, and Church Officers - - -	4	—	—	—	4
Domestic Servants - - - -	58	32	249	207	546
Persons returned as Independent - -	35	2	106	6	149
Almspeople, Pensioners, Paupers, Lunatics, and Prisoners	12	7	34	6	59
RESIDUE OF POPULATION:					
Consisting of the Wives, Children, and others dependent on all Classes - - - - -	88	1,516	1,544	1,577	4,725
Total of all other Classes - - -	860	1,678	2,013	1,804	6,355

Divide " ALL OTHER CLASSES" between the AGRICULTURISTS and the MANUFACTURERS in the proportion which these respectively bear to each other, and the numbers engaged in, and dependent on, each interest will stand thus :—

Engaged in Agriculture - - -	902	
Dependent on ,, - - -	3,506	
AGRICULTURE—Total - -		4,408
Engaged in Manufactures - -	733	
Dependent on ,, - -	2,849	
MANUFACTURES—Total -		3,582
Total of the County - - -		7,990

TAXATION.

		Paid by the	
		LAND.	MANUFACTURERS.
		£	£
Paid exclusively by the Landed Interest :		(*See Summary.*)	
Land Tax - - - - - -		1,129	
Property Tax—on Land, assessed at - - - £38,713			—
Paid in the Proportion of 4-7ths by the Landed Interest, and 3-7ths by the Manufacturers :			
Poor Relief - - - - - £1,000		568	432
Highway Rates			
Church ,, } No Return.			
Turnpike Trusts			
Property Tax—on Dwelling Houses, assessed at - 11,052		184	138
,, on other Property ,, - - -		—	—
		1,881	570
Total of Taxation of the County - - - £2,451			

ENGAGED IN	MALES.		FEMALES.		TOTAL.
	20 years of age and upwards.	Under 20 years of age.	20 years of age and upwards.	Under 20 years of age.	
Agriculture :					
Farmers and Graziers - - -	1,194	15	57	—	1,266
Agricultural Labourers - - - -	3,393	1,349	150	53	4,945
Gardeners, Nurserymen, and Florists - -	178	22	2	2	204
	4,765	1,386	209	55	6,415
Manufactures :					
Cotton Manufacture (all branches) - - -	832	226	440	231	1,729
Printers (Calico) - - - - -	570	330	35	122	1,057
Woollen and Cloth Manufacture (all branches) - -	673	182	53	44	952
Nailers and Nail Makers - - - -	343	180	6	1	530
Weavers (all branches) - - ·· - -	404	71	13	18	506
Factory Workers (branch not specified) -	108	81	94	45	328
Iron Manufacture (all branches) - - -	193	120	3	1	317
Tartan Manufacture (all branches) - - -	113	48	41	21	223
Bleachers - - - - - -	72	17	84	34	207
Moulders (branch not specified) - - -	96	77	—	—	173
Founders (branch not specified) - - -	80	70	—	—	150
Worsted Manufacture (all branches) - -	48	19	34	22	123
Miscellaneous - - - - -	813	133	312	35	1,293
	4,345	1,554	1,115	574	7,588
All other Classes :					
Employed in Retail Trade or in Handicraft, as Masters or Workmen - - - - -	5,165	1,065	994	137	7,361
Labourers - - - - - -	4,006	581	316	49	4,952
Military and Naval - - - - -	393	34	—	—	427
Professional Persons - - - - -	241	—	—	—	241
Other Educated Persons following miscellaneous Pursuits	299	57	66	7	429
Persons engaged in the Government Civil Service -	77	1	4	—	82
Parochial, Town, and Church Officers - - -	56	—	—	—	56
Domestic Servants - - - - -	476	264	1,909	1,649	4,298
Persons returned as Independent - - -	351	15	1,380	74	1,820
Almspeople, Pensioners, Paupers, Lunatics, and Prisoners	180	12	130	24	346
Residue of Population :					
Consisting of the Wives, Children, and others dependent on all Classes - - - - -	1,148	14,542	15,929	16,423	48,042
Total of all other Classes - - -	12,392	16,571	20,728	18,363	68,054

Divide "all other classes" between the Agriculturists and the Manufacturers in the proportion which these respectively bear to each other, and the numbers engaged in, and dependent on, each interest will stand thus :—

Engaged in Agriculture	- - -	6,415	
Dependent on ,,	- - -	31,176	
Agriculture—Total	- -		37,591
Engaged in Manufactures	- - -	7,588	
Dependent on ,,	- -	36,878	
Manufactures—Total	- -		44,466
Total of the County	- - -		82,057

TAXATION.

		Paid by the	
		Land.	Manufacturers.
Paid exclusively by the Landed Interest :		£	£
Land Tax - - - - - - -		(*See Summary.*)	
Property Tax—on Land, assessed at - - £181,147		5,283	—
Paid in the Proportion of 3-7ths by the Landed Interest, and 4-7ths by the Manufacturers :			
Poor Relief - - - - - £4,015		1,719	2,296
Highway Rates ⎫			
Church ,, ⎬ No Return.			
Turnpike Trusts ⎭			
Property Tax—on Dwelling Houses, assessed at - 63,559		792	1,061
,, on other Property ,, - 34,999		438	585
		8,229	3,942
Total of Taxation of the County - - - £12,171			

(*For those engaged in Mines, see "Mining Interest."*)

ENGAGED IN	MALES.		FEMALES.		TOTAL.
	20 years of age and upwards.	Under 20 years of age.	20 years of age and upwards.	Under 20 years of age.	
Agriculture:					
Farmers and Graziers - - - -	399	4	47	—	450
Agricultural Labourers - - -	2,115	241	577	11	2,914
Gardeners, Nurserymen, and Florists - -	16	—	—	—	16
	2,530	215	624	11	3,380
Manufactures:					
Woollen Manufacture (all branches) - - -	37	1	21	—	59
Weavers (all branches) - - - -	49	—	1	—	50
Miscellaneous - - - - -	26	—	3	—	29
	112	1	25	—	138
All other Classes:					
Employed in Retail Trade or in Handicraft, as Masters or Workmen - - - - -	900	85	40	3	1,028
Labourers - - - - -	142	13	16	1	172
Military and Naval - - - - -	361	19	—	—	380
Professional Persons - - - -	31	—	—	—	31
Other Educated Persons following miscellaneous Pursuits	69	12	7	1	89
Persons engaged in the Government Civil Service -	51	—	—	—	51
Parochial, Town, and Church Officers - - -	15	—	—	—	15
Domestic Servants - - - -	172	223	798	442	1,635
Persons returned as Independent - - -	71	3	344	5	423
Almspeople, Pensioners, Paupers, Lunatics, and Prisoners	198	1	185	2	386
Residue of Population:					
Consisting of the Wives, Children, and others dependent on all Classes - - - - -	971	5,192	5,654	5,237	17,054
Total of all other Classes - - -	2,981	5,548	7,044	5,691	21,264

Divide "all other classes" between the Agriculturists and the Manufacturers in the proportion which these respectively bear to each other, and the number engaged in, and dependent on, each interest will stand thus :—

Engaged in Agriculture - - -	3,380		
Dependent on - - - - -	20,430		
Agriculture—Total - - ——		23,810	
Engaged in Manufactures - - -	138		
Dependent on - - - -	834		
Manufactures—Total - - ——		972	
Total of the County - - -		24,782	

TAXATION.

		Paid by the	
		Land.	Manufacturers.
Paid exclusively by the Landed Interest:		£	£
Land Tax - - - - - -		(*See Summary.*)	
Property Tax—on Land, assessed at - - - £33,688		982	—
Paid in the Proportion of 24-25ths by the Landed Interest, and 1-25th by the Manufacturers:			
Poor Relief - - - - - - £556		534	22
Highway Rates ⎫			
Church ,, ⎬ No Return.			
Turnpike Trusts ⎭			
Property Tax—on Dwelling Houses, assessed at - - 860		24	1
,, on other Property ,, - - 564		16	
		1,556	23
Total of Taxation of the County - - - -		£1,579	

ENGAGED IN	MALES.		FEMALES.		TOTAL.
	20 years of age and upwards.	Under 20 years of age.	20 years of age and upwards.	Under 20 years of age.	
Agriculture :					
Farmers and Graziers - - - -	1,128	1	85	—	1,214
Agricultural Labourers - - - -	2,954	680	217	46	3,897
Gardeners, Nurserymen, and Florists - - -	50	6	—	—	56
	4,132	687	302	46	5,167
Manufactures :					
Weavers (all branches) - - -	160	4	2	—	166
Cotton Manufacture (all branches) - - -	68	15	8	1	92
Woollen and Cloth Manufacture (all branches) -	46	1	9	1	57
Muslin Flowerers and Workers - - - -	—	—	37	13	50
Spinners (branch not specified) - - - -	1	—	36	—	37
Miscellaneous - - - - -	144	21	46	1	212
	419	41	138	16	614
All other Classes :					
Employed in Retail Trade or in Handicraft, as Masters or Workmen - - - - - }	2,045	343	450	59	2,897
Labourers - - - - -	361	28	53	3	445
Military and Naval - - - -	255	22	—	—	277
Professional Persons - - - -	103	—	—	—	103
Other Educated Persons following miscellaneous Pursuits -	112	17	32	—	161
Persons engaged in the Government Civil Service	55	—	3	—	58
Parochial, Town, and Church Officers - -	31	—	2	1	34
Domestic Servants - - - -	289	189	1,147	866	2,471
Persons returned as Independent - - -	190	4	549	16	759
Almspeople, Pensioners, Paupers, Lunatics, and Prisoners	63	4	37	4	108
Residue of Population :					
Consisting of the Wives, Children, and others dependent on all Classes - - - - }	763	8,147	8,607	8,564	26,081
Total of all other Classes - - -	4,267	8,754	10,880	9,513	33,414

Divide " **all other classes** " between the **Agriculturists** and the **Manufacturers** in the proportion which these respectively bear to each other, and the numbers engaged in, and dependent on, each interest will stand thus:—

Engaged in Agriculture　-　　　-　　　-　　5,167
Dependent on　　,,　　　-　　　-　　-　29,803

　　　　Agriculture—Total　-　　　————　　34,970

Engaged in Manufactures　-　　-　　　-　　614
Dependent on　　,,　　　-　　　-　　　3,611

　　　　Manufactures—Total　-　　-　　　　4,225

　　　　Total of the County　　-　　　-　　-　39,195

TAXATION.

	Paid by the	
	Land.	Manufacturers.
Paid exclusively by the Landed Interest :	£	£
Land Tax - - - - - -	*(See Summary.)*	
Property Tax—on Land, assessed at - - - £124,807	3,640	—
Paid in the Proportion of 8-9ths by the Landed Interest, and 1-9th by the Manufacturers :		
Poor Relief - - - - - £2,408	2,141	267
Highway Rates }		
Church　　,, } No Return.		
Turnpike Trusts }		
Property Tax—on Dwelling Houses, assessed at - - 10,062	261	32
,,　　　on other Property　　,,　　- - 537	14	1
	6,056	300

　　　　Total of Taxation of the County　-　　-　　-　- £6,356

SCOTLAND—SUMMARY OF POPULATION.

COUNTIES.	AGRICULTURE.			MANUFACTURES.			TOTAL OF THE COUNTY.
	Engaged in :	Dependent on :	TOTAL.	Engaged in :	Dependent on :	TOTAL.	
ABERDEEN - - -	25,224	109,087	134,311	10,907	47,169	58,076	192,387
ARGYLL - - - -	13,187	75,148	88,335	1,349	7,687	9,036	97,371
AYR - - - -	11,160	52,316	63,476	17,736	83,144	100,880	164,356
BANFF - - -	7,581	38,410	45,991	608	3,080	3,688	49,679
BERWICK - - -	6,173	25,685	31,858	500	2,080	2,580	34,438
BUTE - - - -	1,419	9,617	11,036	605	4,099	4,704	15,740
CAITHNESS - -	5,116	27,921	33,037	512	2,794	3,306	36,343
CLACKMANNAN - - -	952	6,339	7,291	1,549	10,315	11,864	19,155
DUMBARTON - -	2,603	8,905	11,508	7,417	25,371	32,788	44,296
DUMFRIES - - -	10,938	47,019	57,957	2,807	12,066	14,873	72,830
EDINBURGH -	7,756	108,649	116,405	7,266	101,783	109,049	225,454
ELGIN OR MORAY - -	5,080	27,604	32,684	362	1,966	2,328	35,012
FIFE - - -	10,041	38,447	48,488	18,979	72,673	91,652	140,140
FORFAR - - - -	10,078	34,747	44,825	28,260	97,435	125,695	170,520
HADDINGTON -	6,168	27,714	33,882	365	1,639	2,004	35,886
INVERNESS - -	13,746	77,595	91,341	972	5,486	6,458	97,799
KINCARDINE -	5,848	19,758	25,606	1,706	5,763	7,469	33,075
KINROSS - - -	1,032	3,247	4,279	1,081	3,403	4,484	8,763
KIRKCUDBRIGHT -	5,256	30,105	35,361	856	4,902	5,758	41,119
LANARK - - -	13,169	62,257	75,426	61,378	290,168	351,546	426,972
LINLITHGOW -	2,456	14,817	17,273	1,365	8,234	9,599	26,872
NAIRN - - - -	1,591	7,302	8,893	58	266	324	9,217
ORKNEY AND SHETLAND -	6,251	39,366	45,617	2,117	13,331	15,448	61,065
PEEBLES - - -	1,669	7,544	9,213	233	1,053	1,286	10,499
PERTH - - -	16,302	64,233	80,535	11,509	45,346	56,855	137,390
RENFREW - - -	5,866	21,776	27,642	27,042	100,388	127,430	155,072
ROSS AND CROMARTY -	10,281	63,115	73,396	741	4,548	5,289	78,685
ROXBURGH - -	6,530	25,621	32,151	2,818	11,056	13,874	46,025
SELKIRK - - -	902	3,506	4,408	733	2,849	3,582	7,990
STIRLING - - -	6,415	31,176	37,591	7,588	36,878	44,466	82,057
SUTHERLAND - -	3,380	20,430	23,810	138	834	972	24,782
WIGTOWN - - -	5,167	29,803	34,970	614	3,611	4,225	39,195
	229,337	1,159,259	1,388,596	220,171	1,011,417	1,231,588	2,620,184

Total of the Agricultural Interest - - - 1,388,596
,,   Manufacturing Interest - - - 1,231,588

Total Population of Scotland - - - - 2,620,184

SCOTLAND—SUMMARY OF DIRECT AND LOCAL TAXATION.

COUNTIES.	Paid by the Landed Interest and those dependent on it.	Paid by the Manufacturing Interest and those dependent on it.	Total Taxation of the County.
	£	£	£
ABERDEEN	28,630	6,508	35,138
ARGYLL	10,388	416	10,304
AYR	17,683	9,351	27,034
BANFF	5,776	212	5,988
BERWICK	13,308	706	14,014
BUTE	1,226	248	1,474
CAITHNESS	2,498	81	2,579
CLACKMANNAN	1,656	947	2,603
DUMBARTON	3,311	3,630	6,941
DUMFRIES	15,522	1,937	17,459
EDINBURGH	35,714	28,738	64,452
ELGIN or MORAY	4,385	137	4,522
FIFE	16,219	9,185	25,404
FORFAR	15,122	18,041	33,163
HADDINGTON	12,128	376	12,504
INVERNESS	6,975	160	7,135
KINCARDINE	6,036	654	6,690
KINROSS	1,388	244	1,632
KIRKCUDBRIGHT	9,304	657	9,961
LANARK	22,874	64,621	87,495
LINLITHGOW	4,154	917	5,071
NAIRN	630	29	659
ORKNEY and SHETLAND	1,737	199	1,936
PEEBLES	3,355	195	3,550
PERTH	23,869	5,178	29,047
RENFREW	9,152	23,467	32,619
ROSS and CROMARTY	5,545	131	5,676
ROXBURGH	13,920	2,827	16,747
SELKIRK	1,881	570	2,451
STIRLING	8,229	3,942	12,171
SUTHERLAND	1,556	23	1,579
WIGTOWN	6,056	300	6,356
Land Tax of the Kingdom (no Return of separate Counties)	47,954	—	47,954
	358,181	184,627	542,808

Total of Direct and Local Taxation paid by the Landed Interest   - -   £358,181

    ,,   ,,   Manufacturing - -   184,627

Total of Direct and Local Taxation of Scotland   - - -   £542,808

ENGAGED IN	MALES.		FEMALES.		TOTAL.
	20 years of age and upwards.	Under 20 years of age.	20 years of age and upwards.	Under 20 years of age.	
Agriculture:					
Farmers and Graziers - - - -	3,752	44	164	—	3,960
Agricultural Labourers - - - -	3,247	626	335	38	4,246
Gardeners, Nurserymen, and Florists - -	276	11	—	—	287
	7,275	681	499	38	8,493
Manufactures:					
Weavers (all branches) - - - -	325	9	5	—	339
Rope and Cord Spinners and Makers - -	106	40	1	—	147
Dyers - - - - - - -	43	7	35	11	96
Hatters - - - - - - -	71	5	3	3	82
Sail Makers - - - - - - -	54	27	—	—	81
Spinners (branch not specified) - -	4	—	73	1	78
Miscellaneous - - - - -	575	103	107	23	808
	1,178	191	224	38	1,631
All other Classes:					
Employed in Retail Trade or in Handicraft, as Masters or Workmen - - - - -	10,596	2,257	2,343	762	15,958
Labourers - - - - - -	1,995	152	1,151	75	3,373
Military and Naval - - - - -	2,738	381	—	—	3,119
Professional Persons - - - -	434	—	—	—	434
Other Educated Persons following miscellaneous Pursuits	480	54	292	33	859
Persons engaged in the Government Civil Service -	88	—	5	1	94
Parochial, Town, and Church Officers - - -	60	—	5	—	65
Domestic Servants - - - -	727	385	4,348	2,075	7,535
Persons returned as Independent - - -	2,263	98	4,596	219	7,176
Almspeople, Pensioners, Paupers, Lunatics, and Prisoners	652	131	319	71	1,173
Residue of Population:					
Consisting of the Wives, Children, and others dependent on all Classes - - - -	1,838	22,911	24,509	24,872	74,130
Total of all other Classes - - -	21,871	26,369	37,568	28,108	113,916

Divide " all other classes" between the Agriculturists and the Manufacturers in the proportion which these respectively bear to each other, and the numbers engaged in, and dependent on, each interest will stand thus :—

Engaged in Agriculture - - -	8,493	
Dependent on ,, - - -	95,564	
Agriculture—Total - - ———		104,057
Engaged in Manufactures - - -	1,631	
Dependent on ,, - - -	18,352	
Manufactures—Total - - ———		19,983
Total of the County - -		124,040

TAXATION.

There is no Return of the Direct and Local Taxation of the several Islands in the British Seas, but it is very trifling in Amount.

ENGAGED IN	MALES.		FEMALES.		TOTAL.
	15 years of age and upwards.	Under 15 years of age.	15 years of age and upwards.	Under 15 years of age.	
Agriculture :					
Farmers - - - - - - -	17,020	- -	844	- -	17,864
Servants, Labourers, and Ploughmen - - -	26,773	3,207	873	122	30,975
Gardeners - - - - - -	256	2	2	- -	260
Graziers - - - - - - -	4	-	-	- -	4
Herdsmen - - - - - -	162	371	18	81	632
Caretakers - - - - - -	53	1	2	- -	56
Land Agents and Stewards - - - - -	94	-	-	- -	94
Gamekeepers - - - - - -	19	- -	-	- -	19
Dairy Keepers - - - - -	4	- -	7	- -	11
	44,385	3,581	1,746	203	49,915
Manufactures:					
Spinners (Flax, Wool, and Cotton) - - -	54	23	5,950	498 }	26,090
,, (Unspecified) - - - -	9	- -	18,093	1,463 }	
Weavers (Linen, Cotton, Woollen, and Silk) - -	4,034	374	590	86 }	17,610
,, (Unspecified) - - - -	9,646	805	1,854	221 }	
Factory Workers - - - - -	410	134	1,059	236	1,839
Winders and Warpers - - - -	30	185	846	387	1,448
Bleachers - - - - - -	828	48	84	7	967
Flax Dressers - - - - -	350	25	67	12	454
Knitters - - - - - -	-	-	223	33	256
Coopers - - - - - -	237	2	- -	- -	239
Nailers - - - - - -	211	17	-	-	228
Cloth Finishers - - - - -	121	7	2	1	131
Paper Makers - - - - -	68	-	49	9	126
Manufacturers (Thread, Linen, and Cotton) -	53	2	27	6	88
Calico Printers - - - - -	73	3	4	- -	80
Turners - - - - - -	49	4	-	- -	53
Dyers - - - - - -	40	-	10	- -	50
Reed Makers - - - - -	39	1	-	- -	40
Rope Makers - - - - -	27	10	-	- -	37
Chandlers and Soap Boilers - - - -	32	2	-	-	34
Basket Makers - - - - -	27	2	2	- -	31
Tanners - - - - - -	18	-	-	- -	18
Mat Makers - - - - - -	1	4	7	4	16
Miscellaneous - - - - -	123	6	25	1	155
	16,480	1,654	28,892	2,964	49,990
All other Classes:					
Employed in Handicraft, as Masters or Workmen. in the production of—					
Food - - - -	1,459	25	224	- -	1,708
Clothing - - - - -	3,123	161	4,891	630	8,805
Lodging, Furniture, Machinery, &c. -	4,295	66	16	- -	4,377
Ministering to Health - - - -	123	-	35	- -	158
,, Charity - - - -	3	-	3	- -	6
,, Justice - - - - -	413	-	1	- -	414
,, Education - - - -	439	-	184	1	624
,, Religion - - - -	242	-	3	- -	245
Unclassified - - - -	3,361	565	8,216	1,065	13,207
	13,458	817	13,573	1,696	29,544
Residue of Population :					
Consisting of the Wives, Children, and others dependent on all Classes - - - - -					146,739
Total of all other Classes - - - - - - - - -					176,283

Divide " all other classes " between the Agriculturists and the Manufacturers in the proportion which these respectively bear to each other, and the numbers engaged in, and dependent on, each interest will stand thus:—

Engaged in Agriculture - -	49,915	
Dependent on ,, - -	88,076	
Agriculture—Total - -	———	137,991
Engaged in Manufactures - -	49,990	
Dependent on ,, - -	88,207	
Manufactures—Total - -	———	138,197
Total of the County - -		276,188

ARMAGH—County of. [Ireland.

ENGAGED IN	MALES.		FEMALES.		TOTAL.
	15 years of age and upwards.	Under 15 years of age.	15 years of age and upwards.	Under 15 years of age.	
AGRICULTURE:					
Farmers	14,839	1,408	421	110	16,778
Servants, Labourers, and Ploughmen	21,085	1	831	-	21,917
Gardeners	158	-	-	-	158
Grazier	-	-	1	-	1
Herdsmen	63	366	17	83	529
Caretakers	13	-	-	-	13
Land Agents and Stewards	60	-	-	-	60
Game Keepers	10	-	-	-	10
Dairy Keepers	-	-	2	-	2
	36,228	1,775	1,272	193	39,468
MANUFACTURES:					
Spinners (Flax and Wool)	-	-	2,719	90 ⎱	⎱ 19,852
,, (Unspecified)	-	-	16,506	537 ⎰	⎰
Weavers (Linen, Cotton, and Woollen)	2,674	76	508	29 ⎱	⎱ 16,361
,, (Unspecified)	10,463	306	2,213	92 ⎰	⎰
Winders and Warpers	14	30	510	93	647
Flax Dressers	317	-	13	-	330
Bleachers	238	5	-	-	243
Knitters	-	-	185	9	194
Factory Workers	52	12	105	19	188
Coopers	149	2	-	-	151
Nailers	142	2	1	-	145
Reed Makers	73	2	-	-	75
Chandlers and Soap Boilers	43	-	-	-	43
Cloth Finishers	30	2	2	-	34
Brick Makers	26	-	1	-	27
Basket Makers	26	-	-	-	26
Turners	23	1	-	-	24
Net Makers	2	-	22	-	24
Lace Workers	-	-	18	5	23
Rope Makers	21	-	-	-	21
Tanners	15	-	-	-	15
Lime Burners	15	-	-	-	15
Miscellaneous	122	1	22	1	146
	14,445	439	22,825	875	38,584
ALL OTHER CLASSES:					
Employed in Handicraft, as Masters or Workmen, in the production of—					
Food	1,155	48	82	7	1,292
Clothing	2,202	45	2,643	83	4,973
Lodging, Furniture, Machinery, &c.	3,331	30	11	-	3,372
Ministering to Health	89	-	40	-	129
,, Charity	4	-	2	-	6
,, Justice	290	-	-	-	290
,, Education	266	-	126	-	392
,, Religion	166	-	2	-	168
Unclassified	2,516	255	5,304	627	8,702
	10,019	378	8,210	717	19,324
RESIDUE OF POPULATION:					
Consisting of the Wives, Children, and others dependent on all Classes					135,017
Total of all other Classes					154,341

Divide "ALL OTHER CLASSES" between the AGRICULTURISTS and the MANUFACTURERS in the proportion which these respectively bear to each other, and the numbers engaged in, and dependent on, each interest will stand thus:—

Engaged in Agriculture	39,468	
Dependent on ,,	78,045	
AGRICULTURE—Total		117,513
Engaged in Manufactures	38,584	
Dependent on ,,	76,296	
MANUFACTURES—Total		114,880
Total of the County		232,393

ENGAGED IN	MALES.		FEMALES.		TOTAL.
	15 years of age and upwards.	Under 15 years of age.	15 years of age and upwards.	Under 15 years of age.	
AGRICULTURE:					
Farmers	93	-	9	-	102
Servants, Labourers, and Ploughmen	851	24	17	1	893
Gardeners	62	2	-	-	64
Herdsmen	3	2	2	-	7
Caretakers	2	-	-	-	2
Land Agents and Stewards	10	-	-	-	10
Dairy Keepers	20	-	6	-	26
	1,041	28	34	1	1,104
MANUFACTURES:					
Factory Workers	651	294	1,661	344	2,950
Weavers (Cotton, Linen, and Silk)	390	25	66	5	2,079
,, (Unspecified)	1,427	49	94	23	
Spinners (Flax, Cotton, and Wool)	62	14	496	63	1,467
,, (Unspecified)	-	-	778	54	
Winders and Warpers	45	50	724	106	925
Flax Dressers	369	15	-	-	384
Coopers	309	1	-	-	310
Bleachers	115	10	12	2	139
Iron Founders	126	8	-	-	134
Rope Makers	120	13	-	-	133
Nailers	104	8	-	-	112
Braziers and Coppersmiths	89	4	-	-	93
Chandlers and Soap Boilers	84	-	-	-	84
Cloth Finishers	75	-	3	-	78
Glass Makers	51	-	24	-	75
Hatters	53	-	12	-	65
Brick Makers	38	10	3	1	52
Turners	48	3	-	-	51
Manufacturers of Cotton and Thread	42	1	3	-	46
Paper Makers	19	-	21	-	40
Basket Makers	31	-	4	-	35
Dyers	21	-	9	-	30
Miscellaneous	253	12	46	5	316
	4,522	517	3,956	603	9,598
ALL OTHER CLASSES:					
Employed in Handicraft, as Masters or Workmen, in the production of—					
Food	1,376	23	213	-	1,612
Clothing	1,754	72	2,993	251	5,070
Lodging, Furniture, Machinery, &c.	3,676	109	58	5	3,848
Ministering to Health	112	1	24	-	137
,, Charity	-	-	14	-	14
,, Justice	292	2	1	-	295
,, Education	133	1	122	-	256
,, Religion	71	-	1	-	72
Unclassified	5,905	245	3,435	194	9,779
	13,319	453	6,861	450	21,083
RESIDUE OF POPULATION:					
Consisting of the Wives, Children, and others dependent on all Classes					43,523
Total of all other Classes					64,606

Divide "ALL OTHER CLASSES" between the AGRICULTURISTS and the MANUFACTURERS in the proportion which these respectively bear to each other, and the numbers engaged in, and dependent on, each interest will stand thus :—

Engaged in Agriculture	1,104	
Dependent on ,,	6,664	
AGRICULTURE—Total		7,768
Engaged in Manufactures	9,598	
Dependent on ,,	57,942	
MANUFACTURES—Total		67,540
Total of the Town		75,308

ENGAGED IN	MALES.		FEMALES.		TOTAL.
	15 years of age and upwards.	Under 15 years of age.	15 years of age and upwards.	Under 15 years of age.	
Agriculture:					
Farmers - - - - - - -	4,432	- -	250	- -	4,682
Servants, Labourers, and Ploughmen - -	12,569	622	2,994	214	16,399
Gardeners - - - - -	116	- -	-	- -	116
Herdsmen - - - - - - -	212	81	3	3	299
Caretakers - - - - - - -	35	2	3	- -	40
Land Agents and Stewards - - - -	89	- -	-	- -	89
Game Keepers - - - - -	4	- -	-	- -	4
Dairy Keepers - - - - - -	7	- -	24	- -	31
	17,464	705	3,274	217	21,660
Manufactures:					
Spinners (Wool and Flax) - - - -	2	- -	1,061	27	1,944
,, (Unspecified) - - - -	-	- -	814	40	
Knitters - - - - - - -	1	- -	279	10	290
Weavers (Linen, Woollen, and Cotton) - -	68	- -	-	-	234
,, (Unspecified) - - - -	157	2	7	-	
Nailers - - - - - - -	95	6	-	- -	101
Hatters - - - - - - -	46	- -	2	- -	48
Carders - - - - - - -	-	- -	22	2	24
Braziers and Coppersmiths - - - -	10	- -	-	- -	10
Clothiers - - - - - -	9	- -	-	- -	9
Lime Burners - - - - - -	9	- -	-	- -	9
Flax Dressers - - - - - -	6	- -	2	- -	8
Skinners - - - - - - -	7	- -	-	- -	7
Rope Makers - - - - - -	6	- -	1	- -	7
Potters - - - - - - -	7	- -	-	- -	7
Basket Makers - - - - - -	-	- -	5	1	6
Winders and Warpers - - - - -	6	- -	-	- -	6
Sieve Makers - - - - - -	-	- -	5	- -	5
Straw Workers - - - - - -	2	- -	2	- -	4
Dyers - - - - - - -	1	- -	3	- -	4
Mat Makers - - - - - -	3	- -	-	- -	3
Comb Makers - - - - - -	2	- -	1	- -	3
Wire Workers - - - - - -	2	- -	-	- -	2
Iron Founders - - - - - -	12	- -	1	- -	13
Miscellaneous - - - - -					
	458	8	2,205	80	2,751
All other Classes:					
Employed in Handicraft, as Masters or Workmen, in the production of—					
Food - - - -	628	10	118	2	758
Clothing - - - -	1,094	36	1,014	21	2,165
Lodging, Furniture, and Machinery, &c.	2,062	17	15	- -	2,094
Ministering to Health - - - - -	43	- -	62	- -	105
,, Charity - - - -	5	- -	18	- -	23
,, Justice - - - -	194	- -	1	- -	195
,, Education - - - -	141	1	87	- -	229
,, Religion - - - -	80	- -	60	- -	140
Unclassified - - - - -	1,876	169	3,755	271	6,071
	6,123	233	5,130	294	11,780
Residue of Population:					
Consisting of the Wives, Children, and others dependent on all Classes - - - -					50,037
Total of all other Classes - - - - - - -					61,817

Divide "all other classes" between the Agriculturists and the Manufacturers in the proportion which these respectively bear to each other, and the numbers engaged in, and dependent on, each interest will stand thus:—

Engaged in Agriculture - - -	21,660	
Dependent on ,, - - - -	54,851	
AGRICULTURE—Total - - -		76,511
Engaged in Manufactures - - -	2,751	
Dependent on ,, - -	6,966	
MANUFACTURES—Total - -		9,717
Total of the County - - - -		86,228

ENGAGED IN	MALES.		FEMALES.		TOTAL.
	15 years of age and upwards.	Under 15 years of age.	15 years of age and upwards.	Under 15 years of age.	
AGRICULTURE:					
Farmers	350	-	26	-	376
Servants, Labourers, and Ploughmen	706	72	23	2	803
Gardeners	11	-	-	-	11
Herdsmen	2	1	-	-	3
Land Steward	1	-	-	-	1
Dairy Keeper	1	-	-	-	1
	1,071	73	49	2	1,195
MANUFACTURES:					
Factory Workers	76	44	230	68	418
Weavers (Cotton, Linen, and Woollen)	30	2	9	-⎰	277
,, (Unspecified)	206	2	28	-⎱	
Spinners (Cotton, Flax, and Wool)	31	-	34	1⎰	180
,, (Unspecified)	-	-	110	4⎱	
Flax Dressers	17	1	-	-	18
Nailers	12	1	-	-	13
Winders and Warpers	-	-	10	2	12
Calico Printers	9	-	-	-	9
Coopers	9	-	-	-	9
Knitters	-	-	8	-	8
Chandlers and Soap Boilers	6	-	-	-	6
Dyers	4	-	1	-	5
Manufacturers of Cotton	3	-	-	-	3
Bleachers	2	-	1	-	3
Brick Makers	2	-	1	-	3
Turners	2	-	-	-	2
Braziers and Coppersmiths	2	-	-	-	2
Distiller	1	-	-	-	1
Cloth Finisher	1	-	-	-	1
Hatter	1	-	-	-	1
Reed Maker	1	-	-	-	1
Ironfounder	1	-	-	-	1
Gunsmith	1	-	-	-	1
	417	50	432	75	974
ALL OTHER CLASSES:					
Employed in Handicraft, as Masters or Workmen, in the production of—					
Food	155	1	23	-	179
Clothing	135	9	432	56	632
Lodging, Furniture, Machinery, &c.	175	3	2	-	180
Ministering to Health	10	-	1	-	11
,, Justice	36	-	2	-	38
,, Education	16	-	13	-	29
,, Religion	19	-	-	-	19
Unclassified	252	37	404	42	735
	798	50	877	98	1,823

RESIDUE OF POPULATION:

Consisting of the Wives, Children, and others dependent on all Classes - - - -   5,387

Total of all other Classes - - - - - - - -   7,210

Divide "ALL OTHER CLASSES" between the AGRICULTURISTS and the MANUFACTURERS in the proportion which these respectively bear to each other, and the numbers engaged in, and dependent on, each interest will stand thus :—

Engaged in Agriculture - - - 1,195
Dependent on ,, - - - - 3,973

AGRICULTURE—Total - - ——— 5,168

Engaged in Manufactures - - - 974
Dependent on ,, - - - 3,237

MANUFACTURES—Total - - ——— 4,211

Total of the Town - - - 9,397

ENGAGED IN	MALES.		FEMALES.		TOTAL.
	15 years of age and upwards.	Under 15 years of age.	15 years of age and upwards.	Under 15 years of age.	
Agriculture :					
Farmers - - - - - -	19,571	3	463	- -	20,037
Servants, Labourers, and Ploughmen - -	31,787	3,534	1,008	300	36,629
Gardeners - - - - - -	116	- -	- -	- -	116
Grazier - - - - - - -	1	- -	- -	- -	1
Herdsmen - - - - - -	222	394	30	165	811
Caretakers - - - - -	31	- -	- -	- -	31
Land Agents and Stewards - - - -	69	-	-	-	69
Game Keepers - - - - -	8	-	-	-	8
Dairy Keepers - - - - -	2	- -	1	- -	3
	51,807	3,931	1,502	465	57,705
Manufactures :					
Spinners (Flax, Wool, and Cotton) - - -	- -	- -	6,363	412 ⎫	29,420
,, (Unspecified) - - - -	- -	- -	20,899	1,746 ⎬	
Weavers (Linen, Woollen, Cotton, Silk) - -	792	5	11	- - ⎱	3,030
,, (Unspecified) - - - -	2,183	17	20	2 ⎰	
Knitters - - - - - -	- -	- -	372	21	393
Coopers - - - - - - -	312	5	- -	- -	317
Flax Dressers - - - - -	143	- -	23	- -	166
Nailers - - - - - - -	163	3	- -	- -	166
Hatters - - - - - -	64	1	1	- -	66
Winders and Warpers - - - -	1	3	25	3	32
Dyers - - - - - -	20	- -	7	- -	27
Basket Makers - - - - -	19	- -	3	- -	22
Carders - - - - - -	- -	- -	20	1	21
Reed Makers - - - - -	18	- -	- -	- -	18
Bleachers - - - - - -	16	- -	- -	- -	16
Clothiers - - - - - -	12	- -	- -	- -	12
Braziers and Coppersmiths - - - -	10	- -	1	- -	11
Chandlers and Soap Boilers - - -	11	- -	- -	- -	11
Sieve Makers - - - - -	7	1	- -	- -	8
Harness Makers - - - - -	7	- -	- -	- -	7
Potters - - - - - -	5	- -	- -	- -	5
Turners - - - - - -	4	- -	1	- -	5
Brick Makers - - - - -	4	- -	- -	- -	4
Miscellaneous - - - - -	18	2	2	1	23
	3,809	37	27,748	2,186	33.780
All other Classes :					
Employed in Handicraft, as Masters or Workmen, in the production of—					
Food - - - -	830	12	143	1	986
Clothing - - - -	2,086	64	1,792	125	4,067
Lodging, Furniture, Machinery, &c. -	2,475	30	19	- -	2,524
Ministering to Health - - - -	98	- -	40	1	139
,, ,, Justice - - - -	278	- -	- -	- -	278
,, ,, Education - - - -	311	- -	122	- -	433
,, ,, Religion - - - -	141	- -	7	- -	148
Unclassified - - - - -	2,293	401	5,813	768	9,275
	8,512	507	7,936	895	17,850
Residue of Population :					
Consisting of the Wives, Children, and others dependent on all Classes - - - -					133,823
Total of all other Classes - - - - - - - -					151,673

Divide "all other classes" between the Agriculturists and the Manufacturers in the proportion which these respectively bear to each other, and the numbers engaged in, and dependent on, each interest will stand thus :—

Engaged in Agriculture	- - -	57,705	
Dependent on ,,	- - -	84,180	
Agriculture—Total	- -	———	141,885
Engaged in Manufactures -	- -	33,780	
Dependent on ,,	- - -	67,493	
Manufactures—Total	-	———	101,273
Total of the County	- - -		243,158

ENGAGED IN	MALES.		FEMALES.		TOTAL.
	15 years of age and upwards.	Under 15 years of age.	15 years of age and upwards.	Under 15 years of age.	
AGRICULTURE:					
Farmers	20,124	23	619	1	20,767
Servants, Labourers, and Ploughmen	45,243	3,645	4,129	860	53,877
Gardeners	138	1	-	-	139
Graziers	2	-	-	-	2
Herdsmen	950	87	14	4	1,055
Caretakers	36	-	1	-	37
Land Stewards	149	-	-	-	149
Game Keepers	2	-	-	-	2
Dairy Keepers	4	-	82	1	87
	66,648	3,756	4,845	866	76,115
MANUFACTURES:					
Spinners (Wool and Flax)	6	-	8,358	402 ⎰	16,511
,, (Unspecified)	5	-	7,206	534 ⎱	
Knitters	-	1	1,110	23	1,134
Weavers (Linen, Woollen, and Cotton)	300	-	9	4 ⎰	1,121
,, (Unspecified)	791	9	8	- ⎱	
Carders	-	2	292	18	312
Coopers	209	2	-	-	211
Nailers	145	7	-	-	152
Manufacturers (Lace and Cotton)	2	-	40	49	91
Haircloth Makers	3	-	54	3	60
Hatters	46	2	7	-	55
Winders and Warpers	2	1	42	4	49
Net Makers	3	-	33	1	37
Flax Dressers	17	2	11	1	31
Chandlers and Soap Boilers	22	-	-	-	22
Dyers	15	-	2	-	17
Clothiers	9	-	2	-	11
Cloth Finishers	10	-	-	-	10
Lime Burners	9	-	-	-	9
Wool Dressers	5	-	2	-	7
Skinners	7	-	-	-	7
Brick Makers	4	-	3	-	7
Miscellaneous	49	1	5	3	58
	1,659	27	17,184	1,042	19,912
ALL OTHER CLASSES:					
Employed in Handicraft, as Masters or Workmen, in the production of—					
Food	962	9	154	2	1,127
Clothing	2,484	72	2,135	99	4,790
Lodging, Furniture, Machinery, &c.	3,098	37	21	3	3,159
Ministering to Health	74	-	131	-	205
,, Charity	4	-	-	-	4
,, Justice	448	-	3	-	451
,, Education	376	-	107	-	483
,, Religion	152	-	4	-	156
Unclassified	3,419	401	8,983	1,279	14,082
	11,017	519	11,538	1,383	24,457
RESIDUE OF POPULATION:					
Consisting of the Wives, Children, and others dependent on all Classes					165,910
Total of all other Classes					190,367

Divide "ALL OTHER CLASSES" between the AGRICULTURISTS and the MANUFACTURERS in the proportion which these respectively bear to each other, and the numbers engaged in, and dependent on, each interest will stand thus:—

Engaged in Agriculture	76,115	
Dependent on ,,	150,893	
AGRICULTURE—Total		227,008
Engaged in Manufactures	19,912	
Dependent on ,,	39,474	
MANUFACTURES—Total		59,386
Total of the County		286,394

ENGAGED IN	MALES.		FEMALES.		TOTAL.
	15 years of age and upwards.	Under 15 years of age.	15 years of age and upwards.	Under 15 years of age.	
Agriculture :					
Farmers -	157	- -	2	- -	159
Servants and Labourers	1,502	16	28	- -	1,546
Gardeners	128	-	- -	- -	128
Grazier	1	-	-	- -	1
Herdsmen	- -	4	-	- -	4
Land Stewards	21	- -	-	- -	21
Game Keeper	1	- -	-	- -	1
Dairy Keepers	1	- -	19	- -	20
	1,811	20	49	- -	1,880
Manufactures :					
Coopers -	712	13	- -	- -	725
Weavers (Cotton, Woollen, and Linen)	150	1	5	- }	329
„ (Unspecified)	171	- -	2	- }	
Glovers	31	- -	235	6	272
Spinners (Wool, Flax, and Cotton)	1	- -	45	- }	252
„ (Unspecified) -	-	- -	206	- }	
Tanners -	151	- -	- -	- -	151
Nailers	131	- -	-	- -	131
Hatters -	97	1	23	- -	121
Rope Makers	109	- -	1	- -	110
Chandlers and Soap Boilers	69	- -	15	- -	84
Wool Dressers	79	1	1	- -	81
Clothiers	30	- -	48	- -	78
Braziers and Coppersmiths	54	- -	-	- -	54
Basket Makers	52	- -	1	- -	53
Ironfounders -	51	1	-	- -	52
Paper Stainers	43	- -	2	- -	45
Turners	41	- -	-	- -	41
Glass Makers	35	- -	4	- -	39
Winders and Warpers -	-	- -	38	- -	38
Comb Makers	31	- -	4	- -	35
Dyers	19	- -	14	- -	33
Skinners	32	- -	-	- -	32
Manufacturers (Lace and Thread)	4	- -	26	- -	30
Miscellaneous	207	3	43	- -	253
	2,300	20	713	6	3,039
All other Classes :					
Employed in Handicraft, as Masters or Workmen, in the production of					
Food -	1,512	12	821	- -	2,345
Clothing	2,555	43	2,721	22	5,341
Lodging, Furniture, Machinery, &c.	3,339	25	130	- -	3,494
Ministering to Health	121	- -	65	- -	186
„ Charity	12	- -	6	- -	18
„ Justice	372	- -	-	- -	372
„ Education	173	- -	126	- -	299
„ Religion	80	- -	66	- -	146
Unclassified	7,218	87	6,577	127	14,009
	15,382	167	10,512	149	26,210
Residue of Population :					
Consisting of the Wives, Children, and others dependent on all Classes	-	-		-	49,591
Total of all other Classes	-	-	-	-	75,801

Divide "all other classes" between the Agriculturists and the Manufacturers in the proportion which these respectively bear to each other, and the numbers engaged in, and dependent on, each interest will stand thus—

Engaged in Agriculture	-	-	1,880
Dependent on „	-	-	28,970
Agriculture—Total	-	-	30,850
Engaged in Manufactures	-	-	3,039
Dependent on „	-	-	46,831
Manufactures—Total	-		49,870
Total of the City -	-	-	80,720

ENGAGED IN	MALES.		FEMALES.		TOTAL.
	15 years of age and upwards.	Under 15 years of age.	15 years of age and upwards.	Under 15 years of age.	
AGRICULTURE:					
Farmers	38,400	2	1,907	-	40,309
Servants, Labourers, and Ploughmen	126,064	6,918	11,154	1,494	145,630
Gardeners	752	5	2	-	759
Graziers	2	-	-	-	2
Herdsmen	1,415	959	34	47	2,455
Caretakers	120	1	5	-	126
Land Agents and Stewards	778	-	-	"	778
Game Keepers	36	-	-	-	36
Dairy Keepers	432	-	244	-	676
	167,999	7,885	13,346	1,541	190,771
MANUFACTURES:					
Spinners (Wool, Flax, and Cotton)	16	-	11,268	375 }	22,566
,, (Unspecified)	4	1	10,089	813 }	
Weavers (Linen, Woollen, Cotton, Lace, Tape, and Corduroy)	923	5	31	18 }	3,384
,, (Unspecified)	2,368	13	23	3 }	
Knitters	3	-	1,490	68	1,561
Nailers	498	24	-	-	522
Coopers	417	7	-	-	424
Carders	2	1	318	6	327
Net Makers	1	-	167	19	187
Paper Makers	103	3	24	-	130
Straw Workers	-	-	105	16	121
Hatters	102	1	4	1	108
Wool Dressers	101	-	4	-	105
Flax Dressers	40	-	60	3	103
Winders and Warpers	3	-	100	-	103
Manufacturers of Lace, Woollen, Cotton, and Thread	7	-	85	-	92
Rope Makers	69	-	-	-	69
Dyers	47	-	6	-	53
Tanners	44	-	-	-	44
Basket Makers	43	1	-	-	44
Chandlers and Soap Boilers	44	-	-	-	44
Factory Workers	7	2	28	4	41
Skinners	38	-	1	-	39
Lime Burners	38	-	-	-	38
Miscellaneous	242	4	34	1	281
	5,160	62	23,837	1,327	30,386
ALL OTHER CLASSES:					
Employed in Handicraft, as Masters or Workmen, in the production of—					
Food	4,513	43	1,081	4	5,641
Clothing	8,782	216	4,930	146	14,074
Lodging, Furniture, Machinery, &c.	11,802	90	55	-	11,947
Ministering to Health	286	-	287	-	573
,, Charity	10	-	4	-	14
,, Justice	1,275	-	-	-	1,275
,, Education	1,090	1	436	1	1,528
,, Religion	511	-	88	-	599
Unclassified	12,564	1,364	29,174	3,639	46,741
	40,833	1,714	36,055	3,790	82,392

RESIDUE OF POPULATION:

Consisting of the Wives, Children, and others dependent on all Classes - - - - 469,849

Total of all other Classes - - - - - - 552,241

Divide "ALL OTHER CLASSES" between the AGRICULTURISTS and the MANUFACTURERS in the proportion which these respectively bear to each other, and the numbers engaged in, and dependent on, each interest will stand thus:—

Engaged in Agriculture - - - 190,771

Dependent on ,, - - - 476,366

AGRICULTURE—Total - - ———— 667,137

Engaged in Manufactures - - - 30,386

Dependent on ,, - - - 75,875

MANUFACTURES—Total - - ———— 106,261

Total of the County - - - 773,398

ENGAGED IN	MALES.		FEMALES.		TOTAL.
	15 years of age and upwards.	Under 15 years of age.	15 years of age and upwards.	Under 15 years of age.	
AGRICULTURE:					
Farmers -	26,181	1	468	-	26,650
Servants, Labourers, and Ploughmen	37,075	4,181	490	89	41,835
Gardeners	88	-	-	-	88
Graziers	4	-	-	-	4
Herdsmen	281	1,589	117	636	2,623
Caretakers	17	-	1	-	18
Land Agents and Stewards -	55	-	-	-	55
Game Keepers	5	-	-	-	5
Dairy Keeper	1	-	-	-	1
	63,707	5,771	1,076	725	71,279
MANUFACTURES:					
Spinners (Flax and Wool)	-	-	12,782	741 }	42,221
,, (Unspecified)	1	-	27,058	1,639 }	
Knitters	-	-	3,144	515	3,659
Weavers (Linen, Wool, Cotton, and Silk)	854	4	71	4 }	3,374
,, (Unspecified) -	2,421	9	11	- }	
Flax Dressers	313	1	32	-	346
Coopers	217	-	-	-	217
Carders -	-	-	112	11	123
Nailers	115	5	-	-	120
Bleachers	39	-	-	-	39
Winders and Warpers -	1	-	30	-	31
Hatters -	30	-	-	-	30
Rope Makers -	19	1	-	-	20
Clothiers -	18	-	-	-	18
Dyers	11	-	3	-	14
Basket Makers	8	-	4	-	12
Reed Makers -	11	-	-	-	11
Braziers and Coppersmiths -	9	1	-	-	10
Chandlers and Soap Boilers	10	-	-	-	10
Net Makers	3	-	7	-	10
Brick Makers	8	-	1	-	9
Turners -	9	-	-	-	9
Miscellaneous	46	1	5	-	52
	4,143	22	43,260	2,910	50,335
ALL OTHER CLASSES:					
Employed in Handicraft, as Masters or Workmen, in the production of—					
Food	1,702	13	257	2	1,974
Clothing	2,732	57	1,839	44	4,672
Lodging, Furniture, Machinery, &c.	2,700	24	14	-	2,738
Ministering to Health	65	-	45	-	110
,, Justice -	736	-	1	-	737
,, Education	351	-	107	-	458
,, Religion	193	-	5	-	198
Unclassified	2,202	370	5,575	727	8,874
	10,681	464	7,843	773	19,761
RESIDUE OF POPULATION:					
Consisting of the Wives, Children, and others dependent on all Classes					155,073
Total of all other Classes					174,834

Divide "ALL OTHER CLASSES" between the AGRICULTURISTS and the MANUFACTURERS in the proportion which these respectively bear to each other, and the numbers engaged in, and dependent on, each interest will stand thus :—

Engaged in Agriculture	71,279	
Dependent on ,,	102,472	
AGRICULTURE—Total -		173,751
Engaged in Manufactures	50,335	
Dependent on ,,	72,362	
MANUFACTURES—Total		122,697
Total of the County		296,448

ENGAGED IN	MALES.		FEMALES.		TOTAL.
	15 years of age and upwards.	Under 15 years of age	15 years of age and upwards.	Under 15 years of age.	
AGRICULTURE:					
Farmers - - - - - -	20,966	2	1,014	- -	21,982
Servants, Labourers, and Ploughmen - - -	35,197	3,159	714	73	39,143
Gardeners - - - - - -	326	2	- -	- -	328
Herdsmen - - - - - -	90	550	16	155	811
Caretakers - - - - -	18	- -	3	- -	21
Land Agents and Stewards - - -	133	5	-	-	138
Game Keepers - - - - -	15	- -	-	-	15
Dairy Keepers - - - - -	3	- -	6	- -	9
	56,748	3,718	1,753	228	62,447
MANUFACTURES:					
Spinners (Flax, Wool, and Cotton) - - -	57	9	3,876	155 ⎰	28,818
,, (Unspecified)	-	- -	24,005	716 ⎱	
Weavers (Linen, Cotton, Woollen, Silk, Fringe) -	4,194	254	554	54 ⎰	22,529
,, (Unspecified) - - - -	13,429	1,122	2,590	332 ⎱	
Winders and Warpers - - - -	120	160	1,981	274	2,535
Factory Workers - - - -	175	129	527	171	1,0 2
Bleachers - - - - -	517	24	42	10	593
Flax Dressers - - - -	486	6	32	- -	524
Nailers - - - - - -	356	33	-	- -	389
Knitters - - - - - -	-	- -	344	16	360
Coopers - - - - - -	288	4	-	-	292
Manufacturers (Thread, Cotton, Linen, Silk, and Tabinet)	118	2	45	-	173
Straw Workers - - - - -	-	8	-	102	110
Chandlers and Soap Boilers - - -	87	- -	-	-	87
Cloth Finishers - - - -	75	1	8	-	84
Reed Makers - - - - -	82	2	-	-	84
Rope Makers - - - - -	55	14	-	1	70
Tanners - - - - -	68	-	-	-	68
Dyers - - - - - -	37	- -	11	-	48
Hatters - - - - -	40	3	3	-	46
Turners - - - - -	38	2	-	-	40
Basket Makers - - - -	35	1	1	1	38
Brick Makers - - - -	29	-	-	-	29
Miscellaneous - - - - -	156	11	52	3	222
	20,442	1,785	34,071	1,843	58,141
ALL OTHER CLASSES:					
Employed in Handicraft, as Masters or Workmen, in the ⎱ production of—					
Food - - - - -	2,516	42	438	- -	2,996
Clothing - - - -	4,542	214	18,250	3,893	26,899
Lodging, Furniture, Machinery, &c. -	6,318	101	41	2	6,462
Ministering to Health - - - -	177	- -	29	-	206
,, Charity - - - -	4	- -	7	-	11
,, Justice - - - -	585	- -	-	-	585
,, Education - - - -	466	2	259	- -	727
,, Religion - - - -	340	-	22	-	362
Unclassified - - - - - -	5,447	854	11,013	1,316	18,630
	20,395	1,213	30,059	5,211	56,878
RESIDUE OF POPULATION:					
Consisting of the Wives, Children, and others dependent on all Classes - - - -					183,980
Total of all other Classes - - - - -					240,858

Divide "ALL OTHER CLASSES" between the AGRICULTURISTS and the MANUFACTURERS in the proportion which these respectively bear to each other, and the numbers engaged in, and dependent on. each interest will stand thus :—

Engaged in Agriculture - - - - 62,447
Dependent on ,, - - - 124,730

AGRICULTURE Total - - ——— 187,177

Engaged in Manufactures - - - 58,141
Dependent on ,, - - - 116,128

MANUFACTURES—Total - - ——— 174,269

Total of the County - - - 361,446

ENGAGED IN	MALES.		FEMALES.		TOTAL.
	15 years of age and upwards.	Under 15 years of age.	15 years of age and upwards.	Under 15 years of age.	
AGRICULTURE:					
Farmers	44	-	2	-	46
Servants, Labourers, and Ploughmen	266	4	9	2	281
Gardeners	14	-	-	-	14
Herdsmen	1	2	-	-	3
Caretakers	2	-	-	-	2
Land Stewards	4	-	-	-	4
Dairy Keepers	10	-	5	-	15
	341	6	16	2	365
MANUFACTURES:					
Weavers (Linen and Cotton)	111	11	4	4 ⎱	931
,, (Unspecified)	753	4	43	1 ⎰	
Spinners (Flax, Cotton, and Wool)	5	-	48	3 ⎱	243
,, (Unspecified)	2	6	163	16 ⎰	
Winders and Warpers	1	5	119	5	130
Machine Makers	49	-	-	-	49
Flax Dressers	32	-	-	-	32
Nailers	29	2	-	-	31
Hatters	15	-	7	-	22
Chandlers and Soap Boilers	11	-	-	-	11
Farmers	10	-	-	-	10
Iron Founders	10	-	-	-	10
Knitters	-	-	9	-	9
Basket Makers	9	-	-	-	9
Rope Makers	9	-	-	-	9
Braziers and Coppersmiths	8	-	-	-	8
Overseers in Factories	6	-	1	-	7
Mat Makers	7	-	-	-	7
Carders	-	-	6	-	6
Brick Makers	6	-	-	-	6
Reed Makers	6	-	-	-	6
Sail Makers	6	-	-	-	6
Dyers	4	-	1	-	5
Lace Makers	-	-	4	-	4
Miscellaneous	32	1	1	-	31
	1,121	29	406	29	1,585

ALL OTHER CLASSES:
Engaged in Handicraft, as Masters or Workmen, in the production of—

Food	283	-	57	-	340
Clothing	395	6	293	2	696
Lodging, Furniture, and Machinery, &c.	600	1	1	-	602
Ministering to Health	18	-	6	-	24
,, Justice	44	-	1	-	45
,, Education	19	-	23	-	42
,, Religion	19	-	36	-	55
Unclassified	1,277	36	793	31	2,137
	2,655	43	1,210	33	3,941

RESIDUE OF POPULATION:
Consisting of the Wives, Children, and others dependent on all Classes   - - - -   10,370

Total of all other Classes   - - - - - - -   **14,311**

Divide "ALL OTHER CLASSES" between the AGRICULTURISTS and the MANUFACTURERS in the proportion which these respectively bear to each other, and the numbers engaged in, and dependent on, each interest will stand thus:—

Engaged in Agriculture	- - -	365
Dependent on ,,	- - -	2,678
AGRICULTURE—Total	- - ————	3,043
Engaged in Manufactures	- - -	1,585
Dependent on ,,	- - -	11,633
MANUFACTURES—Total	- ————	13,218
Total of the County	- - -	16,261

ENGAGED IN.	MALES.		FEMALES.		TOTAL.
	15 years of age and upwards.	Under 15 years of age.	15 years of age and upwards.	Under 15 years of age.	
AGRICULTURE:					
Farmers -	171	- -	5	- -	176
Servants, Labourers, and Ploughmen	792	- -	37	- -	829
Gardeners	331	- -	1	- -	332
Graziers	4	- -	-	- -	4
Herdsmen	3	- -	-	- -	3
Caretakers	32	- -	6	- -	38
Land Agents and Stewards -	44	- -	-	- -	44
Game Keeper	1	- -	-	- -	1
Dairy Keepers	522	3	176	- -	701
	1,900	3	225	- -	2,128
MANUFACTURES:					
Hatters	389	3	158	- -	550
Weavers (Silk, Ribbon, Lace, Cotton, Woollen, Linen, Fringe, Tabinet, Tape, and Corduroy) -	620	19	470	11	1,593
,, (unspecified) -	365	4	103	1	
Winders and Warpers	10	-	368	11	389
Chandlers and Soap Boilers	307	1	13	- -	321
Tanners -	311	7	1	- -	319
Braziers and Coppersmiths	245	7	-	- -	252
Pin Makers	40	10	160	18	228
Tin Plate Workers	214	3	3	- -	220
Paper Stainers	189	14	4	- -	207
Nailers	190	8	-	- -	198
Dyers	166	4	14	- -	184
Rope Makers	150	- -	-	- -	150
Glass Makers	134	9	3	- -	146
Brush Makers	91	6	44	3	144
Spinners (Wool, Cotton, and Flax) -	20	- -	43	-	201
,, (unspecified) -	5	5	108	20	
Turners -	132	4	-	- -	136
Comb Makers	106	5	24	- -	135
Iron Founders	132	- -	-	- -	132
Basket Makers	114	1	9	1	125
Corduroy Cutters -	64	- -	45	- -	109
Gunsmiths -	100	4	-	- -	104
Miscellaneous	1,183	47	341	18	1,589
	5,277	161	1,911	83	7,432
ALL OTHER CLASSES:					
Employed in Handicraft, as Masters or Workmen, in the production of—					
Food	4,000	64	1,480	6	5,550
Clothing	7,819	171	10,939	476	19,405
Lodging, Furniture, Machinery, &c.	12,590	231	572	14	13,407
Ministering to Health -	837	- -	374	- -	1,211
,, Charity	12	- -	15	- -	27
,, Justice -	3,001	- -	1	- -	3,002
,, Education -	460	- -	583	- -	1,043
,, Religion	305	- -	180	- -	485
Unclassified	22,892	486	22,954	675	47,007
	51,916	952	37,098	1,171	91,137
RESIDUE OF POPULATION:					
Consisting of the Wives, Children, and others dependent on all Classes -	-	-	-	-	132,029
Total of all other Classes -	-	-	-	-	223,166

The City of Dublin being the representative of every other interest in the Kingdom of Ireland, we divide "ALL OTHER CLASSES" between the AGRICULTURISTS and the MANUFACTURERS in the proportion which these bear to each other in the entire population of the Kingdom irrespective of the City of Dublin, and this gives 4-5ths to the Agriculturists and 1-5th to the Manufacturers.

Engaged in Agriculture -	-	-	2,128
Dependent on ,, -	-	-	178,532
AGRICULTURE—Total -	-	-	180,660
Engaged in Manufactures -	-	-	7,432
Dependent on ,, -	-	-	44,634
MANUFACTURES—Total -	-	-	52,066
Total of the City -	-	-	232,726

ENGAGED IN	MALES.		FEMALES.		TOTAL.
	15 years of age and upwards.	Under 15 years of age.	15 years of age and upwards.	Under 15 years of age.	
Agriculture:					
Farmers - - - - - - -	2,055	- -	163	- -	2,218
Servants, Labourers, and Ploughmen - -	15,943	882	1,538	147	18,510
Gardeners - - - - - - -	1,054	12	2	- -	1,068
Graziers - - - - - - -	4	- -	- -	- -	4
Herdsmen - - - - - - -	229	89	4	2	324
Caretakers - - - - - -	99	1	7	1	108
Land Agents and Stewards - - - -	281	- -	- -	- -	281
Game Keepers - - - - - -	10	- -	- -	- -	10
Dairy Keepers - - - - - -	287	3	127	3	420
	19,962	987	1,841	153	22,943
Manufactures:					
Weavers (Woollen, Cotton, Linen, Lace, Corduroy, Ribbon, Fringe, and Tape) - - - }	238	3	82	2 }	756
,, (Unspecified) - - - -	334	14	80	3 }	
Spinners (Wool, Flax. and Cotton) - - -	27	1	415	4 }	710
,, (Unspecified) - - - -	3	- -	234	26 }	
Factory Workers - - - - - -	76	50	215	66 }	407
Paper Makers - - - - - -	151	7	102	6	266
Knitters - - - - - - -	1	- -	158	4	163
Nailers - - - - - - -	146	12	1	- -	159
Calico Printers - - - - - -	109	2	38	3	152
Hatters - - - - - - -	71	- -	18	- -	89
Winders and Warpers - - - - -	1	4	37	2	44
Manufacturers (Cotton, Silk Tabinet, Cloth, Glass, and Rope) - - - - - - }	109	5	11	- -	125
Flax Dressers - - - - - -	33	- -	3	- -	36
Pin Makers - - - - - -	19	2	13	1	35
Button Makers - - - - - -	22	- -	8	- -	30
Wool Dressers - - - - - -	24	- -	5	- -	29
Bleachers - - - - - - -	23	- -	- -	- -	23
Dyers - - - - - - -	20	- -	3	- -	23
Brick Makers - - - - - -	21	- -	- -	- -	21
Carders- - - - - - - -	6	- -	14	- -	20
Iron Founders - - - - - -	19	1	- -	- -	20
Tin-plate Workers - - - - - -	17	2	- -	- -	19
Gunsmiths - - - - - - -	18	- -	- -	- -	18
Miscellaneous - - - - -	168	3	16	1	188
	1,656	106	1,453	118	3,333
All other Classes:					
Employed in Handicraft, as Masters or Workmen, in the production of—					
Food - - - - -	1,671	28	333	2	2,034
Clothing - - - - -	1,251	39	1,976	157	3,423
Lodging, Furniture, Machinery, &c. -	3,752	61	20	1	3,834
Ministering to Health - - - -	226	-	53	- -	279
,, Charity - - - - -	4	- -	2	- -	6
,, Justice - - - - -	1,289	- -	2	- -	1,291
,, Education - - - -	290	- -	350	2	642
,, Religion - - - -	222	- -	156	- -	378
Unclassified - - - - - -	5,314	345	9,988	476	16,123
	14.019	473	12,880	638	28,010
Residue of Population:					
Consisting of the Wives, Children, and others dependent on all Classes - - - -					85,761
Total of all other Classes - - - - - - -					113,771

Divide "all other classes" between the Agriculturists and the Manufacturers in the proportion which these respectively bear to each other, and the numbers engaged in, and dependent on, each interest will stand thus:—

Engaged in Agriculture - - -	22,943	
Dependent on ,, - - -	99,340	
Agriculture—Total - -		122,283
Engaged in Manufactures - - -	3,333	
Dependent on ,, - - -	14,431	
Manufactures—Total - - -		17,764
Total of the County - -		140,047

ENGAGED IN	MALES.		FEMALES.		TOTAL.
	15 years of age and upwards.	Under 15 years of age.	15 years of age and upwards.	Under 15 years of age.	
AGRICULTURE:					
Farmers -	13,058	2	240	-	13,300
Servants, Labourers, and Ploughmen	19,575	2,002	249	46	21,872
Gardeners	75	-	-	-	75
Graziers	5	-	-	-	5
Herdsmen	324	62	17	31	434
Caretakers	31	-	3	-	34
Land Stewards	30	-	-	-	30
Game Keepers	8	-	-	-	8
Dairy Keepers	-	-	14	-	14
	33,106	2,066	523	77	35,772
MANUFACTURES:					
Spinners (Flax and Wool)	-	-	4,834	155 ⎫	21,596
,, (Unspecified)	-	-	15,507	1,100 ⎬	
Weavers (Linen, Woollen, and Cotton)	370	-	2	- ⎫	1,661
,, (Unspecified)	1,281	2	6	- ⎬	534
Knitters	-	-	512	22	274
Coopers	271	3	-	-	128
Flax Dressers	106	-	22	-	70
Nailers	67	3	-	-	23
Hatters	23	-	-	-	15
Basket Makers	12	-	1	2	14
Clothiers	12	-	2	-	12
Gunsmiths	12	-	-	-	11
Dyers	4	-	7	-	10
Straw Workers	-	-	-	10	10
Turners	9	1	-	-	9
Potters	9	-	-	-	9
Reed Makers	8	-	1	-	9
Sieve Makers	9	-	-	-	7
Carders	-	-	7	-	7
Block Makers	4	-	3	-	7
Chandlers and Soap Boilers	7	-	-	-	7
Miscellaneous	41	-	6	-	47
	2,245	9	20,910	1,289	24,453
ALL OTHER CLASSES:					
Employed in Handicraft, as Masters or Workmen, in the production of—					
Food	488	4	117	2	611
Clothing	1,445	40	1,840	69	3,394
Lodging, Furniture, Machinery, &c.	1,822	24	16	3	1,865
Ministering to Health	41	-	33	-	74
,, Charity	-	-	1	-	1
,, Justice	217	-	1	-	218
,, Education	245	1	70	-	316
,, Religion	88	-	3	-	91
Unclassified	1,430	283	4,101	413	6,227
	5,776	352	6,182	487	12,797
RESIDUE OF POPULATION:					
Consisting of the Wives, Children, and others dependent on all Classes	-	-	-	-	83,459
Total of all other Classes	-	-	-	-	96,256

Divide " ALL OTHER CLASSES " between the AGRICULTURISTS and the MANUFACTURERS in the proportion which these respectively bear to each other, and the numbers engaged in, and dependent on, each interest will stand thus :—

Engaged in Agriculture	35,772	
Dependent on ,,	57,174	
AGRICULTURE—Total		92,946
Engaged in Manufactures	24,453	
Dependent on ,,	39,082	
MANUFACTURES—Total		63,535
Total of the County		156,481

ENGAGED IN	MALES.		FEMALES.		TOTAL.
	15 years of age and upwards.	Under 15 years of age.	15 years of age and upwards.	Under 15 years of age.	
Agriculture :					
Farmers	20	-	-	-	20
Servants and Labourers	263	9	5	2	279
Gardeners	12	-	-	-	12
Herdsmen	1	4	-	-	5
Caretakers	3	-	-	-	3
Land Stewards	8	-	-	-	8
	307	13	5	2	327
Manufactures :					
Net Makers	-	-	-	-	
Spinners (Flax and Wool)	-	-	490	8	498
,, (Unspecified)	-	-	51	18 ⎫	155
Weavers (Linen)	2	-	63	21 ⎬	
,, (Unspecified)	8	-	-	- ⎭	48
Nailers	40	-	-	-	
Coopers	41	1	-	-	42
Rope Makers	32	-	-	-	32
Hatters	30	-	-	-	30
Chandlers and Soap Boilers	24	-	2	-	26
Knitters	15	-	-	-	15
Braziers and Coppersmiths	-	-	9	3	12
Clothiers	8	-	-	-	8
Tanners	6	-	-	-	6
Sail Makers	6	-	-	-	6
Paper Makers	5	-	-	-	5
Lime Burners	4	-	-	-	4
Comb Makers	3	-	-	-	3
Carders	3	-	-	-	3
Dyers	-	-	1	2	3
Block Makers	1	-	1	-	2
Card Makers	2	-	-	-	2
Iron Founders	2	-	-	-	2
Starch Manufacturers	2	-	-	-	2
Miscellaneous	10	-	-	-	10
	246	1	617	52	916
All other Classes :					
Employed in Handicraft, as Masters or Workmen, in the production of—					
Food	807	15	136	-	958
Clothing	420	6	365	1	792
Lodging, Furniture, Machinery, &c.	592	4	3	-	599
Ministering to Health	24	-	18	-	42
,, Justice	110	-	-	-	110
,, Education	35	-	21	-	56
,, Religion	26	-	48	-	74
Unclassified	1,522	49	1,102	68	2,741
	3,536	74	1,693	69	5,372
Residue of Population :					
Consisting of the Wives, Children, and others dependent on all Classes					10,660
Total of all other Classes					16,032

Divide " all other classes" between the Agriculturists and the Manufacturers in the proportion which these respectively bear to each other, and the numbers engaged in, and dependent on, each interest will stand thus :—

Engaged in Agriculture   - - -   327
Dependent on ,,   - - -   4,217

     Agriculture—Total - -   4,544

Engaged in Manufactures   - -   916
Dependent on ,,   - - -   11,815

     Manufactures—Total - -   12,731

Total of the Town   - - -   17,275

ENGAGED IN	MALES.		FEMALES.		TOTAL.
	15 years of age and upwards.	Under 15 years of age.	15 years of age and upwards.	Under 15 years of age.	
AGRICULTURE:					
Farmers - - - - - - -	21,197	3	632	- -	21,832
Servants, Labourers, and Ploughmen - - -	73,211	7,080	7,633	1,455	89,379
Gardeners, - - - - -	286	- -	- -	- -	286
Graziers - - - - - - -	3	- -	- -	- -	3
Herdsmen - - - - - -	1,745	92	30	27	1,894
Caretakers - - - - - -	35	1	- -	- -	36
Land Agents and Stewards - - - -	245	- -	- -	- -	245
Game Keepers - - - - -	23	- -	- -	- -	23
Dairy Keepers - - - - -	- -	- -	4	1	5
	96,745	7,176	8,299	1,483	113,703
MANUFACTURES:					
Spinners (Wool, Cotton, and Flax) - - -	6	- -	16,935	742 ⎱	30,555
,, (Unspecified) - - -	3	6	12,044	819 ⎰	
Weavers (Linen, Woollen, and Cotton) - - -	554	- -	8	- ⎱	2,119
,, (Unspecified) - - - -	1,531	4	22	- ⎰	
Knitters - - - - - -	1	4	1,808	106	1,919
Carders - - - - - -	- -	- -	477	53	530
Nailers - - - - - -	229	11	- -	- -	240
Coopers - - - - - -	223	- -	- -	- -	223
Net Makers - - - - - -	1	- -	80	45	126
Flax Dressers - - - - -	53	- -	16	- -	69
Hatters - - - - - -	51	- -	3	- -	54
Winders and Warpers - - - -	2	1	40	3	46
Dyers - - - - - -	15	- -	10	- -	25
Braziers and Coppersmiths - - - -	17	3	- -	- -	20
Chandlers and Soap Boilers - - - -	17	- -	2	- -	19
Clothiers - - - - - -	15	- -	1	- -	16
Turners - - - - - -	16	- -	- -	- -	16
Gunsmiths - - - - - -	13	- -	- -	- -	13
Sieve Makers - - - - -	12	- -	1	- -	13
Skinners - - - - - -	11	- -	- -	- -	11
Basket Makers - - - - -	8	- -	1	- -	9
Straw Workers - - - - -	- -	- -	7	- -	7
Rope Makers - - - - -	6	- -	- -	- -	6
Reed Makers - - - - -	5	- -	- -	- -	5
Bleachers - - - - - -	2	- -	2	- -	4
Glovers - - - - - -	3	- -	1	- -	4
Tanners - - - - - -	3	- -	- -	- -	3
Brick Makers - - - - -	3	- -	- -	- -	3
Lime Burners - - - - -	3	- -	- -	- -	3
Cutlers - - - - - -	3	- -	- -	- -	3
Hair Cloth Makers - - - -	2	- -	1	- -	3
Distillers - - - - - -	2	- -	- -	- -	2
Miscellaneous - - - - -	9	- -	1	- -	10
	2,819	29	31,460	1,768	36,076
ALL OTHER CLASSES:					
Employed in Handicraft, as Masters or Workmen, in the production of—					
Food - - - -	1,211	51	290	4	1,556
Clothing - - -	3,274	67	2,335	77	5,753
Lodging, Furniture, Machinery, &c. -	4,450	22	20	4	4,496
Ministering to Health - - - - -	74	- -	135	- -	209
,, Justice - - - -	749	- -	1	- -	750
,, Education - - - -	398	- -	153	- -	551
,, Religion - - - -	206	- -	45	- -	251
Unclassified - - - - - -	5,009	601	10,356	1,224	17,190
	15,371	741	13,335	1,309	30,756
RESIDUE OF POPULATION:					
Consisting of the Wives, Children, and others dependent on all Classes - - - -					242,388
Total of all other Classes - - - - - - -					273,144

Divide " ALL OTHER CLASSES " between the AGRICULTURISTS and the MANUFACTURERS in the proportion which these respectively bear to each other, and the numbers engaged in, and dependent on, each interest will stand thus:—

Engaged in Agriculture - - -	113,703	
Dependent on ,, - - -	207,355	
AGRICULTURE—Total - - -		321,058
Engaged in Manufactures - - -	36,076	
Dependent on ,, - - -	65,789	
MANUFACTURES—Total - - -		101,865
Total of the County - - -		422,923

ENGAGED IN	MALES.		FEMALES.		TOTAL.
	15 years of age and upwards.	Under 15 years of age.	15 years of age and upwards.	Under 15 years of age.	
Agriculture:					
Farmers - - - - - -	19,131	1	542	- -	19,674
Servants, Labourers, and Ploughmen - - -	45,803	3,011	1,977	419	51,210
Gardeners - - - - -	122	-	-	- -	122
Herdsmen - - - - - -	901	682	47	114	1,744
Caretakers - - - - - -	35	-	-	- -	35
Land Agents and Stewards - - -	156	-	-	- -	156
Gamekeepers - - - -	6	-	-	- -	6
Dairykeepers - - - -	29	-	86	1	116
	66,183	3,694	2,652	534	73,063
Manufactures:					
Spinners (Flax, Wool, and Cotton) - - -	4	3	7,532	363 }	15,308
„ (Unspecified) - - - - -	2	1	6,830	573 }	
Weavers (Woollen, Linen, and Cotton) - -	253	-	15	-	1,370
„ (Unspecified) - - - -	1,092	3	6	1 }	
Knitters - - - - - -	-	-	567	36	603
Carders - - - - -	-	-	256	21	277
Coopers - - - - - -	229	1	-	-	230
Nailers - - - - - -	144	11	-	-	155
Hatters - - - - - -	64	-	1	-	65
Net Makers - - - - -	1	1	22	1	25
Dyers - - - - - -	21	1	1	-	23
Flax Dressers - - - -	9	-	12	-	21
Turners - - - - - -	17	-	-	-	17
Basket Makers - - - -	11	-	-	-	11
Winders and Warpers - - - -	-	-	8	1	9
Cloth Finishers - - - -	9	-	-	-	9
Salt Manufacturers - - - -	7	-	1	-	8
Lace Manufacturers - - - -	1	-	7	-	8
Clothiers - - - - -	8	-	-	-	8
Chandlers and Soap Boilers - - -	7	-	-	-	7
Wool Dressers - - - - -	3	-	3	-	6
Glovers - - - - - -	5	-	1	-	6
Reed Makers - - - - -	6	-	-	-	6
Tanners - - - - - -	5	-	-	-	5
Brick Makers - - - - -	5	-	-	-	5
Cutlers - - - - -	5	-	-	-	5
Gun Smiths - - - - -	4	-	-	-	4
Rope Makers - - - - -	4	-	-	-	4
Sieve Makers - - - - -	4	-	-	-	4
Distillers - - - - -	2	-	-	-	2
Bleachers - - - - -	2	-	-	-	2
Comb Makers - - - -	2	-	-	-	2
Iron Founders - - - - -	2	-	-	-	2
Lamp Makers - - - - -	2	-	-	-	2
Miscellaneous - - - - -	6	-	2	-	8
	1,936	21	15,264	996	18,217
All other Classes:					
Employed in Handicraft, as Masters or Workmen, in the production of—					
Food - - - -	1,048	23	189	4	1,264
Clothing - - - -	2,630	96	1,732	45	4,503
Lodging, Furniture, Machinery, &c. -	3,096	22	9	1	3,128
Ministering to Health - - - - -	94	-	135	-	229
„ Charity - - - -	1	-	1	-	2
„ Justice - - - -	450	-	2	-	452
„ Education - - - -	403	-	92	-	495
„ Religion - - - -	167	-	23	-	190
Unclassified - - - - -	3,703	637	10,275	1,292	15,907
	11,592	778	12,458	1,342	26,170

Residue of Population:					
Consisting of the Wives, Children, and others dependent on all Classes - - - -					176,430
Total of all other Classes - - - - - -					202,600

Divide "all other classes" between the Agriculturists and the Manufacturers in the proportion which these respectively bear to each other, and the numbers engaged in, and dependent on, each interest will stand thus:—

Engaged in Agriculture - - - -	73,063	
Dependent on „ - - - -	162,167	
Agriculture—Total - -		235,230
Engaged in Manufactures - - -	18,217	
Dependent on „ - - -	40,433	
Manufactures—Total - -		58,650
Total of the County - - -		293,880

ENGAGED IN	MALES.		FEMALES.		TOTAL.
	15 years of age and upwards.	Under 15 years of age.	15 years of age and upwards.	Under 15 years of age.	
Agriculture :					
Farmers - - - - - -	3,857	-	235	-	4,092
Servants, Labourers, and Ploughmen -	20,247	1,164	2,692	265	24,368
Gardeners - - - - - -	179	1	-	-	180
Graziers - - - - - - -	2	-	-	-	2
Herdsmen - - - - - -	606	119	2	2	729
Caretakers - - - - -	20	1	1	-	22
Land Agents and Stewards - - -	143	-	-	-	143
Game Keepers - - - - -	18	-	-	-	18
Dairy Keepers - - - - -	11	1	4	3	19
	25,083	1,286	2,934	270	29.573
Manufactures :					
Spinners (Wool, Flax, and Cotton) - -	14	3	909	30 ⎰	2,523
,, (Unspecified) - - -	-	2	1,509	56 ⎱	
Knitters - - - - -	-	-	560	28	588
Weavers (Linen, Cotton, Woollen, and Lace) -	89	1	4	2 ⎰	328
,, (Unspecified) - - - -	209	1	22	- ⎱	
Factory Workers - - - - -	61	9	120	24	214
Nailers - - - - - -	106	4	-	-	110
Flax Dressers - - - - -	39	5	7	2	53
Hatters - - - - - -	36	-	1	-	37
Straw Workers - - - - -	-	-	33	-	33
Carders - - - - - -	-	-	17	-	17
Braziers and Coppersmiths - - -	14	1	-	-	15
Chandlers and Soap Boilers - - -	12	-	-	-	12
Winders and Warpers - - - -	-	1	9	-	10
Iron Founders - - - - -	8	2	-	-	10
Brick Makers - - - - -	9	-	-	-	9
Basket Makers - - - - -	8	-	1	-	9
Sickle Makers - - - - -	9	-	-	-	9
Sieve Makers - - - - -	8	-	1	-	9
Glovers - - - - - -	5	-	2	-	7
Lime Burners - - - - -	6	-	-	-	6
Distillers - - - - - -	5	-	-	-	5
Skinners - - - - - -	4	-	-	-	4
Turners - - - - - -	4	-	-	-	4
Mat Makers - - - - -	2	-	2	-	4
Dyers - - - - - -	1	-	2	-	3
Manufacturers (Cotton and Woollen) -	3	-	-	-	3
Clothiers - - - - - -	2	-	-	-	2
Tanners - - - - - -	2	-	-	-	2
Comb Makers - - - - -	2	-	-	-	2
Button Makers - - - - -	2	-	-	-	2
Glass Makers - - - - -	2	-	-	-	2
Miscellaneous - - - - -	5	-	-	1	6
	667	29	3,199	143	4.038
All other Classes :					
Employed in Handicraft, as Masters or Workmen, in the production of—					
Food - - - - -	806	-	124	-	930
Clothing - - - - -	1,349	44	1,186	48	2,627
Lodging, Furniture, Machinery, &c. -	2,188	33	13	-	2,234
Ministering to Health - - - -	50	-	44	-	94
,, Charity - - - - -	2	-	11	-	13
,, Justice - - - - -	306	-	2	-	308
,, Education - - - -	167	-	111	-	278
,, Religion - - - -	98	-	19	-	117
Unclassified - - - - - -	2,673	328	5,314	450	8.765
	7,639	405	6,824	498	15,366
Residue of Population :					
Consisting of the Wives, Children, and others dependent on all Classes - - - -					65,511
Total of all other Classes - - - - - - - -					80,877

Divide "ALL OTHER CLASSES" between the AGRICULTURISTS and the MANUFACTURERS in the proportion which these respectively bear to each other, and the numbers engaged in, and dependent on, each interest will stand thus :—

Engaged in Agriculture - - -	29,573		
Dependent on ,, - - -	71,161		
AGRICULTURE—Total - -	———	100,734	
Engaged in Manufactures - -	4,038		
Dependent on ,, - -	9,716		
MANUFACTURES—Total - -	———	13,754	
Total of the County - - -		114,488	

ENGAGED IN	MALES.		FEMALES.		TOTAL.
	15 years of age and upwards.	Under 15 years of age.	15 years of age and upwards.	Under 15 years of age.	
AGRICULTURE :					
Farmers -	59	-	4	-	63
Servants and Labourers	356	28	63	11	458
Gardeners	45	-	-	-	45
Herdsmen -	1	1	-	-	2
Caretaker	1	-	-	-	1
Land Agents and Stewards	7	-	-	-	7
Game Keeper -	1	-	-	-	1
Dairy Keepers -	3	-	9	-	12
	473	29	76	11	589
MANUFACTURES :					
Spinners (Wool and Flax) -	9	2	19	-	} 70
„ (Unspecified) -	8	-	32	-	}
Weavers (Woollen, Linen, Cotton, and Silk) -	68	-	-	-	} 184
„ (Unspecified) -	115	1	-	-	}
Knitters -	-	-	39	3	42
Nailers -	38	3	-	-	41
Hatters -	33	-	2	-	35
Braziers and Coppersmiths	27	-	-	-	27
Cloth Finishers -	22	-	-	-	22
Rope Makers -	18	1	-	-	19
Glovers -	3	1	13	1	18
Chandlers and Soap Boilers	17	-	1	-	18
Harness Makers -	16	-	-	-	16
Wool Dressers -	11	-	4	-	15
Skinners -	14	-	-	-	14
Manufacturers (Woollen, Lace, and Starch) -	17	-	8	-	25
Dyers -	5	1	4	-	10
Flax Dressers -	6	-	3	-	9
Clothiers -	9	-	-	-	9
Turners -	8	1	-	-	9
Carders -	-	-	7	-	7
Winders and Warpers -	-	-	6	1	7
Card Makers -	4	-	2	1	7
Wire Workers -	6	1	-	-	7
Brush Makers -	5	-	1	-	6
Distillers -	5	-	-	-	5
Factory Workers -	1	-	4	-	5
Tanners -	5	-	-	-	5
Leather Dressers -	4	-	1	-	5
Brick Makers -	5	-	-	-	5
Basket Makers -	5	-	-	-	5
Iron Founders -	5	-	-	-	5
Comb Makers -	4	-	-	-	4
Gun Smiths -	4	-	-	-	4
Miscellaneous -	18	-	-	-	18
	515	11	146	6	678
ALL OTHER CLASSES :					
Employed in Handicraft, as Masters or Workmen, in the production of—					
Food -	326	6	80	1	413
Clothing -	732	29	534	16	1,311
Lodging, Furniture, Machinery, &c. -	709	6	8	-	723
Ministering to Health -	27	-	12	-	39
„ Charity -	1	-	6	-	7
„ Justice -	103	-	1	-	104
„ Education -	38	-	22	-	60
„ Religion -	32	-	14	-	46
Unclassified -	1,811	20	1,327	77	3,235
	3,779	61	2,004	94	5,938

RESIDUE OF POPULATION :

Consisting of the Wives, Children, and others dependent on all Classes - - - - 11,866

Total of all other Classes - - - - - - - 17,804

Divide " ALL OTHER CLASSES" between the AGRICULTURISTS and the MANUFACTURERS in the proportion which these respectively bear to each other, and the numbers engaged in, and dependent on, each interest will stand thus :—

Engaged in Agriculture - - - 589
Dependent on - - - 8,232

AGRICULTURE—Total - - ——— 8,821

Engaged in Manufactures - - 678
Dependent on „ - - - 9,572

MANUFACTURES—Total - - ——— 10,250

Total of the City - - - 19,071

ENGAGED IN	MALES.		FEMALES.		TOTAL.
	15 years of age and upwards.	Under 15 years of age.	15 years of age and upwards.	Under 15 years of age.	
AGRICULTURE:					
Farmers - - - - - -	10,787	- -	920	- -	11,707
Servants, Labourers, and Ploughmen - -	27,983	1,381	9,992	731	40,087
Gardeners - - - - - - -	134	1	1	- -	136
Graziers - -	2	- -	- -	- -	2
Herdsmen - - - - - - -	301	87	8	- -	396
Caretakers - - - - - -	35	1	5	- -	41
Land Agents and Stewards - - - -	108	- -	- -	- -	108
Game Keepers - - - - - -	13	- -	- -	- -	13
Dairy Keepers - - - - -	8	- -	82	1	91
	39,371	1,470	11,008	732	52,581
MANUFACTURES:					
Spinners (Wool and Flax) - - - -	2	3	937	16 ⎫	1,769
,, (Unspecified) - -	1	1	788	21 ⎬	
Weavers (Linen, Woollen, and Cotton) - -	135	- -	3	- ⎱	500
,, (Unspecified) -	359	- -	3	- ⎰	
Knitters - - - - - - -	- -	- -	330	12	342
Nailers - - - - - - -	189	- -	- -	- -	189
Manufacturers (Lace and Woollen) - -	3	- -	30	- -	33
Hatters - - - - - - -	14	1	7	1	23
Carders - - - - - - -	2	- -	16	1	19
Chandlers and Soap Boilers - - -	18	- -	- -	- -	18
Basket Makers - - - - -	17	- -	- -	- -	17
Straw Workers - - - - -	- -	- -	16	- -	16
Lime Burners - - - - - -	16	- -	- -	- -	16
Braziers and Coppersmiths - - -	15	- -	- -	- -	15
Winders and Warpers - - - -	1	1	9	1	12
Sieve Makers - - - - - -	7	2	3	- -	12
Flax Dressers - - - - -	10	- -	1	- -	11
Wool Dressers - - - - -	10	- -	1	- -	11
Turners - - - - - - -	9	- -	- -	- -	9
Distillers - - - - - -	8	- -	- -	- -	8
Brick Makers - - - - -	4	1	- -	- -	5
Musical Instrument Makers - - -	5	- -	- -	- -	5
Dyers - - - - - - -	3	- -	1	- -	4
Iron Founders - - - - -	4	- -	- -	- -	4
Factory Workers - - - - -	3	- -	- -	- -	3
Skinners - - - - - -	3	- -	- -	- -	3
Tanners - - - - - - -	3	- -	- -	- -	3
Potters - - - - - - -	3	- -	- -	- -	3
Clothiers - - - - - -	2	- -	- -	- -	2
Bleacher - - - - - -	1	- -	- -	- -	1
Glover - - - - - - -	1	- -	- -	- -	1
Rope Maker - - - - - -	1	- -	- -	- -	1
Mat Maker - - - - - -	1	- -	- -	- -	1
Starch Manufacturer - - - -	1	- -	- -	- -	1
	851	9	2,145	52	3,057
ALL OTHER CLASSES:					
Employed in Handicraft, as Masters or Workmen, in the production of—					
Food	769	4	185	- -	958
Clothing - - - -	1,878	28	1,321	24	3,251
Lodging, Furniture, Machinery, &c. -	3,795	10	8	- -	3,813
Ministering to Health - - - -	42	- -	92	- -	134
,, Justice - - - -	441	- -	- -	- -	441
,, Education - - - -	272	- -	101	- -	373
,, Religion - - - -	130	- -	5	- -	135
Unclassified - - - - - -	2,939	214	6,219	479	9,851
	10,266	256	7,931	503	18,956
RESIDUE OF POPULATION:					
Consisting of the Wives, Children, and others dependent on all Classes - -			- -	- -	108,755
Total of all other Classes - - - - - -					127,711

Divide " ALL OTHER CLASSES " between the AGRICULTURISTS and the MANUFACTURERS in the proportion which these respectively bear to each other, and the numbers engaged in, and dependent on, each interest will stand thus :—

Engaged in Agriculture - - -	52 581	
Dependent on ,, - - -	120,694	
AGRICULTURE—Total - -		173,275
Engaged in Manufactures - - -	3,057	
Dependent on ,, - -	7,017	
MANUFACTURES—Total - -		10,074
Total of the County - - -		183,349

ENGAGED IN	MALES.		FEMALES.		TOTAL.
	15 years of age and upwards.	Under 15 years of age.	15 years of age and upwards.	Under 15 years of age.	
AGRICULTURE:					
Farmers -	8,806	- -	374	- -	9,180
Servants, Labourers, and Ploughmen - - -	22,546	2,431	3,506	671	29,154
Gardeners - - - - -	123	- -	- -	- -	123
Graziers - - - - - -	2	- -	- -	- -	2
Herdsmen - - - - - -	314	8	7	1	330
Caretakers - - - - - -	1	- -	1	- -	2
Land Agents and Stewards -	143	- -	- -	- -	143
Game Keepers - - - - -	6	- -	- -	- -	6
	31,941	2,439	3,888	672	38,940
MANUFACTURES:					
Spinners (Wool, Flax, and Cotton) - - -	1	1	1,896	36 ⎰	4,555
,, (Unspecified) - - - - -	-	4	2,385	232 ⎱	
Weavers (Linen, Woollen, Cotton, Corduroy, Lace, Silk, ⎰ and Stuff) - - - - - ⎱	220	- -	4	- -	705
,, (Unspecified) - - - - -	479	- -	- -	1 ⎰	
Knitters - - - - - -	-	- -	513	47	560
Coopers - - - - - -	125	3	- -	- -	128
Nailers - - - - - -	98	2	- -	- -	100
Carders - - - - - -	-	- -	64	4	68
Hatters - - - - - -	31	- -	2	- -	33
Brick Makers - - - - -	26	- -	6	- -	32
Chandlers and Soap Boilers - - -	21	- -	- -	- -	21
Flax Dressers - - - -	12	- -	- -	1	13
Wool Dressers - - - -	13	- -	- -	- -	13
Dyers - - - - - -	7	- -	5	- -	12
Distillers - - - - - -	11	- -	- -	- -	11
Braziers and Coppersmiths - - -	11	- -	- -	- -	11
Tanners - - - - -	10	- -	- -	- -	10
Lime Burners - - - -	10	- -	- -	- -	10
Turners - - - - - -	10	- -	- -	- -	10
Gunsmiths - - - - -	10	- -	- -	- -	10
Glovers - - - - -	5	- -	3	- -	8
Rope Makers - - - - -	7	- -	- -	- -	7
Winders and Warpers - - - -	-	4	- -	2	6
Reed Makers - - - - -	6	- -	- -	- -	6
Basket Makers - - - -	6	- -	- -	- -	6
Mat Makers - - - - -	4	- -	2	- -	6
Manufacturers (Lace and Woollen) - -	5	- -	- -	- -	5
Tobacco Pipe Makers - - - -	5	- -	- -	- -	5
Wire Workers - - - -	4	- -	- -	- -	4
Comb Makers - - - - -	2	- -	- -	- -	2
Iron Founders - - - - .-	2	- -	- -	- -	2
Corduroy Cutter - - - -	1	- -	- -	- -	1
Starch Manufacturer - - - -	1	- -	- -	- -	1
Pin Maker - - - - -	1	- -	- -	- -	1
	1,144	14	4,880	323	6,361
ALL OTHER CLASSES:					
Employed in Handicraft, as Masters or Workmen, in the production of—					
Food - - - -	796	6	239	1	1,042
Clothing - - -	1,598	37	1,491	55	3,181
Lodging, Furniture, Machinery, &c.	2,371	31	16	-	2,418
Ministering to Health - - - - -	64	- -	53	-	117
,, Charity - - -	-	- -	1	-	1
,, Justice - - - -	489	- -	2	-	491
,, Education - - - -	249	- -	119	-	368
,, Religion - - - -	126	- -	24	-	150
Unclassified - - - -	3,065	256	5,361	487	9,169
	8,758	330	7,306	543	16,937
RESIDUE OF POPULATION:					
Consisting of the Wives, Children, and others dependent on all Classes - - - -					84,619
Total of all other Classes - - - - -					101,556

Divide "ALL OTHER CLASSES" between the AGRICULTURISTS and the MANUFACTURERS in the proportion which these respectively bear to each other, and the numbers engaged in, and dependent on, each interest will stand thus :—

Engaged in Agriculture - - -	38,940	
Dependent on ,, - - -	87,296	
AGRICULTURE—Total - -		126,236
Engaged in Manufactures - -	6,361	
Dependent on ,, - -	14,260	
MANUFACTURES—Total - -		20,621
Total of the County - - -		146,857

ENGAGED IN	MALES.		FEMALES.		TOTAL.
	15 years of age and upwards.	Under 15 years of age.	15 years of age and upwards.	Under 15 years of age.	
AGRICULTURE:					
Farmers - - - - - - -	13,326	1	179	- -	13,506
Servants, Labourers, and Ploughmen - - -	21,924	2,585	470	154	25,133
Gardeners - - - - - -	48	- -	- -	- -	48
Graziers - - - - - -	2	- -	- -	- -	2
Herdsmen - - - - - -	163	40	2	13	218
Caretakers - - - - - -	20	- -	1	- -	21
Land Agents and Stewards - - - -	25	- -	- -	- -	25
Game Keepers - - - - -	3	- -	- -	- -	3
Dairy Keepers - - - - -	2	- -	3	- -	5
	35,513	2,626	655	167	38,961
MANUFACTURES:					
Spinners (Flax and Wool) - - - -	- -	- -	7,583	505 ⎱	21,302
,, (Unspecified) - - -	- -	- -	11,850	1,364 ⎰	
Weavers (Linen and Woollen) - - -	274	1	2	- ⎱	986
,, (Unspecified) - - -	707	1	1	- ⎰	
Knitters - - - - - -	- -	- -	521	22	543
Coopers - - - - - -	243	3	- -	- -	246
Nailers - - - - - -	119	3	- -	- -	122
Flax Dressers - - - - -	61	- -	13	- -	74
Carders - - - - - -	- -	- -	14	7	21
Bleachers - - - - - -	12	- -	- -	- -	12
Winders and Warpers - - - - -	- -	- -	9	- -	9
Dyers - - - - - -	7	- -	2	- -	9
Hatters - - - - - -	9	- -	- -	- -	9
Basket Makers - - - - -	5	- -	1	1	7
Lime Burners - - - - -	6	- -	- -	- -	6
Potters - - - - - -	5	- -	- -	- -	5
Clothiers - - - - - -	4	- -	- -	- -	4
Braziers and Coppersmiths - - - -	4	- -	- -	- -	4
Tanners - - - - - -	3	- -	- -	- -	3
Reed Makers - - - - -	3	- -	- -	- -	3
Chandlers and Soap Boilers - - - -	3	- -	- -	- -	3
Turners - - - - - -	2	- -	- -	- -	2
Card Makers - - - - -	2	- -	- -	- -	2
Cutlers - - - - - -	2	- -	- -	- -	2
Sieve Makers - - - - -	2	- -	- -	- -	2
Skinner - - - - - -	1	- -	- -	- -	1
Rope Maker - - - - -	1	- -	- -	- -	1
Brick Maker - - - - -	1	- -	- -	- -	1
	1,476	8	19,996	1,899	23,379
ALL OTHER CLASSES:					
Employed in Handicraft, as Masters or Workmen, in the production of—					
Food - - - - -	353	1	113	- -	467
Clothing - - - -	1,164	38	929	31	2,162
Lodging, Furniture, Machinery, &c. -	1,128	11	5	- -	1,144
Ministering to Health - - - -	37	- -	27	- -	64
,, Charity - - -	1	- -	- -	- -	1
,, Justice - - - -	297	- -	- -	- -	297
,, Education - - -	205	1	61	- -	267
,, Religion - - - -	71	- -	2	- -	73
Unclassified - - - - -	1,239	3,134	225	443	5,041
	4,495	3,185	1,362	474	9,516
RESIDUE OF POPULATION:					
Consisting of the Wives, Children, and others dependent on all Classes - - - - -					83,441
Total of all other Classes - - - - - - -					92,957

Divide "ALL OTHER CLASSES" between the AGRICULTURISTS and the MANUFACTURERS in the proportion which these respectively bear to each other, and the numbers engaged in, and dependent on, each interest will stand thus :—

Engaged in Agriculture - - -	38,961	
Dependent on ,, - - -	58,096	
AGRICULTURE—Total - -		97,057
Engaged in Manufactures - -	23,379	
Dependent on ,, - -	34,861	
MANUFACTURES—Total - -		58,240
Total of the County - - -		155,297

ENGAGED IN	MALES.		FEMALES.		TOTAL.
	15 years of age and upwards.	Under 15 years of age.	15 years of age and upwards.	Under 15 years of age.	
AGRICULTURE:					
Farmers - - - - - -	119	- -	5	- -	124
Servants, Labourers, and Ploughmen - - -	1,011	23	28	4	1,066
Gardeners - - - - - - -	73	- -	- -	- -	73
Herdsmen - - - - - -	2	1	- -	- -	3
Caretakers - - - - - -	2	- -	- -	- -	2
Land Stewards - - - - - -	23	- -	- -	- -	23
Dairy Keepers - - - - - -	2	- -	9	- -	11
	1,232	24	42	4	1,302
MANUFACTURES:					
Spinners (Wool, Flax, and Cotton) - - -	1	- -	49	1 }	342
,, (Unspecified) - - -	1	- -	278	12 }	
Factory Workers - - - - -	-	- -	207	72	279
Coopers - - - - -	240	2	- -	- -	242
Weavers (Linen, Cotton, and Woollen) - -	36	1	1	- }	206
,, (Unspecified) - - -	163	2	3	- }	
Nailers - - - - - -	86	4	- -	- -	90
Rope Makers - - - - -	66	3	2	- -	71
Chandlers and Soap Boilers - - -	58	- -	1	- -	59
Hatters - - - - -	40	- -	7	- -	47
Wool Dressers - - - - -	38	- -	- -	- -	38
Glovers - - - - -	2	- -	29	- -	31
Knitters - - - - - -	-	- -	30	- -	30
Iron Founders - - - - -	25	4	- -	- -	29
Dyers - - - - -	14	12	- -	- -	26
Tobacco Pipe Makers - - - -	15	- -	7	- -	22
Basket Makers - - - - -	15	3	4	- -	22
Braziers and Coppersmiths - - -	21	- -	- -	- -	21
Cutlers - - - - - -	19	- -	- -	- -	19
Straw Workers - - - - -	-	- -	17	1	18
Sail Makers - - - - -	18	- -	- -	- -	18
Turners - - - - -	17	- -	- -	- -	17
Comb Makers - - - - -	15	- -	- -	- -	15
Gunsmiths - - - - -	12	1	- -	- -	13
Clothiers - - - - - -	10	- -	1	- -	11
Salt Manufacturers - - - -	8	- -	1	- -	9
Manufacturers (Lace and Thread) - - -	9	- -	- -	- -	9
Skinners - - - - -	9	- -	- -	- -	9
Cloth Finishers - - - - -	8	- -	- -	- -	8
Paper Makers - - - - -	8	- -	- -	- -	8
Mat Makers - - - - -	4	- -	4	- -	8
Paper Stainers - - - - -	7	- -	- -	- -	7
Block Makers - - - - -	7	- -	- -	- -	7
Miscellaneous - - - - -	46	- -	10	- -	56
	1,018	20	663	86	1,787
ALL OTHER CLASSES:					
Employed in Handicraft, as Masters or Workmen, in the production of—					
Food - - - - -	891	15	286	4	1,196
Clothing - - - - -	1,158	27	2,234	198	3,617
Lodging, Furniture, Machinery, &c. -	1,865	42	50	- -	1,957
Ministering to Health - - - -	77	- -	44	- -	121
,, Charity - - - -	5	- -	7	- -	12
,, Justice - - - -	192	- -	1	- -	193
,, Education - - - -	104	- -	63	- -	167
,, Religion - - - -	60	- -	13	- -	73
Unclassified - - - - -	5,119	116	3,652	147	9,034
	9,471	200	6,350	349	16,370
RESIDUE OF POPULATION:					
Consisting of the Wives, Children, and others dependent on all Classes - - - -					28,932
Total of all other Classes - - - - - - - -					45,302

Divide " ALL OTHER CLASSES " between the AGRICULTURISTS and the MANUFACTURERS in the proportion which these respectively bear to each other, and the numbers engaged in, and dependent on, each interest will stand thus :—

Engaged in Agriculture - - -	1,302		
Dependent on ,, - - -	19,241		
AGRICULTURE—Total - -		20,543	
Engaged in Manufactures - -	1,787		
Dependent on ,, - -	26,061		
MANUFACTURES—Total - -		27,848	
Total of the City - - -		48,391	

ENGAGED IN	MALES.		FEMALES.		TOTAL.
	15 years of age and upwards.	Under 15 years of age.	15 years of age and upwards.	Under 15 years of age.	
AGRICULTURE:					
Farmers	14,489	-	567	-	15,056
Servants, Labourers, and Ploughmen	47,300	2,237	3,630	521	53,688
Gardeners	217	-	-	-	217
Herdsmen	688	86	10	-	784
Caretakers	75	-	3	-	78
Land Agents and Stewards	241	-	-	-	241
Game Keepers	13	-	-	-	13
Dairy Keepers	188	-	477	6	671
	63,211	2,323	4,687	527	70,748
MANUFACTURES:					
Spinners (Wool and Flax)	1	1	5,713	183 ⎱	13,791
,, (Unspecified)	5	-	7,235	653 ⎰	
Weavers (Linen, Woollen, Corduroy, and Cotton)	363	-	15	- ⎱	1,276
,, (Unspecified)	886	2	10	- ⎰	
Knitters	-	-	637	22	659
Coopers	360	5	-	1	366
Nailers	135	4	-	-	139
Carders	1	-	61	1	63
Winders and Warpers	2	2	23	2	29
Paper Makers	24	1	-	-	25
Flax Dressers	4	-	13	1	18
Wool Dressers	15	1	1	-	17
Chandlers and Soap Boilers	17	-	-	-	17
Lime Burners	14	-	-	-	14
Hatters	13	-	-	-	13
Dyers	9	-	2	-	11
Bleachers	9	-	1	-	10
Brick Makers	10	-	-	-	10
Manufacturers (Thread and Worsted)	8	-	1	-	9
Cloth Finishers	7	-	-	-	7
Skinners	6	-	1	-	7
Glovers	4	-	3	-	7
Turners	7	-	-	-	7
Basket Makers	5	-	1	-	6
Factory Workers	-	-	3	2	5
Clothiers	4	-	-	-	4
Gunsmiths	4	-	-	-	4
Salt Manufacturers	3	-	-	-	3
Tanners	3	-	-	-	3
Reed Makers	3	-	-	-	3
Cutlers	2	-	-	-	2
Tool Makers	2	-	-	-	2
Braziers and Coppersmiths	2	-	-	-	2
Miscellaneous	7	-	1	-	8
	1,935	16	13,721	865	16,537
ALL OTHER CLASSES:					
Employed in Handicraft, as Masters or Workmen, in the production of—					
Food	766	3	122	1	892
Clothing	2,800	52	2,090	92	5,034
Lodging, Furniture, Machinery, &c.	3,413	22	17	-	3,452
Ministering to Health	63	-	96	-	159
,, Charity	2	-	2	-	4
,, Justice	459	-	-	-	459
,, Education	407	-	109	-	516
,, Religion	179	-	7	-	186
Unclassified	3,945	407	11,288	1,236	16,876
	12,034	484	13,731	1,329	27,578
RESIDUE OF POPULATION:					
Consisting of the Wives, Children, and others dependent on all Classes	-	-	-		166,775
Total of all other Classes	-	-	-		194,353

Divide " ALL OTHER CLASSES" between the AGRICULTURISTS and the MANUFACTURERS, in the proportion which these respectively bear to each other, and the numbers engaged in and dependent on each interest will stand thus :—

Engaged in Agriculture	70,748	
Dependent on ,,	157,531	
AGRICULTURE—Total		228,279
Engaged in Manufactures	16,537	
Dependent on ,,	36,822	
MANUFACTURES—Total		53,359
Total of the County		281,638

ENGAGED IN	MALES.		FEMALES.		TOTAL.
	15 years of age and upwards.	Under 15 years of age.	15 years of age and upwards.	Under 15 years of age.	
Agriculture:					
Farmers - - - - - -	15,023	-	665	-	15,688
Servants, Labourers, and Ploughmen - -	22,339	2,518	442	75	25,374
Gardeners - - - - - -	138	1	-	-	139
Grazier - - - - - - -	1	-	-	-	1
Herdsmen - - - - - -	156	953	38	251	1,398
Caretakers - - - - - -	34	-	1	-	35
Land Agents and Stewards - - - -	80	-	-	-	80
Game Keepers - - - - - -	4	-	-	-	4
Dairy Keepers - - - - - -	1	-	3	-	4
	37,776	3,472	1,149	326	42,723
Manufactures:					
Spinners (Flax and Wool) - - - -	-	-	6,939	466	} 27,556
,, (Unspecified) - - - - -	2	-	19,661	1,488	
Weavers (Linen, Cotton, and Woollen) - -	1,869	93	74	18	} 8,847
,, (Unspecified) - - - - -	5,915	208	634	36	
Flax Dressers - - - - - -	349	-	52	1	402
Winders and Warpers - - - - -	16	35	138	78	267
Bleachers - - - - - -	229	8	-	-	237
Coopers - - - - - - -	222	6	-	-	228
Knitters - - - - - - -	-	-	178	39	217
Nailers - - - - - - -	181	18	-	-	199
Factory Workers - - - - - -	16	-	68	-	84
Rope Makers - - - - - -	53	3	1	-	57
Mat Makers - - - - - -	8	8	19	4	39
Chandlers and Soap Boilers - - - -	38	-	-	-	38
Reed Makers - - - - - -	34	-	-	-	34
Braziers and Coppersmiths - - - -	28	1	-	-	29
Hatters - - - - - - -	28	-	-	-	28
Cloth Finishers - - - - - -	26	-	-	-	26
Dyers - - - - - - -	12	-	8	-	20
Iron Founders - - - - - -	17	-	-	-	17
Turners - - - - - - -	9	5	-	-	14
Basket Makers - - - - - -	12	-	2	-	14
Paper Makers - - - - - -	12	-	2	-	14
Distillers - - - - - - -	13	-	-	-	13
Tanners - - - - - - -	12	-	-	-	12
Potters - - - - - - -	12	-	-	-	12
Tobacco Pipe Makers - - - - -	10	-	1	-	11
Carders - - - - - - -	-	-	10	-	10
Gunsmiths - - - - - -	9	-	-	-	9
Sail Makers - - - - - -	8	-	-	-	8
Cutlers - - - - - - -	6	-	-	-	6
Manufacturers (Linen, Cotton, Silk, and Tabinet) - -	3	1	1	-	5
Miscellaneous - - - - -	40	1	3	2	46
	9,189	387	27,791	2,132	39,499
All other Classes:					
Employed in Handicraft, as Masters or Workmen, in the production of—					
Food - - - - -	1,277	13	160	-	1,450
Clothing - - - - -	2,442	101	2,783	177	5,503
Lodging, Furniture, Machinery, &c. -	3,561	52	16	-	3,629
Ministering to Health - - - -	113	-	18	-	131
,, Charity - - - - -	2	-	3	-	5
,, Justice - - - - -	282	-	2	-	284
,, Education - - - -	340	1	169	-	510
,, Religion - - - -	200	-	3	-	203
Unclassified - - - - - -	3,295	408	6,225	712	10,640
	11,512	575	9,379	889	22,355

Residue of Population:
Consisting of the Wives, Children, and others dependent on all Classes -   -   117,597

Total of all other Classes   -   -   -   -   -   -   -   139,952

Divide "ALL OTHER CLASSES" between the AGRICULTURISTS and the MANUFACTURERS in the proportion which these respectively bear to each other, and the numbers engaged in, and dependent on, each interest will stand thus :—

Engaged in Agriculture	-	-	-	42,723
Dependent on ,,	-	-	-	72,720
AGRICULTURE—Total -	-	-	115,443
Engaged in Manufactures	-	-	-	39,499
Dependent on ,,	-	-	-	67,252
MANUFACTURES—Total	-	-	106,731
Total of the County	-	-	-	222,174

ENGAGED IN	MALES.		FEMALES.		TOTAL.
	15 years of age and upwards.	Under 15 years of age.	15 years of age and upwards.	Under 15 years of age.	
AGRICULTURE:					
Farmers	6,922	-	269	-	7,191
Servants, Labourers, and Ploughmen	18,911	1,927	930	182	21,950
Gardeners	58	-	-	-	58
Graziers	6	-	-	-	6
Herdsmen	123	-	2	-	125
Caretakers	12	-	1	-	13
Land Agents and Stewards	40	-	-	-	40
Gamekeepers	3	-	-	-	3
Dairykeepers	1	-	13	-	14
	26,076	1,927	1,215	182	29,400
MANUFACTURES:					
Spinners (Flax and Wool)	-	-	3,937	256 ⎫	9,368
,, (Unspecified)	-	7	4,788	380 ⎭	
Weavers (Linen, Woollen, and Silk)	347	-	2	- ⎫	989
,, (Unspecified)	638	-	1	1 ⎭	
Knitters	-	-	274	35	309
Nailers	88	4	-	-	92
Flax Dressers	34	-	6	-	40
Carders	-	-	24	8	32
Hatters	31	-	-	-	31
Dyers	12	-	5	-	17
Winders and Warpers	-	-	8	3	11
Braziers and Coppersmiths	9	1	-	-	10
Reed Makers	9	-	-	-	9
Distillers	7	-	-	-	7
Manufacturers of Lace	-	-	7	-	7
Tanners	6	-	-	-	6
Turners	5	-	-	-	5
Card Makers	3	-	2	-	5
Basket Makers	2	1	2	-	5
Sieve Makers	5	-	-	-	5
Gunsmiths	3	1	-	-	4
Bleachers	2	-	1	-	3
Brick Makers	3	-	-	-	3
Potters	3	-	-	-	3
Net Makers	2	-	1	-	3
Wool Dresser	-	-	1	-	1
Skinner	1	-	-	-	1
Glover	1	-	-	-	1
Lime Burner	1	-	-	-	1
Iron Founder	1	-	-	-	1
Tool Maker	1	-	-	-	1
Miscellaneous	5	-	-	-	5
	1,219	14	9,059	683	10,975
ALL OTHER CLASSES:					
Employed in Handicraft, as Masters or Workmen, in the production of—					
Food	390	4	99	-	493
Clothing	1,108	32	855	17	2,012
Lodging, Furniture, Machinery, &c.	1,555	14	8	-	1,577
Ministering to Health	47	-	32	-	79
,, Charity	1	-	-	-	1
,, Justice	232	-	2	-	234
,, Education	157	-	55	-	212
,, Religion	87	-	3	-	90
Unclassified	1,287	73	3,420	272	5,052
	4,864	123	4,474	289	9,750

RESIDUE OF POPULATION:						
Consisting of the Wives, Children, and others dependent on all Classes	-	-	-	-		65,366
Total of all other Classes	-	-	-	-	-	75,116

Divide "ALL OTHER CLASSES" between the AGRICULTURISTS and the MANUFACTURERS in the proportion which these respectively bear to each other, and the numbers engaged in, and dependent on, each interest will stand thus:—

Engaged in Agriculture	-	-	-	29,400
Dependent on ,,	-	-	-	54,698
AGRICULTURE—Total	-	-		84,098
Engaged in Manufactures	-	-	-	10,975
Dependent on ,,	-	-	-	20,418
MANUFACTURES—Total	-	-		31,393
Total of the County	-			115,491

ENGAGED IN	MALES.		FEMALES.		TOTAL.
	15 years of age and upwards.	Under 15 years of age.	15 years of age and upwards.	Under 15 years of age.	
AGRICULTURE:					
Farmers - - - - - -	4,560	- -	325	- -	4,885
Servants, Labourers, and Ploughmen - - -	14,218	831	1,280	176	16,505
Gardeners - - - - -	169	- -	- -	- -	169
Graziers - - - - - -	2	- -	- -	- -	2
Herdsmen - - - - -	177	147	4	30	358
Caretakers - - - - - -	22	- -	- -	- -	22
Land Agents and Stewards - - - -	139	- -	- -	- -	139
Game Keepers - - - - -	16	- -	- -	- -	16
Dairy Keepers - - - - -	5	- -	6	- -	11
	19,308	978	1,615	206	22,107
MANUFACTURES:					
Spinners (Flax and Wool) - - - -	- -	2	2,300	30 ⎫	5,042
,, (Unspecified) - - -	1	6	2,522	181 ⎭	
Weavers (Linen, Woollen, and Cotton) - - -	351	- -	6	4 ⎫	1,927
,, (Unspecified) - - - -	1,522	11	33	- ⎭	
Knitters - - - - - -	- -	- -	303	12	315
Winders and Warpers - - - ▪ -	4	2	93	16	115
Pin Makers - - - - - -	20	4	61	24	109
Nailers - - - - - ▪	69	2	- -	- -	71
Coopers - - - - - -	60	- -	- -	- -	60
Flax Dressers - - - - -	38	6	5	1	50
Factory Workers - - - - -	7	3	34	1	45
Basket Makers - - - - -	37	- -	2	- -	39
Net Makers - - - - - -	1	4	22	12	39
Bleachers - - - - - -	32	- -	3	- -	35
Rope Makers - - - - -	24	- -	- -	- -	24
Chandlers and Soap Boilers - - - -	17	- -	1	- -	18
Dyers - - - - - -	12	- -	4	- -	16
Hatters - - - - - -	15	1	- -	- -	16
Iron Founders - - - - -	14	1	- -	- -	15
Tanners - - - - - -	12	- -	1	- -	13
Brick Makers - - - ▪ - -	13	- -	- -	- -	13
Carders - - - - - -	- -	2	8	- -	10
Tool Makers - - - - - -	10	- -	- -	- -	10
Braziers and Coppersmiths - - - -	8	1	- -	- -	9
Sieve Makers - - - - -	7	- -	- ▪	1	8
Distillers - - - - - -	6	- -	- -	- -	6
Potters - - - - - -	6	- -	- -	- -	6
Turners - - - - - -	5	- -	- -	- -	5
Wire Drawers - - - - -	5	- -	- -	- -	5
Salt Manufacturers - - - - -	4	- -	- -	- -	4
Lace Manufacturers - - - - -	- -	- -	4	- -	4
Lime Burners - - - - -	4	- -	- -	- -	4
Gunsmiths - - - - - -	3	- -	3	- -	3
Miscellaneous - - - - - -	8	- -	3	- -	11
	2,315	45	5,405	282	8,047
ALL OTHER CLASSES:					
Employed in Handicraft, as Masters or Workmen, in the production of—					
Food - - - -	1,393	19	215	4	1,631
Clothing - - - -	1,292	24	1,052	45	2,413
,, Lodging, Furniture, Machinery, &c. -	2,063	20	19	2	2,104
Ministering to Health - - - -	54	- -	34	- -	88
,, Charity - - - -	- -	- -	1	- -	1
,, Justice - - - -	331	- -	1	- -	332
,, Education - - - -	131	- -	87	- -	218
,, Religion - - - -	88	- -	2	- -	90
Unclassified - - - - - -	2,908	243	4,513	452	8,116
	8,260	306	5,924	503	14,993
RESIDUE OF POPULATION:					
Consisting of the Wives, Children, and others dependent on all Classes - - - -					66,832
Total of all other Classes - - - - - -					81,825

Divide "ALL OTHER CLASSES" between the AGRICULTURISTS and the MANUFACTURERS in the proportion which these respectively bear to each other, and the numbers engaged in, and dependent on, each interest will stand thus:—

Engaged in Agriculture - - -	22,107	
Dependent on ,, - - -	59,989	
AGRICULTURE—Total - -		82,096
Engaged in Manufactures - - -	8,047	
Dependent on ,, - -	21,836	
MANUFACTURES—Total - -		29,883
Total of the County - - -		111,979

ENGAGED IN	MALES.		FEMALES.		TOTAL.
	15 years of age and upwards.	Under 15 years of age.	15 years of age and upwards.	Under 15 years of age.	
AGRICULTURE :					
Farmers -	22,049	2	426	-	22,477
Servants, Labourers, and Ploughmen	67,172	8,941	6,215	1,777	84,105
Gardeners	161	-	-	-	161
Graziers	9	-	-	-	9
Herdsmen	677	297	67	234	1,275
Caretakers -	7	-	1	-	8
Land Agents and Stewards -	101	-	-	-	101
Game Keepers	12	-	-	-	12
Dairy Keepers	-	-	3	1	4
	90,188	9,240	6,712	2,012	108,152
MANUFACTURES :					
Spinners (Flax and Wool) -	-	-	15,480	919 ⎱	31,196
,, (Unspecified) -	1	-	13,766	1,030 ⎰	
Weavers (Linen, Woollen, and Ribbon)	601	-	26	- ⎱	3,441
,, (Unspecified) -	2,684	10	108	12 ⎰	
Knitters -	-	-	1,883	164	2,047
Carders	-	-	442	52	494
Coopers -	277	1	-	-	278
Nailers	143	11	-	-	154
Flax Dressers	53	-	54	-	107
Hatters	92	-	1	-	93
Winders and Warpers	5	-	66	2	73
Clothiers	28	-	-	-	28
Turners -	27	-	-	-	27
Braziers and Coppersmiths	25	-	-	-	25
Chandlers and Soap Boilers	22	-	2	-	24
Bleachers	14	-	2	-	16
Straw Workers	-	-	13	2	15
Dyers	5	-	6	-	11
Reed Makers -	10	-	-	-	10
Rope Makers -	9	-	1	-	10
Gunsmiths	8	-	-	-	8
Brick Makers -	6	-	-	-	6
Potters -	5	-	-	-	5
Net Makers -	2	-	3	-	5
Sieve Makers	5	-	-	-	5
Distillers	4	-	-	-	4
Glovers -	4	-	-	-	4
Tanners	3	-	-	-	3
Comb Makers	3	-	-	-	3
Basket Makers	3	-	-	-	3
Salt Manufacturers	2	-	-	-	2
Skinners	2	-	-	-	2
Cutlers -	2	-	-	-	2
Miscellaneous	7	-	-	-	7
	4,052	22	31,853	2,181	38,108
ALL OTHER CLASSES :					
Employed in Handicraft, as Masters or Workmen, in the production of—					
Food	995	3	328	2	1,328
Clothing	2,710	96	2,044	80	4,930
Lodging, Furniture, Machinery, &c.	2,925	26	8	-	2,959
Ministering to Health -	82	-	58	-	140
,, Charity	2	-	1	-	3
,, Justice -	725	-	-	-	725
,, Education	334	3	107	-	444
,, Religion	191	1	2	-	194
Unclassified	3,446	497	7,580	1,158	12,681
	11,410	626	10,128	1,240	23,404
RESIDUE OF POPULATION :					
Consisting of the Wives, Children, and others dependent on all Classes					219,223
Total of all other Classes					242,627

Divide "ALL OTHER CLASSES" between the AGRICULTURISTS and the MANUFACTURERS in the proportion which these respectively bear to each other, and the numbers engaged in, and dependent on, each interest will stand thus :—

Engaged in Agriculture	108,152	
Dependent on ,,	179,411	
AGRICULTURE—Total		287,563
Engaged in Manufactures	38,108	
Dependent on ,,	63,216	
MANUFACTURES—Total		101,324
Total of the County		388,887

ENGAGED IN	MALES.		FEMALES.		TOTAL.
	15 years of age and upwards.	Under 15 years of age.	15 years of age and upwards.	Under 15 years of age.	
Agriculture:					
Farmers	7,084	-	501	-	7,585
Servants, Labourers, and Ploughmen	31,104	1,901	1,830	295	35,130
Gardeners	302	-	-	-	302
Graziers	39	-	-	-	39
Herdsmen	1,355	201	11	8	1,575
Caretakers	108	1	5	-	114
Land Agents and Stewards	276	-	-	-	276
Game Keepers	34	-	-	-	34
Dairy Keepers	31	-	26	-	57
	40,333	2,103	2,373	303	45,112
Manufactures:					
Spinners (Wool, Flax, and Cotton)	4	1	2,877	61	7,539
,, (Unspecified)	-	9	4,272	315	
Weavers (Linen, Lace, Woollen, and Cotton)	326	-	95	1	1,453
,, (Unspecified)	1,003	4	20	4	
Knitters	1	-	652	60	713
Nailers	116	2	-	-	118
Coopers	109	-	-	-	109
Flax Dressers	50	1	32	2	85
Factory Workers	3	-	58	7	68
Carders	-	2	58	5	65
Winders and Warpers	5	5	22	8	40
Hatters	33	2	3	-	38
Basket Makers	36	-	-	-	36
Turners	33	-	-	-	33
Chandlers and Soap Boilers	21	-	1	-	22
Tanners	19	-	-	-	19
Dyers	17	-	1	-	18
Mat Makers	9	1	6	2	18
Paper Makers	13	-	2	-	15
Sieve Makers	14	-	-	-	14
Lime Burners	12	-	-	-	12
Brick Makers	11	-	-	-	11
Potters	9	-	-	-	9
Bleachers	8	-	-	-	8
Wool Dressers	3	-	4	-	7
Straw Workers	-	-	5	1	6
Iron Founders	6	-	-	-	6
Manufacturers (Lace and Woollen)	3	-	1	-	4
Cloth Finishers	3	-	1	-	4
Rope Makers	4	-	-	-	4
Gunsmiths	3	-	-	-	3
Braziers and Coppersmiths	3	-	-	-	3
Glovers	2	-	-	-	2
Miscellaneous	10	-	-	-	10
	1,889	27	8,110	466	10,492
All other Classes:					
Employed in Handicraft, as Masters or Workmen, in the production of—					
Food	990	12	139	1	1.142
Clothing	1,713	27	1,277	38	3,055
Lodging, Furniture, Machinery, &c.	3,152	22	7	1	3,182
Ministering to Health	73	-	46	-	119
,, Charity	4	-	1	-	5
,, Justice	404	-	1	-	405
,, Education	253	-	125	-	378
,, Religion	155	-	10	-	165
Unclassified	3,430	394	7,711	791	12,326
	10,174	455	9,317	831	20,777
Residue of Population:					
Consisting of the Wives, Children, and others dependent on all Classes					107,447
Total of all other Classes					128,224

Divide "ALL OTHER CLASSES" between the Agriculturists and the Manufacturers in the proportion which these respectively bear to each other, and the numbers engaged in, and dependent on, each interest will stand thus:—

Engaged in Agriculture	45,112	
Dependent on ,,	104,030	
AGRICULTURE—Total		149,142
Engaged in Manufactures	10,492	
Dependent on ,,	24,194	
MANUFACTURES—Total		34,686
Total of the County		183,828

ENGAGED IN	MALES.		FEMALES.		TOTAL.
	15 years of age and upwards.	Under 15 years of age.	15 years of age and upwards.	Under 15 years of age.	
AGRICULTURE:					
Farmers	16,127	1	448	-	16,576
Servants, Labourers, and Ploughmen	25,399	3,010	1,181	208	29,798
Gardeners	74	1	-	-	75
Graziers	2	-	-	-	2
Herdsmen	74	236	18	145	473
Caretakers	15	-	-	-	15
Land Agents and Stewards	71	-	-	-	71
Game Keepers	9	-	-	-	9
Dairy Keepers	.	-	2	-	2
	41,771	3,248	1,649	353	47,021
MANUFACTURES:					
Spinners (Flax and Wool)	1	-	3,990	165 }	25,559
,, (Unspecified)	3	-	19,921	1,479 }	
Weavers (Linen, Woollen, and Cotton)	522	8	14	- }	3,321
,, (Unspecified)	2,655	26	90	6 }	
Knitters	11	-	209	16	236
Coopers	198	3	-	-	201
Flax Dressers	169	-	22	-	191
Nailers	120	8	-	-	128
Winders and Warpers	10	3	29	11	53
Bleachers	35	7	-	1	43
Brick Makers	35	2	-	-	37
Basket Makers	35	1	-	-	36
Hatters	30	-	1	-	31
Dyers	25	-	3	-	28
Chandlers and Soap Boilers	19	1	-	-	20
Reed Makers	17	-	1	-	18
Tool Makers	10	-	-	-	10
Gunsmiths	10	-	-	-	10
Cloth Finishers	9	-	-	-	9
Turners	8	-	-	-	8
Carders	-	-	7	-	7
Manufacturers (Linen and Cotton)	7	-	-	-	7
Lime Burners	6	-	-	-	6
Rope Makers	6	-	-	-	6
Braziers and Coppersmiths	4	-	-	-	4
Tanners	3	-	-	-	3
Quill Manufacturer	2	1	-	-	3
Sieve Makers	3	-	-	-	3
Distillers	2	-	-	-	2
Skinners	2	-	-	-	2
Straw Workers	-	-	2	-	2
Glovers	2	-	-	-	2
Miscellaneous	7	1	2	-	10
	3,966	61	24,291	1,678	29,996
ALL OTHER CLASSES:					
Employed in Handicraft, as Masters or Workmen, in the production of—					
Food	808	11	108	-	927
Clothing	1,818	70	2,080	93	4,061
Lodging, Furniture, Machinery, &c.	2,511	33	23	2	2,569
Ministering to Health	73	-	40	-	113
,, Charity	-	-	1	-	1
,, Justice	253	-	2	-	255
,, Education	254	1	74	2	331
,, Religion	116	-	1	-	117
Unclassified	1,949	4,835	472	749	8,005
	7,782	4,950	2,801	846	16,379
RESIDUE OF POPULATION:					
Consisting of the Wives, Children, and others dependent on all Classes	-	-	-	-	107,046
Total of all other Classes	-	-	-	-	123,425

Divide "ALL OTHER CLASSES" between the AGRICULTURISTS and the MANUFACTURERS in the proportion which these respectively bear to each other, and the numbers engaged in, and dependent on, each interest will stand thus :—

Engaged in Agriculture	47,021	
Dependent on ,,	75,355	
AGRICULTURE—Total		122,376
Engaged in Manufactures	29,996	
Dependent on ,,	48,070	
MANUFACTURES—Total		78,066
Total of the County		200,442

QUEEN'S COUNTY.

ENGAGED IN	MALES.		FEMALES.		TOTAL.
	15 years of age and upwards.	Under 15 years of age.	15 years of age and upwards.	Under 15 years of age.	
AGRICULTURE:					
Farmers - - - - - -	7,985	- -	678	- -	8,663
Servants, Labourers, and Ploughmen - -	24,470	1,912	5,675	663	32,720
Gardeners - - - - - -	143	- -	1	- -	144
Grazier - - - - - -	1	- -	- -	- -	1
Herdsmen - - - - - -	299	53	6	2	360
Caretakers - - - - -	56	- -	7	- -	63
Land Agents and Stewards - - -	128	- -	- -	- -	128
Game Keepers - - - - -	13	- -	- -	- -	13
Dairy Keepers - - - - -	5	- -	23	- -	28
	33,100	1,965	6,390	665	42,120
MANUFACTURES:					
Spinners (Wool and Flax) - - -	16	2	1,469	45 ⎫	2,435
,, (Unspecified) - -	5	1	846	51 ⎭	
Weavers (Cotton, Woollen, Linen, Lace, and Silk) -	697	6	216	2 ⎫	1,657
,, (Unspecified) - - - -	570	4	159	3 ⎭	
Knitters - - - - -	- -	3	682	58	743
Wool Dressers - - - - -	269	4	5	1	279
Coopers - - - - - -	181	- -	- -	- -	181
Nailers - - - - - -	140	1	1	- -	142
Factory Workers - - - -	21	1	103	11	136
Winders and Warpers - - - -	3	6	87	22	118
Carders - - - - - -	- -	- -	69	2	71
Iron Founders - - - - -	23	- -	- -	- -	23
Braziers and Coppersmiths - - -	19	1	- -	- -	20
Hatters - - - - - -	15	- -	4	- -	19
Potters - - - - - -	14	1	1	- -	16
Chandlers and Soap Boilers - - -	14	- -	- -	- -	14
Dyers - - - - - -	11	- -	1	- -	12
Basket Makers - - - - -	10	- -	- -	- -	10
Turners - - - - - -	9	- -	- -	- -	9
Flax Dressers - - - - -	3	- -	- -	- -	9
Manufacturers (Woollen) - - -	6	- -	5	- -	8
Lime Burners - - - - -	8	- -	2	- -	8
Sieve Makers - - - - -	8	- -	- -	- -	8
Cutlers - - - - - -	6	- -	- -	- -	6
Tanners - - - - - -	5	- -	- -	- -	5
Straw Workers - - - - -	- -	- -	- -	5	5
Glovers - - - - -	5	- -	- -	- -	5
Brick Makers - - - - -	5	- -	- -	- -	5
Comb Makers - - - - -	3	- -	- -	1	4
Wire Workers - - - - -	3	- -	- -	- -	3
Rope Makers - - - - -	2	- -	1	- -	3
Cloth Finishers - - - -	2	- -	- -	- -	2
Miscellaneous - - - - -	15	- -	- -	1	16
	2,088	30	3,651	202	5,971
ALL OTHER CLASSES:					
Employed in Handicraft, as Masters or Workmen, in the production of—					
Food - - - - -	666	2	145	- -	813
Clothing - - -	1,549	36	1,579	65	3,229
Lodging, Furniture, Machinery, &c. -	2,775	24	18	- -	2,817
Ministering to Health - - - -	50	- -	61	- -	111
,, Charity - - - -	8	- -	12	- -	20
,, Justice - - - -	417	- -	3	- -	420
,, Education - - -	210	- -	144	- -	354
,, Religion - - - -	95	- -	26	- -	121
Unclassified - - - - - -	2,620	320	5,137	501	8,578
	8,390	382	7,125	566	16,463
RESIDUE OF POPULATION:					
Consisting of the Wives, Children, and others dependent on all Classes - - - -					89,376
Total of all other Classes - - - - - - -					105,839

Divide "ALL OTHER CLASSES" between the AGRICULTURISTS and the MANUFACTURERS in the proportion which these respectively bear to each other, and the numbers engaged in, and dependent on, each interest will stand thus:—

Engaged in Agriculture - - -	42,120	
Dependent on ,, - - -	92,698	
AGRICULTURE—Total - -		134,818
Engaged in Manufactures - -	5,971	
Dependent on ,, - - -	13,141	
MANUFACTURES—Total - -		19,112
Total of the County - -		153,930

ENGAGED IN	MALES.		FEMALES.		TOTAL.
	15 years of age and upwards.	Under 15 years of age.	15 years of age and upwards.	Under 15 years of age.	
AGRICULTURE:					
Farmers	10,529	1	333	- -	10,863
Servants, Labourers, and Ploughmen -	46,363	3,583	3,023	568	53,537
Gardeners	115	- -	- -	- -	115
Graziers -	13	- -	- -	- -	13
Herdsmen	973	34	16	1	1,024
Caretakers	6	- -	- -	- -	6
Land Agents and Stewards	94	- -	- -	- -	94
Game Keepers	14	- -	-	- -	14
Dairy Keepers	3	- -	34	- -	37
	58,110	3,618	3,406	569	65,703
MANUFACTURES:					
Spinners (Flax, Wool, and Cotton)	- -	- -	7,131	283 }	15,251
,, (Unspecified) -	- -	- -	7,327	510 }	
Weavers (Linen, Woollen, and Cotton)	320	- -	10	- }	1,296
,, (Unspecified) -	953	8	5	- }	
Knitters -	- -	-	375	9	384
Coopers	197	1	- -	- -	198
Nailers -	168	4	- -	.	172
Carders -	- -	-	100	8	108
Hatters -	72	-	1	- -	73
Tobacco Pipe Makers -	49	4	5	- -	58
Flax Dressers	47	-	-	- -	47
Potters -	23	-	-	- -	23
Winders and Warpers	-	-	13	3	16
Braziers and Coppersmiths	15	-	-	- -	15
Dyers -	6	-	6	- -	12
Turners -	11	-	-	- -	11
Card Makers	11	-	-	- -	11
Chandlers and Soap Boilers	11	-	-	- -	11
Glovers -	8	-	2	- -	10
Cloth Finishers	4	-	3	- -	7
Sieve Makers	7	-	-	- -	7
Skinners -	6	-	-	- -	6
Clothiers -	5	-	-	- -	5
Basket Makers	4	-	1	- -	5
Gunsmiths -	5	-	-	- -	5
Distillers -	4	-	-	- -	4
Comb Makers	4	-	-	- -	4
Cutlers -	4	-	-	- -	4
Lime Burners	3	-	-	- -	3
Reed Makers	3	-	-	- -	3
Rope Makers	3	-	-	- -	3
Tanners -	2	-	-	- -	2
Miscellaneous	4	-	2	- -	6
	1,949	17	14,981	813	17,760
ALL OTHER CLASSES:					
Employed in Handicraft, as Masters or Workmen, in the production of—					
Food -	620	3	202	- -	825
Clothing	1,890	44	1,167	10	3,111
Lodging, Furniture, Machinery, &c. -	2,339	17	12	- -	2,368
Ministering to Health	62	-	39	- -	101
,, Charity -	1	-	-	- -	1
,, Justice	393	-	2	- -	395
,, Education	295	-	96	- -	391
,, Religion	119	-	2	- -	121
Unclassified -	2,464	380	5,444	701	8,989
	8,183	444	6,964	711	16,302

RESIDUE OF POPULATION:		
Consisting of the Wives, Children, and others dependent on all Classes - - - -		153,826
Total of all other Classes - - - - -		170,128

Divide " ALL OTHER CLASSES " between the AGRICULTURISTS and the MANUFACTURERS in the proportion which these respectively bear to each other, and the numbers engaged in, and dependent on, each interest will stand thus:—

Engaged in Agriculture - - -	65,703	
Dependent on ,, - - -	133,927	
AGRICULTURE—Total - - -		199,630
Engaged in Manufactures - - -	17,760	
Dependent on ,, - - -	36,201	
MANUFACTURES—Total - - -		53,961
Total of the County - - -		253,591

ENGAGED IN	MALES.		FEMALES.		TOTAL.
	15 years of age and upwards.	Under 15 years of age.	15 years of age and upwards.	Under 15 years of age.	
AGRICULTURE:					
Farmers - - - - - -	12,975	1	194	-	13,170
Servants, Labourers, and Ploughmen - - -	25,283	3,236	1,192	375	30,086
Gardeners - - - - - -	111	-	-	-	111
Graziers - - - - - -	7	-	-	-	7
Herdsmen - - - - -	376	107	16	39	538
Caretakers - - - - - -	19	-	3	-	22
Land Stewards - - - - -	58	-	-	-	58
Game Keepers - - - - -	4	-	-	-	4
	38,833	3,344	1,405	414	43,996
MANUFACTURES:					
Spinners (Flax and Wool)	-	2	6,624	266 }	15,539
,, (Unspecified) - - - -	1	1	7,952	693 }	
Weavers (Linen and Woollen) - - -	337	-	2	- }	1,110
,, (Unspecified) - - -	765	1	5	- }	
Knitters - - - - -	-	-	419	29	448
Coopers - - - - - -	361	1	-	-	362
Carders - - - - -	-	-	88	9	97
Nailers - - - - - -	91	4	-	-	95
Flax Dressers - - - - -	50	-	2	-	52
Winders and Warpers - - - -	2	-	28	2	32
Hatters - - - - - -	31	-	-	-	31
Clothiers - - - - -	17	-	3	-	20
Cutlers - - - - -	16	-	-	-	16
Chandlers and Soap Boilers - - -	14	-	-	-	14
Rope Makers - - - - -	13	-	-	-	13
Bleachers - - - - -	12	-	-	-	12
Dyers - - - - -	9	-	3	-	12
Braziers and Coppersmiths - - -	12	-	-	-	12
Tobacco Pipe Makers - - - -	11	-	-	-	11
Sieve Makers - - - -	9	-	-	-	9
Cloth Finishers - - - -	5	-	-	-	5
Gunsmiths - - - - -	5	-	-	-	5
Comb Makers - - - -	4	-	-	-	4
Glovers - - - - -	4	-	-	-	4
Turners - - - - -	4	-	-	-	4
Lime Burners - - - -	3	-	-	-	3
Net Makers - - - - -	-	-	3	-	3
Sail Makers - - - -	3	-	-	-	3
Block Makers - - - -	2	-	-	-	2
Reed Makers - - - -	2	-	-	-	2
Card Makers - - - - -	2	-	-	-	2
Distiller - - - - -	1	-	-	-	1
Miscellaneous - - - -	5	-	1	-	6
	1,791	9	15,130	999	17,929
ALL OTHER CLASSES:					
Employed in Handicraft, as Masters or Workmen, in the production of—					
Food - - - -	612	5	180	1	798
Clothing - - - -	1,733	42	1,344	77	3,196
Lodging, Furniture, Machinery, &c. -	1,709	9	6	1	1,725
Ministering to Health - - - -	49	-	33	-	82
,, Charity - - - -	-	-	5	-	5
,, Justice - - -	346	-	3	-	349
,, Education - - -	244	-	76	-	320
,, Religion - - - -	116	-	2	-	118
Unclassified - - - - - -	2,427	277	4,790	680	8,174
	7,236	333	6,439	759	14,767
RESIDUE OF POPULATION:					
Consisting of the Wives, Children, and others dependent on all Classes - - - -					104,194
Total of all other Classes - - - - - - -					118,961

Divide " ALL OTHER CLASSES " between the AGRICULTURISTS and the MANUFACTURERS in the proportion which these respectively bear to each other, and the numbers engaged in, and dependent on, each interest will stand thus :—

         Engaged in Agriculture - - - 43,996
         Dependent on ,, - - - - 84,519

            AGRICULTURE—Total - - 128,515

         Engaged in Manufactures - - - 17,929
         Dependent on ,, - - - 34,442

            MANUFACTURES—Total - - 52,371

         Total of the County - - - 180,886

ENGAGED IN	MALES.		FEMALES.		TOTAL.
	15 years of age and upwards.	Under 15 years of age.	15 years of age and upwards.	Under 15 years of age.	
Agriculture:					
Farmers - - - - - - -	25,630	122	1,585	7	27,344
Servants, Labourers, and Ploughmen - - -	64,830	3,654	9,963	1,135	79,582
Gardeners - - - - - -	397	1	-	-	398
Graziers - - - - - -	15	-	3	-	18
Herdsmen - - - - - -	963	253	8	3	1,227
Caretakers - - - - - -	138	2	10	-	150
Land Agents and Stewards - - - -	412	1	-	-	413
Game Keepers - - - - -	24	-	-	-	24
Dairy Keepers - - - - -	39	-	260	-	299
	92,448	4,033	11,829	1,145	109,455
Manufactures:					
Spinners (Flax and Wool) - - - -	2	-	3,505	93 ⎰	7,886
,, (Unspecified) - - -	4	-	3,969	313 ⎱	
Weavers (Linen, Woollen, and Cotton) - -	276	1	37	1 ⎰	1,186
,, (Unspecified) - -	826	17	26	2 ⎱	
Knitters - - - - - -	1	-	690	26	717
Coopers - - - - - -	585	10	-	-	595
Nailers - - - - - -	427	30	-	-	457
Hatters - - - - - -	118	-	13	-	131
Carders - - - - - -	1	-	87	6	94
Chandlers and Soap Boilers - - - -	85	-	2	-	87
Braziers and Coppersmiths - - - -	55	1	5	-	61
Basket Makers - - - - -	44	3	3	-	50
Lime Burners - - - - -	47	1	-	-	48
Flax Dressers - - - - -	27	-	20	-	47
Wool Dressers - - - - -	42	-	-	-	42
Dyers - - - - - -	29	-	9	-	38
Factory Workers - - - - -	3	-	31	1	35
Turners - - - - - -	22	1	1	-	24
Tanners - - - - - -	20	-	-	-	20
Cutlers - - - - - -	20	-	-	-	20
Rope Makers - - - - -	16	-	2	-	18
Clothiers - - - - - -	13	-	4	-	17
Skinners - - - - - -	15	-	-	-	15
Winders and Warpers - - - - -	-	-	12	2	14
Straw Workers - - - - -	1	-	12	1	14
Brick Makers - - - - -	14	-	-	-	14
Comb Makers - - - - -	13	-	-	-	13
Gunsmiths - - - - - -	12	1	-	-	13
Distillers - - - - - -	11	-	-	-	11
Glovers - - - - - -	6	-	4	-	10
Sieve Makers - - - - -	9	-	1	-	10
Wire Workers - - - - -	8	-	1	-	9
Miscellaneous - - - - -	42	-	6	-	48
	2,794	65	8,440	445	11,744
All other Classes:					
Employed in Handicraft, as Masters or Workmen, in the production of—					
Food - - - -	1,900	15	352	3	2,270
Clothing - - - -	5,195	153	3,425	101	8,874
Lodging, Furniture, Machinery, &c. -	7,561	95	53	1	7,710
Ministering to Health - - - -	181	-	209	-	390
,, Charity - - - -	5	-	4	-	9
,, Justice - - - -	1,062	-	5	-	1,067
,, Education - - - -	666	-	235	-	901
,, Religion - - - -	280	-	50	-	330
Unclassified - - - - -	8,030	664	18,401	1,879	28,974
	24,880	927	22,734	1,984	50,525
Residue of Population:					
Consisting of the Wives, Children, and others dependent on all Classes - - - -					263,829
Total of all other Classes - - - - - - -					314,354

Divide " all other classes" between the Agriculturists and the Manufacturers in the proportion which these respectively bear to each other, and the numbers engaged in, and dependent on, each interest will stand thus:—

Engaged in Agriculture - - - 109,455
Dependent on ,, - - - 283,894
    Agriculture—Total - - - 393,349
Engaged in Manufactures - - - 11,744
Dependent on ,, - - - 30,460
    Manufactures—Total - - 42,204

        Total of the County - - - 435,553

TYRONE—County of. [Ireland.

ENGAGED IN	MALES.		FEMALES.		TOTAL.
	15 years of age and upwards.	Under 15 years of age.	15 years of age and upwards.	Under 15 years of age.	
Agriculture:					
Farmers - - - - - -	23,799	3	503	-	24,305
Servants, Labourers, and Ploughmen - -	34,697	4,027	784	104	39,612
Gardeners - - - - - - -	148	-	1	-	149
Graziers - - - - - - -	2	-	-	-	2
Herdsmen - - - - - - -	314	1,936	118	887	3,255
Caretakers - - - - - -	30	6	5	-	41
Land Agents and Stewards - - - -	75	-	-	-	75
Game Keepers - - - - - -	18	-	-	-	18
Dairy Keepers - - - - - -	3	-	14	-	17
	59,086	5,972	1,425	991	67,474
Manufactures:					
Spinners (Flax and Wool) - - - -	-	-	10,145	525 ⎱	46,736
,, (Unspecified) - - - - -	-	-	33,360	2,706 ⎰	
Weavers (Linen, Woollen, Cotton, and Fringe) -	2472	47	250	18 ⎱	11,373
,, (Unspecified) - - - -	7587	141	842	16 ⎰	
Flax Dressers - - - - - -	541	10	51	4	606
Knitters - - - - - - -	-	-	378	24	402
Coopers - - - - - - -	259	6	-	-	265
Nailers - - - - - - -	206	9	-	-	215
Factory Workers - - - - - -	21	20	109	27	177
Winders and Warpers - - - - -	9	19	104	33	165
Bleachers - - - - - - -	83	-	1	-	84
Reed Makers - - - - - -	80	-	3	-	83
Carders - - - - - - -	1	-	67	1	69
Hatters - - - - - - -	47	1	3	-	51
Chandlers and Soap Boilers - - - -	35	-	1	-	36
Potters - - - - - - -	27	-	3	-	30
Cloth Finishers - - - - - -	26	2	-	-	28
Basket Makers - - - - - -	20	1	.7	-	28
Rope Makers - - - - - -	19	3	-	-	22
Brick Makers - - - - - -	20	-	-	-	20
Dyers - - - - - - -	15	-	3	-	18
Paper Makers - - - - - -	18	-	-	-	18
Lime Burners - - - - - -	17	-	-	-	17
Turners - - - - - - -	17	-	-	-	17
Clothiers - - - - - - -	16	-	-	-	16
Manufacturers (Linen and Cotton) - - -	11	-	-	-	11
Gunsmiths - - - - - -	11	-	-	-	11
Braziers and Coppersmiths - - - -	10	-	-	-	11
Skinners - - - - - - -	10	1	-	-	10
Net Makers - - - - - -	1	3	4	2	10
Tanners - - - - - - -	9	-	-	-	9
Button Makers - - - - - -	2	-	5	-	7
Miscellaneous - - - - - -	22	1	5	-	28
	11,612	264	45,341	3,356	60,573
All other Classes:					
Employed in Handicraft, as Masters or Workmen, in the production of—					
Food - - - - -	1,306	10	203	-	1,519
Clothing - - - -	2,826	111	2,787	128	5,852
Lodging, Furniture, and Machinery, &c.	4,001	34	22	2	4,059
Ministering to Health - - - -	120	-	30	-	150
,, Charity - - - -	1	-	1	-	2
,, Justice - - - -	322	-	2	-	324
,, Education - - - -	431	1	131	-	563
,, Religion - - - -	238	-	5	-	243
Unclassified - - - - -	2,643	699	6,854	1,023	11,219
	11,888	855	10,035	1,153	23,931

Residue of Population:

Consisting of the Wives, Children, and others dependent on all Classes - - - - -					160,978
Total of all other Classes - - - - - - -					184,909

Divide " all other classes " between the Agriculturists and the Manufacturers in the proportion which these respectively bear to each other, and the numbers engaged in, and dependent on, each interest will stand thus :—

Engaged in Agriculture - - -	67,474		
Dependent on ,, - - -	97,438		
Agriculture—Total - -		164,912	
Engaged in Manufactures - -	60,573		
Dependent on ,, - -	87,471		
Manufactures—Total -		148,044	
Total of the County - - -		312,956	

ENGAGED IN	MALES.		FEMALES.		TOTAL.
	15 years of age and upwards.	Under 15 years of age.	15 years of age and upwards.	Under 15 years of age.	
AGRICULTURE:					
Farmers	18	-	2	-	20
Servants and Labourers	362	17	87	2	468
Gardeners	28	-	-	-	28
Caretakers	3	-	2	-	5
Land Agent and Stewards	15	-	-	-	15
Game Keeper	1	-	-	-	1
Dairy-Keepers	1	-	15	-	16
	428	17	106	2	553
MANUFACTURES:					
Coopers	130	1	1	-	132
Weavers (Linen, Cotton, Woollen, Lace)	10	-	23	-⎫	111
„ (Unspecified)	51	-	26	1⎬	56
Nailers	53	3	-	-⎭	
Spinners (Flax and Wool)	-	-	14	-⎫	47
„ (Unspecified)	-	-	26	7⎬	47
Knitters	-	-	46	1⎭	
Assistants in Factories	1	4	31	2	38
Glass Makers	35	3	-	-	38
Chandlers and Soap Boilers	32	-	2	-	34
Rope Makers	19	4	-	-	23
Iron Founders	20	1	1	-	22
Tanners	19	-	-	-	19
Sail Makers	17	2	-	-	19
Basket Makers	16	1	-	-	17
Manufacturers of Sundries	5	4	7	-	16
Tobacco Pipe Makers	9	-	6	-	15
Braziers and Coppersmiths	14	-	-	-	14
Hatters	9	-	3	-	12
Glovers	2	-	7	1	10
Turners	8	1	1	-	10
Lime Burners	8	-	-	-	8
Winders and Warpers	1	-	4	1	6
Dyers	5	-	1	-	6
Glue and Size Makers	6	-	-	-	6
Blockmakers	5	-	-	-	5
Cutlers	5	-	-	-	5
Gunsmiths	5	-	-	-	5
Wool Dressers	3	-	-	-	3
Skinners	3	-	-	-	3
Starch Manufacturers	3	-	-	-	3
Musical Instrument Makers	3	-	-	-	3
Manufacturers (Thread and Woollen)	2	-	-	-	2
Flax Dressers	2	-	-	-	2
Paper Stainers	2	-	-	-	2
Miscellaneous	6	-	-	-	6
	509	24	199	13	745
ALL OTHER CLASSES:					
Employed in Handicraft, as Masters or Workmen, in the production of—					
Food	622	6	191	1	820
Clothing	736	18	797	27	1,578
Lodging, Furniture, Machinery, &c.	1,014	12	19	-	1,045
Ministering to Health	42	-	14	-	56
„ Charity	1	-	2	-	3
„ Justice	142	-	3	-	145
„ Education	33	-	54	-	87
„ Religion	35	-	55	-	90
Unclassified	2,378	94	2,203	75	4,750
	5,003	130	3,338	103	8,574
RESIDUE OF POPULATION:					
Consisting of the Wives, Children, and others dependent on all Classes	-	-	-	-	13,344
Total of all other Classes	-	-	-	-	21,918

Divide "ALL OTHER CLASSES" between the AGRICULTURISTS and the MANUFACTURERS in the proportion which these respectively bear to each other, and the numbers engaged in, and dependent on, each interest will stand thus:—

Engaged in Agriculture	553	
Dependent on „	9,337	
AGRICULTURE—Total		9,890
Engaged in Manufactures	745	
Dependent on „	12,581	
MANUFACTURES—Total		13,326
Total of the City		23,216

ENGAGED IN	MALES.		FEMALES.		TOTAL.
	15 years of age and upwards.	Under 15 years of age.	15 years of age and upwards.	Under 15 years of age.	
Agriculture:					
Farmers - - - -	7,071	-	352	-	7,423
Servants, Labourers, and Ploughmen -	29,809	2,066	9349	936	42,160
Gardeners - - - - -	165	1	1	-	167
Herdsmen - - - -	316	305	-	-	630
Caretakers - - - - -	47	-	-	9	50
Land Agent and Stewards - -	172	-	3	-	172
Game Keepers - - - -	19	-	-	-	19
Dairy Keepers - - - -	25	-	95	-	120
	37,624	2,372	9,800	945	50,741
Manufactures:					
Spinners (Flax, Wool, and Cotton) -	54	-	1,340	39 ⎫	
,, (Unspecified) - - -	1	6	528	32 ⎬	2,000
Weavers (Cotton, Woollen, and Linen) -	198	7	327	14 ⎭	
,, (Unspecified) - - -	344	2	14	2 ⎱	908
Knitters - - - - -	1	-	311	11	323
Coopers - - - - -	190	3	-	-	193
Nailers - - - - -	121	4	-	-	125
Assistants in Factories - - -	9	25	29	39	102
Carders - - - - -	17	-	45	2	64
Winders and Warpers - - -	8	2	42	1	53
Rope Makers - - - -	44	2	-	-	46
Lime Burners .. - - -	23	-	-	-	23
Flax Dressers - - - -	20	-	2	-	22
Turners - - - - -	19	2	-	-	21
Bleachers - - - - -	16	2	1	-	19
Hatters - - - - -	11	-	6	1	18
Wool Dressers - - - -	9	-	3	2	14
Chandlers and Soap Boilers - -	14	-	-	-	14
Basket Makers - - - -	13	-	-	-	13
Braziers and Coppersmiths - -	12	-	1	-	13
Dyers - - - - -	9	-	3	-	12
Manufacturers of Sundries - -	5	3	1	1	10
Tanners - - - - -	8	-	-	-	8
Sail Makers - - - -	8	-	-	-	8
Iron Founders - - - -	6	-	-	-	6
Skinners - - - - -	5	-	-	-	5
Straw Workers - - - -	-	-	5	-	5
Brick Makers - - - -	4	-	-	-	4
Gunsmiths - - - - -	4	-	-	-	4
Sieve Makers - - - -	1	-	3	-	4
Cloth Finishers - - - -	3	-	-	-	3
Glovers - - - - -	3	-	-	-	3
Paper Makers - - - -	3	-	-	-	3
Net Makers - - - -	-	-	1	2	3
Miscellaneous - - - -	6	-	2	-	8
	1,189	58	2,664	146	4,057
All other Classes:					
Employed in Handicraft, as Masters or Workmen, in the production of—					
Food - - - -	1,511	8	211	-	1,730
Clothing - - - - -	1,759	65	1,423	68	3,315
Lodging, Furniture, Machinery, &c. -	3,159	37	9	2	3,207
Ministering to Health - - -	41	-	67	-	108
,, Charity - - - -	8	-	15	-	23
,, Justice - - - - -	346	-	1	-	347
,, Education - - - -	203	-	102	-	305
,, Religion - - - -	192	-	98	-	290
Unclassified - - - - -	3,127	322	7,366	923	11,738
	10,346	432	9,292	993	21,063
Residue of Population:					
Consisting of the Wives, Children, and others dependent on all Classes - - - -					97,110
Total of all other Classes - - - - - - -					118,173

Divide " all other classes " between the Agriculturists and the Manufacturers in the proportion which these respectively bear to each other, and the numbers engaged in, and dependent on, each interest will stand thus:—

Engaged in Agriculture - - -	50,741	
Dependent on ,, - - -	109,424	
Agriculture—Total .. -		160,165
Engaged in Manufactures - -	4,057	
Dependent on ,, - -	8,749	
Manufactures—Total -		12,806
Total of the County - - -		172,971

ENGAGED IN	MALES.		FEMALES.		TOTAL.
	15 years of age and upwards.	Under 15 years of age.	15 years of age and upwards.	Under 15 years of age.	
AGRICULTURE:					
Farmers - - - - - -	6,251	-	398	-	6,649
Servants, Labourers, and Ploughmen - -	23,453	2,245	2,892	526	29,116
Gardeners - - - - - -	136	-	-	-	136
Graziers - - - - - -	16	-	-	-	16
Herdsmen - - - - - -	595	82	12	6	695
Caretakers - - - - -	45	-	1	-	46
Land Agents and Stewards - - - -	117	-	-	-	117
Game Keepers - - - - -	30	-	-	-	30
Dairy Keepers - - - - -	2	-	14	-	16
	30,645	2,327	3317	532	36,821
MANUFACTURES:					
Spinners (Flax and Wool) - - - -	1	4	3,206	103 }	8,121
,, (Unspecified) - - -	3	18	4,407	379 }	
Weavers (Linen, Woollen, Cotton, and Corduroy) -	296	1	4	- }	933
,, (Unspecified) - - - -	615	7	9	1 }	
Knitters - - - - - -	-	-	376	16	392
Coopers - - - - - -	213	2	-	-	215
Nailers - - - - - -	105	7	2	-	114
Carders - - - - - -	1	-	54	7	62
Winders and Warpers - - - - -	3	6	31	9	49
Flax Dressers - - - - -	20	-	7	1	28
Hatters - - - - - -	24	1	1	-	26
Dyers - - - - - -	19	-	5	-	24
Wool Dressers - - - - -	6	2	7	-	15
Turners - - - - - -	13	-	-	-	13
Chandlers and Soap Boilers - - - -	13	-	-	-	13
Basket Makers - - - - -	8	-	4	-	12
Braziers and Coppersmiths - - - -	12	-	-	-	12
Japanners - - - - - -	12	-	-	-	12
Lime Burners - - - - -	11	-	-	-	11
Bleachers - - - - - -	7	-	-	-	7
Rope Makers - - - - -	6	-	1	-	7
Distillers - - - - - -	6	-	-	-	6
Cutlers - - - - - -	5	-	-	-	5
Manufacturers (Lace and Cotton) - - -	1	-	3	-	4
Cloth Finishers - - - - -	4	-	-	-	4
Tanners - - - - - -	4	-	-	-	4
Skinners - - - - - -	3	-	-	-	3
Comb Makers - - - - -	2	1	-	-	3
Brick Makers - - - - -	3	-	-	-	3
Iron Founders - - - - -	3	-	-	-	3
Wire Workers - - - - -	3	-	-	-	3
Sieve Makers - - - - -	3	-	-	-	3
Miscellaneous - - - - -	10	-	3	-	13
	1,435	49	8,120	516	10,120
ALL OTHER CLASSES:					
Employed in Handicraft, as Masters or Workmen, in the production of—					
Food - - - - -	605	4	144	2	755
Clothing - - - -	1,378	41	1,128	49	2,596
Lodging, Furniture, Machinery, &c.	2,175	37	18	-	2,230
Ministering to Health - - - -	60	-	38	-	98
,, Justice - - - -	350	-	2	-	352
,, Education - - - -	198	-	93	-	291
,, Religion - - - -	109	-	14	-	123
Unclassified - - - - - -	2,391	349	5,743	669	9,152
	7,266	431	7,180	720	15,597
RESIDUE OF POPULATION:					
Consisting of the Wives, Children, and others dependent on all Classes - - - - -					78,762
Total of all other Classes - - - - - - - - -					94,359

Divide "ALL OTHER CLASSES" between the AGRICULTURISTS and the MANUFACTURERS in the proportion which these respectively bear to each other, and the numbers engaged in, and dependent on, each interest will stand thus:—

Engaged in Agriculture - - -	36,821	
Dependent on ,, - - - -	74,017	
AGRICULTURE—Total - - ————		110,838
Engaged in Manufactures - -	10,120	
Dependent on ,, - -	20,342	
MANUFACTURES—Total - - ————		30,462
Total of the County - - -		141,300

ENGAGED IN	MALES.		FEMALES.		TOTAL.
	15 years of age and upwards.	Under 15 years of age.	15 years of age and upwards.	Under 15 years of age.	
AGRICULTURE:					
Farmers	11,903	-	1,103	-	13,006
Servants, Labourers, and Ploughmen	27,700	1,561	6,225	512	35,998
Gardeners	193	-	-	-	193
Graziers	3	-	-	-	3
Herdsmen	83	56	4	7	150
Caretakers	66	1	11	-	78
Land Agents and Stewards	166	-	-	-	166
Game Keepers	19	-	-	-	19
Dairy Keepers	26	-	89	2	117
	40,159	1,618	7,432	521	49,730
MANUFACTURES:					
Spinners (Flax, Wool, and Cotton)	2	3	3,452	103 }	6,622
„ (Unspecified)	6	5	2,938	113 }	
Knitters	-	-	905	58	963
Weavers (Linen, Woollen, and Cotton)	208	3	4	- }	755
„ (Unspecified)	509	4	27	- }	
Coopers	318	3	-	-	321
Straw Workers	3	-	227	35	265
Nailers	214	10	2	-	226
Carders	3	-	76	1	80
Hatters	61	-	10	-	71
Net Makers	1	-	54	1	56
Chandlers and Soap Boilers	52	-	1	-	53
Rope Makers	33	3	-	-	36
Braziers and Coppersmiths	34	1	-	-	35
Flax Dressers	24	-	10	-	34
Factory Workers	15	5	11	2	33
Manufacturers (Lace)	-	-	28	4	32
Basket Makers	32	-	-	-	32
Clothiers	26	1	1	-	28
Glovers	7	-	20	-	27
Lime Burners	23	-	1	-	24
Brick Makers	19	2	1	-	22
Winders and Warpers	-	8	11	1	20
Sieve Makers	17	2	-	-	19
Tanners	18	-	-	-	18
Mat Makers	2	-	13	-	15
Skinners	11	-	1	-	12
Potters	12	-	-	-	12
Dyers	7	-	4	-	11
Turners	9	-	-	-	9
Block Makers	7	-	-	-	7
Miscellaneous	33	1	-	-	34
	1,706	51	7,797	318	9,872
ALL OTHER CLASSES:					
Employed in Handicraft, as Masters or Workmen, in the production of—					
Food	1,701	14	353	2	2,070
Clothing	3,234	103	3,241	122	6,700
Lodging, Furniture, Machinery, &c.	4,544	43	37	1	4,625
Ministering to Health	95	-	134	-	229
„ Charity	2	-	-	-	2
„ Justice	483	-	2	-	485
„ Education	347	-	162	-	509
„ Religion	188	-	25	-	213
Unclassified	4,291	430	9,030	714	14,465
	14,885	590	12,984	839	29,298

RESIDUE OF POPULATION:

Consisting of the Wives, Children, and others dependent on all Classes	-	-	-	-	113,133
Total of all other Classes	-	-	-	-	142,431

Divide "ALL OTHER CLASSES" between the AGRICULTURISTS and the MANUFACTURERS in the proportion which these respectively bear to each other, and the numbers engaged in, and dependent on, each interest will stand thus:—

Engaged in Agriculture	49,730	
Dependent on „	118,840	
AGRICULTURE—Total		168,570
Engaged in Manufactures	9,872	
Dependent on „	23,591	
MANUFACTURES—Total		33,463
Total of the County		202,033

ENGAGED IN	MALES.		FEMALES.		TOTAL.
	15 years of age and upwards.	Under 15 years of age.	15 years of age and upwards.	Under 15 years of age.	
Agriculture :					
Farmers	5,762	-	449	-	6,211
Servants, Labourers, and Ploughmen	18,443	1,130	2,210	259	22,042
Gardeners	177	1	1	-	179
Graziers	2	-	-	-	2
Herdsmen	265	197	7	8	477
Caretakers	110	-	12	-	122
Land Agents and Stewards	142	-	-	-	142
Game Keepers	17	-	-	-	17
Dairy Keepers	41	1	50	3	95
	24,959	1,329	2,729	270	29,287
Manufactures :					
Spinners (Wool, Flax, and Cotton)	2	-	1,213	36 }	2,086
,, (Unspecified)	-	2	788	45 }	
Knitters	1	1	709	71	782
Weavers (Cotton, Woollen, and Linen)	76	2	71	7 }	320
,, (Unspecified)	138	5	8	13 }	
Nailers	142	5	-	-	147
Coopers	91	1	-	-	92
Carders	-	-	64	6	70
Net Makers	1	1	50	2	54
Hatters	46	1	4	-	51
Straw Workers	-	-	30	4	34
Chandlers and Soap Boilers	24	-	1	-	25
Winders and Warpers	-	4	15	-	19
Basket Makers	15	-	-	-	15
Braziers and Coppersmiths	15	-	-	-	15
Flax Dressers	3	-	4	-	7
Turners	7	-	-	-	7
Mat Makers	4	-	3	-	7
Bleachers	6	-	-	-	6
Lime Burners	6	-	-	-	6
Wool Dressers	1	-	4	-	5
Clothiers	5	-	-	-	5
Glovers	4	-	1	-	5
Calico Printers	4	-	-	-	4
Brick Makers	4	-	-	-	4
Factory Workers	-	-	-	3	3
Iron Founders	3	-	-	-	3
Sieve Makers	3	-	-	-	3
Manufacturers (Lace)	-	-	2	-	2
Dyers	2	-	-	-	2
Skinners	2	-	-	-	2
Cutlers	2	-	-	-	2
Gunsmiths	2	-	-	-	2
Miscellaneous	7	1	-	1	9
	616	23	2,967	188	3,794
All other Classes :					
Employed in Handicraft, as Masters or Workmen, in the production of—					
Food	1,312	14	183	-	1,509
Clothing	1,414	49	1,370	61	2,894
Lodging, Furniture, Machinery, &c.	3,216	45	14	2	3,277
Ministering to Health	67	-	54	-	121
,, Charity	1	-	1	-	2
,, Justice	319	-	2	-	321
,, Education	231	-	137	-	368
,, Religion	121	-	6	-	127
Unclassified	2,662	367	5,640	492	9,161
	9,343	475	7,407	555	17,780

Residue of Population :
Consisting of the Wives, Children, and others dependent on all Classes - - - - 75,282

Total of all other Classes - - - - - - 93,062

Divide "all other classes" between the Agriculturists and the Manufacturers in the proportion which these respectively bear to each other, and the numbers engaged in, and dependent on, each interest will stand thus :—

Engaged in Agriculture - - - 29,287
Dependent on ,, - - - 82,389
    Agriculture—Total - - 111,676

Engaged in Manufactures - - - 3,794
Dependent on ,, - - - 10,673
    Manufactures—Total - 14,467

Total of the County - - - 126,143

138

IRELAND—SUMMARY OF POPULATION.

COUNTIES.	AGRICULTURE.			MANUFACTURES.			TOTAL OF THE COUNTY.
	Engaged in :	Dependent on :	TOTAL.	Engaged in:	Dependent on :	TOTAL.	
ANTRIM	49,915	88,076	137,991	49,990	88,207	138,197	276,188
ARMAGH	39,468	78,045	117,513	38,584	76,296	114,880	232,393
BELFAST (Town)	1,104	6,664	7,768	9,598	57,942	67,540	75,308
CARLOW	21,660	54,851	76,511	2,751	6,966	9,717	86,228
CARRICKFERGUS (Town)	1,195	3,973	5,168	974	3,237	4,211	9,379
CAVAN	57,705	84,180	141,885	33,780	67,493	101,273	243,158
CLARE	76,115	150,893	227,008	19,912	39,474	59,386	286,394
CORK (City)	1,880	28,970	30,850	3,039	46,831	49,870	80,720
CORK (County)	190,771	476,366	667,137	30,386	75,875	106,261	773,398
DONEGAL	71,279	102,472	173,751	50,335	72,362	122,697	296,448
DOWN	62,447	124,730	187,177	58,141	116,128	174,269	361,446
DUBLIN (City)	2,128	178,532	180,660	7,432	44,634	52,066	232,726
DUBLIN (County)	22,943	99,340	122,283	3,333	14,431	17,764	140,047
DROGHEDA	365	2,678	3,043	1,585	11,633	13,218	16,261
FERMANAGH	35,772	57,174	92,946	24,453	39,082	63,535	156,481
GALWAY (County)	113,703	207,355	321,058	36,076	65,789	101,865	422,923
GALWAY (Town)	327	4,217	4,544	916	11,815	12,731	17,275
KERRY	73,063	162,167	235,230	18,217	40,433	58,650	293,880
KILDARE	29,573	71,161	100,734	4,038	9,716	13,754	114,488
KILKENNY (City)	589	8,232	8,821	678	9,572	10,250	19,071
KILKENNY (County)	52,581	120,694	173,275	3,057	7,017	10,074	183,349
KING'S COUNTY	38,940	87,296	126,236	6,361	14,260	20,621	146,857
LEITRIM	38,961	58,096	97,057	23,379	34,861	58,240	155,297
LIMERICK (City)	1,302	19,241	20,543	1,787	26,061	27,848	48,391
LIMERICK (County)	70,748	157,531	228,279	16,537	36,822	53,359	281,638
LONDONDERRY	42,723	72,720	115,443	39,499	67,232	106,731	222,174
LONGFORD	29,400	54,698	84,098	10,975	20,418	31,393	115,491
LOUTH	22,107	59,989	82,096	8,047	21,836	29,883	111,979
MAYO	108,152	179,411	287,563	38,108	63,216	101,324	388,887
MEATH	45,112	104,030	149,142	10,492	24,194	34,686	183,828
MONAGHAN	47,021	75,355	122,376	29,996	48,070	78,066	200,442
QUEEN'S COUNTY	42,120	92,698	134,818	5,971	13,141	19,112	153,930
ROSCOMMON	65,703	133,927	199,630	17,760	36,201	53,961	253,591
SLIGO	43,996	84,519	128,515	17,929	34,442	52,371	180,886
TIPPERARY	109,455	283,894	393,349	11,744	30,460	42,204	435,553
TYRONE	67,474	97,438	164,912	60,573	87,471	148,044	312,956
WATERFORD (City)	553	9,337	9,890	745	12,581	13,326	23,216
WATERFORD (County)	50,741	109,424	160,165	4,057	8,749	12,806	172,971
WESTMEATH	36,821	74,017	110,838	10,120	20,342	30,462	141,300
WEXFORD	49,730	118,840	168,570	9,872	23,591	33,463	202,033
WICKLOW	29,287	82,389	111,676	3,794	10,673	14,467	126,143
	1,844,929	4,065,620	5,910,549	*725,021	1,539,554	2,264,575	8,175,124

Total of the Agricultural Interest - - 5,910,549
    ,, Manufacturing Interest - - 2,264,575

Total Population of Ireland - - - 8,175,124

* See note at page 150.

IRELAND—SUMMARY OF DIRECT AND LOCAL TAXATION.

	Paid by the Landed Interest and those dependent on it.	Paid by the Manufacturing Interest and those dependent on it.
Paid exclusively by the Landed Interest. TITHES - - - - - - -	£ 500,000	£
* *Paid in the Proportion of 5-7ths by the Landed Interest, and 2-7ths by the Manufacturing Interest.* COUNTY CESS - - - - £1,158,198 Annual average amount ordered to be levied in the years 1841, 1842, 1843.	827,995	330,203
POOR RATES - - - - - £256,658 Collected in the year ended 29th Sept. 1844.	183,325	73,333
	1,511,320	403,536

	£
Total paid by the Landed Interest - - - - - 1,511,320	
„ Manufacturing Interest - - - - 403,536	
Total of Direct and Local Taxation paid in Ireland - £1,914,856	

* There is no return of the assessment of the separate counties, and it is therefore impossible to ascertain the exact proportion of the Direct and Local Taxation paid by each after the manner of the Counties in Great Britain. Nor does there appear to be any return of the exact amount collected as Tithe; but it is generally estimated at about £500,000, the whole revenue of the Church of Ireland being £854,129. The proportion which the Landed and Manufacturing Interests bear to each other in the entire population, as shown on the other side, is consequently the only division that can be made of these items.

UNITED KINGDOM—SUMMARY OF POPULATION.

	See Page	AGRICULTURE.			MANUFACTURES.			TOTAL.
		Engaged in :	Dependent on :	TOTAL.	Engaged in :	Dependent on :	TOTAL.	
ENGLAND	46	1,157,816	8,154,495	9,312,311	943,998	4,738,829	5,682,827	14,995,138
WALES	60	103,632	650,748	754,380	19,517	137,706	157,223	911,603
SCOTLAND	94	229,337	1,159,259	1,388,596	220,171	1,011,417	1,231,588	2,620,184
BRITISH ISLANDS	96	8,493	95,564	104,057	1,631	18,352	19,983	124,040
IRELAND	138	1,844,929	4,065,620	5,910,549	725,021	1,539,554	2,264,575	8,175,124
		3,344,207	14,125,686	17,469,893	1,910,338	7,445,858	9,356,196	26,826,089

Total of the Agricultural Interest - - - - - 17,469,893
,, Manufacturing Interest - - - - 9,356,196
Travelling on the right of the Census - - - - - 5,016

Total of the United Kingdom - - - - - 26,831,105

UNITED KINGDOM—SUMMARY OF DIRECT AND LOCAL TAXATION.

	See Page	Paid by the Landed Interest and those dependent on it.	Paid by the Manufacturing Interest and those dependent on it.	TOTAL.
		£	£	£
ENGLAND - - - - -	46	11,278,954	3,751,713	15,030,667
WALES - - - - -	60	733,456	93,121	826,577
SCOTLAND - - - -	95	358,181	184,627	542,808
BRITISH ISLES - - - -	96	*(No Return.)*		
IRELAND - - - -	139	1,511,320	403,536	1,954,856
		13,881,911	4,432,997	18,314,908

Total of Direct and Local Taxation paid by the Agricultural Interest - £13,881,911

     ,,   ,,   Manufacturing Interest - 4,432,997

Total paid by the United Kingdom - - - - - £18,314,908

UNITED KINGDOM—SUMMARY OF PERSONS ENGAGED IN AGRICULTURE.

COUNTIES.		Farmers and Graziers.	Agricultural Labourers, Servants, and Ploughmen.	Gardeners, Nurserymen, and Florists.	TOTAL.
ENGLAND.					
BEDFORD	See Page 1	1,458	12,861	614	14,933
BERKS	2	1,876	18,649	724	21,249
BUCKS	3	2,465	18,860	572	21,897
CAMBRIDGE	4	3,341	18,916	661	22,918
CHESTER	5	7,454	18,455	895	26,804
CORNWALL	6	8,201	18,003	658	26,862
CUMBERLAND	7	5,254	10,079	278	15,611
DERBY	8	6,991	11,776	566	19,333
DEVON	9	12,032	41,054	1,436	54,522
DORSET	10	2,854	15,876	462	19,192
DURHAM	11	3,538	10,089	735	14,362
ESSEX	12	5,110	44,208	1,798	51,116
GLOUCESTER	13	4,953	24,725	1,592	31,270
HEREFORD	14	3,513	12,831	272	16,616
HERTFORD	15	1,780	17,541	824	20,145
HUNTINGDON	16	1,121	7,112	247	8,480
KENT	17	5,477	39,611	2,497	47,585
LANCASTER	18	16,646	30,585	2,338	49,569
LEICESTER	20	3,669	12,770	653	17,092
LINCOLN	21	11,288	45,394	879	57,561
MIDDLESEX	22	1,205	11,668	5,291	18,164
MONMOUTH	24	2,597	5,853	235	8,685
NORFOLK	25	7,447	41,275	1,643	50,365
NORTHAMPTON	26	3,315	21,792	624	25,731
NORTHUMBERLAND	27	3,065	13,659	615	17,339
NOTTINGHAM	28	3,787	15,926	645	20,358
OXFORD	29	2,365	17,909	515	20,789
RUTLAND	30	616	2,629	71	3,316
SALOP	31	5,024	22,361	618	28,003
SOMERSET	32	8,687	34,338	1,442	44,467
SOUTHAMPTON	33	3,614	30,535	1,392	35,541
STAFFORD	34	6,515	21,568	1,037	29,120
SUFFOLK	35	5,382	37,351	1,125	43,858
SURREY	36	2,030	19,282	4,040	25,352
SUSSEX	37	4,042	30,522	1,144	35,708
WARWICK	38	3,799	19,284	1,156	24,239
WESTMORELAND	39	2,478	3,975	113	6,566
WILTS	40	4,456	31,099	835	36,390
WORCESTER	41	3,356	19,243	950	23,549
YORK (EAST RIDING)	42	4,475	18,378	653	23,506
YORK (CITY AND AINSTY)	42	495	1,519	165	2,179
YORK (NORTH RIDING)	43	7,946	19,752	479	28,177
YORK (WEST RIDING)	44	16,738	30,321	2,238	49,297
		212,355	899,734	45,727	1,157,816
WALES.					
ANGLESEY	48	2,348	5,299	73	7,720
BRECON	49	2,107	3,410	72	5,589
CARDIGAN	50	3,467	5,478	51	8,996
CARMARTHEN	51	5,503	8,936	72	14,611
CARNARVON	52	3,496	6,195	122	9,813
DENBIGH	53	3,467	7,767	207	11,441
FLINT	54	1,771	3,586	134	5,491
GLAMORGAN	55	3,191	6,643	252	10,086
MERIONETH	56	2,367	3,262	48	5,677
MONTGOMERY	57	3,483	6,669	77	10,229
PEMBROKE	58	2,993	6,384	93	9,470
RADNOR	59	1,584	3,008	17	4,609
		35,777	66,637	1,218	103,632
SCOTLAND.					
ABERDEEN	62	8,677	15,974	573	25,224
ARGYLE	63	4,546	8,522	119	13,187
AYR	64	3,028	7,829	303	11,160
BANFF	65	2,553	4,925	103	7,581
BERWICK	66	579	5,501	93	6,173
BUTE	67	612	764	43	1,419
CAITHNESS	68	1,915	3,164	37	5,116
CLACKMANNAN	69	126	771	55	952
DUMBARTON	70	521	1,941	141	2,603
DUMFRIES	71	1,858	8,919	161	10,938
EDINBURGH	72	657	5,865	1,234	7,756
ELGIN OR MORAY	73	1,483	3,471	126	5,080
FIFE	74	1,195	8,485	361	10,041
FORFAR	75	1,771	7,905	402	10,078
HADDINGTON	76	321	5,714	133	6,168
INVERNESS	77	3,766	9,800	180	13,746
KINCARDINE	78	1,332	4,419	97	5,848
KINROSS	79	160	857	15	1,032
KIRKCUDBRIGHT	80	1,123	4,007	126	5,257
LANARK	81	2,552	10,029	588	13,169
LINLITHGOW	82	372	2,007	77	2,456
NAIRN	83	393	1,183	15	1,591
ORKNEY AND SHETLAND	84	4,013	2,229	9	6,251
PEEBLES	85	252	1,374	43	1,669
PERTH	86	3,879	11,980	443	16,302
RENFREW	87	1,128	4,410	328	5,866
ROSS AND CROMARTY	88	2,340	7,826	115	10,281
ROXBURGH	89	698	5,634	198	6,530
SELKIRK	90	93	785	24	902
STIRLING	91	1,266	4,945	204	6,415
SUTHERLAND	92	450	2,914	16	3,380
WIGTOWN	93	1,214	3,897	56	5,167
		54,873	168,046	6,418	229,337
ISLANDS IN THE BRITISH SEAS	96	3,960	4,246	287	8,493

UNITED KINGDOM—SUMMARY OF PERSONS ENGAGED IN AGRICULTURE.
(*Continued.*)

COUNTIES.		Farmers and Graziers.	Agricultural Labourers, Servants, and Ploughmen.	Gardeners, Nurserymen, and Florists.	Herdsmen, Caretakers, Land Agents and Stewards, Gamekeepers, Dairykeepers.	TOTAL.
IRELAND.	See Page					
ANTRIM	97	17,868	30,975	260	812	49,915
ARMAGH	98	16,779	21,917	158	614	39,468
BELFAST (Town)	99	102	893	64	45	1,104
CARLOW	100	4,682	16,399	116	463	21,660
CARRICKFERGUS (Town)	101	376	803	11	5	1,195
CAVAN	102	20,038	36,629	116	922	57,705
CLARE	103	20,769	53,877	139	1,330	76,115
CORK (City)	104	160	1,546	128	46	1,880
CORK (County)	105	40,311	145,630	759	4,071	190,771
DONEGAL	106	26,654	41,835	88	2,702	71,279
DOWN	107	21,982	39,143	328	994	62,447
DROGHEDA (Town)	108	46	281	14	24	365
DUBLIN (City)	109	180	829	332	787	2,128
DUBLIN (County)	110	2,222	18,510	1,068	1,143	22,943
FERMANAGH	111	13,305	21,872	75	520	35,772
GALWAY (Town)	112	20	279	12	16	327
GALWAY (County)	113	21,835	89,379	286	2,203	113,703
KERRY	114	19,674	51,210	122	2,057	73,063
KILDARE	115	4,094	24,368	180	931	29,573
KILKENNY (City)	116	63	458	45	23	589
KILKENNY (County)	117	11,709	40,087	136	649	52,581
KING'S COUNTY	118	9,182	29,154	123	481	38,940
LEITRIM	119	13,508	25,133	48	272	38,961
LIMERICK (City)	120	124	1,066	73	39	1,302
LIMERICK (County)	121	15,056	53,688	217	17,87	70,748
LONDONDERRY	122	15,689	25,374	139	1,521	42,723
LONGFORD	123	7,197	21,950	58	195	29,400
LOUTH	124	4,887	16,505	169	546	22,107
MAYO	125	22,486	84,105	161	1,400	108,152
MEATH	126	7,624	35,130	302	2,056	45,112
MONAGHAN	127	16,578	29,798	75	570	47,021
QUEEN'S COUNTY	128	8,664	32,720	144	592	42,120
ROSCOMMON	129	10,876	53,537	115	1,175	65,703
SLIGO	130	13,177	30,086	111	622	43,996
TIPPERARY	131	27,362	79,582	398	2,113	109,455
TYRONE	132	24,307	39,612	149	3,406	67,474
WATERFORD (City)	133	20	468	28	37	553
WATERFORD (County)	134	7,423	42,160	165	991	50,741
WESTMEATH	135	6,665	29,116	136	904	36,821
WEXFORD	136	13,009	35,998	193	530	49,730
WICKLOW	137	6,213	22,042	179	853	29,287
		472,916	1,324,144	7,422	40,447	1,844,929

GENERAL SUMMARY.

	Farmers and Graziers.	Agricultural Labourers, Servants, and Ploughmen.	Gardeners, Nurserymen, and Florists.	Herdsmen, Caretakers, Land Agents and Stewards, Gamekeepers, Dairykeepers.	TOTAL.
ENGLAND	212,355	899,734	45,727	-	1,157,816
WALES	35,777	66,637	1,218	-	103,632
SCOTLAND	54,873	168,046	6,418	-	229,337
ISLANDS IN THE BRITISH SEAS	3,960	4,246	287	-	8,493
IRELAND	472,916	1,324,144	7,422	40,447	1,844,929
TOTAL	779,881	2,462,807	61,072	40,447	3,344,207

TOTAL AMOUNT OF PERSONS ENGAGED IN AGRICULTURE IN THE UNITED KINGDOM - - 3,344,207

UNITED KINGDOM—AGRICULTURE—AGE AND SEX.

SUMMARY OF THE AGE AND SEX OF ALL PERSONS ENGAGED IN AGRICULTURE.

OCCUPATIONS.	MALES.		FEMALES.		TOTAL.
	20 years of age and upwards in Great Britain, and 15 in Ireland.	Under 20 years of age in Great Britain, and 15 in Ireland.	20 years of age and upwards in Great Britain, and 15 in Ireland.	Under 20 years of age in Great Britain, and 15 in Ireland.	
FARMERS AND GRAZIERS:					
ENGLAND	194,596	2,467	15,392	- -	212,455
WALES	31,807	190	3,780	- -	35,777
ISLES IN THE BRITISH SEAS	3,752	44	164	- -	3,960
SCOTLAND	50,732	354	3,787	- -	54,873
IRELAND	453,096	168	18,126	8	471,398
	733,983	3,223	41,249	8	778,463
AGRICULTURAL LABOURERS:					
ENGLAND	724,625	139,661	26,888	8,460	899,634
WALES	47,447	17,155	1,300	735	66,637
ISLES IN THE BRITISH SEAS	3,247	626	335	38	4,246
SCOTLAND	109,550	39,854	13,528	5,114	168,046
IRELAND	1,127,484	102,739	108,173	18,481	1,356,877
	2,012,353	300,035	150,224	32,828	2,495,440
GARDENERS, NURSERYMEN, AND FLORISTS:					
ENGLAND	42,364	2,165	1,074	124	45,727
WALES	1,141	59	16	2	1,218
ISLES IN THE BRITISH SEAS	276	11	-	-	287
SCOTLAND	5,727	615	65	11	6,418
IRELAND	7,378	31	12	-	7,421
	57,886	2,881	1,167	137	61,071
ALL OTHER CLASSES; more particularly enumerated in the Irish Abstract, viz.:					
LAND AGENTS	174	- -	-	- -	174
„ STEWARDS	4,829	- -	6	- -	4,835
GAME KEEPERS	439	- -	-	- -	439
DAIRY KEEPERS	1,720	2,034	8	23	3,785
	7,162	2,034	14	23	9,233
	2,810,384	308,173	192,654	32,996	3,344,207

RECAPITULATION.

MALES.—20 years of age and upwards in Great Britain, and 15 in Ireland - 2,810,384

„   Under 20 years of age in Great Britain, and 15 in Ireland - - 308,173

    TOTAL—MALES - - - - 3,118,557

FEMALES.—20 years of age and upwards in Great Britain, and 15 in Ireland 192,654

„   Under 20 years of age in Great Britain, and 15 in Ireland - 32,996

    TOTAL—FEMALES - - - - 225,650

    TOTAL—MALES and FEMALES of all ages employed in AGRICULTURE - - 3,344,207

UNITED KINGDOM—MANUFACTURES.

THE MANUFACTURING INTEREST

OF THE

UNITED KINGDOM.

GREAT BRITAIN—MANUFACTURES.

TABLE SHOWING THE NUMBER OF PERSONS IN GREAT BRITAIN ENGAGED IN
THE SIX MOST IMPORTANT BRANCHES OF THE TEXTILE FABRICS, viz. :
THE MANUFACTURE OF COTTON, HOSE, LACE, WOOL AND WORSTED, SILK, AND FLAX AND LINEN.

	MALES.		FEMALES.		TOTAL.
COTTON.	20 years of age and upwards.	Under 20 years of age.	20 years of age and upwards.	Under 20 years of age.	
England and Wales, and Isles in the British Seas	73,819	36,727	67,182	50,440	228,168
Scotland	31,991	12,241	16,648	13,328	74,208
Total	105,810	48,968	83,830	63,768	302,376
Add proportion of Fabric not specified	32,302	10,203	20,640	12,141	75,286
Total of Great Britain	138,112	59,171	104,470	75,909	377,662
HOSE.					
England and Wales, and Isles in the British Seas	23,820	3,726	6,071	2,371	35,988
Scotland	1,632	416	2,066	99	3,943
Total	25,182	4,142	8,137	2,470	39,931
Add proportion of Fabric not specified	7,688	863	2,003	470	11,024
Total of Great Britain	32,870	5,005	10,140	2,940	50,955
LACE.					
England and Wales, and Isles in the British Seas	5,330	1,072	14,425	5,655	26,482
Scotland	43	10	1,451	429	1,933
Total	5,373	1,082	15,876	6,084	28,415
Add proportion of Fabric not specified	1,640	225	3,909	1,158	6,932
Total of Great Britain	7,013	1,307	19,785	7,242	35,347
WOOL AND WORSTED.					
England and Wales, and Isles in the British Seas	66,092	17,758	21,819	15,580	121,249
Scotland	6,508	1,753	1,510	1,123	10,894
Total	72,600	19,511	23,329	16,703	132,143
Add proportion of Fabric not specified	22,164	4,065	5,744	3,180	35,153
Total of Great Britain	94,764	23,576	29,073	19,883	167,296
SILK.					
England and Wales, and Isles in the British Seas	22,267	7,170	20,723	12,509	62,669
Scotland	2,191	521	767	743	4,222
Total	24,458	7,691	21,490	13,252	66,891
Add proportion of Fabric not specified	7,466	1,602	5,291	2,523	16,882
Total of Great Britain	31,924	9,293	26,781	15,775	83,773
FLAX AND LINEN.					
England and Wales, and Isles in the British Isles	8,819	2,817	3,504	4,008	19,148
Scotland	21,395	6,211	13,203	7,791	48,600
Total	30,214	9,028	16,707	11,799	67,748
Add proportion of Fabric not specified	9,224	1,880	4,114	2,247	17,465
Total of Great Britain	39,438	10,908	20,821	14,846	85,213
FABRIC NOT SPECIFIED.					
England and Wales, and Isles in the British Seas	65,462	14,932	28,483	15,927	124,804
Scotland	15,022	3,906	13,218	5,792	37,938
Total of Great Britain	80,484	18,838	41,701	21,719	162,742
TOTAL OF TEXTILE FABRICS.					
England and Wales, and Isles in the British Seas	265,609	84,202	162,207	106,490	618,508
Scotland	78,512	25,058	48,863	29,305	181,738
Total of Great Britain	344,121	109,260	211,070	135,795	800,246

UNITED KINGDOM—MANUFACTURES.

SUMMARY OF PERSONS ENGAGED IN MANUFACTURES,

SHOWING THE NUMBER ENGAGED IN EACH SEPARATE BRANCH.

OCCUPATIONS.	ENGLAND, WALES, and ISLES IN THE BRITISH SEAS.	SCOTLAND.	IRELAND.	TOTAL.
Alkali Manufacture - - - - -	118	5	- -	123
Alum ,, - - - - - -	220	2	- -	222
Anchor Smiths and Chain Makers - - -	1,737	115	- -	1,852
Annatto Makers - - - - -	4	- - -	- -	4
Anti-dry-rot Works - - - -	1	- -	- -	1
Anvil Makers - - - - -	119	- -	- -	119
Asphalte Manufactures - - - -	5	- -	- -	5
Basket Makers - - - - -	5,726	297	849	6,872
Bayonet Forgers and Makers - - -	28	- -	- -	28
Bead Makers - - - - -	55	- -	- -	55
Bell Founders - - - - -	27	1	- -	28
Bit Makers (all branches) - - -	843	4	- -	847
Blacklead Manufactures - - - -	23	- -	- -	23
Blade Makers and Forgers - - -	333	- -	- -	333
Bleachers (branch not specified) - -	4,070	3,126	2,547	9,743
Block and Print Cutters - - -	1,195	539	88	1,822
Blue Manufacturers - - - -	61	1	10	72
Bobbin Makers and Turners - - -	1,010	26	- -	1,036
Boiler Makers - - - - -	2,752	727	- -	3,479
Bolt Makers - - - - -	253	6	- -	259
Bombazine Manufacturers - -	41	- -	- -	41
Bone Crushers and Millers - - -	34	11	- -	45
Bone Turners, Cutlers, and Workers - -	206	7	- -	213
Bow-string Makers - - - -	17	2	- -	19
Brace and Belt Makers - - - -	622	16	42	680
Braid Makers - - - - -	78	4	- -	82
Brass Founders and Moulders - - -	5,459	933	- -	6,392
Brick and Tile Makers - - - -	17,221	1,142	426	18,789
Brimstone Manufacturers - -	7	-	- -	7
Buckle Makers - - - - -	252	- -	- -	252
Buhl Cutters and Workers - - -	26	- -	- -	26
Button Makers (all branches) - -	3,915	40	156	4,111
Candlestick Makers - - - -	64	1	- -	65
Candle-wick and Lamp-wick Makers - -	48	15	- -	63
Cane Dressers and Workers - - -	192	1	- -	193
Canvas Makers and Weavers - - -	329	748	3	1,080
Card Makers - - - - -	2,052	103	3,249	5,404
Card (Paper) Makers - - - -	164	- -	- -	164
Carpet and Rug Manufacturers - -	3,023	1,094	16	4,133
Castor Makers - - - - -	54	- -	- -	54
Catgut Makers and Gut Blowers and Spinners -	9	1	- -	10
Cement Grinders - - - - -	100	6	- -	106
Chain (Curb) Makers - - - -	76	- -	- -	76
Chair Makers - - - - -	4,905	218	- -	5,123
Charcoal Burners - - - -	216	63	- -	279
Chemists (Manufacturing) - - -	544	140	- -	684
Chocolate Manufactures - - -	37	- -	- -	37
Clasp Makers - - - - -	17	- -	- -	17
Clay Workers - - - - -	365	10	- -	375
Coach-lace Makers and Weavers - -	133	12	- -	145
Coach-lamp Makers - - - -	36	- -	- -	36
Cock Founders - - - - -	162	- -	- -	162
Coke Burners - - - - -	930	7	- -	937
Colour Manufacturers - - - -	473	165	- -	638
Comb Makers - - - - -	1,752	369	277	2,398
Composition Makers - - - -	34	- -	- -	34
Copper Manufacturers - - - -	2,126	14	- -	2,140
Copperplate Makers and Workers - -	26	7	- -	33
Copper Smiths - - - - -	1,100	219	- -	1,319
Copperas Manufacturers - - -	33	19	- -	52
Corduroy Cutters and Weavers - - -	- -	- -	150	150
Cork screw Makers - - - -	70	- -	- -	70
Cotton-band Makers - - - -	40	- -	- -	40
Cotton Manufactures (all branches) - -	213,944	66,945	6,033	286,922
Cover Makers - - - - -	19	- -	- -	19
Cover (Table) Makers - - - -	12	- -	- -	12
Coverlet Makers - - - -	17	- -	- -	17
Crape Manufacturers (all branches) - -	323	7	- -	330
Crate Makers - - - - -	550	7	- -	557
Crucible and Casting Pot Makers - -	36	- -	- -	36
Curry Comb Makers - - - -	80	- -	- -	80
Distillers and Rectifiers - - -	313	400	204	917
Drug Grinders and Manufacturers - -	21	9	- -	30
Dye Manufacturers (all branches) - -	123	142	- -	265
Dyers (Calico and Cotton) - - -	1,451	201		
,, (Fur) - - - - -	22	-		
,, (Fustian) - - - -	104	-		
,, (Leather) - - - -	167	2	899	4,930
,, (Linen) - - - -	24	8		
,, (Silk) - - - -	1,072	91		
,, (Wool and Woollen) - - -	772	117		
Engine and Machine Makers - - -	6,264	925	1,324	8,513
Engine Turners - - - - -	104	4	- -	108

UNITED KINGDOM—SUMMARY OF MANUFACTURES.

(*Continued.*)

OCCUPATIONS.	ENGLAND, WALES, and ISLES IN THE BRITISH SEAS.	SCOTLAND.	IRELAND.	TOTAL.
Engineers - - - - - -	21,419	3,951	434	25,804
Eye (Artificial) Makers - - - -	9	-	-	9
Factory Workers (Manufactures not specified) - -	16,245	6,233	8,193	30,671
Fancy Goods Manufacturers - - -	3,573	52	-	3,625
Felt Makers - - - - -	201	6	-	207
Fence and Hurdle Makers - - -	256	16	-	272
Fender Makers - - - -	462	-	-	462
Fent (Cotton) Makers - - - -	38	-	-	38
File Makers (all branches) - - -	4,267	31	-	4,298
Filter Makers - - - - -	16	-	-	16
Fire-iron Makers - - - -	130	-	-	130
Fire-work Makers - - - -	96	-	-	96
Fish-hook Makers - - - -	192	21	-	213
Flannel Manufacturers (all branches) - -	628	2	-	630
Flask Makers - - - - -	5	-	-	5
Flask (Powder) Makers - - - -	50	-	-	50
Flax and Linen Manufacturers (all branches) - -	15,917	45,837	135,303	197,057
Flint Millers - - - - -	85	10	-	95
Flock Manufacturers - - - -	70	-	-	70
Floor Cloth Manufacturers - - -	299	7	-	306
Fork Makers - - - - -	571	-	-	571
Founders (branch not specified) - - -	958	351	-	1,309
Fringe Manufacturers - - -	643	87	64	794
Fullers - - - - -	1,219	12	-	1,231
Fustian Manufacturers - - -	3,554	4	-	3,558
Gauze Manufacturers - - - -	49	4	-	53
Gimp Spinners and Weavers - - -	10	-	-	10
Girth Web Makers and Weavers - - -	77	16	-	93
Glass and Emery Paper Makers - - -	69	4	-	73
Glass and Glass Bottle Manufacturers - -	6,745	662	358	7,765
Glass Painters and Stainers - - -	100	8	-	108
Glass Plate Makers - - - -	57	-	-	57
Glove Makers - - - -	8,835	72	777	9,684
Glove (Silk) Makers - - - -	318	-	-	318
Glue and Size Makers - - - -	198	25	24	247
Gold Beater's Skin Makers - - -	2	-	-	2
Gold Lace Makers - - - -	94	4	-	98
Grate, Range, and Stove Makers - - -	212	5	-	217
Grease Makers - - - -	46	2	-	48
Grinders - - - - -	2,841	33	-	2,874
Guard-chain Makers - - - -	26	-	-	26
Gun Makers - - - -	4,868	183	362	5,413
Gun (Air) Makers - - - -	2	-	-	2
Gun (Barrel) Makers - - -	307	-	-	307
Gun Flint Makers - - - -	76	-	-	76
Gun Implement and Cartridge Makers - -	42	-	-	42
Gunpowder Makers - - - -	153	49	-	202
Hackle Makers - - - - -	55	44	28	127
Haft and Scale Makers and Turners - -	760	-	-	760
Hair Manufacturers (all branches) - -	854	257	103	1,214
Hat Box Makers - - - -	271	43	-	314
Hat Block Makers - - - -	25	7	-	32
Hatters and Hat Manufacturers (all branches) - -	17,194	818	2,310	20,322
Heald Makers - - - - -	199	142	6	347
Hemp Manufacturers (all branches) - -	353	518	-	871
Hinge Makers - - - -	769	31	-	800
Hook and Eye Makers - - - -	114	1	-	115
Hoop Makers - - - - -	726	30	-	756
Horn Turners and Workers - - -	82	15	-	97
Hose (Stockings) Manufacturers (all branches) -	35,988	3,943	-	39,931
Hot Pressers - - - - -	142	5	-	147
India Rubber and Mackintosh Manufacturers -	157	3	-	160
Ink Makers - - - - -	87	18	-	105
Ink-stand Makers - - - -	60	-	-	60
Instrument Makers - - - -	154	-	-	154
Iron Box Makers - - - -	8	-	-	8
Iron Manufacturers - - -	25,878	3,618	546	30,042
Iron Masters - - - -	202	24	-	226
Isinglass Makers - - - -	16	-	-	16
Ivory Cutters and Workers - - -	486	4	-	490
Jack Makers - - - - -	47	-	-	47
Jack (Bottle) Makers - - - -	34	-	-	34
Jack (Coach) Makers - - - -	2	-	-	2
Japanners - - - - -	1,649	84	13	1,746
Jet Carvers and Workers - - -	36	-	-	36
Kelp Manufacturers (all branches) - -	-	26	-	26
Knife Makers (all branches) - - -	1,878	-	-	1,878
Knitters - - - - -	1,441	142	23,019	24,602
Knitters (Frame Work) - - -	312	9	-	321
Label Makers - - - - -	2	-	-	2
Lace Manufacturers - - -	26,482	1,933	1,862	30,277
Lamp, Lantern, and Chandelier Makers - -	423	-	12	435
Lamp Black Makers - - - -	13	-	-	13
Lead Manufacturers (all branches) - -	1,178	115	-	1,293
Leather Embossers and Gilders - - -	42	-	-	42

UNITED KINGDOM—SUMMARY OF MANUFACTURES.

(Continued.)

OCCUPATIONS.	ENGLAND, WALES, and ISLES IN THE BRITISH SEAS.	SCOTLAND.	IRELAND.	TOTAL.
Letter Cutters and Makers - - - - -	41	- -	- -	41
Lime Burners - - - - - -	1,801	310	360	2,471
Lint Manufacturers - - - - - -	125	504	- -	629
Looking Glass Makers - - - - -	183	12	15	210
Mangle Makers - - - - - -	31	- -	- -	31
Marble Turners and Workers - - -	15	- -	18	33
Mat Makers - - - - - - -	833	39	245	1,117
Metal Manufacturers (all branches, including White and Britannia Metal and German Silver) -}	1,583	13	- -	1,596
Millstone Makers - - - - -	45	9	1	55
Miscellaneous Manufacturers - - - -	- -	- -	107	107
Morocco Leather Manufacturers - - -	13	- -	- -	13
Mould Makers - - - - - -	171	5	- -	176
Moulders (branch not specified) - - -	3,465	893	- -	4,358
Musical Instrument Makers - - - -	1,929	180	105	2,214
Musical String Makers - - - - -	48	1	- -	49
Muslin Embroiderers - - - - -	- -	3,326	- -	3,326
Muslin Manufacturers - - - - -	139	735	- -	874
Mustard Manufacturers - - - - -	118	1	2	121
Nail Makers - - - - - -	18,691	1,620	6,276	26,587
Needle Makers - - - - - -	2,509	15	5	2,529
Net Makers - - - - - -	236	355	1,147	1,738
Oil Miliers - - - - - -	283	2	- -	285
Organ Builders - - - - - -	378	16	- -	394
Ormolu Maker - - - - - -	1	- -	- -	1
Oven Makers - - - - - -	8	- -	- -	8
Pan Makers - - - - - -	36	- -	- -	36
Pan Smiths (Salt) - - - - -	26	- -	- -	26
Paper Manufacturers - - - - -	5,690	1,470	713	7,873
Paper Stainers - - - - - -	1,335	32	296	1,663
Papier-maché and Tray Manufacturers - -	194	- -	- -	194
Parchment Makers - - - - -	337	2	33	372
Pasteboard Makers - - - - -	44	3	- -	47
Pattern Designer and Makers - - - -	1, 47	625	23	1,795
Pattern Card Makers - - - - -	91	- -	- -	91
Peg Makers - - - - - -	20	- -	- -	20
Pen and Penholder Makers - - - -	234	2	- -	236
Pen (Steel) Makers - - - - -	327	- -	- -	327
Pencil Makers - - - - - -	250	4	- -	254
Pencil-case Makers - - - - -	45	1	- -	46
Percussion and Metal Cap Maker - - -	46	- -	- -	46
Pewterers and Pewter Pot Makers - - -	311	10	- -	321
Pin Manufacturers (all branches) - - -	1,306	24	385	1,715
Pipe Makers - - - - - -	2,721	111	- -	2,832
Pipe (Tobacco) Makers - - - - -	174	35	234	443
Plaister and Strapping Makers - - -	5	- -	- -	5
Plaster Manufacturers - - - - -	26	- -	3	29
Plated Ware Manufacturers - - - -	56	- -	- -	56
Platers - - - - - - -	1,583	9	10	1,602
Plush and Shag Manufacturers - - -	260	6	- -	266
Polishing Paste Makers - - - - -	4	- -	- -	4
Pottery, China, and Earthenware Manufacturers -	23,811	963	218	24,992
Press Makers - - - - - -	42	- -	- -	42
Press Workers - - - - - -	65	- -	- -	65
Printers (Cotton and Calico) - - - -	8,976	6,327	345	15,648
Print Cutters - - - - - -	- -	- -	48	48
Printers (Silk) - - - - - -	171	6	- -	177
Printers (Woollen) - - - - -	940	- -	- -	940
Purse Makers - - - - - -	23	- -	- -	23
Quill Cutters - - - - - -	104	37	58	199
Quilter and Quilt Makers - - - -	204	6	- -	210
Rack Makers - - - - - -	3	- -	- -	3
Razor Makers - - - - - -	581	- -	- -	581
Razor-case Makers - - - - -	23	- -	- -	23
Red Lead Makers - - - - -	8	1	- -	9
Reed Makers - - - - - -	515	144	472	1,131
Reel Makers - - - - - -	13	5	- -	18
Refiners - - - - - - -	184	5	- -	189
Ribbon Manufacturers (all branches) - -	6,826	5	168	6,999
Ring Makers and Turners - - - -	44	- -	- -	44
Rivet Makers - - - - - -	25	11	- -	36
Roller Makers and Turners - - - -	602	27	- -	629
Rope and Cord Spinners and Makers - -	9,485	1,834	1,081	12,400
Sail, Sail-cloth, and Tarpaulin Manufacturers -	3,384	499	205	4,088
Salt Manufacturers - - - - -	604	32	52	688
Scagliola Makers - - - - -	18	- -	- -	18
Scissors Makers - - - - - -	1,042	- -	- -	1,042
Screw Cutter and Makers - - - -	1,242	7	- -	1,249
Scum Boilers - - - - - -	5	- -	- -	5
Scuttle Makers - - - - - -	5	- -	- -	5
Sealing-wax Makers - - - - -	55	8	- -	63
Shawl Manufacturers - - - - -	204	1,055	1	1,260
Shot Makers - - - - - -	23	- -	- -	23
Shovel Makers - - - - - -	67	- -	- -	68
Shuttle Makers - - - - - -	365	1	- -	418
Sickle Makers - - - - - -	- -	43	10	26
		- -	26	

UNITED KINGDOM—SUMMARY OF MANUFACTURES.

(*Continued.*)

OCCUPATIONS.	ENGLAND, WALES, and ISLES IN THE BRITISH SEAS.	SCOTLAND.	IRELAND.	TOTAL.
Sieve Makers - - - - -	360	63	234	657
Silk Manufacturers - - - - -	54,144	4,101	602	58,847
Sinker Makers - - - - -	207	-	-	207
Skate Makers - - - - -	3	-	-	3
Skewer Makers - - - - -	15	1	-	16
Skin Dressers and Skinners - - - -	1,604	437	304	2,345
Slate Manufacturers - - - -	271	22	-	293
Small-ware Manufacturers - - - -	600	11	-	611
Smelters (ore not specified) - - -	664	-	-	664
Snuff and Tobacco Box Makers - -	6	130	-	136
Snuffer Makers - - - -	180	-	-	180
Soap Boilers and Makers - - -	680	58	1,416	2,154
Soda Manufacturers - - -	36	3	-	39
Spile Makers - - - - -	14	-	-	14
Spindle Makers - - - - -	240	16	-	256
Spinners (branch not specified) - -	9,350	3,630	*334,201	347,181
Spoon Makers - - - -	487	51	-	538
Spring Makers - - - -	331	4	-	335
Spring (Door) Makers - - - -	13	-	-	13
Spring (Secret) Makers - - -	64	-	-	64
Spur Makers - - - - -	136	-	10	146
Stamp Makers - - - - -	6	1	-	7
Starch Manufacturers - - - -	141	18	70	229
Steel Workers - - - - -	147	2	-	149
Steelyard Makers - - - -	50	-	-	50
Stereotype Founders - - - -	15	8	-	23
Stirrup Makers - - - -	158	1	-	159
Straw Plait Manufacturers - - -	9,800	1,417	704	11,921
Stuff Manufacturers - - - -	6,574	-	1	6,575
Sugar Bakers and Boilers - - -	912	170	-	1,082
Swivel Makers - - - - -	4	-	-	4
Sword Cutlers and Makers - - -	116	-	-	116
Tag Makers and Dealers - - -	13	-	-	13
Tambour Workers - - - -	-	-	882	882
Tank Makers - - - - -	13	-	-	13
Tanners - - - - -	5,826	775	852	7,453
Tape Manufacturers (all branches) - -	937	59	21	1,017
Tar and Rosin Makers - - -	23	-	-	23
Tartan Manufacturers - - -	-	241	-	'241
Tassel Makers - - - -	87	9	25	121
Tea and Coffee Pot Makers - - -	19	-	-	19
Thimble Makers - - - -	97	-	-	97
Thread Manufacturers - - -	757	800	166	1,723
Thread (Shoe) Makers and Winders -	57	-	-	57
Tin Manufacturers (all branches) - -	1,320	-	-	1,320
Tinfoil Makers - - - -	18	-	-	18
Tip Makers - - - - -	39	-	-	39
Tonbridge Ware Manufacturers - -	23	-	-	23
Tool Dealers and Makers - - -	4,685	233	108	5,026
Treenail Makers - - - -	21	-	-	21
Trimming Makers - - - -	399	3	-	402
Turners - - - - -	6,117	1,042	722	7,881
Turpentine Distillers and Makers - -	24	2	-	26
Type Founders - - - -	635	292	35	962
Urn Makers - - - - -	57	-	-	57
Varnish Makers - - - -	140	2	-	142
Vinegar Makers - - - -	54	6	1	61
Vitriol Manufacturers - - - -	106	9	3	118
Wadding Makers - - - -	67	-	-	67
Wafer Makers - - - -	35	2	-	37
Weavers (Tabinet) - - - -	-	-	19	19
Weavers (branch not specified) - -	88,415	21,616	*91,086	201,117
Weighing Machine Makers - - -	12	-	-	12
Whalebone Workers - - - -	82	-	-	82
White-lead Makers - - - -	47	-	-	47
Whiting Manufacturers - - -	84	-	-	84
Willow Weavers and Workers - -	208	-	-	208
Winders and Warpers - - - -	-	-	7,564	7,564
Wire Drawers and Makers - - -	1,324	35	32	1,391
Wire Rope Makers - - - -	4	-	-	4
Wire Workers and Weavers - - -	1,480	63	101	1,644
Woollen and Cloth Manufacturers (all branches) - -	88,436	8,917	77,650	175,003
Worsted Manufactures (all branches) - -	20,835	523	11	21,369
Yarn Manufactures - - - -	334	2,058	-	2,392
Zinc Manufacturers and Workers - -	230	2	-	232
Unclassified - - - - -	-	-	-	5,682
TOTAL - - - -	924,096	216,810	*725,021	1,865,927

See note at page 152.

UNITED KINGDOM—MANUFACTURES—AGE AND SEX.

SUMMARY OF THE AGE AND SEX OF ALL PERSONS ENGAGED IN MANUFACTURES.

	MALES.		FEMALES.		
	20 years of age and upwards in Great Britain, and 15 in Ireland.	Under 20 years of age in Great Britain, and 15 in Ireland.	20 years of age and upwards in Great Britain, and 15 in Ireland.	Under 20 years of age in Great Britain, and 15 in Ireland.	TOTAL.
ENGLAND AND WALES, AND ISLES IN THE BRITISH SEAS	479,774	130,443	191,968	121,911	924,096
SCOTLAND - - -	99,672	31,983	53,894	31,261	216,810
GREAT BRITAIN - - -	579,446	162,426	245,862	153,172	1,140,906
IRELAND - - -	138,334	6,538	542,384	37,765	*725,021
TOTAL - - - -	717,780	168,964	788,246	190,937	1,865,927

RECAPITULATION.

MALES—20 years of age and upwards in Great Britain, and 15 in Ireland - - 717,780
  ,,   Under 20 years of age in Great Britain, and 15 in Ireland - - - 168,964
FEMALES—20 years of age and upwards in Great Britain, and 15 in Ireland - - 788,246
  ,,   Under 20 years of age in Great Britain, and 15 in Ireland - - - 190,937
                                                                        ───────
                                                                       1,865,927

* From the above statement, which is corroborated by the Summaries of the several Counties given in this work, and by the Summary of Manufactures at page 151, the number of persons employed in the Manufactures of Ireland is stated at 725,021. Of these, 699,485 are returned as "Ministering to Clothing," of whom no less than 573,860 are stated to be females. This item, however, requires further explanation. The only branches of Manufactures of any importance in Ireland employ about 215,000 persons, viz. :

Flax and Linen - - - - - - - 135,303
Woollen - - - - - - - - 77,650
Silk, Tabbinet, Ribbon, Fringe, &c. - - - - 1,776
                                              ───────
                                              214,729
Miscellaneous Manufactures of every kind - - - 85,005
                                                        ───────
                                                        299,734
To this is added, in the Government Summary,—
Spinners (branch not specified) - - - - 334,201
Weavers   ,, - - - - 91,086
                                        ───────
                                        425,287
                                        ───────
                                        725,021

In what branch of Manufactures these 425,287 persons are engaged does not appear, and it is clear that the produce of their labour does not form the staple of any important branch of Manufactures carried on in Ireland. The only solution of the difficulty is, that, after the fashion of the English Counties in the olden time, there is a large amount of spinning and weaving done in private houses for the consumption of the particular individual or family, and these do in truth belong to the Agricultural Interest, and are supported by it.

Instead, therefore, of estimating the number of persons engaged in Manufactures in Ireland at 725,021, according to the Government return, we estimate it in round numbers at 300,000, and the number of persons dependent on these at 700,000, leaving to be supported by and dependent on the Agricultural Interest in Ireland, 7,175,124 persons; and with this correction the Agricultural and Manufacturing Population of the United Kingdom will stand thus :

		AGRICULTURE.	MANUFACTURES.
	See Page		
ENGLAND - - - - 46		9,312,311	5,682,827
WALES - - - - 60		754,380	157,223
SCOTLAND - - - - 94		1,388,596	1,231,588
BRITISH ISLES - - 96		104,057	19,983
IRELAND, corrected as above stated -		7,175,124	1,00 ,000
		18,714,468	8,091,621
			26,826,089
Persons travelling on the night of the Census - -			5,016
TOTAL POPULATION OF THE UNITED KINGDOM -			26,831,105

UNITED KINGDOM—ALL OTHER CLASSES

DEPENDENT ON, AND SUPPORTED BY, AGRICULTURE AND MANUFACTURES,

IN THE PROPORTION WHICH THESE RESPECTIVELY BEAR TO EACH OTHER,
IN THE WHOLE POPULATION OF THE UNITED KINGDOM;

VIZ.,

TRADE AND COMMERCE—ALL PERSONS EMPLOYED IN RETAIL TRADE OR IN HANDICRAFT,
AS MASTERS OR WORKMEN.

THE MINING INTEREST.

THE SHIPPING INTEREST.

PROFESSIONAL PERSONS.

OTHER EDUCATED PERSONS, FOLLOWING MISCELLANEOUS PURSUITS.

PERSONS RETURNED AS INDEPENDENT.

PERSONS ENGAGED IN THE GOVERNMENT CIVIL SERVICE.

PAROCHIAL, TOWN, AND CHURCH OFFICERS.

DOMESTIC SERVANTS.

LABOURERS.

ALMSPEOPLE, PENSIONERS, PAUPERS, LUNATICS, AND PRISONERS.

UNITED KINGDOM—TRADE AND COMMERCE.

SUMMARY OF PERSONS ENGAGED IN TRADE AND COMMERCE,

DEPENDENT ON AGRICULTURE AND MANUFACTURES IN THE PROPORTION WHICH THESE RESPECTIVELY BEAR TO EACH OTHER.

OCCUPATIONS.	ENGLAND, WALES, and ISLES IN THE BRITISH SEAS.	SCOTLAND.	IRELAND.	TOTAL.
Accoutrement Makers - - - -	133	- -	7	140
Agents and Factors - - - - - -	5,030	557	895	6,482
Agricultural Implement Makers - - -	1,048	32	- -	1,080
Animal and Bird Dealers - - - -	83	18	- -	101
Animal and Bird Preservers - - - -	77	- -	- -	77
Archery Goods Dealers and Makers - - -	44	19	- -	63
Armourers - - - - - -	14	- -	- -	14
Army Agents - - - - - -	23	3	- -	26
Army Clothiers - - - - -	37	- -	- -	37
Army Contractors - - - - - -	11	- -	- -	11
Articulators (Anatomical Instrument Makers) -	1	1	- -	2
Assay Masters - - - - - -	4	- -	- -	4
Assayers - - - - - -	66	2	- -	68
Auctioneers, Appraisers, and House Agents - -	3,061	242	241	3,544
Axletree Makers - - - - -	34	- -	- -	34
Baby Linen Dealers and Makers - - -	77	16	- -	93
Bacon and Ham Dealers and Factors - -	287	45	11	343
Bakers - - - - - -	37,143	7,334	6,698	51,175
Ball Makers - - - - - -	54	7	- -	61
Bark Dealers - - - - - -	5	- -	- -	5
Barm Makers - - - - - -	- -	- -	10	10
Barometer and Thermometer Makers - - -	125	7	- -	132
Bat Makers - - - - -	35	1	- -	36
Bath Keepers - - - - - -	195	17	33	245
,, Makers - - - - -	7	- -	- -	7
Bazaar Keepers - - - - -	44	1	- -	45
Bed and Mattress Makers - - - -	363	18	- -	381
Bedstead Makers - - - - -	396	- -	- -	396
Bee Dealer - - - - - -	1	- -	- -	1
Bee Hive Makers - - - - -	49	1	- -	50
Bellows Makers - - - - -	234	1	93	328
Billiard Table Makers - - - -	11	- -	1	12
,, Keepers - - - -	100	10	- -	110
Bird Stuffers - - - - -	- -	- -	4	4
,, Dealers - - - - -	- -	- -	1	1
Blacking Makers and Dealers - - - -	379	23	44	446
Blacksmiths - - - - - -	82,180	15,160	25,185	122,525
Bladder Dealers and Merchants - - -	5	- -	- -	5
Blind Makers - - - - - -	341	13	- -	354
Block, Oar, and Mast Makers - - - -	1,247	241	- -	1,488
Boat Builders - - - - -	2,444	480	1	2,925
,, and Barge Owners - - - -	185	2	- -	187
Bone Merchants - - - - -	182	10	- -	192
Bonnet Makers - - - - -	5,007	611	5,669	11,287
Booksellers, Bookbinders, and Publishers - -	10,908	2,447	1,028	14,383
Boot and Shoe Makers - - - -	187,943	26,837	50,334	265,114
Bottle Dealers and Merchants - - -	136	- -	- -	136
Braziers, Brass Finishers and Workers, and Tinkers -	6,332	340	1,764	8,436
Brewers - - - - - -	9,357	1,085	367	10,809
Bricklayers - - - - - -	39,411	395	1,331	41,137
Bridge and Canal Contractors - - -	6	- -	- -	6
Brogue Makers - - - - -	- -	- -	5,394	5,394
Brokers (all branches) - - - -	3,945	677	857	5,479
Bronzers - - - - - -	20	- -	- -	20
Brush (Artists') and Hair Pencil Makers - -	13	- -	- -	13
Brush and Broom Makers - - - -	5,945	332	834	7,111
Builders - - - - -	8,555	633	792	9,980
Building Material Dealers - - - -	6	- -	- -	6
Bullion Brokers and Merchants - - -	10	- -	- -	10
Burnishers - - - - - -	255	- -	- -	255
Butchers - - - - - -	44,683	3,194	5,332	53,209
,, (Pork) - - - - -	812	8	- -	820
Butter Dealers, Merchants, and Factors - -	311	15	81	407
,, Inspectors - - - -	- -	- -	3	3
Button Dealers and Merchants - - -	46	- -	- -	46
Cabinet Makers and Upholsterers - - -	26,387	4,325	3,086	33,798
Cage Makers - - - - -	71	- -	8	79
Canal Agents - - - - -	26	1	- -	27
Cane Merchants - - - - -	6	1	- -	7
Cap Makers and Dealers - - - -	1,499	154	456	2,109
Carpenters and Joiners - - - -	138,515	24,462	38,891	201,868
Carpet Dealers and Warehousemen - - -	558	1	- -	559
Carpet Bag Makers - - - - -	17	- -	- -	17
Carriers, Carters, and Waggoners - - -	26,494	7,802	8,318	42,614
Cart Makers - - - - -	- -	- -	722	722
Carvers and Gilders - - - - -	4,098	533	258	4,889
Case Makers - - - - -	256	2	- -	258
Cattle and Sheep Dealers and Salesmen - -	2,263	703	919	3,885
Cellarmen - - - - -	427	33	- -	460
Chaff Cutters - - - - -	67	- -	- -	67

156

UNITED KINGDOM—SUMMARY OF PERSONS ENGAGED IN TRADE, &c.
(Continued.)

OCCUPATIONS.	ENGLAND, WALES, and ISLES IN THE BRITISH SEAS.	SCOTLAND.	IRELAND.	TOTAL.
Chair Letters	113	-	15	128
Chasers	449	11	-	460
„ (Herald)	32	-	-	32
Cheesemongers and Factors	2,426	31	3	2,460
Chemists and Druggists	10,122	731	177	11,030
Chimney Sweepers	4,697	331	642	5,670
China, Earthenware, and Glass Dealers	2,643	451	179	3,273
Cider Merchants and Dealers	56	2	9	67
Clay Agents and Merchants	40	5	-	45
Clerks of Works	-	-	5	5
Clock and Watch Makers	13,577	1,202	885	15,664
Cloth Merchants and Salesmen	47	144	-	191
Clothes Dealers and Outfitters	518	62	-	580
Clothiers	11,022	562	-	11,584
Coach Makers (all branches)	11,802	801	1,425	14,028
Coach, Cab, and Omnibus Owners	1,520	55	122	1,697
Coal and Colliery Agents and Bailiffs	635	302	-	937
„ Fitters	120	-	-	120
„ Labourers, Heavers, and Porters	8,752	472	132	9,356
„ Merchants and Dealers	6,346	634	316	7,296
„ Meters	282	10	-	292
„ Owners	338	85	-	423
Coffee Dealers and Merchants	44	-	-	44
„ and Cocoa Roasters	135	9	-	144
„ House Keepers	809	26	-	835
Coffin Makers	-	-	8	8
Collar (Dog) Makers	4	-	-	4
Colonial Agents and Brokers	52	-	-	52
Colourmen (Artists')	37	-	-	37
Compass Makers	14	2	-	16
Commission Agents and Factors	496	154	-	650
Contractors of Public Works	-	-	8	8
Cooks	-	-	40	40
Coopers	14,554	3 825	-	18,379
Cooper (Back) Makers	41	-	-	41
Copper Agents	48	-	-	48
„ Merchants	17	-	-	17
Coral Carvers and Workers	5	-	-	5
Cordial Makers	-	-	14	14
Cork Cutters	1,459	451	-	1,910
„ Merchants	10	-	-	10
Corn Agents	50	11	-	61
„ Merchants, Dealers, and Factors	3,148	452	728	4,328
„ Meters	172	25	-	197
Cornice Makers	5	-	-	5
Cotton Agents and Brokers	161	24	-	185
„ Merchants and Dealers	412	81	-	493
Curiosity Dealers	40	-	-	40
Curriers and Leather Sellers	9,629	1,024	877	11,530
Custom House Agents	28	-	-	28
Cutlers	6,089	229	-	6,318
Diamond Merchants	10	-	-	10
„ Setters and Workers	62	-	-	62
Die Engravers and Sinkers	266	15	-	281
Dog Breakers and Dealers	18	6	-	24
Drapers	21,167	1,800	185	23,152
„ (Linen)	5,421	125	733	6,279
Draughtsmen	-	-	4	4
Dress Makers and Milliners	94,349	12,452	45,745	152,546
Dressing and Writing Case Makers	58	3	-	61
Drysalters	281	38	-	319
Drug Brokers and Merchants	37	-	-	37
Dulse Dealers	-	3	-	3
Dyers, Callenderers, and Scourers	11,839	2,138	-	13,977
East India Agents, Brokers, and Merchants	15	-	-	15
Eating House Keepers	733	86	-	819
Egg Merchants and Dealers	213	70	1,768	2,051
Embossers	78	-	-	78
Embroiderers	843	507	-	1,350
Enamellers	74	-	-	74
Engravers (all branches)	4,540	681	249	5,470
Exhibition (Show) Keepers	119	13	-	132
Fan Makers	41	-	-	41
Fancy Goods Warehousemen and Dealers	199	-	-	199
Farriers and Cattle Doctors	5,180	316	92	5,588
Feather Makers, Dealers, and Dressers	206	16	465	687
Fellmongers	1,461	20	-	1,481
Figure and Image Makers	266	21	7	294
Firemen	-	-	125	125
Fish Contractors	47	-	-	47
„ Curers	38	858	-	896
Fishermen	-	-	9,211	9,211
Fishing Rod and Tackle Makers	182	47	-	229
Fishmongers and Dealers	5,070	765	672	6,507
Flannel Agents and Merchants	20	-	-	20

UNITED KINGDOM—SUMMARY OF PERSONS ENGAGED IN TRADE, &c.
(Continued.)

OCCUPATIONS.	ENGLAND, WALES, and ISLES IN THE BRITISH SEAS.	SCOTLAND.	IRELAND.	TOTAL.
Flax Merchants and Staplers - - - -	21	13	54	88
Flock Dealers and Merchants - - -	18	-	-	18
Flour Dealers and Mealmen - - -	1,675	316	30	2,021
Flower (Artificial) Makers - - -	1,112	26	11	1,149
Frame Makers - - - -	1,150	33	29	1,212
French Polishers - - - -	1,362	52	-	1,414
Fruit Brokers and Merchants - - -	130	-	-	130
Furriers - - - -	1,818	73	143	2,034
Gas Fitters - - - -	831	12	51	894
Gas Meter Makers - - -	19	-	-	19
Ginger Beer, Soda, and Mineral Water Makers - -	541	55	65	661
Glass Merchants - - - -	30	3	4	37
Globe Makers - - - -	12	5	-	17
Gold Beaters - - - -	539	31	-	570
Golf Ball Makers - - -	-	10	-	10
„ Club Makers - - -	-	2	-	2
Green Grocers and Fruiterers - - -	7,908	466	433	8,807
Grindery Dealers - - -	14	-	-	14
Grocers and Tea Dealers - - -	41,929	7,277	3,434	52,640
Haberdashers and Hosiers - - -	3,536	527	1,260	5,323
Hair Dealers and Merchants - - -	53	33	-	86
Hair (Artists in) - - -	17	-	-	17
Hair Dressers and Barbers - - -	9,543	770	691	11,004
Hardwaremen and Dealers - - -	454	84	-	538
Hawkers, Hucksters, and Pedlars - - -	14,709	2,561	6,022	23,292
Hay and Straw Dealers - - -	447	23	12	482
Hemp Dealers and Merchants - - -	79	2	-	81
Herb Distillers - - -	6	1	-	7
Herbalists - - - -	78	2	-	80
Hop Dealers - - - -	199	5	-	204
Horse Dealers and Trainers - - -	2,238	125	427	2,790
Ice Dealers - - - -	5	-	-	5
India Rubber Merchants - - -	3	-	-	3
Indigo Brokers and Merchants - - -	11	-	-	11
Instrument Case Makers - - -	7	-	-	7
Insurance Agents and Brokers - - -	84	30	-	114
Iron Agents - - - -	24	1	-	25
„ Dealers and Merchants - - -	296	83	-	379
Ironmongers - - - -	5,658	766	574	6,998
„ (Saddler's) - - -	45	-	-	45
Jewel Case Makers - - -	50	7	-	57
Jewellers, Goldsmiths, and Silversmiths - -	8,463	644	431	9,538
Knackers - - - -	48	-	-	48
Lace Agents - - - -	67	1	-	68
Lace Dealers and Lacemen - - -	454	15	-	469
Lamp Contractors - - -	15	-	-	15
Lapidaries - - - -	278	58	3	339
Last Makers - - - -	401	50	60	511
Lath Makers and Renders - - -	1,246	137	94	1,477
Lead Agents - - - -	42	1	-	43
Lead Merchants - - - -	-	6	-	6
Leather Case Makers - - -	37	-	-	37
„ Dealers - - -	-	-	334	334
Leather Pipe Makers - - -	30	-	-	30
Leech Bleeders and Dealers - - -	74	3	2	79
Librarians - - - -	253	39	-	292
Limb (Artificial) Makers - - -	5	-	-	5
Lime Dealers and Merchants - - -	216	25	-	241
Linen Agents and Merchants - - -	40	39	87	166
Lithographers and Lithographic Printers - -	220	201	20	441
Livery Stable Keepers - - -	1,099	39	3	1,141
Locksmiths and Bellhangers - - -	5,429	92	55	5,576
Lodging and Boarding House Keepers - -	7,557	2,693	1,411	11,661
Maltsters - - - -	7,965	498	104	8,567
Manchester Warehousemen - - -	27	-	-	27
Manure Dealers - - -	29	1	-	30
Map Makers and Publishers - - -	132	17	7	156
Marble Merchants and Dealers - - -	12	4	1	17
Marine Store Dealers - - -	465	6	-	471
Mark Makers - - - -	18	-	-	18
Mask Makers - - - -	10	-	-	10
Masons (Marble) - - -	547	147	-	694
Masons (Paviors and Stone Cutters) - -	64,068	18,585	20,473	103,126
Match Sellers - - -	236	43	-	279
Mathematical Instrument Makers - - -	310	8	-	318
Measure Makers - - -	130	3	-	133
Measurers - - - -	-	-	83	83
Measuring Tape Makers - - -	6	1	-	7
Medalists and Medal Makers - - -	26	1	-	27
Medicine Venders - - -	115	9	-	124
Merchants (General) - - -	12,315	6,472	-	18,787
„ (Unspecified) - - -	-	-	3,257	3,257
Mercury Dealers - - - -	4	-	-	4
Metal Agents, Merchants, and Dealers - -	45	5	-	50
Meters (branch not specified) - - -	45	-	-	45

158

UNITED KINGDOM—SUMMARY OF PERSONS ENGAGED IN TRADE, &c.
(*Continued.*)

OCCUPATIONS.	ENGLAND, WALES. and ISLES IN THE BRITISH SEAS.	SCOTLAND.	IRELAND.	TOTAL.
Milk Sellers and Cow Keepers -	8,112	1,215	- -	9,327
Millers -	22,599	3,143	4,309	30,051
Millwrights -	6,869	2,030	968	9,867
Mine Agents -	343	2	-	345
Mineralogists and Mineral Dealers -	43	3	-	46
Miscellaneous Dealers -	-	-	15	15
Modellers -	379	2	-	381
Mop Makers -	125	8	-	133
Music Copyists -	7	-	-	7
Music Engravers and Printers -	61	2	-	63
Music Sellers and Publishers -	258	33	-	291
Muslin Agents and Dealers -	-	47	-	47
Naturalists -	64	-	-	64
Nautical Instrument Makers -	25	1	-	26
Navy Agents -	35	-	-	35
News Agents and Venders -	609	15	156	780
Oil and Colourmen -	1,506	15	-	1,521
Oil Merchants -	100	14	-	114
Old Clothes Dealers -	-	-	318	318
Opticians -	1,009	86	33	1,128
Ornament Makers -	83	7	-	90
Outfitters -	104	-	-	104
Packers and Pressers -	1,584	65	-	1,649
Painters, Plumbers, and Glaziers, and Varnishers -	44,144	4,056	5,389	53,589
Painters (Herald) -	101	3	-	104
Paper Hangers -	1,077	22	-	1,099
Paper Merchants and Dealers -	77	9	14	100
Paper Rulers -	139	69	-	208
Paper Box Makers -	141	3	-	144
Pastry Cooks and Confectioners -	6,270	706	1,312	8,288
Patten and Clog Makers -	3,327	158	-	3,485
Pawnbrokers -	2,584	109	-	2,693
Pearl Workers -	266	-	-	266
Peat Dealers -	20	67	-	87
Peel Makers -	4	-	-	4
Perfumers -	657	54	19	730
Philosophical Instrument Makers -	16	7	-	23
Picture Cleaners and Dealers -	169	5	-	174
,, Frame Makers -	108	9	-	117
Pig Dealers -	662	9	949	1,620
Pitch and Tar Merchants -	7	-	-	7
Plasterers -	12,038	1,403	1,425	14,866
Pocket Book and Card Case Makers -	312	30	-	342
Pole Dealers and Makers -	10	-	-	10
Polishers -	575	78	-	653
Porter and Ale Merchants -	168	8	-	176
Potato Dealers and Merchants -	368	28	-	416
Poulterers and Game Dealers -	1,395	127	221	1,743
Print Colourers -	175	1	-	176
,, Sellers -	158	14	12	184
Printers -	15,846	2,467	1,717	20,030
,, (Copperplate) -	460	34	18	512
Provision Curers -	7	13	-	20
,, Dealers -	1,034	755	-	1,789
Pump Makers -	548	6	173	727
Quarry Agents -	6	-	-	6
,, Owners -	34	2	-	36
Quarrymen -	-	-	549	549
Quill Merchants -	15	3	-	18
Rag Cutters, Dealers, and Gatherers -	1,316	108	881	2,305
Railway Agents and Contractors -	196	49	-	245
Reed Merchants -	3	-	-	3
Register Office (Servants) Keepers -	21	-	-	21
Respirator Makers -	4	-	-	4
Ribbon Merchants and Dealers -	11	-	-	11
Rice Millers -	2	3	-	5
Road Contractors -	133	278	412	823
Robe Makers -	47	7	12	66
Rocket Makers -	-	-	1	1
Rule Makers -	320	1	-	321
Rush Dealers -	39	-	-	39
Russia Merchants and Brokers -	21	-	-	21
Sack and Bag Dealers and Makers -	781	124	-	905
Saddlers and Harness and Collar Makers -	14,091	1,632	3,135	18,858
Saddletree Makers -	171	15	7	193
Salesmen and Saleswomen -	1,667	148	121	1,936
Salt Agents -	6	-	-	6
Salt Dealers and Merchants -	115	46	-	161
Salt Proprietors -	15	-	-	15
Salters -	-	-	230	230
Sand Merchants -	192	7	-	199
Sauce and Pickle Makers -	35	-	-	35
Sawyers -	25,043	4,550	3,866	33,459
Scale Makers -	433	4	-	437

UNITED KINGDOM—SUMMARY OF PERSONS ENGAGED IN TRADE, &c.

(*Continued.*)

OCCUPATIONS.	ENGLAND, WALES, and ISLES IN THE BRITISH SEAS.	SCOTLAND.	IRELAND.	TOTAL.
Scavengers and Nightmen	526	83	- -	609
Screen Makers	6	-	- -	6
Screw (Wood) Makers	85	- -	- -	85
Seal Makers and Polishers	23	1	14	38
Seamstresses and Seamsters	18,780	9,531	47,283	75,594
Seedsmen and Seed Merchants	771	135	88	994
Shawl Merchants and Dealers	42	15	- -	57
Shell Dealers	44	1	- -	45
Ship Agents and Brokers	682	100	68	850
,, Builders, Carpenters, and Wrights	17,198	2,926	1,768	22,192
,, Breakers	10	-	- -	10
,, Caulkers	612	2	- -	614
,, Chandlers	197	14	- -	211
,, Riggers	701	26	- -	727
,, and Smack Owners	938	215	- -	1,153
,, Smiths	177	3	- -	180
Shoe (Carpet and List) Makers	17	5	-	22
Shop Keepers and General Dealers	25,394	1,412	31,693	58,499
,, Assistants	- -	,,	7,672	7,672
Shot Dealers and Factors	2	1	- -	3
Shroud Makers	18	-	- -	18
Silk Agents and Brokers	59	4	-	63
Silk Mercers	1,670	228	115	2,013
Silk Merchants	103	6	- -	109
Skylight and Sash Makers	22	-	-	22
Slate Agents and Merchants	123	7	6	136
Slaters	3,329	2,247	3,285	8,861
Slop Makers and Sellers	519	7	- -	526
Small Wire Dealers	173	109	- -	282
Smelting Agents	5	-	-	5
Snuff Grinders	-	-	20	20
Spanish Leather Makers	- -	-	3	3
Spar Cutters and Turners	32	-	-	32
Spectacle Makers	200	3	- -	203
Spice Merchants	6	-	- -	6
Sponge Dealers and Merchants	12	-	-	12
Stationers	3,092	228	153	3,473
,, (Law)	726	-	-	726
Statuaries	- -	-	23	23
Stay and Corset Makers	5,758	812	1,152	7,722
Steel Merchants	4	-	- -	4
Stevedores	6	-	- -	6
Stencillers	113	-	- -	113
Stewards and Stewardesses (Ship)	91	35	- -	126
Stock Makers	17	13	21	51
,, (Men's) Makers	529	4	- -	533
Store Agents	11	-	-	11
,, Merchants and Dealers	255	29	- -	284
Store Keepers	159	147	- -	306
Straw Bonnet and Hat Makers	8,977	1,589	. 553	11,119
Straw Plait Dealers and Merchants	354	-	- -	354
Strop Makers	37	1	- -	38
Surgical Instrument Maker	224	12	- -	236
Tailors and Breeches Makers	108,945	17,192	36,866	163,003
Tallow and Wax Chandlers	3,239	426	- -	3,665
Tavern Keepers viz.:—				
Beer Shop Keepers	5,629	13	- -	5,642
Hotel and Innkeepers	15,441	1,612	1,736	18,789
Publicans and Victuallers	37,805	2,556	10,914	51,275
Spirit Merchants	904	4,365	2	5,271
Tea Brokers and Merchants	91	42	- -	133
Tea Dealers	74	-	-	74
Teazle Merchants	6	-	- -	6
Tennis Court Keepers	3,777	262	1,018	5,057
Thatchers	8	-	- -	8
Theatrical Property Makers	667	111	- -	778
Tilers	62	7	- -	69
Tilt Makers	39	-	-	39
Timber Agents and Brokers	22	-	- -	22
,, Benders	1,706	97	67	1,870
,, Merchants and Dealers	25	-	-	25
Tin Dealers and Agents	6,946	1,404	1,282	9,632
Tin Plate Workers and Tinmen	5,003	972	536	6,511
Tobacconists	-	-	548	548
Tobacco Twisters	49	3	-	52
Toll Contractors	44	-	- -	44
Tortoiseshell Dealers and Workers	1,823	43	2	1,891
Toy Dealers and Makers	74	-	- -	74
Trap Makers	1,252	276	41	1,569
Travellers (Commercial)	63	2	18	83
Trimming Dealers	334	2	- -	336
Tripe Dealers and Dressers	1,627	80	105	1,812
Trunk and Box Makers	125	1	8	134
Truss Makers	31	7	- -	38
Tube Makers				

UNITED KINGDOM—SUMMARY OF PERSONS ENGAGED IN TRADE, &c.
(*Continued.*)

OCCUPATIONS.	ENGLAND, WALES, and ISLES IN THE BRITISH SEAS.	SCOTLAND.	IRELAND.	TOTAL.
Turf Cutters, Dealers, and Merchants - - -	171	- -	34	205
Umbrella, Parasol, and Walking-stick Makers -	1,749	204	88	2,041
Undertakers - - - - -	918	33	21	972
Vellum Binders - - ... - -	134	- -	- -	134
Venders of Soft Goods - - - -	- -	- -	905	905
Waiters (Hotel and Tavern) - - -	- -	- -	100	100
Warehousemen and Women - - - -	11,690	1,184	- -	12,874
Waste Dealers - - - - -	254	4	- -	258
Water Carriers and Dealers - - -	29	- -	157	186
Water Gilders - - - - -	50	- -	- -	50
Wax Merchants - - - ... -	3	- -	- -	3
,, Modellers and Workers - - -	21	13	- -	34
Weaving Agents - - - - -	- -	63	- -	63
Well Sinkers - - - - -	316	2	- -	318
West India Agents and Merchants - - -	9	- -	- -	9
Whalebone Merchants - - - -	2	- -	- -	2
Wharfingers - - - - -	730	1	- -	731
Wheelwrights - - - - -	25,219	1,055	1,973	28,247
Whetstone Cutters and Makers - - -	76	4	- -	80
Whip Makers - - - - -	1,353	62	- -	1,415
Whitesmiths - - - - -	6,507	22	1,240	7,769
Willow Merchants - - - -	2	- -	- -	2
Wine Agents and Merchants - - -	2,590	244	184	3,018
,, Coopers - - - -	573	3	5	581
,, Merchants - - - -	3	3	- -	6
Wood Merchants - - - - -	310	230	- -	540
,, Polishers - - - - -	- -	- -	54	54
Wool Agents, Merchants, and Staplers - -	1,684	34	17	1,735
,, (Berlin) Dealers and Workers - -	33	- -	- -	33
Woollen Agents and Factors - - -	42	5	- -	47
,, Drapers - - - -	1,419	330	1,086	2,835
Worsted Dealers and Merchants - - -	73	12	- -	85
Yarn Agents - - - - -	13	- -	- -	13
,, Dealers - - - -	12	13	71	96
Yeast Dealers and Merchants - - -	179	2	- -	181
Zinc Agents and Merchants - - -	5	- -	- -	5
Other Persons engaged in Trade (branch not specified) -	50,976	6,136	527	57,636
TOTAL - - - -	1,712,699	256,771	443,981	2,413,951

UNITED KINGDOM.

THE MINING INTEREST.

UNITED KINGDOM—THE MINING INTEREST.

TABLE SHOWING THE NUMBER OF PERSONS EMPLOYED IN WORKING THE MINES OF THE UNITED KINGDOM.

COAL.

	MALES.		FEMALES.		TOTAL.
	20 years of age and upwards.	Under 20 years of age.	20 years of age and upwards.	Under 20 years of age.	
ENGLAND and WALES, and ISLES IN THE BRITISH SEAS	72,090	27,641	789	794	101,314
SCOTLAND	11,318	4,834	396	371	16,919
TOTAL of GREAT BRITAIN	83,408	32,475	1,185	1,165	118,233

COPPER.

ENGLAND and WALES, and ISLES IN THE BRITISH SEAS	9,852	3,428	913	1,200	15,393
SCOTLAND	14	- -	- -	- -	14
TOTAL of GREAT BRITAIN	9,866	3,428	913	1,200	15,407

LEAD.

ENGLAND and WALES, and ISLES IN THE BRITISH SEAS	9,006	1,875	40	20	10,941
SCOTLAND	421	57	- -	- -	478
TOTAL of GREAT BRITAIN	9,427	1,932	40	20	11,419

IRON.

ENGLAND and WALES, and ISLES IN THE BRITISH SEAS	5,933	2,174	399	53	8,559
SCOTLAND	1,840	505	25	20	2,390
TOTAL of GREAT BRITAIN	7,773	2,679	424	73	10,949

TIN.

ENGLAND and WALES, and ISLES IN THE BRITISH SEAS	4,601	1,349	68	82	6,100
SCOTLAND	1	- -	- -	- -	1
TOTAL of GREAT BRITAIN	4,602	1,349	68	82	6,101

MANGANESE.

ENGLAND and WALES, and ISLES IN THE BRITISH SEAS	224	43	4	1	272
SCOTLAND	2	1	- -	- -	3
TOTAL of GREAT BRITAIN	226	44	4	1	275

SALT.

ENGLAND and WALES, and ISLES IN THE BRITISH SEAS	242	24	2	- -	268
SCOTLAND	-	- -	- -	- -	-
TOTAL of GREAT BRITAIN	242	24	2	- -	268

MINERAL NOT SPECIFIED.

ENGLAND and WALES, and ISLES IN THE BRITISH SEAS	23,111	6,385	447	478	30,421
SCOTLAND	583	138	19	12	752
TOTAL of GREAT BRITAIN	23,694	6,523	466	490	31,173
IRELAND	-	- -	- -	- -	3,096
TOTAL of the UNITED KINGDOM	23,694	6,523	466	490	34,269

TOTAL OF PERSONS EMPLOYED IN MINES.

ENGLAND and WALES, and ISLES IN THE BRITISH SEAS	125,059	42,919	2,662	2,628	173,268
SCOTLAND	14,179	5,535	440	403	20,557
TOTAL of GREAT BRITAIN	139,238	48,454	3,102	3,031	193,825
IRELAND	-	- -	- -	- -	3,096
TOTAL of the UNITED KINGDOM	139,238	48,454	3,102	3,031	196,921

UNITED KINGDOM—THE MINING INTEREST.

COUNTIES.	COAL MALES	COAL FEMALES	COPPER MALES	COPPER FEMALES	LEAD MALES	LEAD FEMALES	IRON MALES	IRON FEMALES	TIN MALES	TIN FEMALES	MANGANESE MALES	MANGANESE FEMALES	SALT MALES	SALT FEMALES	MINERAL NOT SPECIFIED MALES	MINERAL NOT SPECIFIED FEMALES	TOTAL OF THE COUNTY
ENGLAND.																	
CHESTER	1,932	18			5								263	2	192	1	2,413
CORNWALL			11,639	2,098	419	21	85		5,706	130	69				533	27	20,727
CUMBERLAND	1,823	6	27		1,420	6	59								297	2	3,640
DERBY	4,467	19			1,455	6	591								233	13	6,784
DEVON	15	2	456	3	187	2	17		145	5	197	5			291	14	1,339
DURHAM	15,156	46			1,458	3	7								1,319	5	17,998
GLOUCESTER	2,748	8					121	9							292	7	3,177
HEREFORD	33	3					2								27		65
LANCASTER	15,218	762	246	2	15		262								547	50	17,111
LEICESTER	702	3			2										28		736
MONMOUTH	5,037	68					1,134	27							3,133	149	9,584
NORTHUMBERLAND	7,527	20			940	1	49	1							277	6	8,821
NOTTINGHAM	1,074	5															1,079
SALOP	3,780	73	6		486		451		1						1,512	42	6,325
SOMERSET	3,321	110			51		6	2	22						143	2	3,596
STAFFORD	9,827	47	37		52		2,549	21	1	1					6,070	68	18,736
SURREY															172		172
SUSSEX	15														47		62
WARWICK	782	2	2				42								178		1,006
WESTMORELAND	57				199										16		272
WILTS	11	4							1						48		59
WORCESTER	908						52		4				2		1,058	8	2,030
YORK (North Riding)	254				1,046	2	45								91		1,439
YORK (West Riding)	11,441	125	1		569	2	1,152	339							670	7	14,310
Total—ENGLAND	**86,137**	**1,321**	**12,419**	**2,103**	**8,304**	**43**	**6,624**	**399**	**5,879**	**150**	**266**	**5**	**265**	**2**	**17,174**	**402**	**141,493**
WALES.																	
ANGLESEY	113	1	256	1											327	1	699
BRECON	1,071	22					81	44							1,952	145	3,315
CARDIGAN	5				534	11									216	8	774
CARMARTHEN	1,490	9			71	3	13	1							46	4	1,637
CARNARVON	5		432	7	11		10				1				114		581
DENBIGH	1,981	10			84	2	11								344		2,439
FLINT	1,684	14			1,437		13								785	8	3,941
GLAMORGAN	6,498	39	97				1,340	7							3,407	58	11,450
MERIONETH			47		52	2									111		212
MONTGOMERY			5		83										76		167
PEMBROKE	684	167													23		874
ISLES IN THE BRITISH SEAS			15		364		14		71				1		104	3	501
Miscellaneous	60		2				1								4,817	296	5,248
Total—ENGLAND and WALES, and ISLES IN THE BRITISH SEAS	**99,731**	**1,583**	**13,280**	**2,113**	**10,944**	**60**	**8,107**	**452**	**5,950**	**150**	**267**	**5**	**266**	**2**	**29,496**	**925**	**173,331**

UNITED KINGDOM—THE MINING INTEREST.

(Continued.)

COUNTIES.	COAL		COPPER		LEAD		IRON		TIN		MANGANESE		SALT		MINERAL NOT SPECIFIED.		TOTAL OF THE COUNTY.
	MALES.	FEMALES.	MALES.	FEMALES.	MALES.	FEMALES.	MALES.	FEMALES.	MALES.	FEMALES.	MALES.	FEMALES.	MALES.	FEMALES.	MALES.	FEMALES.	
SCOTLAND.																	
ARGYLL	76	-	1	-	51	-	-	-	-	-	-	-	-	-	5	-	133
AYR	2,318	2	-	-	3	-	172	-	-	-	-	-	-	-	33	1	2,529
CLACKMANNAN	581	39	-	-	-	-	115	-	-	-	-	-	-	-	22	-	757
DUMBARTON	202	3	-	-	-	-	31	-	-	-	-	-	-	-	15	-	251
DUMFRIES	113	-	-	-	155	-	-	-	-	-	-	-	-	-	-	-	268
EDINBURGH	1,180	187	-	-	-	-	51	-	-	-	-	-	-	-	25	-	1,443
FIFE	1,809	259	-	-	-	-	-	-	-	-	-	-	-	-	22	-	2,090
HADDINGTON	352	46	-	-	-	-	-	-	-	-	-	-	-	-	-	-	398
KIRKCUDBRIGHT	-	-	1	-	94	-	13	-	-	-	-	-	-	-	-	-	108
LANARK	7,226	165	10	-	143	-	1,671	31	1	-	-	-	-	-	528	13	9,788
LINLITHGOW	261	12	-	-	-	-	142	12	-	-	-	-	-	-	9	-	436
PEEBLES	31	26	-	-	-	-	-	-	-	-	-	-	-	-	-	-	57
PERTH	26	-	-	-	29	-	29	-	-	-	-	-	-	-	6	-	90
RENFREW	907	3	-	-	-	-	5	1	-	-	-	-	-	-	9	-	925
STIRLING	1,030	25	2	-	-	-	112	1	-	-	-	-	-	-	27	17	1,234
MISCELLANEOUS	20	-	-	-	-	-	-	-	-	-	3	-	-	-	20	-	50
TOTAL—SCOTLAND	16,152	767	14	-	478	-	2,345	45	1	-	3	-	-	-	721	31	20,557
IRELAND.																	
ANTRIM	-	-	-	-	-	-	-	-	-	-	-	-	-	-	5	-	5
A'MAGH	-	-	-	-	-	-	-	-	-	-	-	-	-	-	25	-	25
CARLOW	-	-	-	-	-	-	-	-	-	-	-	-	-	-	17	-	17
CLARE	-	-	-	-	-	-	-	-	-	-	-	-	-	-	13	-	13
CORK (CITY)	-	-	-	-	-	-	-	-	-	-	-	-	-	-	3	-	3
CORK (COUNTY)	-	-	-	-	-	-	-	-	-	-	-	-	-	-	310	11	321
DONEGAL	-	-	-	-	-	-	-	-	-	-	-	-	-	-	1	-	1
DOWN	-	-	-	-	-	-	-	-	-	-	-	-	-	-	72	-	72
DUBLIN	-	-	-	-	-	-	-	-	-	-	-	-	-	-	14	-	14
FERMANAGH	-	-	-	-	-	-	-	-	-	-	-	-	-	-	4	-	4
GALWAY	-	-	-	-	-	-	-	-	-	-	-	-	-	-	1	-	1
KERRY	-	-	-	-	-	-	-	-	-	-	-	-	-	-	21	3	24
KILKENNY	-	-	-	-	-	-	-	-	-	-	-	-	-	-	416	-	416
KING'S COUNTY	-	-	-	-	-	-	-	-	-	-	-	-	-	-	1	-	1
LEITRIM	-	-	-	-	-	-	-	-	-	-	-	-	-	-	12	-	12
LIMERICK	-	-	-	-	-	-	-	-	-	-	-	-	-	-	18	-	18
MEATH	-	-	-	-	-	-	-	-	-	-	-	-	-	-	2	-	2
MONAGHAN	-	-	-	-	-	-	-	-	-	-	-	-	-	-	37	-	37
QUEEN'S COUNTY	-	-	-	-	-	-	-	-	-	-	-	-	-	-	298	-	298
ROSCOMMON	-	-	-	-	-	-	-	-	-	-	-	-	-	-	55	-	55
TIPPERARY	-	-	-	-	-	-	-	-	-	-	-	-	-	-	426	13	439
TYRONE	-	-	-	-	-	-	-	-	-	-	-	-	-	-	171	-	171
WATERFORD	-	-	-	-	-	-	-	-	-	-	-	-	-	-	381	4	385
WEXFORD	-	-	-	-	-	-	-	-	-	-	-	-	-	-	39	2	41
WICKLOW	-	-	-	-	-	-	-	-	-	-	-	-	-	-	721	-	721
TOTAL—IRELAND	-	-	-	-	-	-	-	-	-	-	-	-	-	-	3,063	33	3,096

UNITED KINGDOM—THE MINING INTEREST.

GENERAL SUMMARY.

	COAL.		COPPER.		LEAD.		IRON.		TIN.		MANGANESE.		SALT.		MINERAL NOT SPECIFIED.		TOTAL.
	Males.	Females.	Males.	Females.	Males.	Females.	Males.	Females.	Males.	Females.	Males.	Females.	Males.	Females.	Males.	Females.	
ENGLAND AND WALES, AND ISLES IN THE BRITISH SEAS	99,731	1,583	13,280	2,113	10,944	60	8,107	452	5,950	150	267	5	266	2	29,496	925	173,331
SCOTLAND	16,152	767	14	-	478	-	2,345	45	1	-	3	-	-	-	721	31	20,557
IRELAND	-	-	-	-	-	-	-	-	-	-	-	-	-	-	3,063	33	3,096
TOTAL—UNITED KINGDOM	115,883	2,350	13,294	2,113	11,422	60	10,452	497	5,951	150	270	5	266	2	33,280	989	196,984

UNITED KINGDOM.

THE SHIPPING INTEREST.

UNITED KINGDOM—SHIPPING.

VESSELS BELONGING TO THE BRITISH EMPIRE.

STATEMENT of the NUMBER, TONNAGE, and CREWS of VESSELS belonging to the BRITISH EMPIRE, on the 31st December, 1844.

	ON 31ST DECEMBER, 1844.		
	Vessels.	Tons.	Men.
UNITED KINGDOM - - - -	23,253	2,994,166	170,162
ISLES OF GUERNSEY, JERSEY, and MAN - -	763	50,226	5,529
BRITISH PLANTATIONS - - -	7,304	592,839	40,659
Total - - - -	31,320	3,637,231	216,350

VESSELS EMPLOYED IN THE COASTING TRADE OF THE UNITED KINGDOM.

STATEMENT of the NUMBER and TONNAGE of VESSELS which ENTERED INWARDS and CLEARED OUTWARDS with CARGOES, at the several Ports of the UNITED KINGDOM, during the Year ending 5th January, 1845; distinguishing the Vessels employed in the Intercourse between GREAT BRITAIN and IRELAND from other Coasters.

COASTING TRADE.	ENTERED INWARDS.		CLEARED OUTWARDS.	
	YEAR ENDING 5TH JAN. 1845.		YEAR ENDING 5TH JAN. 1845.	
	Vessels.	Tons.	Vessels.	Tons.
Employed in the Intercourse between GREAT BRITAIN and IRELAND - -	10,147	1,349,273	16,948	1,817,756
Other Coasting Vessels - - - -	123,751	9,615,434	128,294	9,877,105
Total - - -	133,898	10,964,707	145,242	11,694,861

VESSELS EMPLOYED IN THE FOREIGN TRADE OF THE UNITED KINGDOM.

STATEMENT of the NUMBER and TONNAGE of VESSELS, distinguishing the Countries to which they belonged, which ENTERED INWARDS and CLEARED OUTWARDS, in the Year ending 5th January, 1845; stated exclusively of Vessels in Ballast, and of those employed in the Coasting Trade between GREAT BRITAIN and IRELAND.

COUNTRIES TO WHICH THE VESSELS BELONGED.	ENTERED INWARDS.		CLEARED OUTWARDS.	
	YEAR ENDING 5TH JAN. 1845.		YEAR ENDING 5TH JAN. 1845.	
	Vessels.	Tons.	Vessels.	Tons.
United Kingdom and its Dependencies - -	14,681	3,087,437	13,842	2,604,243
Russia - - - - - - -	199	53,272	136	37,426
Sweden - - - - - -	267	35,346	237	33,960
Norway - - - - - -	871	147,959	386	45,949
Denmark - - - - - -	1,559	115,287	1,527	115,307
Prussia - - - - - - -	1,104	207,490	821	145,725
Other German States - - - -	1,003	85,535	1,132	107,264
Holland - - - - - -	565	46,199	641	59,319
Belgium - - - - - -	280	41,479	350	51,865
France - - - - - -	631	34,570	1,206	102,387
Spain - - - - - - -	75	9,722	98	13,089
Portugal - - - - - -	31	3,105	27	2,898
Italian States - - - - -	56	14,324	63	17,715
Other European States - - - -	1	196	-	-
United States of America - - -	600	348,548	572	342,254
Other States in America, Africa, or Asia - -	6	865	4	665
Total - - - -	21,929	4,231,334	21,042	3,680,066

UNITED KINGDOM—SHIPPING.

BRITISH PLANTATIONS.

Statement of the Number, Tonnage, and Crews of Vessels that belonged to the several British Plantations in the Year 1844.

COUNTRIES.	VESSELS.	TONS.	CREWS.
EUROPE:			
Malta - - - - -	85	15,326	892
AFRICA:			
Bathurst - - - - -	25	1,169	215
Sierra Leone - - - -	17	1,148	111
Cape of Good Hope, Cape Town - -	27	3,090	265
,, Port Elizabeth - -	2	201	19
Mauritius - - - - -	124	12,079	1,413
ASIA:			
Bombay - - - - -	113	50,767	3,393
Cochin - - - - -	15	5,674	275
Tanjore - - - - -	33	5,070	257
Madras - - - - -	32	5,474	248
Malacca - - - - -	2	288	13
Coringa - - - - -	17	3,384	136
Calcutta - - - - -	186	51,779	2,604
Singapore - - - - -	13	2,543	289
Ceylon - - - - -	674	30,076	2,696
Prince of Wales Island - - -	7	996	51
NEW HOLLAND:			
Sydney - - - - -	293	28,051	2,128
Melbourne - - - - -	29	1,240	147
Adelaide - - - - -	17	864	60
Hobart Town - - - -	103	7,152	724
Launceston - - - -	42	3,150	257
NEW ZEALAND:			
Auckland - - - - -	13	305	32
Wellington - - - -	12	262	42
AMERICA:			
Canada, Quebec - - - -	509	45,361	2,590
,, Montreal - - -	60	10,097	556
Cape Breton, Sydney - - -	360	15,048	1,296
,, Arichat - - -	96	4,614	335
New Brunswick, Miramichi - - -	81	10,143	509
,, St. Andrew's - -	193	18,391	918
,, St. John's - -	398	63,676	2,480
Newfoundland, St. John's - -	847	53,944	4,576
Nova Scotia, Halifax - - -	1,657	82,890	5,292
,, Liverpool - - -	31	2,641	163
,, Pictou - - -	60	6,929	354
,, Yarmouth - - -	146	11,724	637
Prince Edward's Island - - -	237	13,861	856
West Indies, Antigua - - -	55	833	220
,, Bahamas - - -	140	3,252	686
,, Barbadoes - - -	37	1,640	305
,, Berbice - - -	18	854	89
,, Bermuda - - -	54	3,623	323
,, Demerara - - -	54	2,353	250
,, Dominica - - -	14	502	85
,, Grenada - - -	48	812	198
,, Jamaica, Antonio - -	5	95	22
,, ,, Annotto Bay -	2	79	13
,, ,, Falmouth -	5	107	29
,, ,, Kingston -	68	2,659	359
,, , Montego Bay -	18	849	105
,, ,, Morant Bay -	9	251	51
,, ,, Port Maria -	3	86	18
,, ,, St. Ann's -	1	20	4
,, ,, Savannah la Mar -	3	153	22
,, ,, St. Lucea -	2	64	10
,, Montserrat - - -	4	100	19
,, Nevis - - -	11	178	45
,, St. Kitt's - - -	35	546	114
,, St. Lucia - - -	19	913	132
,, St. Vincent's - - -	27	1,164	180
,, Tobago - - -	7	189	46
,, Tortola - - -	48	278	127
,, Trinidad - - -	61	1,832	378
Total - - -	7,304	592,839	40,659

UNITED KINGDOM—SHIPPING.

FOREIGN TRADE – INWARDS.

STATEMENT of the SHIPPING employed in the TRADE of the UNITED KINGDOM, exhibiting the NUMBER, TONNAGE, and CREWS of VESSELS that ENTERED INWARDS (including their repeated Voyages), separating BRITISH from FOREIGN VESSELS, and distinguishing the Trade with each Country, in the year 1844.

COUNTRIES.	INWARDS.					
	BRITISH.			FOREIGN.		
	Vessels.	Tons.	Crews.	Vessels.	Tons.	Crews.
EUROPE, *viz.* :						
Russia	1,799	351,215	15,361	212	53,667	2,417
Sweden	78	12,806	581	344	59,835	2,941
Norway	16	1,315	89	779	125,011	6,339
Denmark	59	7,423	350	1,667	123,674	8,250
Prussia	786	108,626	5,047	1,286	220,202	10,539
Germany	900	181,322	9,845	1,123	113,209	6,924
Holland	1,239	173,247	9,796	843	80,217	5,226
Belgium	656	76,690	6,772	484	72,207	4,524
France	4,177	463,548	35,792	1,988	163,869	14,777
Portugal, Proper	448	43,271	2,650	27	2,746	233
,, Azores	218	17,458	1,254	5	444	44
,, Madeira	24	5,196	348	1	123	10
Spain and Balearic Islands	447	45,994	2,669	87	9,512	773
,, Canaries	6	590	34	5	487	50
Gibraltar	84	19,856	1,554	1	218	13
Italy and Italian Islands	497	76,602	3,819	56	14,866	697
Malta	39	5,365	282	-	-	-
Ionian Islands	51	6,250	356	-	-	-
Turkey and Continental Greece	177	29,708	1,717	14	2,843	141
Morea and Greek Islands	51	7,339	387	-	-	-
AFRICA. *viz.* :						
Egypt	115	31,354	1,652	-	-	-
Tripoli, Barbary, and Morocco	47	6,155	330	-	-	-
Senegal and Coast from Morocco to the River Gambia	1	56	5	-	-	-
Sierra Leone and Coast from the Gambia to the Mesurado	43	9,686	475	-	-	-
Windward Coast	1	190	14	-	-	-
Cape Coast Castle	31	4,864	291	-	-	-
Coast from Rio Volta to Cape of Good Hope	269	78,162	4,274	-	-	-
Cape of Good Hope	35	7,269	379	-	-	-
Eastern Coast	15	3,024	188	-	-	-
Ports in the Red Sea	-	-	-	-	-	-
Madagascar	-	-	-	-	-	-
Bourbon	-	-	-	-	-	-
Mauritius	82	23,593	1,115	-	-	-
Cape Verd Islands	1	84	8	-	-	-
St Helena and Ascension	1	196	9	-	-	-
ASIA, *viz.*:						
Arabia	-	-	-	-	-	-
East India Company's Territories, Singapore, and Ceylon	440	197,979	9,634	-	-	-
Java	16	5,597	220	1	387	22
Philippine Islands	21	7,891	351	1	250	12
Other Islands of the Indian Seas	-	-	-	-	-	-
China	104	45,605	2,174	-	-	-
Japan	-	-	-	-	-	-
New Holland	103	34,779	1,698	-	-	-
New Zealand	6	1,348	77	-	-	-
South Sea Islands	2	327	19	-	-	-
AMERICA, *viz.* :						
British Northern Colonies	2,284	789,410	30,222	-	-	-
,, West Indies	714	195,440	10,716	-	-	-
Hayti	36	6,810	355	-	-	-
Cuba and other Foreign West Indies	135	39,993	2,010	41	10,243	470
United States	373	206,183	8,170	575	338,737	11,157
Mexico	70	25,011	1,641	2	408	22
Columbia	72	13,698	633	2	334	22
Brazil	200	45,649	2,333	14	2,589	128
Rio de la Plata	63	13,134	621	-	-	-
Chili	100	29,343	1,421	2	367	31
Peru	52	16,279	747	1	407	20
Falkland Isles	-	-	-	-	-	-
Whale Fisheries	49	14,781	1,940	-	-	-
Guernsey, Jersey, and Man	2,454	159,752	13,303	47	5,286	309
Total	19,687	3,647,463	195,728	9,608	1,402,138	76,091

UNITED KINGDOM—SHIPPING.

FOREIGN TRADE—OUTWARDS.

STATEMENT of the SHIPPING employed in the TRADE of the UNITED KINGDOM, exhibiting the NUMBER, TONNAGE, and CREWS of VESSELS that CLEARED OUTWARDS (including their repeated Voyages), separating BRITISH from FOREIGN VESSELS, and distinguishing the Trade with each Country, in the Year 1844.

COUNTRIES.	OUTWARDS.					
	BRITISH.			FOREIGN.		
	Vessels.	Tons.	Crews.	Vessels.	Tons.	Crews.
EUROPE, *viz.*:						
Russia	1,310	261,780	11,560	216	48,775	2,212
Sweden	72	13,366	598	239	28,841	1,676
Norway	13	1,230	83	757	129,990	6,370
Denmark	476	78,753	3,699	2,326	212,621	12,410
Prussia	584	75,226	3,920	1,039	198,016	8,693
Germany	902	180,815	9,478	1,191	98,297	6,269
Holland	1,154	157,708	9,058	742	60,979	4,287
Belgium	628	65,829	6,396	397	54,847	3,639
France	4,226	494,762	36,990	1,651	127,096	12,956
Portugal, Proper	381	38,598	2,544	59	7,468	454
„ Azores	186	16,076	1,177	3	295	22
„ Madeira	36	7,869	523	-	-	-
Spain and Balearic Islands	582	84,424	4,577	142	21,429	1,086
„ Canaries	6	793	54	7	741	70
Gibraltar	256	44,118	3,534	4	1,233	50
Italy and Italian Islands	535	85,411	4,445	122	25,337	1,249
Malta	143	28,101	1,364	67	12,349	638
Ionian Islands	68	9,418	536	1	150	8
Turkey and Continental Greece	237	44,571	2,537	37	10,285	453
Morea and Greek Islands	23	3,812	200	1	252	11
AFRICA, *viz.*:						
Egypt	91	25,859	1,561	14	3,150	147
Tripoli, Barbary, and Morocco	58	12,605	545	6	1,935	75
Senegal and Coast from Morocco to the River Gambia	-	-	-	1	85	8
Sierra Leone and Coast from the Gambia to the Mesurado	49	11,563	594	-	-	-
Windward Coast	1	240	11	-	-	-
Cape Coast Castle	35	6,424	406	-	-	-
Coast from Rio Volta to Cape of Good Hope	579	165,345	9,432	1	310	11
Cape of Good Hope	289	76,249	4,272	-	-	-
Eastern Coast	14	2,515	165	1	187	12
Ports in the Red Sea	2	630	30	-	-	-
Madagascar	4	1,061	54	-	-	-
Bourbon	2	571	36	-	-	-
Mauritius	73	21,206	1,106	-	-	-
Cape Verd Islands	9	1,514	93	1	161	11
St Helena and Ascension	26	6,318	339	-	-	-
ASIA, *viz.*:						
Arabia	22	9,817	437	-	-	-
East India Company's Territories, Singapore, and Ceylon	469	219,640	12,127	1	710	24
Java	21	7,273	352	4	1,477	90
Philippine Islands	4	1,347	66	1	589	24
Other Islands of the Indian Seas	2	1,242	83	-	-	-
China	78	32,534	1,691	5	2,110	98
Japan	1	180	12	-	-	-
New Holland	107	43,037	2,265	-	-	-
New Zealand	6	2,212	105	-	-	-
South Sea Islands	6	2,113	95	-	-	-
AMERICA, *viz.*						
British Northern Colonies	2,060	722,299	29,333	2	882	27
„ West Indies	822	231,667	12,949	-	-	-
Hayti	32	5,169	304	4	940	49
Cuba and other Foreign West Indies	137	38,633	1,561	92	22,494	1,121
United States	428	238,889	9,229	621	355,344	12,117
Mexico	46	15,222	1,081	1	104	8
Columbia	39	9,521	524	6	1,180	64
Brazil	255	60,521	3,143	47	12,574	559
Rio de la Plata	42	10,177	500	3	389	26
Chili	100	25,915	1,370	3	637	49
Peru	39	9,782	532	-	-	-
Falkland Isles	1	208	13	-	-	-
Whale Fisheries	49	14,513	2,019	-	-	-
Guernsey, Jersey, and Man	1,972	126,051	11,216	1	87	6
Total	19,788	3,582,822	212,924	9,816	1,444,346	77,109

UNITED KINGDOM—SHIPPING.

ENTRIES AND CLEARANCES.

STATEMENT of the NUMBER, TONNAGE, and CREWS of VESSELS (including their repeated Voyages) that ENTERED INWARDS and CLEARED OUTWARDS, at the several PORTS of the UNITED KINGDOM, from and to FOREIGN PARTS, during each of the three years ending 5th January, 1845.

	YEARS.	BRITISH and IRISH VESSELS.			FOREIGN VESSELS.			TOTAL.		
		Vessels.	Tons.	Crews.	Vessels.	Tons.	Crews.	Vessels.	Tons.	Crews.
INWARDS	1842	18,987	3,294,725	178,884	8,054	1,205,303	65,952	27,041	4,500,028	244,836
	1843	19,500	3,545,346	191,326	8,541	1,301,950	69,791	28,041	4,847,296	261,117
	1844	19,687	3,647,463	195,728	9,608	1,402,138	76,091	29,295	5,049,601	271,819
OUTWARDS	1842	18,785	3,375,270	186,816	8,375	1,252,176	68,493	27,160	4,627,446	255,309
	1843	19,334	3,635,833	197,976	8,709	1,341,433	71,718	28,043	4,977,266	269,694
	1844	19,788	3,852,822	212,924	9,816	1,444,346	77,109	29,604	5,297,168	290,033

STATEMENT of the NUMBER and TONNAGE of VESSELS which ENTERED the undermentioned PORTS in the Year ending 5th January, 1845.

PORTS.	BRITISH.		FOREIGN.	
	Vessels.	Tons.	Vessels.	Tons.
London	4,741	1,008,463	2,144	353,346
Liverpool	2,671	760,597	939	367,918
Bristol	347	72,847	56	9,382
Hull	1,085	234,361	1,388	156,308
Newcastle	1,229	184,413	945	109,862
Plymouth	340	40,110	47	8,508
Leith	250	38,458	489	42,455
Glasgow	238	44,938	46	9,942
Greenock	209	67,353	3	963
Cork	165	30,444	17	1,807
Belfast	177	41,119	40	5,489
Dublin	243	43,062	43	5,644

STEAM VESSELS (BRITISH AND FOREIGN).

STATEMENT of the NUMBER and TONNAGE of STEAM VESSELS which ENTERED and CLEARED at PORTS in each division of the UNITED KINGDOM ; distinguishing the FOREIGN from the COASTING TRADE, and the COUNTRIES to which the VESSELS belonged in the year 1844.

COUNTRIES TO WHICH THE VESSELS BELONGED.	COASTING TRADE.				FOREIGN TRADE.			
	ENTERED.		CLEARED.		ENTERED.		CLEARED.	
	Vessels.	Tons.	Vessels.	Tons.	Vessels.	Tons.	Vessels.	Tons.
UNITED KINGDOM:								
ENGLAND	9,611	1,887,846	9,656	1,821,946	3,122	507,271	3,061	490,837
SCOTLAND	2,827	716,353	2,523	617,741	–	–	–	–
IRELAND	3,115	783,961	3,321	830,812	2	278	2	278
	15,553	3,388,160	15,500	3,270,499	3,124	507,549	3,063	491,115
FRANCE	–	–	–	–	398	40,078	406	40,663
HOLLAND (To and from ENGLAND.)	–	–	–	–	35	7,846	38	8,626
BELGIUM	–	–	–	–	78	23,007	78	20,782
GERMANY	–	–	–	–	47	11,986	47	15,105

UNITED KINGDOM—SHIPPING.

SUMMARY OF THE SHIPPING INTEREST OF THE UNITED KINGDOM.

	VESSELS.	TONS.	MEN.
VESSELS BELONGING TO THE BRITISH EMPIRE on the 31st December, 1844 - - - - - -	31,320	3,637,231	216,350
COASTING TRADE.			
VESSELS ENTERED INWARDS during the year ending Jan. 5, 1845	133,898	10,964,707	
VESSELS CLEARED OUTWARDS ,, ,, ,,	145,242	11,694,861	
COLONIES.			
VESSELS BELONGING TO THE BRITISH PLANTATIONS in the year 1844 - - - - - - -	7,304	592,839	40,659
FOREIGN TRADE.			
VESSELS ENTERED INWARDS in the year 1844 :			
BRITISH - - - - - -	19,687	3,647,463	195,728
FOREIGN - - - - - -	9,608	1,402,138	76,091
	29,295	5,049,601	271,819
VESSELS CLEARED OUTWARDS in the year 1844 :			
BRITISH - - - - - -	19,788	3,852,822	212,924
FOREIGN - - - - - -	9,816	1,444,346	77,109
	29,604	5,297,168	29·,033
STEAM VESSELS.			
COASTING TRADE :			
ENTERED in the year 1844 - - -	15,553	3,388,160	
CLEARED ,, - - -	15,500	3,270,499	
FOREIGN TRADE :			
ENTERED ,, - - -	3,124	567,549	
CLEARED ,, - - -	3,063	491,115	

PROFESSIONAL PERSONS.

THE NUMBER of PROFESSIONAL PERSONS in the UNITED KINGDOM is returned as follows :—

	CLERICAL.	LEGAL.	MEDICAL.	TOTAL.
ENGLAND - - -	18,840	13,759	17,745	50,344
WALES - • - -	1,610	396	691	2,697
SCOTLAND - - -	2,956	3,185	3,568	9,709
ISLES IN THE BRITISH SEAS -	137	114	183	434
IRELAND - - - -	7,192	*3,852	6,871	17,915
	30,735	21,306	29,058	81,099

And these are supported by, and derive their incomes from, the AGRICULTURAL and MANUFACTURING DISTRICTS, in the following proportions :—

MANUFACTURING COUNTIES.	CLERICAL.	LEGAL.	MEDICAL.	TOTAL.
CHESTER - - - -	321	221	326	868
DERBY - - - -	331	136	225	692
LANCASTER - - -	1,082	959	1,454	3,495
LEICESTER - - - -	419	105	210	734
NOTTINGHAM - - -	332	118	214	664
STAFFORD - - - -	355	227	372	954
WARWICK - - - -	351	288	438	1,077
YORKSHIRE - - - -	1,632	860	1,389	3,881
	4,823	2,914	4,628	12,365
Leaving to be supported by the AGRICULTURAL INTEREST of ENGLAND and WALES - - -	15,627	11,241	13,808	40,676
	20,450	14,155	18,436	53,041

And inasmuch as the AGRICULTURAL INTEREST of these Counties is numerically much greater than that of the MANUFACTURING in every other County of England and Wales, it follows that the MANUFACTURING INTEREST supports about 1-4th of the CLERICAL, LEGAL, and MEDICAL PROFESSIONS, in England and Wales, and that the remaining 3-4ths are resident in, and dependent on, the AGRICULTURAL DISTRICTS and INTERESTS for their support.

In SCOTLAND the population is equally divided between AGRICULTURE and MANUFACTURES. (See Page 94.)

In IRELAND the proportion which MANUFACTURES bear to AGRICULTURE is as 1 to 8. (See Page 152.)

This rule, although not quite conclusive, is sufficient for our present purpose; and we shall therefore adopt it in all instances where a more minute investigation is rendered impossible by the defective returns of the Census.

We have therefore the following results :—

	AGRICULTURE.	MANUFACTURES.	TOTAL.
ENGLAND AND WALES - -	40,676	12,365	53,041
SCOTLAND - - - -	4,854	4,855	9,709
ISLES IN THE BRITISH SEAS -	354	80	434
IRELAND - - - -	15,675	2,240	17,915
	61,559	19,540	81,099

There is nothing connected with or arising out of Statistics, that could better illustrate the relative importance of the two interests than this, that the number of PROFESSIONAL PERSONS resident in and supported by our Manufacturing Towns and Counties are but one-fourth of the whole number spread throughout the length and breadth of the United Kingdom.

* This number is returned as Ministering to Justice, independent of those engaged in the Government and Civil Service; but if the classification had been carried out on the same rule as the English, this item would no doubt have been much greater.

OTHER EDUCATED PERSONS

FOLLOWING MISCELLANEOUS PURSUITS.

Under this head are classed—

| BANKERS, | BROKERS, | CLERKS, | LITERATURE, |
| MERCHANTS, | AGENTS, | SHOPMEN, | SCIENCE, |

THE FINE ARTS,

and, in fact, every class that ministers to the wants of the community by any profession or calling requiring an education, and not otherwise specifically enumerated.

These are distributed as follows:—

In ENGLAND	-	-	-	-	120,788
WALES	-	-	-	-	3,090
SCOTLAND	-	-	-	-	18,099
BRITISH ISLES	-	-	-	-	859
IRELAND	-	-	-	-	32,660
Total	-	-	-	-	175,496

It must of course be obvious to every one that these classes would be principally located in our Cities and Towns, and in the Metropolis of each Kingdom; and thus we find that—

MIDDLESEX contains 29,672; or 1-4th of the number returned for all ENGLAND.

EDINBURGH contains 3,585; or 1-5th of the number returned for all SCOTLAND.

DUBLIN contains 5,524; or 1-6th of the number returned for all IRELAND.

The numbers returned in the eight Manufacturing Counties stand thus:—

CHESTER	-	-	-	-	2,590
DERBY	-	-	-	-	1,528
LANCASTER	-	-	-	-	13,804
LEICESTER	-	-	-	-	1,051
NOTTINGHAM	-	-	-	-	1,302
STAFFORD	-	-	-	-	3,207
WARWICK	-	-	-	-	4,031
YORKSHIRE	-	-	-	-	9,603
					37,116

And if to these we add one-half of those returned for Scotland, and one-eighth of those returned for Ireland, we arrive at the following conclusion:—

	AGRICULTURE.	MANUFACTURES.	TOTAL.
ENGLAND AND WALES - -	86,762	37,116	123,878
SCOTLAND - - -	9,049	9,050	18,099
BRITISH ISLES - - -	687	172	859
IRELAND - - -	28,578	4,082	32,660
	125,076	50,420	175,496

It will thus be seen that of "*Other Educated Persons following Miscellaneous Pursuits,*" 5-7ths of the whole number in the United Kingdom are supported by the AGRICULTURISTS, and 2-7ths by the MANUFACTURERS.

PERSONS RETURNED AS INDEPENDENT.

The COMMISSIONERS for taking the CENSUS, in their Report, say that, "With respect to the term 'INDEPENDENT,' we should premise that the numbers included under that head are not merely the wealthy, or even those in easy circumstances, but all who support themselves upon their own means without any occupation. It will, therefore, afford no test of the relative amount of wealthy persons in different localities, or throughout Great Britain, as while it includes in the more rural districts many poor widows or aged men living upon their savings, it omits many large capitalists, who are returned under their proper heads in the list of 'OCCUPATIONS.'"

The numbers returned are as follows:—

In ENGLAND	-	-	-	421,995
WALES	-	-	-	23,978
BRITISH ISLES	-	-	-	7,176
SCOTLAND	-	-	-	58.291
Total of GREAT BRITAIN	-			511,440

With respect to Ireland, it is an extraordinary fact, that the Commissioners do not recognise or enumerate any class as "INDEPENDENT," and we are therefore left in utter darkness of the number of persons of independent means living in the Kingdom of Ireland.

That they are a very large number there can be no doubt, as the resident Nobility and Gentry form a very influential and important section of society.

Independent of Ireland, however, it will be seen that the number for Great Britain is no less than 511,440, and if to these we add the large number of DOMESTIC SERVANTS, supported by persons of independent means (see page 179), we have a class which, in number, exceeds that of the whole number of persons of all ages employed in the Manufacture of the Textile Fabrics (see page 147), and but little inferior to the whole number *employed* by the Manufacturing Interest of the United Kingdom (see page 152.)

For the eight Manufacturing Counties the return is as follows:—

CHESTER	-	-	-	8,444
DERBY	-	-	-	5,193
LANCASTER	-	-	-	33,207
LEICESTER	-	-	-	4,377
NOTTINGHAM	-	-	-	4,818
STAFFORD	-	-	-	8,173
WARWICK	-	-	-	8,976
YORKSHIRE	-	-	-	35,573
Total	-	-	-	108,761

These amount to one-fourth of the whole number returned for England and Wales, but inasmuch as the population of the eight counties is 4,867,028, or nearly one-third of the population of England and Wales, it follows that, in proportion to population, the amount of resident independence is below the average of the other parts of the kingdom.

Of the sources from whence this important class derive their incomes, we have no statistical knowledge to guide us.

The Rental of the Land of the United Kingdom is about 52 millions; that of Houses, 40 millions; Government Annuitants, 30 millions;—making together 122 millions per annum: and there can be no question but that these are the principal sources of income.

On the other hand, but very few persons living in a state of independence draw their supplies from any branch of Trade or Manufactures; for in nearly all cases, an individual, after spending a long life in business, on his retiring from it takes the precaution to withdraw his capital, and invests it in one or the other of the interests above-mentioned.

Notwithstanding the deficiency of the Government Statistics in this particular, there is, however, a rule which may be applied with great fairness to test not only the relative importance of each interest, but also to fix with some degree of certainty the proportion which each contributes to the support of the "INDEPENDENCE" resident in the United Kingdom.

We refer to the value of the annual productions of each, or, in other words, the amount of contribution which each Interest makes to the common stock, as shown at pages 183 and 184, from which it will be seen that the productions of our Manufacturers do not constitute more than about one-third of the whole. And if to this we add, that the effect of machinery is to give almost unlimited power to one individual to produce great results, it comes in confirmation of the fact, that the Master Manufacturers, as a class, are, numerically speaking, the smallest of any in the Kingdom, not amounting to 1-50th of those living in independence within the United Kingdom.

Indirectly, Manufactures of course contribute to the taxation of the country and the support of the population, in the proportions which are shown at pages 140 and 141; but, for the foregoing reasons, we apprehend that in about the same proportion do "*Persons returned as Independent,*" draw their respective incomes or means of support *directly* from the Manufacturing Interest, and those of course only in respect of capital not withdrawn from, or monies lent to, the Manufacturers.

PERSONS ENGAGED IN THE GOVERNMENT CIVIL SERVICE.

The numbers returned in the Census are as follows:

ENGLAND	13,557
WALES	531
BRITISH ISLES	94
SCOTLAND	2,777
IRELAND	4,990
	21,949

These, for the greater part, consist of persons employed by the Government in the departments of the Customs, Excise, Post Office, and the collection of the Stamps and Taxes; and it might reasonably be expected that the great marts for Manufactures in the eight Manufacturing Counties would find employment for a large proportion of the whole. The return for these counties is, however, as follows:—

CHESTER	181
DERBY	110
LANCASTER	1,234
LEICESTER	83
NOTTINGHAM	95
STAFFORD	238
WARWICK	209
YORKSHIRE	905
	3,055

Add to these one-half the number returned for Scotland, and one-eighth of those returned for Ireland, and we have the following result:

	AGRICULTURE.	MANUFACTURES	TOTAL.
ENGLAND AND WALES	11,033	3,055	14,088
SCOTLAND	1,388	1,389	2,777
BRITISH ISLES	94	-	94
IRELAND	4,366	624	4,990
	16,811	5,068	21,949

So far, therefore, as the Civil Service of the Government is concerned, it is apparent that not more than one-fourth is employed in or supported by the Manufacturing Interests, and that the remaining three-fourths are supported by Interests other than the Manufacturing, and arise out of the necessity of keeping up establishments of the Customs, Excise, and Post Office, for the transaction and despatch of business in all the cities, towns, and villages of the United Kingdom.

PAROCHIAL, TOWN, AND CHURCH OFFICERS,

INCLUDING POLICE AND LAW OFFICERS.

Of these the total number returned is 38,208, and they are thus distributed:—

ENGLAND	21,443
WALES	682
BRITISH ISLES	65
SCOTLAND	3,085
IRELAND	12,933
	38,208

The eight Manufacturing Counties are returned as follows:—

CHESTER	423
DERBY	206
LANCASTER	2,541
LEICESTER	193
NOTTINGHAM	234
STAFFORD	376
WARWICK	661
YORKSHIRE	1,311
	5,945

If to these we add one-half the number returned for Scotland, and one-eighth of those in Ireland, we have the following result:—

	AGRICULTURE.	MANUFACTURES.	TOTAL.
ENGLAND AND WALES -	16,180	5,945	22,125
SCOTLAND -	1,540	1,545	3,085
BRITISH ISLES	65	-	65
IRELAND -	11,317	1,616	12,933
	29,102	9,106	38,208

From the above it will be seen that the Agricultural Districts support about 3-4ths, and the Manufacturing 1-4th of the whole.

It is necessary, however, here to draw a distinction which marks in a very decided manner the peculiar character of each pursuit.

Agriculture supports a larger number of Parochial and Church Officers, because large masses of mankind congregated in cities and towns do not require the same number to manage their Parochial and Church affairs as when the same amount of population is spread throughout the small towns and villages in agricultural districts.

For instance, Liverpool, Manchester, Leeds, and Halifax, have a population of 812,267; and the number of Parochial and Church Officers returned for these places is only 154, while the County of Norfolk, with a population of 412,664, has 147, or, as compared with the Manufacturing districts, 2 to 1.

On the other hand, the same towns of Liverpool, Manchester, Leeds, and Halifax find employment for 1,163 persons, returned as Police Officers, Constables, and Watchmen.

The Agricultural Counties of Devon and Suffolk, with a population of 36,000 more, return only 305, or, as compared with the Manufacturing districts, as 1 is to 4.

It follows that for Parochial and Church Government the Agricultural Districts support a very large proportion of the whole number returned under that head; and for the protection of property, the detection, suppression, and punishment of crime, the Manufacturing Districts find employment for 3-4ths, and the Agricultural 1-4th of the Police and Law Officers, as compared with their respective populations.

DOMESTIC SERVANTS.

For the United Kingdom, this class may be estimated in round numbers at one million and a half. As a class, numerically speaking, they rank next to the number of persons employed in Manufactures (see page 152); but inasmuch as they only represent themselves, and have no wives, children, servants, or tradespeople dependant on them for support, they are, in truth, the weakest of all classes in the body politic. They are thus distributed :—

	MALES.	FEMALES.	TOTAL.
ENGLAND - - -	223,040	712,792	935,832
WALES - - - -	10,489	5 ,727	63,216
BRITISH ISLES - -	1,112	6,423	7,535
SCOTLAND - - - -	21,767	136,883	158,650
IRELAND - - -			328,889
			1,494,122

For the eight Manufacturing Counties the return is as follows :—

	MALES.	FEMALES.	TOTAL.
CHESTER - - -	6,953	17,048	24,001
DERBY - - - -	5,484	9,751	15,235
LANCASTER - - -	11,746	61,252	72,998
LEICESTER - - -	4,652	8,895	13,547
NOTTINGHAM - - -	2,805	10,478	13,283
STAFFORD - - - -	4, 51	19,080	23,331
WARWICK - - -	4,667	19,258	23,925
YORKSHIRE - - - -	13,070	59,527	72,597
	53,628	205,289	258,917

Add to these one-half the number returned for Scotland, and one-eighth those returned for Ireland. and the account stands thus : —

	AGRICULTURE.	MANUFACTURES.	TOTAL.
ENGLAND AND WALES - -	740,131	258,917	999,048
SCOTLAND - - - -	79,325	79,325	158,650
BRITISH ISLES - -	7,535	- -	7,535
IRELAND - - -	287,778	41,111	328,889
	1,114,769	379,353	1,494,122

The Commissioners observe that "We have reason to believe that, in some instances, servants kept in farm houses and employed generally about the premises have been returned as Domestic Servants, whereas, in 1831, such persons were included as Agricultural Labourers. Our directions were very precise on this point, as all Farm Servants were to be returned as Agricultural Labourers."

If this be true that the Domestic Servants employed at all the farm houses, with the exceptions the Commissioners here refer to, are returned as Agricultural Labourers, it is a very remarkable fact, that the Agricultural Counties, independent of Agriculture, give employment to a much larger number of Domestic Servants than the Manufacturing Counties, if we compare the respective amount of their populations thus:—

	POPULATION.	DOMESTIC SERVANTS.
LANCASTER - - - - -	1,667,054	72,998
DEVON - - - - - -	533,460	41,585
NORFOLK - - - - -	412,664	23,118
SUFFOLK - - - - -	315,073	17,817
LINCOLN - - - - -	362,602	26,534
	1,623,799	109,054

This gives a more unfavourable result to the Manufacturing Interest than the statement above, but when we consider that Domestic Servants are principally supported by the resident gentry or by persons in easy circumstances, and that the great mass of a manufacturing population are servants themselves of another kind, it proves most conclusively that the estimate here given, as regards the amount of employment afforded to this class by the Manufacturers, is much overstated.

Whether this conclusion be correct or not, one fact is evident enough, that the Manufacturing Counties do not give employment to more than *one-fourth* of the persons returned as "Domestic Servants."

LABOURERS.

Under this head are included Labourers whose employment is not otherwise specified, also Miners, Quarriers, Porters, Messengers, and other persons engaged in laborious occupations.

These are returned as follows :—

ENGLAND	620,492
WALES	53,430
BRITISH ISLES	3,373
SCOTLAND	84,573
IRELAND	31,252
	793,120

It will be necessary, however, to deduct from these the number engaged in the working of our mines, as in this work we treat them as a separate and distinct interest, and these amount to 196,984 (see page 166), leaving 596,136 to be accounted for.

The return for the eight Manufacturing Counties is as follows :—

CHESTER	14,544
DERBY	15,477
LANCASTER	76,079
LEICESTER	3,676
NOTTINGHAM	5,460
STAFFORD	34,917
WARWICK	11,804
YORKSHIRE	51,743
	213,700

Add to these one-half the number returned for Scotland, and one-eighth those returned for Ireland, and the numbers supported by each interest will stand thus :—

	AGRICULTURE.	MANUFACTURES.	TOTAL.
ENGLAND AND WALES BRITISH ISLES	290,264	213,700	503,964
SCOTLAND	32,008	32,008	64,016
IRELAND	24,637	3,519	28,156
	346,909	249,227	596,136

From this it will be seen that the Manufacturing Interest, in proportion to its population, gives employment to a much larger amount of the labour classed under this particular head than the Agricultural, and for this very obvious reason—that Porters, Messengers, Carmen, and Boatmen, are principally required in Manufacturing localities.

ALMSPEOPLE, PENSIONERS, PAUPERS, LUNATICS, AND PRISONERS

In the Government abstract these several classes are included under one head, and the return for the United Kingdom is as follows :—

ENGLAND - - - -	168,376
WALES - - -	7,830
BRITISH ISLES - -	1,173
SCOTLAND - - - -	21,690
IRELAND - - -	36,032
	235,101

The eight Manufacturing Counties supply the following numbers :—

CHESTER - - - -	2,355
DERBY - - - - -	1,585
LANCASTER - - -	12,717
LEICESTER - - -	2,134
NOTTINGHAM - - -	1,923
STAFFORD - - -	3,669
WARWICK - - -	3,499
YORKSHIRE - - -	10,896
	38,778

If to these we add one-half the number returned for Scotland, and one-eighth of those returned for Ireland, we have the following results :—

	AGRICULTURE.	MANUFACTURES.	TOTAL.
ENGLAND AND WALES -	137,428	38,778	176,206
BRITISH ISLANDS - - -	1,173	- -	1,173
SCOTLAND - - -	10,845	10,8·5	21,690
IRELAND - -	31,528	4,504	36,032
	180,974	54,127	235,101

It is impossible for us to draw any general conclusion from the above figures, but the Commissioners have furnished us with another table that will enable us to form some idea of the relative contribution which each interest makes to the inmates of the following institutions.

	PERSONS ENGAGED IN COMMERCE, TRADE, AND MANUFACTURE.					PERSONS ENGAGED IN AGRICULTURE.					TO EVERY 10,000 PERSONS ENGAGED IN	
	MALES.		FEMALES.			MALES.		FEMALES.				
	20 years of age and upwards.	Under 20 years of age.	20 years of age and upwards.	Under 20 years of age	TOTAL.	20 years of age and upwards.	Under 20 years of age.	20 years of age and upwards.	Under 20 years of age.	TOTAL.	COMMERCE, TRADE, & MANUFACTURES.	AGRICULTURE.
Workhouses - - -	5,492	479	2,532	404	8,907	3,466	137	252	18	3,873	33·7	30·4
Hospitals - - -	1,603	312	451	185	2,551	573	146	22	5	746	8·2	5·0
Gaols - - -	4,928	1,227	569	148	6,872	1,634	316	15	4	1,969	22·0	11·1
Lunatic Asylums - -	1,759	13	457	8	2,237	620	5	43	- -	668	7·2	4·5

CRIMINALS.

COMPARATIVE TABLE showing the NUMBER OF PERSONS COMMITTED FOR TRIAL or BAILED in each of the last Ten Years, and the numbers in each County separately.

COUNTIES.	1836.	1837.	1838.	1839.	1840.	1841.	1842.	1843.	1844.	1845.
BEDFORD	162	123	134	108	175	191	229	202	188	155
BERKS	205	270	290	324	347	306	333	328	287	260
BUCKS	193	258	237	251	246	287	277	313	280	286
CAMBRIDGE	279	260	237	219	220	240	241	257	297	239
CHESTER	554	616	645	775	1,042	943	1,086	1,018	777	688
CORNWALL	198	281	264	289	339	295	282	301	269	272
CUMBERLAND	143	154	155	146	131	151	115	109	138	118
DERBY	192	228	262	239	247	277	322	322	279	186
DEVON	527	671	578	658	717	687	716	740	715	720
DORSET	193	256	255	294	274	284	241	252	203	218
DURHAM	164	202	164	206	171	215	266	300	276	203
ESSEX	619	747	636	542	683	647	758	710	596	554
GLOUCESTER (including BRISTOL)	823	906	1,021	935	1,045	1,236	1,252	1,186	1,071	929
HEREFORD	154	186	190	214	237	245	259	238	230	226
HERTFORD	324	335	343	258	303	319	338	265	271	244
HUNTINGDON	68	67	97	53	83	62	68	68	79	88
KENT	872	896	1,024	956	903	962	1,155	977	911	831
LANCASTER	2,265	2,809	2,585	2,901	3,506	3,987	4,497	3,677	2,893	2,852
LEICESTER	310	432	365	412	466	466	492	509	481	328
LINCOLN	411	412	383	388	409	349	507	563	542	389
MIDDLESEX (including LONDON)	3,350	3,273	3,488	3,649	3,577	3,586	4,094	4,260	4,027	4,440
MONMOUTH	120	154	197	230	330	364	264	261	278	196
NORFOLK	739	659	588	732	693	666	808	782	788	642
NORTHAMPTON	187	298	268	250	290	342	346	270	294	302
NORTHUMBERLAND	170	189	159	139	196	226	245	290	294	189
NOTTINGHAM	302	307	250	314	356	329	374	353	348	267
OXFORD	244	272	286	309	359	323	334	328	296	309
RUTLAND	24	27	13	13	9	14	48	39	23	28
SALOP	228	252	271	310	387	416	470	534	449	308
SOMERSET	796	1,028	858	843	1,128	991	1,148	967	1,039	873
SOUTHAMPTON	545	622	632	642	735	677	702	676	517	619
STAFFORD	636	909	768	930	923	1,059	1,485	1,175	885	717
SUFFOLK	528	493	505	527	484	482	527	585	630	407
SURREY	984	950	898	1,016	988	923	1,017	867	941	942
SUSSEX	381	420	529	504	543	539	550	493	409	409
WARWICK	728	880	884	778	1,001	1,046	1,003	1,045	894	769
WESTMORELAND	20	25	36	37	38	33	39	44	24	46
WILTS	354	482	407	428	462	506	548	464	432	379
WORCESTER	328	409	427	460	627	566	609	679	603	563
YORK	1,252	1,376	1,324	1,621	1,867	1,895	2,598	2,304	1,691	1,417
ANGLESEY	19	16	9	16	16	13	21	20	7	23
BRECON	27	29	21	43	58	48	56	62	58	37
CARDIGAN	5	13	16	27	13	17	14	26	31	47
CARMARTHEN	19	49	61	36	67	32	49	171	117	87
CARNARVON	32	22	45	47	66	33	33	21	32	39
DENBIGH	55	76	62	48	55	81	79	89	89	66
FLINT	31	39	18	25	36	44	61	49	50	62
GLAMORGAN	82	103	94	126	184	189	197	174	225	159
MERIONETH	12	5	6	7	11	5	12	21	9	12
MONTGOMERY	48	54	48	93	85	75	73	94	96	67
PEMBROKE	67	54	46	44	44	58	48	88	54	66
RADNOR	15	18	15	31	15	33	23	25	29	30
TOTAL	20,984	23,612	23,094	24,443	27,187	27,760	31,309	29,591	26,542	24,303

From the foregoing table we extract the following figures in reference to the eight Manufacturing Counties :—

	1836.	1837.	1838.	1839.	1840.	1841.	1842.	1843.	1844.	1845.
CHESTER	554	616	645	775	1,042	943	1,086	1,018	777	688
DERBY	192	228	262	239	247	277	322	322	279	186
LANCASTER	2,265	2,809	2,585	2,901	3,506	3,987	4,497	3,677	2,893	2,852
LEICESTER	310	432	365	412	466	466	492	509	481	328
NOTTINGHAM	302	307	250	314	356	329	874	353	348	267
STAFFORD	636	909	768	930	923	1,059	1,485	1,175	885	717
WARWICK	728	880	884	778	1,001	1,046	1,003	1,045	894	769
YORKSHIRE	1,232	1,376	1,324	1,621	1,867	1,895	2,598	2,304	1,691	1,417
TOTAL	6,219	7,557	7,083	7,970	9,408	10,002	11,857	10,403	8,248	7,224

CRIMINALS—(*Continued.*)

It will be seen from this, that in the 10 years from 1836 to 1845, these Counties with a population of 4,867,028, out of 15,906,741 have produced one-third of the Criminals in England and Wales.

In seasons of distress it will also be seen that crime increases in a much greater degree in a Manufacturing than in an agricultural population ; thus in the years 1841, 1842, and 1843, the proportion was nearly three-eighths of the whole, or 32,262 out of 88,680.

	TOTAL.	EIGHT MANUFACTURING COUNTIES.
1841 - -	27,780	10,002
1842 - - - -	31,309	11,857
1843 - - -	29,591	10,403
	88,680	32,262

PUBLIC CHARITIES.

SUMMARY OF CHARITIES reported upon by the Commissioners, and included in the two Digests of 1832 and 1835.

From which it appears that there is held in trust, for various charitable purposes, the following property :—

A. R. P.		£ s. d.
279,497 2 11	Land, producing an Annual Rental of - - - - -	540,565 14 9
15,797	Houses and Cottages - - - - - - -	56,963 1 0
£3,060,684 17 6	Three per Cent. Stock - - - ⎫	
154,247 5 1	Three and a half ditto - - - - ⎪	
291,981 2 0	Four ditto - - - - - ⎬ producing annually -	150,649 9 3
81,031 13 0	Five ditto - - - - - ⎪	
63,041 13 4	Bank and India Stock - - - ⎪	
782,611 19 7	Mortgage, Personal, and Turnpike - - ⎭	
£4,433,598 10 6	Total Annual Income - - -	£784,178 5 0

which, valued at 4 per cent. would make the Fee Simple of the Property held in trust for Charitable } Purposes, amount to - - - - - - - - - } £19,604,150 0 0

APPLICATION OF THE ABOVE.

	£ s. d.
To Endowed Schools - - - - - - - - - -	180,309 12 5
For Education not in Endowed Schools - - - - - - -	16,938 17 5
Total for Education - - - - - - -	197,248 9 10
,, other purposes - - - - -	491,536 3 4
,, Chartered Companies - - - - -	59,393 11 10
Total - - - - - -	748,178 5 0

RENTAL OF LAND.

ENGLAND AND WALES.

Account showing the Area of the different Counties of England and Wales; the Gross Rentals of each in 1814-15 and in 1842-43, as determined by the Assessments under the Property and Income Tax Acts, with the Rent per Acre of each in 1814-15 and in 1842-43.

COUNTIES.	Acres.	Gross Rental for 1814-15.	Rent per Acre in 1814-15.	Gross Rental for 1842-43.	Rent per Acre in 1842-43.	Increase of Rent per Acre in 1842-43 over Rent per Acre in 1814-15.	Decrease of Rent per Acre in 1842-43 below Rent per Acre in 1814-15.
		£	£ s. d.		£ s. d.	£ s. d.	£ s. d.
Bedford - -	296,320	316,595	1 1 4½	377,995	1 5 5	0 4 10¾	—
Berks - -	481,280	502,096	1 0 10½	594,903	1 4 8½	0 3 10	—
Bucks - -	472.320	548,630	1 3 2¾	597,736	1 5 3½	0 2 0¾	—
Cambridge - -	548 480	541,325	0 19 8¾	774,658	1 8 2¾	0 8 6	—
Chester - -	673 280	805,141	1 3 11	962,857	1 8 7	0 4 8	—
Cornwall - -	851,200	629,259	0 14 9½	774,692	0 18 2¼	0 3 4¾	—
Cumberland -	974,720	561,468	0 11 6¼	603,725	0 12 4½	0 0 10¼	—
Derby - -	657,920	707,250	1 1 5¾	845,681	1 5 8¼	0 4 2½	—
Devon - -	1,654,400	1,360,812	0 16 5½	1,556,181	0 18 9¾	0 2 4¼	—
Dorset - -	643,840	564,377	0 17 6¼	613.507	0 19 0½	0 1 6¼	—
Durham - -	702,080	543,411	0 15 5¾	538,781	0 15 4	—	0 0 1¾
Essex - -	981,120	1,109,829	1 2 7½	1,289,645	1 6 3¼	0 3 7¾	—
Gloucester - -	805,120	971,410	1 4 1½	1,121,125	1 7 10	0 3 8½	—
Hereford - -	552,320	524,781	0 19 0	629,981	1 2 9½	0 3 9½	—
Hertford - -	403,200	397,539	0 19 8½	438,226	1 1 8¾	0 2 0¼	—
Huntingdon -	238,080	277,463	1 3 3¾	312,083	1 6 2½	0 2 10¾	—
Kent - - -	996,480	961,368	0 19 3½	1,327,491	1 6 7½	0 7 4	—
Lancaster - -	1,130,240	1,463,183	1 5 10½	1,636,416	1 8 11½	0 3 1	—
Leicester - -	515,840	807,558	1 11 3¾	899,063	1 14 10¼	0 3 6½	—
Lincoln - -	1,671,040	1,865,086	1 2 4	2,340,625	1 8 0	0 5 8	—
Middlesex - -	180,480	517,669	2 17 4½	387,861	2 2 11	—	0 14 5½
Monmouth - -	317,440	231,113	0 14 6¾	290,334	0 18 3½	0 3 8¾	—
Norfolk - -	1,295,360	1,102,352	0 17 0¼	1.644,994	1 5 4¾	0 8 4½	—
Northampton -	650,240	846.172	1 6 0¼	973,144	1 9 1	0 3 0¾	—
Northumberland -	1,197,440	999,951	0 16 8½	835.856	0 13 11½	—	0 2 9
Nottingham -	535,680	604.220	1 2 6½	707,756	1 6 5	0 3 10½	—
Oxford - -	483,840	589,594	1 4 4½	602,396	1 4 1¾	—	0 0 2¾
Rutland - -	95,360	123,296	1 5 10¼	130,935	1 7 5½	0 1 7¼	—
Salop - -	859,520	823,845	0 19 2	1,050,132	1 4 5	0 5 3	—
Somerset - -	1,052,800	1,491,734	1 8 4	1,715.497	1 12 7	0 4 3	—
Southampton - -	1,040,000	707,127	0 13 7¼	777,636	0 14 11¼	0 1 4	—
Stafford - -	757,760	862,973	1 2 9¼	1,104,151	1 9 1½	0 6 4¼	—
Suffolk - -	969,600	826,228	0 17 0½	1,147,536	1 3 8	0 6 7½	—
Surrey - -	485,760	437,958	0 18 0¼	433,505	0 17 10	—	0 0 2¼
Sussex - -	938,240	641,736	0 13 8	855,373	0 18 2¾	0 4 6¾	—
Warwick - -	574,080	838,993	1 9 2¾	905,869	1 11 6½	0 2 3¾	—
Westmoreland -	487,680	260,945	0 10 8½	269,418	0 11 0½	0 0 4	—
Wilts - -	874,880	964,611	1 2 0	1,021,706	1 3 4¼	0 1 4¼	—
Worcester - -	462,720	609,746	1 6 4¼	716,498	1 10 11½	0 4 7¼	—
York - -	3,735,040	3,563,980	0 19 1	3,989,937	1 1 4¼	0 2 3¼	—
Totals for England -	32,243,200	32,502,824		37,795,905			
Average Rent per Statute Acre of England - -	- -	- -	1 0 2	- -	1 3 5½	0 3 3½	—

RENTAL OF LAND.

ENGLAND AND WALES.—(*Continued.*)

COUNTIES.	Acres.	Gross Rental for 1814-15.	Rent per Acre in 1814-15.	Gross Rental for 1842-43.	Rent per Acre in 1842-43.	Increase of Rent per Acre in 1842-43 over Rent per Acre in 1814-15.	Decrease of Rent per Acre in 1842-43 below Rent per Acre in 1814-15.
WALES.		£	£ s. d.	£	£ s. d.	£ s. d.	£ s. d.
Anglesea - -	173,440	76,105	0 8 9¼	129,063	0 14 10½	0 6 1¼	—
Brecon - -	482,560	135,191	0 5 7¼	139,225	0 5 9	0 0 1¾	—
Cardigan - -	432,000	126,399	0 5 10¼	159,949	0 7 4¾	0 1 6½	—
Carmarthen - -	623,360	240,714	0 7 8¾	315,761	0 10 1¾	0 2 4¾	—
Carnarvon - -	348,160	105,852	0 6 1	150,047	0 8 7¾	0 2 6¼	—
Denbigh - -	405,120	224,678	0 11 1	284,346	0 14 0¼	0 2 11¼	—
Flint - -	156,160	139,753	0 17 10¾	193,505	1 4 9¼	0 6 10½	—
Glamorgan - -	506,880	229,013	0 9 0	258,470	0 10 2¼	0 1 2¼	—
Merioneth - -	424,320	96,343	0 4 6½	108,237	0 5 1	0 0 6½	—
Montgomery - -	536 960	181,881	0 6 9¼	258,068	0 9 7	0 2 9¾	—
Pembroke - -	390,400	181,057	0 9 3	266,865	0 11 1¼	0 1 10¼	—
Radnor - -	272,640	90,652	0 6 7¾	107,648	0 7 1¾	0 0 6	—
Totals for Wales -	4,752,200	1,827,638	- -	2,371,184			
Average Rent per Statute Acre of Wales -	- -	- -	0 7 8¼	- -	0 9 11¾	0 2 3½	—
Add for England as before -	32,243,200	32,502,824	- -	37,795,905			
Totals for England and Wales -	36,995,000	34,330,462	- -	40,167,088			
Average Rent per Statute Acre of England and Wales	- -	- -	0 18 6¾	- -	1 1 8½		

SUMMARY OF THE UNITED KINGDOM.

	Acres.	Average per Acre.	Gross Rental.
		£ s. d.	£
England and Wales - - - - -	36,995,000	1 1 8½	40,167,088
Scotland (See page 186) - - - -	18,944,000	0 5 10¾	5,586,628
Ireland (See page 187) - - - -	20,177,446	0 13 5¼	13,562,946
	76,116,446		59,316,662
Deductions - - - - - - - -			563,047
Net Rental - - - - - - - -			58,753,615

RENTAL OF LAND.—(*Continued.*)

SCOTLAND.

ACCOUNT, showing the AREA of the different COUNTIES of SCOTLAND, the RENT PER ACRE of each in 1810-11, and GROSS RENTAL and RENT per Acre of each in 1842-43, as determined by the Assessments under the Property and Income Tax Acts, showing the INCREASE or DIMINUTION of the RENT per Acre in 1842-43, as compared with that for 1810-11.

COUNTIES.	Imperial Acres.	Rent per Acre in 1810-11.	Gross Rental in 1842-3.	Rent per Acre in 1842-43.	Increase of Rent per Acre in 1842-3 over Rent per Acre in 1810-11.	Decrease of Rent per Acre in 1842-3 below Rent per Acre in 1810-11.
		£ s. d.	£	£ s. d.	£ s. d.	£ s. d.
Aberdeen - -	1,254,400	0 3 8¾	423,389	0 6 9	0 3 0¼	—
Argyle and Isles -	2,002,560	0 1 11	232,441	0 2 3¾	0 0 4¾	—
Ayr - -	664,960	0 10 1½	390,278	0 11 8¾	0 1 7½	—
Banff - -	412,800	0 3 10¼	110,608	0 5 4¼	0 1 6	—
Berwick - -	282,880	0 16 5	237,042	0 16 9¾	0 0 4¾	—
Caithness - -	439,680	0 1 5	57,982	0 2 7½	0 1 2½	—
Clackmannan -	30,720	1 0 10¼	35,249	1 2 11¼	0 2 1	—
Cromarty - -	163,840	0 1 4	5,857	0 0 8½	—	0 0 7½
Dumfries - -	801,920	0 6 1½	266,547	0 6 7¾	0 0 6¼	—
Dumbarton - -	145,920	0 7 9¾	72,041	0 9 10½	0 2 0¾	—
Edinburgh - -	226,560	1 4 6¼	239,189	1 1 7½	—	0 2 10¾
Elgin - -	302,720	0 4 1¼	84,082	0 5 6½	0 1 5¼	—
Fife - -	298,880	1 2 5¼	381 572	1 5 6¼	0 3 1	—
Forfar (Angus) -	568,320	0 9 1¾	312,201	0 10 11¾	0 1 10	—
Haddington - -	174,080	1 0 9	221,714	1 5 5½	0 4 8½	—
Inverness and Isles -	2,594,560	0 1 1½	161,499	0 1 2¾	0 0 1¼	—
Kincardine -	243,200	0 13 1¾	128,469	0 10 6¾	—	0 2 7
Kinross - -	46,080	0 9 10½	38,892	0 16 10½	0 7 0	—
Kirkcudbright -	525,760	0 7 3¾	182,926	0 6 11¼	—	0 0 4½
Lanark - -	602,880	0 9 10½	341,122	0 11 3¾	0 1 5¼	—
Linlithgow -	76,800	1 1 7¼	82,842	1 2 1	0 0 5¾	—
Nairn - -	124,800	0 1 10½	15,202	0 2 5	0 0 6½	—
Peebles - -	204,160	0 5 7½	67,675	0 6 7½	0 1 0	—
Perth - -	1,656,320	0 5 6¾	551,078	0 6 7½	0 1 0¾	—
Renfrew - -	144,000	0 17 7¾	152,924	1 1 2¾	0 3 7	—
Ross and Isles -	1,682,560	0 1 1	120,824	0 1 5	0 0 4	—
Roxburgh - -	457,600	0 10 1	235,041	0 10 3¼	0 0 2¼	—
Selkirk - -	168,320	0 4 8¾	38,714	0 4 7	—	0 0 1¾
Stirling - -	312,960	0 11 4¼	181,147	0 11 6¾	0 0 2½	—
Sutherland -	1,122,560	0 0 6	33,689	0 0 7	0 0 1	—
Wigtown - -	288,960	0 8 6¾	124,807	0 8 7½	0 0 0¾	—
	18,021,760		5,527,043			
ISLANDS.						
Bute, Arran, &c. - (Isles of Argyle, Inverness, and Cromarty, included in Counties.)	103,040	0 3 7¼	20,597	0 3 11¾	0 0 4½	—
Orkney Isles -	272,000	0 0 8½	21,431	0 1 6¾	0 0 10¼	—
Shetland - -	547,200	0 0 3	17,457	0 0 7½	0 0 4½	—
	18,944,000		5,586,628			
Average Rent per Imperial Acre in Scotland -	- -	0 5 1½	- -	0 5 10¾	0 0 9¼	—

RENTAL OF LAND.—(*Continued.*)

IRELAND.

Table of the **Extent** of the Several **Counties** and **Provinces** of **Ireland**, exclusive of Lakes, distinguishing the **Cultivated Land** from the **Unimproved Mountain** and **Bog**; showing also the **Proportion** of **Cultivated Land** in each **County**, assuming 1,000 to represent the total extent of Cultivated Land in Ireland; with the estimated **Gross Rental** of the **Land** in the several Counties and Provinces, and the **Average Rent** per Statute Acre.

PROVINCES AND COUNTIES.	Cultivated Acres, including Towns and Plantations.	Unimproved Mountain and Bog.	Total Extent of Acres, exclusive of Lakes.	Proportion of Cultivated Acres, assuming 1000 as the whole cultivated Land of Ireland.	Gross Annual Value of Land.	Average Rent per Acre.
LEINSTER.	Acres.	Acres.	Acres.	Acres.	£	£ s. d.
Carlow - -	189,588	31,249	220,837	13,657	222,319	1 0 1½
Dublin - -	207.102	19,312	226,414	14,919	250,201	1 2 1
Kildare - -	365,565	51,854	417,419	26,334	387,401	0 18 7
Kilkenny - -	485,550	21,126	506,676	34,978	393,280	0 15 6
King's County -	346,416	145,836	492,252	24,955	354,131	0 14 5
Longford - -	196.797	58,937	255,734	14,177	201,061	0 15 8½
Louth - -	185,490	15,603	201,093	13,362	280,650	1 7 11
Meath .. -	560,622	16,033	576,655	40,386	703,458	1 14 5
Queen's County -	355,169	69,289	424,458	25,585	202,500	0 11 11
Westmeath -	374,649	56,392	431,041	26,989	387,597	0 18 0
Wexford - -	527,419	45,501	572,920	37,994	531,916	0 18 7
Wicklow - - -	298,334	200,754	499,088	21,491	310,305	0 12 5
	4,092.701	731,886	4,824,587	294,827	4,224.819	
Average Rent per Statute Acre in Leinster -	- -	- -	- -	- -	- -	0 17 6
MUNSTER.						
Clare - -	464,041	296,033	760,074	33,428	351,582	0 9 3
Cork - -	1,367,577	465,889	1,833,466	98,517	1,203,936	0 13 1
Kerry - -	426,590	726,775	1,153,365	30,731	421,759	0 7 2¼
Limerick - -	541.210	121,101	662,311	38,987	777,386	1 3 5½
Tipperary - -	870,025	178,183	1,048,208	62,674	1,041,214	0 19 10¼
Waterford - -	350,278	105,496	455,774	25,233	346,949	0 15 2½
	4,019,721	1,893,477	5 913,198	289,570	4,142,826	
Average Rent per Statute Acre in Munster -	- -	- -	- -	- -	- -	0 14 0
ULSTER.						
Antrim - -	528,166	180,423	708,589	38,048	650,509	0 18 4¼
Armagh - -	275,017	35,117	310,134	19,812	322,673	1 0 9½
Cavan - -	383,300	71,918	455.218	27,611	334,699	0 14 8¼
Donegal - -	400,749	769,587	1,170,336	28,869	300,065	0 5 1¼
Down - -	530,746	78,317	609,063	38,233	607,619	0 19 11¼
Fermanagh - -	295,593	114,847	410,440	21,294	228,195	0 11 1¼
Londonderry -	327,559	180,709	508,268	23,596	293,907	0 11 6¾
Monaghan - -	292,005	21,585	313,590	21,035	271,147	0 17 3½
Tyrone - -	462,977	311 867	774,844	33,352	370,075	0 9 6½
	3,496,112	1,764,370	5,260,482	251,850	3,378,889	
Average Rent per Statute Acre in Ulster -	- -	- -	- -	- -	- -	0 12 10
CONNAUGHT.						
Galway - -	768,324	708,000	1,476.324	55,348	614,208	0 8 3¾
Leitrim - -	252,746	115,869	368,615	18,207	161,338	0 8 9
Mayo - -	506,795	800,111	1,306,906	36,508	400,412	0 6 1½
Roscommon -	448,022	130,299	578,321	32,274	385,818	0 13 4
Sligo - -	297,290	151,723	449,013	21,416	254,336	0 11 4
	2,273,177	1,906,002	4,179.179	163,753	1,816,112	
Average Rent per Statute Acre in Connaught -	- -	- -	- -	- -	- -	0 8 8¼
Grand Total -	13,881,711	6,295,735	20,177,446	1,000,000	13,562,646	—
Average Rent per Statute Acre in the Whole Kingdom -	- -	- -	- -	- -	- -	0 13 5¼